Apocalyptic Sentimentalism

Apocalyptic Sentimentalism

Love and Fear in U.S. Antebellum Literature

KEVIN PELLETIER

THE UNIVERSITY OF GEORGIA PRESS   Athens

Paperback edition, 2018
© 2015 by the University of Georgia Press
Athens, Georgia 30602
www.ugapress.org
All rights reserved
Set in Adobe Caslon Pro by Graphic Composition, Inc.

Most University of Georgia Press titles are
available from popular e-book vendors.

Printed digitally

The Library of Congress has cataloged the hardcover
edition of this book as follows:
Pelletier, Kevin, 1975–
Apocalyptic sentimentalism : love and fear in U.S. antebellum literature / Kevin Pelletier.
xii, 256 pages ; 24 cm
Includes bibliographical references (pages 229–243) and index.
ISBN 978-0-8203-3948-1 (hardback) — ISBN 978-0-8203-4773-8 (e-book) 1. American literature—19th century—History and criticism. 2. Slavery in literature. 3. Antislavery movements in literature. 4. Apocalyptic literature. 5. African Americans in literature. 6. Emotions in literature. 7. Literature and society—United States—History—19th century. I. Title. II. Title: Love and fear in U.S. antebellum literature.
PS217.S55P45 2015
810.9'003—dc23

2014021694

Paperback ISBN 978-0-8203-5467-5

For Kendra

Contents

Acknowledgments *ix*

Introduction: The Sentimental Apocalypse *1*

PART ONE. BLACK ABOLITION AND THE IDEOLOGICAL ROOTS
OF APOCALYPTIC SENTIMENTALISM

One. David Walker, Nat Turner, and the Logic of Sentimental Terror *35*

Two. "The Wrath of the Lamb": Maria W. Stewart and the
Domestication of Apocalypse *59*

PART TWO. SALVATION THROUGH MOTHERLY VENGEANCE: THE
SENTIMENTALITY OF HARRIET BEECHER STOWE

Three. Uncle Tom's Cabin and the Fictionalization of
Apocalyptic Sentimentalism *97*

Four. "Can Fear of Fire Make Me Love?": *Dred* and the Incarnation
of Apocalypse *120*

PART THREE. JOHN BROWN AND THE LEGACY OF
APOCALYPTIC SENTIMENTALISM

Five. Sentimental John Brown *153*

Coda: The Civil War and Modern Apocalyptic Sentimentalism *181*

Notes *193*
Bibliography *229*
Index *245*

Acknowledgments

Having spent so long thinking and writing about vengeance and wrath and terror, I am relieved finally to be able to express my affection and gratitude for the colleagues, teachers, students, family, and friends that helped make this book possible.

I began to develop this project at SUNY Buffalo, and I received expert guidance from many gifted teachers, especially Neil Schmitz, Robert Daly, and Stacy Hubbard. I am particularly indebted to Carrie Tirado Bramen, who provided indispensable instruction and support as this project evolved. I hope this book lives up to her expectations.

I could not have completed this manuscript without generous financial support from the University of Richmond and the intellectual support of my incredible department. My thanks to Suzanne Jones who, as my department chair, always made sure I had enough time to research and write, and to Bert Ashe, Laura Browder, Abigail Cheever, Daryl Dance, Terryl Givens, Libby Gruner, Brian Henry, Ray Hilliard, Peter Lurie, Joyce MacAllister, Anthony Russell, Ilka Saal, Louis Schwartz, Julietta Singh, Nathan Snaza, David Stevens, Louis Tremaine, Nicole Sackley, Eric Yellin, and Doug Winiarski, who have all enhanced my intellectual life and selflessly provided emotional sustenance when I needed it. My ideas for this book were sharpened over many lunches (and even more desserts) with Rob Nelson. He is a valued friend and dependable interlocutor. Thanks to Marcia Whitehead, Lucretia McCulley, and the entire library staff at the University of Richmond for locating and retrieving essential documents.

I have taught some extraordinary students at the University of Richmond. However, my fall 2012 U.S. Apocalyptic Literature and Culture seminar—which included Scott Rockensies, Miles McKemy, Denise Parker, Austin

Carter, Rachel Ringgold, Ryann Dannelly, Gino Grieco, Rachel Bevels, Starr Miyata, and Aromi Lee—was a once-in-a-career group. They dazzled me daily with their insights and charmed me with their warm and caring natures. The coda to this book came into focus as a direct result of the many conversations I had with them about the contemporary apocalyptic moment.

I have benefited enormously from the generosity of many scholars who contributed in meaningful ways to the development of this book. Mary Foltz, Chris Leise, and Angela Szczepaniak provided valuable commentary on early chapter drafts, and Clay Hooper offered important clarifications about the Scottish Common Sense tradition. Mike Hurst has been an abiding presence in the unfolding of this project. I continue to profit from his remarkable mind. Wai Chee Dimock, Claudia Stokes, and Cindy Weinstein helped me focus pivotal aspects of my argument (and avoid some terrible blunders). And Tracy Fessenden, at a key moment in the process, reminded me of how good I really have it. Jim Hersh taught me the important lesson that intellectual work is always about the ideas, never the ego. In addition to everything else they have given me, Bill Burns, Jamie Carr, and Maglina Lubovich continue to lift my spirits with their friendship and humor.

From among this very generous community of scholars, I must single out several colleagues who have been with this project since its inception and have read every word of every draft and revision. Arthur Riss has left an indelible mark on this book as well as my understanding of early American literature. I am continually inspired by his brilliant mind and moved by his limitless generosity. And to the members of my writing group—Amy Howard, Elizabeth Outka, and Monika Siebert—I offer my deepest thanks. So many hours we spent in each other's company—exchanging ideas, expressing frustrations, celebrating successes, and consoling for setbacks. These three extraordinary scholars provided an invaluable habitat to work in, one that was as compassionate as it was intellectually demanding. Without them, this book never gets off the ground.

Working with the University of Georgia Press has been a supremely gratifying experience. My thanks to Nancy Grayson for supporting this project in its early stages, and to Walter Biggins for overseeing the completion of the manuscript. Walter was a reassuring presence at every stage of the book's development. As the manuscript went to production, Beth Sneed fielded my many inquiries with an impressive amount of patience. I am indebted to the outside readers for UGA Press who engaged my argument with such care and whose feedback allowed me to make significant improvements to the manuscript. Jackie Penny at the American Antiquarian Society and Nancy Sherbert at the Kansas State Historical Society kindly offered their help locating and scanning images for the book. Laura Holliday and Daniel Simon provided meticulous editorial feedback on the initial draft of the manuscript. And Union Theological Seminary in Richmond offered me resources and a much-needed workspace during my leave.

I am extremely fortunate to have family and friends who never tired of hearing my grumblings as I worked to complete this book and who were always quick to offer reassurance when I was overcome with doubt. I cannot stress enough how much I have been fortified by their love. Ever since we were young, my brother, Chris, has given me his unfailing support, and this has not gone unnoticed. I remain his biggest fan. His wife, Heather, and their children, Ameilia and Nathan Pelletier, have been an abiding source of comfort, especially in some very difficult moments. My sincerest thanks go to Jack and Aggie Walsh for opening their home to me (which I often turned into an office space). Mark Silvia and Todd Brayton were my first intellectual inspirations. Greg and Michelle Bressler have been an extension of my own family, and Greg's unique take on the nineteenth century has certainly informed my own. Jason Ritz is truly a master in the art of conversation; my life has been profoundly enriched by our many discussions over the years.

I completed many of the final edits to this book on long train rides from Richmond, Virginia, to Northfield, Massachusetts. My mother, Francine Pelletier, who has been integral to every success I have ever enjoyed, was diagnosed with a terminal illness not long before the manuscript was due. Despite her failing health, she continued to ask me a question she had been asking throughout the previous five years: "Have you finished your book yet?" And I would always respond, with a laugh, "Not yet, but soon." I remain deeply saddened that she passed away before the publication of this book, for it is as much her achievement as it is mine. *Apocalyptic Sentimentalism* is a testament to her life and to the life of my father, Roland Pelletier, who passed away while I was a graduate student. They were an enormous presence in my life, and I feel their loss all the more as a result.

My son, Emerson, and my daughter, Lisette, made up for the lows I experienced along the way. I absolutely adore their goofy personalities and am often overwhelmed by their great big hearts. They are an endless source of laughter and joy.

Finally, I owe everything to Kendra Vendetti, who gave more to this project than I had any right to ask or expect. Her influence extends well beyond this book, and I can never hope to repay all that she has done for me (though I will try). The life I currently enjoy is due in large measure to Kendra's presence in it. This book is lovingly dedicated to her.

Parts of this book have been previously published in different form. A portion of chapter 3 appeared in "*Uncle Tom's Cabin* and Apocalyptic Sentimentalism,"

Lit: Literature Interpretation Theory 20, no. 4 (2009): 266–87. Portions of chapters 1 and 4 appeared in "David Walker, Harriet Beecher Stowe, and the Logic of Sentimental Terror," *African American Review* 46, nos. 2–3 (Summer–Fall 2014): 255–69. My thanks to Taylor & Francis and the Johns Hopkins University Press for permission to republish material in these works.

Apocalyptic Sentimentalism

INTRODUCTION

The Sentimental Apocalypse

> There is no need of entering upon a laboured proof of the doctrine so plainly declared, *That there will be a day of Judgment for mankind.* It is what seems written by the finger of God himself upon the consciences of men.
> —Elihu Baldwin, "The Final Judgment," *1827*

> Though in many of its aspects this visible world seems formed in love, the invisible spheres were formed in fright.
> —*Herman Melville,* Moby-Dick, *1851*

In an 1829 entry from the *New-York Gospel Herald* titled "Remarks on the Term Vengeance," a writer identifying himself as PAULUS expresses frustration at how "orthodox christians" have manipulated ideas of God's vengeance to justify their own vengeful natures. By "orthodox christians," PAULUS mostly likely means Calvinists, and his entry exemplifies larger shifts that were rapidly taking place within American religious culture, where practitioners of more "liberal" faiths were beginning to contest the authority of their Calvinist predecessors.[1] "The vengeance of an orthodox christian...," PAULUS observes, "is *only* to consign his enemies to an endless future *hell*, and then to laugh at them" as they suffer eternal torment. Because this application of vengeance has no redemptive aim, it fails to accord with the example first established by the Christian God who, says PAULUS, exacts vengeance for a very specific purpose: to "*vindicate* the cause of the oppressed." Eager to challenge orthodox accounts, which seem unduly sadistic, the writer of this entry cannot simply repudiate vengeance as an unnecessary evil, in part because he has already conceded that the "Christian Lord" promises to engage in acts of vengeance to defend and deliver the oppressed. As troubling as the orthodox view might be, vengeance nevertheless remains an organizing force within a providentially designed universe. PAULUS resolves this dilemma by insisting on an apparent paradox: if, as Christ's apostles once asserted, "GOD IS LOVE," then, concludes PAULUS, "the vengeance of God is the vengeance of *Love* ... it is the vengeance of a *Saviour*." Rather than reject or marginalize vengeance, PAULUS affirms it as a characteristic of God and a sign of his loving nature. "As 'God is love,'" he reasons, "and as 'God is our Saviour,' his vengeance is compatible with love; is the reverse of hatred, and is, also, in his wonder working hand, a means of effecting the lasting good and happiness of his creatures."[2] What initially seem like inherently distinct and antagonistic impulses, PAULUS sees as perfectly compatible, arguing that examples of God's vengeance are a reflection of God's love and a sign of his redemptive power. Indeed, he goes so far as to conflate the two, suggesting that vengeance is an *expression* of God's love. When God commits acts of retribution against the reprobate, he is displaying compassion for those he chooses to redeem. The Christian God, in this writer's view, is simultaneously a God of love and vengeance, compassion and wrath. By suggesting that love and vengeance are cooperative and even interchangeable urges, PAULUS is able to counter what he sees as the orthodox Christian view, which treats vengeance as an end in and of itself. In its place, he offers a perspective that regards God's vengeance as a means to some greater end, namely, "effecting the lasting good and happiness of his creatures."[3]

While PAULUS's account might initially seem to modern readers like a singular instance of illogic, the pairing of love and vengeance was common in early-nineteenth-century religious, political, and aesthetic culture. Vengeance played a crucial role in attempts to construct a moral world; reminders of God's possible vengeance, and the fear that these reminders produced, served as an incentive to be good and were meant to guide individuals to live righteously. Antebellum readers were surrounded by appeals to the most radical form of moral vengeance—namely, depictions of religious apocalypse—and representations of God's apocalyptic wrath were ubiquitous in the first half of the nineteenth century. From mainstream best-sellers to other forms of cultural production, including broadsides, emblem books, juvenile literature, ballads, religious hymns, and political caricatures, depictions of apocalypse made up a foundational part of antebellum religious culture. While Christian orthodoxy enjoined its followers to nurture a compassionate heart and to follow God's mandate to love one's neighbor, it also warned of his impending wrath and judgment for those who failed to abide by God's laws. Vengeance, in short, was the repercussion for failing to love.

Nowhere is this dynamic—in which the fear of God's wrath is used to bolster compassionate feelings—more visible than in the foremost discourse of love in the nineteenth century: sentimentalism. This claim may surprise readers who have come to view nineteenth-century sentimentality as a philosophy of sympathetic affections. While the scholarly tradition has thoroughly delineated the ways in which sentimentalism is both premised on and promotional of feelings of deep-seated love to facilitate interpersonal connections as well as generate widespread social transformation, it has tended to overlook how foundational threats of God's vengeance, and the terror these threats inspire, are within the nineteenth-century culture of sentiment.[4] When, for example, Harriet Beecher Stowe famously asserted that the moral growth of the nation ultimately depended on each citizen's ability to "feel right," she voiced a sentiment shared by many of her contemporaries who felt that most Americans were insufficiently sympathetic toward Negro slaves. And it is no surprise that scholars have assumed Stowe's injunction to "feel right" was a call to feel compassion and love, for it was ostensibly through a rhetoric of Christian love that Stowe was able to foment a passionate outcry against slavery among many of her Northern readers. Indeed, sentimentalism's transformative potential is best expressed in Stowe's antislavery writing, and scholars continue to uphold her fiction as the paradigmatic example of nineteenth-century abolitionist sentimentality. What made sentimentalism powerful, as evinced by Stowe's best-selling novels, was that it fostered a community whose members were bonded together by an abiding sense of sympathetic love. "Compassion," Philip Fisher succinctly puts it, "is, of course, the primary emotional goal of sentimental narration,"[5] and critics continue to read Stowe's novels specifically, and the sentimental tradition more generally, as confirmation that the nineteenth-century culture of sentiment remained deeply committed to love's transformative capabilities, especially as a means to challenge an institution as hegemonic and pernicious as slavery.[6]

The problem with this widely shared view, however, is that while scholars continue to treat love as the autonomous force of the sentimental tradition, nineteenth-century sentimentalists, including Stowe, expressed profound misgivings about the capacity of love to establish the kinds of sympathetic bonds contemporary critics now take for granted. *Apocalyptic Sentimentalism* reevaluates this scholarly view by investigating a crucial but neglected dimension of the nineteenth-century culture of sentiment: its passionate investment in fear as an indispensable engine of cultural and political transformation. When sentimental writers like Stowe could not depend on love to produce a sympathetic response in readers, fear often served as an incentive to love, energizing love's power and underwriting its potential to convert Americans from fallible sinners into moral beings. Fear exists at the center of nineteenth-century sentimental strategies for effecting social change and cohering disparate communities, often bolstering love when love falters and operating as a principal mechanism for establishing sympathetic connections across lines of difference. In order to inspire a profound sense of fear in their audience, nineteenth-century sentimentalists often deployed prophecies of God's apocalyptic vengeance, a familiar source of dread in Protestant America and one of the most efficient ways to politicize terror in the antebellum period.[7] Rather than existing outside of or in conflict with sentimentalism, apocalyptic vengeance helped to shape the very formation of the nineteenth-century sentimental tradition. The preceding example of PAULUS illustrates the sentimental dynamic I elaborate in the following pages. PAULUS links love and vengeance—an unsurprising move within an evolving Calvinist/Puritan religious tradition. What *is* surprising is how this tradition has been removed and segregated from sentimental discourse. I seek to reestablish the link between this religious tradition and the sentimental tradition, to recover how during the antebellum period antislavery advocates worked to connect sympathy for the slave to an apocalyptic tradition, and to reveal how this linkage came to be erased in modern accounts of the relationship between sentimentality and antislavery reform. Investigating this intersection of love and fear, *Apocalyptic Sentimentalism* proposes a new genealogy for understanding literary sentimentalism as a complex negotiation of seemingly oppositional emotional economies. I read love and fear not as competing and fundamentally separate emotional impulses but as imbricated. I call this imbrication "apocalyptic sentimentalism" to emphasize that sentimental writers did not simply construct a self-generating and self-sustaining account of sympathetic love, but instead used the fear of an imminent apocalypse to augment love's force. Conversely, these writers often saw sympathetic love as inspiring a fearful vengeance, both on the part of God and in those they saw as his messengers on earth. The threat of God's vengeful wrath and the terror that this threat produces are what ultimately ensure the culture of sentiment's confidence in sympathy.[8]

Taking my cue from Stowe, whose early writing brought a powerful sentimental aesthetic to bear on antebellum debates over slavery, I focus my investigation by specifically attending to nineteenth-century antislavery writing and the tradition of abolitionist sentimentality. Perhaps no reform movement was more effective at marshaling a rhetoric of wrath than Northern abolition, with abolitionists often using ideas of divine vengeance as the ultimate penalty for a nation that held other human beings in abject bondage. For most antislavery reformers, slavery constituted an egregious violation against God and a breach of the nation's political and moral foundations, and thus it required an urgent response. Among their many shortcomings, slaveholders lacked a compassionate heart toward their slaves. Antislavery reformers employed a range of tactics to challenge the logic of race-based slavery, one of which was to encourage a greater emotional connection between defenders of slavery and enslaved blacks, a strategy that might, in turn, persuade the slaveholder to relinquish his slaveholding practices. To this end, they frequently reminded audiences of the fearful consequences of failing to establish a sympathetic bond with slaves. In William Lloyd Garrison's preface to Frederick Douglass's *Narrative*, for example, Garrison remarks that a reader "who can peruse" Douglass's narrative "without a tearful eye, a heaving breast, an afflicted spirit" and who is not "filled with an unutterable abhorrence of slavery and all its abettors ... —without trembling for the fate of this country in the hands of a righteous God, who is ever on the side of the oppressed, and whose arm is not shortened that it cannot save,— must have a flinty heart, and be qualified to act the part of a trafficker 'in slaves and the souls of men.'"[9] Garrison calls for a classic sentimental response, with the requisite tearful eyes and afflicted spirit. It is when readers with hardened hearts remain unmoved, however, that Garrison reminds them that God will not let the sins of slavery go unpunished, invoking God's wrath in order to incite a sympathetic connection that will lead to some form of action against slavery. If sympathetic love is Garrison's goal, vengeance is his vehicle.

Readers already familiar with nineteenth-century sentimentality can appreciate why Garrison would use its conventions in his prefatory comments. Sentimentality was thought by its practitioners to encourage intersubjective relations predicated on sympathy and love, offering a powerful mechanism for reformers to imagine egalitarian forms of social exchange and for antislavery activists in particular to argue for interracial bonds based on deep affect.[10] What reformers who used sentimental conventions also knew, and what is missing from the scholarly narrative, was the extent to which vengeance and terror helped energize calls for sympathy and love, and how love might generate acts of vengeance. It is not only the tearful eye and afflicted spirit, but also the warning of God's wrath, that mark Garrison's preface as sentimental. I chart the development of apocalyptic sentimentality by tracing a surprising genealogy, one that begins with David Walker, Nat Turner, and Maria Stewart, moves through the antislavery fiction of Harriet Beecher Stowe, and culminates in 1859 at Harpers Ferry with John Brown. Each of these figures makes critical contributions to the evolution of apocalyptic sentimentalism in the thirty years leading up to the Civil War precisely by treating God's love and his vengeance not as antithetical but, in the spirit of PAULUS, necessarily cooperative and inseparably intermingled.

While I argue that fear occupies an essential place within the nineteenth-century culture of sentiment, I am not suggesting that every work of sentimental narration is necessarily predicated on the deployment of terror as part of its structure of affect. As Cindy Weinstein has incisively observed, the structure of sympathy is not always the same among the many works comprising the vast tradition of literary sentimentalism. There was, rather, an "extraordinarily rich and ideologically diverse debate about sympathy that was taking place in the antebellum period."[11] Following Weinstein, I recognize that there are multiple sentimental traditions circulating during this period, and one in particular— abolitionist sentimentality—that becomes increasingly linked and indebted to an apocalyptic account of love and judgment. I aim in *Apocalyptic Sentimentalism* to recover how sympathy was produced within antislavery discourses without making broad claims about all works of sentimental literature.[12] Some works, for example, like Catharine Maria Sedgwick's *Hope Leslie*, explicitly disavow ideas of vengeance and reject fear as part of their sentimental makeup. In *Hope Leslie*, Puritan forebears like Governor Winthrop, generally viewed as synonymous with an austere Calvinism, are represented more like benevolent patriarchs. For Sedgwick, the type of theological terror embodied by the Puritans runs counter to the aims of domestic fiction.[13]

Conversely, Harriet Beecher Stowe was deeply committed to fear as a sentimental register, especially in her early antislavery fiction. Throughout *Uncle Tom's Cabin* and *Dred*, expressions of love and reminders of God's retribution appear together, suggesting that terror is just as fundamental as love to Stowe's theory of sentimentality. Susan Warner's *The Wide Wide World* occupies a middle ground between *Hope Leslie* and Stowe's antislavery fiction. Unlike Sedgwick, Warner does not completely discount the usefulness of fear in establishing a moral worldview and nurturing intimate bonds between persons, but she does not go so far as to organize her novel around the vibrant interplay between love and terror like Stowe does. For instance, in a scene from Warner's best-seller that portrays a crucial moment in Ellen Montgomery's religious education, Ellen listens to her mentor and confidant, Alice Humphreys, explain how important it is to be "full of love to our Saviour." When Ellen laments that she does not know precisely how to ensure that she remain loving toward God and others, Alice replies, first, by gently warning Ellen that they must remain "mindful to do nothing we shall not wish to remember in the great day of account," and, second, by asking Ellen to open her Bible to the book of Revelation, chapter 20: "And the sea gave up the dead which were in it; and death and hell delivered up the dead which were in them; and they were judged every man according to their works. And death and hell were cast into the lake of fire.... And whosoever was not found written in the book of life was cast into the lake of fire." Alice affirms Ellen's understandable response of "That is dreadful!" by noting, "It will be a dreadful day to all but those whose names are written in the Lamb's book of life."[14] Instead of turning to the Gospels so that Ellen might see examples of Jesus's loving and merciful nature, Alice instead looks to the concluding book of the New Testament, with its descriptions of death and everlasting hellfire, to encourage Ellen to cultivate a properly loving heart. Warner's depictions of judgment as an incentive for greater love fall along a continuum with Sedgwick on one end, Stowe on the other, and this continuum within the sentimental tradition serves as a microcosm of the highly turbulent religious context of antebellum culture, where Americans in religious, political, and artistic circles were wrestling with complex and, for some, contradictory scriptural representations of God's mercy and wrath.[15]

By returning apocalyptic terror to the sentimental tradition, I challenge the way scholars often read the development of sentimentalism within the

American context. Scholars have argued that because of its roots in the Scottish Enlightenment, sentimentalism exists in opposition to the more severe and pessimistic dimensions of Calvinist theology.[16] In contrast to Calvinism's deeply negative view of human nature, the Scottish Common Sense tradition offered a more optimistic vision of sociality in which individuals cohere into communities, in part, through acts of sympathetic identification, and it is this impulse that strongly influenced U.S. sentimental culture.[17] Many scholars see the rise of sentimentalism to be coterminous with and even partly responsible for the decline of Calvinist thought. This view has been most forcefully articulated by Ann Douglas, who maintained that the "sentimentalization of theological and secular culture" subverted the scrupulously intellectual Calvinism that characterized American Protestant thought until the 1820s.[18] It is for Douglas an "obvious historical fact" that "American Calvinism possessed in the seventeenth and eighteenth centuries, and lost in the nineteenth, a sternness, an intellectual rigor which our society then and since has been accustomed to identify with 'masculinity' in some not totally inaccurate if circular sense."[19] Such sentimentalizing trends precipitated a crisis of masculinity, a sign for Douglas of American culture's vitiated intellectual and theological foundations. "For economic and social reasons," Douglas explains, "Calvinism was largely defeated by an anti-intellectual sentimentalism purveyed by men and women whose victory did not achieve their finest goals; America lost its male-dominated theological tradition without gaining a comprehensive feminism or an adequately modernized religious sensibility."[20]

Douglas's seminal work, *The Feminization of American Culture*, is a book that has set the terms of the critical debate for over thirty years and, in my view, misreads the sentimental tradition as emerging in opposition to a strong masculinist Calvinism. Indeed, modern scholarship on sentimentalism is, via Douglas, born out of this false opposition between nineteenth-century sentimentality and Calvinist theology. The many critics who have challenged Douglas for her unfair treatment of sentimentalism's feminist underpinnings have nevertheless accepted her animating premise that Calvinism and the sentimental are opposed rather than often working in close concert. Some critics, like Jane Tompkins and Gregg Camfield, have recognized, along with Douglas, the apocalypticism of *Uncle Tom's Cabin*, for example, without reading this theological dimension as a part of the novel's sentimentality. Most critics, however, tend to ignore the apocalyptic altogether. What was fundamental to antislavery sentimentality—the energizing force of vengeance—has fallen completely out of scholarly view. Recuperating this relationship between love and vengeance within abolitionist discourses, I demonstrate that a prominent strand of sentimentalism actually included much of the same Puritanical authoritativeness that Douglas lauds in a writer like Herman Melville. This authority and sternness is expressed within an apocalyptic register, suggesting that the so-called feminization of American culture does not exclude the apocalyptic but is, at times, thoroughly dependent on it. Indeed, antislavery discourse stands as the clearest example of the fact that this period was not as religiously liberal as is commonly thought.

By ignoring the dynamic between sentiment and hardline religious orthodoxy, or treating their interaction as an intractable tension, scholars of the sentimental tradition have unwittingly generated a rigid binary, with wrath on one side and love on the other, that ultimately fails to explain fully the ongoing interaction between calls for love and threats of divine retribution within nineteenth-century religious and sentimental culture. Modern readers often impose the same broad binary onto the Christian Bible, locating wrath exclusively in the Old Testament, love in the New. This view obscures the many instances in which the New Testament foretells an apocalyptic end to history, most notably in the book of Revelation. Such a view also elides the many narratives of love that pervade the Old Testament. Nineteenth-century Americans, however, perceived a far greater continuity between the Old and New Testaments than the scholarly tradition appreciates, especially regarding apocalyptic prophecy.[21]

Rather than separate the sentimental from the apocalyptic or disregard their linkage, I consider how the apocalyptic fundamentally shaped abolitionist narratives and antislavery politics. When love and vengeance are reconsidered as a mutually reinforcing pair, our understanding of the religious entanglements of sentimentalism, as well as our views on the organizing principles of abolition, must shift to accommodate a far deeper engagement with apocalyptic wrath. I examine the writings of antislavery activists who felt an overwhelming resolve to transform America's moral landscape and who often warned of God's coming judgment to inspire in their readers a sense of urgency to reform their hearts. Indeed, a discourse of apocalyptic sentimentalism is deployed first and foremost to incite action and galvanize a complacent nation to finally address the evils of slavery. Many antislavery reformers and sentimental writers understood that too few white Americans were sympathizing strongly enough with slaves, despite how wretched the slaves' conditions on the plantations were. The decade leading up to the war saw the expanding reach of slavery, first with the Fugitive Slave Act (1850) and then with the Kansas-Nebraska Act (1854). Chief Justice Taney's ruling in *Dred Scott v. Sandford* (1857), moreover, inscribed into law what was already the operating assumption among most whites in the South as well as in the North: blacks not only lacked the legal status to sue in a court of law, but they also failed to meet the legal criteria for citizenship in antebellum America. "We think," Taney writes in his ruling, "that [Negroes] are not included, and were not intended to be included, under the word 'citizens' in the Constitution, and can therefore claim none of the rights and privileges which that instrument provides for and secures to citizens of the United States."[22] Alongside a government that legislated the expansion of slavery and a Supreme Court that sided with the Slave Power, Protestant clergy failed to offer a consensus on the morality of slaveholding, with many instead defending slavery as a reflection of God's will.[23] Indeed, the major institutions in America either supported slavery or avoided the debate altogether. Given this reality, many antislavery sentimentalists appreciated that merely calling for sympathy, or representing scenes of sorrowful slaves that were meant to elicit an emotional response from white readers, was not necessarily going to compel white Americans to feel compassion for Negro slaves. Sympathy, in other words, was not sufficiently powerful on its own to enact the kind of transformation that it was deployed to achieve. The terror of being a potential victim of God's wrath served as a prerequisite to sympathy when sympathy was not an automatic or guaranteed response.

Religion, Terror, Sentiment

Apocalyptic terror's place within antebellum political and aesthetic discourse is not without its historical precedents. Indeed, a rhetoric of terror has been a central part of America's religious culture since the arrival of Anglo-Protestants. The New England Puritans believed that they were a covenantal nation chosen by God to establish his earthly church, and Puritan ministers frequently warned of the severe penalties for backsliding. Such warnings served as a powerful incentive for believers within these Bible commonwealths to fulfill their covenantal obligations and abide by God's word lest they find themselves in a perilous moral state. The Puritans understood from the start what antebellum Americans came to realize in their efforts to challenge slavery: forming a just community sometimes takes some coercion. One of the principal traits of the Puritan sermon, then, was fear, specifically fear of God's retributive wrath. Such depictions, while designed to terrify congregants into choosing a life of righteousness over sin, are also intended to foster a communal attachment among congregants. In what is still the defining study of the Puritan sermon, Sacvan Bercovitch argues that the jeremiad "made anxiety its end as well as its means. Crisis was the social norm it sought to inculcate.... The future, though divinely assured, was never quite there, and New England's Jeremiahs set out to provide the sense of insecurity that would ensure the outcome."[24] By creating an atmosphere of crisis and alarm, the Puritan minister attempted to make certain that his Bible commonwealth would fulfill its religious duties. God's displeasure with his chosen community and his subsequent retribution—two defining themes of the jeremiad—produced the requisite fear and anxiety to bind the Puritan society to its theological obligations and to compel its communicants to act with Christian virtue. Crisis, alarm, and fear—together with Christian love—were for the Puritans essential components of a communal-building economy.

Consider, for example, what is perhaps the most famous Puritan sermon: Jonathan Edwards's "Sinners in the Hands of an Angry God." Edwards's exhortation is recognized for the depths to which he imagines human depravity and his extended descriptions of the extreme and vivid forms of violence God plans to inflict on sinners. For much of the sermon, Edwards instructs his listeners to reflect on their sins and appreciate that "were it not that so is the sovereign pleasure of God, the earth would not bear you one moment; for you are a burden to it."[25] Edwards warns that "there are the black clouds of God's wrath now hanging directly over your heads, full of the dreadful storm, and big with thunder; and were it not for the restraining hand of God it would immediately burst forth upon you."[26] Threats like these are pervasive in "Sinners," but they are meant to serve a greater spiritual purpose for members of the Enfield congregation where he first delivered the sermon.[27] At a crucial moment near the end of his discourse, Edwards redirects his listeners' attention away from their personal sins and asks them to consider the spiritual well-being of the entire church. "There is reason to think," says Edwards, "that there are many in this congregation now hearing this discourse, that will actually be the subjects of this very misery to all eternity." Up until this point, Edwards has encouraged his listeners to fixate on their own sinfulness, isolating each congregant from every other congregant, and therefore creating a false separation between a congregant's spiritual health and the spiritual health of the entire commonwealth. He aims to mend this division by imploring his audience to remain mindful of the entire community of believers: "If we knew that there was one person, and but one, in the whole congregation that was to be the subject of this misery, what an awful thing would it be to think of! If we knew who it was, what an awful sight would it be to see such a person! How might all the rest of the congregation *lift up a lamentable and bitter cry over him!*"[28] Edwards suggests that the very thought of a congregant's everlasting damnation might unify the entire congregation in a collective expression of grief and sorrow, presumably because each congregant would be able to feel the sinner's fear and despair, or at the very least imagine himself or herself in a similar state of anguish. Edwards asks his listeners to extend themselves in an act of compassion, and while he does not use the term "sympathy," he appears to be making a claim about the importance of fostering sympathetic bonds within a covenantal community.[29] This is not, of course, an example of sentimentality; Puritan accounts of love differ markedly from sentimental ones.[30] But the structure of Edwards's sermon serves as an ideological precursor to the structure of apocalyptic sentimentalism that I examine throughout this book. In order to motivate sentiments of sympathy, Edwards spends considerable time focusing on the consequences of failing to be sufficiently sympathetic, and nineteenth-century sentimental writers will do the same.[31]

Edwards's sermon not only exemplifies the dimension of affect within the apocalyptic sentimental tradition, but it also illustrates the directional logic of two different but nevertheless entangled emotional impulses that the authors discussed throughout this study deploy in order to generate antislavery sentiment. Love, in the examples that follow, is inherently other-oriented; it brings a person into contact with another through an affective extension of the self. It is precisely because of the sentimental tradition's emphasis on sociality and promotion of intersubjective relations that some scholars have read it as an important component in the expansion of American democratic culture.[32] Conversely, fear encourages self-interest and self-preservation.[33] Warnings of God's wrath like the one we see in Edwards's sermon are designed to promote introspection and a careful consideration of one's sins so that one might make the requisite changes to avoid God's disapproving judgment. For Edwards, as well as for the writers working within the tradition of abolitionist sentimentality, introspection energized by fear could lead to a renunciation of sin and might even generate a loving connection between oneself and another that was previously inhibited by some form of selfish interest or moral profligacy. That is, while love is the goal, it must at times be compelled by the threat of eternal torment. This is the sentimental structure that writers like David Walker and Harriet Beecher Stowe elaborate and depend on, a structure that was first expressed by America's Puritan forebears.

The tradition of apocalyptic sentimentalism I chart in this book develops alongside several major overlapping nineteenth-century religious and cultural transformations: the decline of Calvinist thought, the rise of evangelical Protestantism, and the advent of religious liberalism, running parallel to and intersecting with the period's denominational diversification.[34] While the antebellum period is often noted for the way evangelical and liberal Protestant churches challenged some of the more gloomy and orthodox tenets of Calvinism (i.e., total depravity in human beings, the absence of free will, and limited salvation for the elect), many of these denominations continued to believe in a revised (and often muted) version of apocalyptic theology, even as they emphasized the more loving and merciful aspects of Christ.[35] This amalgamation of end-times theology with an emphasis on God's redemptive power and promise of salvation was an especially prominent feature within the revivalist fervor of the Second Great Awakening, where ministers attempted to facilitate widespread conversion experiences and usher in God's millennial kingdom. Revivalist ministers exuberantly promoted ideas of Christ's second coming and enjoined their listeners to live piously as a way of ushering in a new heaven and a new earth.

They continued, however, to warn of the consequences of failing to reform one's heart and repudiate sin, inspiring in attendees a profound sense of dread at the prospect of being cast into hell. "It is vain for men to think of keeping destruction at a distance," one Congregationalist minister announced at the height of the Second Great Awakening, "and keeping the uplifted arm of vengeance long suspended, by wavering, and hesitating, and deferring the time of decision:—vain indeed to think of delaying the hour of their doom."[36] In short, there is no clean break between hard-line Calvinist theology and the more moderate forms of belief that sought to replace it. *Apocalyptic Sentimentalism* narrates this uneven and often messy shift away from Calvinism by featuring texts from various religious denominations and backgrounds that depict the Christian God as simultaneously loving and wrathful, suggesting that these two impulses were fundamental to how many nineteenth-century believers understood God's authority.

Apocalypse in the Antebellum Period

I use variations of the term *apocalypse* throughout this study, even though the figures that I examine never do. While terms like wrath, vengeance, and judgment were the more common idiom among antebellum Protestants, I have deliberately chosen apocalypse to serve as an umbrella category that encompasses each of these related ideas. The apocalypse in this book is intended to signify a threat suspended, regardless of the specific lexicon a given writer chooses to deploy in his or her text. Apocalypse is a warning that God will scourge reprobates for their sinful ways but never an actual depiction of this scourging.

The threat in suspension is what generates continuous feelings of terror meant to motivate readers' abandonment of sin. The suspended nature of the apocalyptic threat is ultimately the source of its power because it locates the reader on the threshold of doom without ever condemning him or her to everlasting misery and woe. In this respect, the apocalypse is actually more reformatory than it is apocalyptic. It is not about the end as such, but about creating a temporal opening in the present in which readers have time to change their hearts before the actual end arrives. Of course, many antebellum Americans did not view apocalyptic theology as exclusively negative or punitive. Indeed, many nineteenth-century believers eagerly looked forward to Christ's second coming as a glorious event that would rid the world of sin.[37] In the chapters that follow, however, I mainly emphasize the coercive and disciplinary uses of apocalyptic theology, for this was how abolitionists used threats of God's vengeance in their writing. And while exegetical debates about Revelation and apocalyptic prophecy appeared in religious periodicals or were elaborated from the church pulpit throughout the antebellum period, the figures I consider employ the apocalyptic as a political, sentimental, or aesthetic category, and most often as some combination of the three. As a style of narrative (aesthetic) marshaled to effect social change (political) and inspire a powerful emotional response from readers (sentimental), the apocalypse displays a versatility that scholars do not often appreciate or recognize in their discussions of antislavery writing, sentimentality, and America's complex religious culture. *Apocalyptic Sentimentalism* offers new ways of understanding how the figure of the apocalypse helped form nineteenth-century sentimental culture and how a sentimental apocalypse bears on the political efforts of abolitionists and antislavery writers who were not strict Calvinists but who nevertheless understood how central warnings of God's coming vengeance were in shaping debates over slavery.

Despite the regularity with which depictions of God's wrath were used in the antebellum period to encourage various forms of political and cultural transformation, my focus on this particular style of apocalyptic representation is comparatively narrow when considered among the great diversity of apocalyptic figurations that characterize the first half of the nineteenth century. In one important overarching sense, the apocalypse is a religious master narrative that organizes the dramatic unfolding and ultimate fulfillment of providential history. For evangelicals, the second coming of Christ was an ordained and highly climatic event for this privileged redeemer nation.[38] In this sense, faith in a coming apocalypse remained a vital force in shaping the way Americans lived their lives, for in one's daily existence, nothing less than the eternal salvation of souls and the longevity of America as a covenantal nation were at stake. Within this eschatological framework, the apocalypse is the most dramatic of categories, and there was no shortage of guides to understanding apocalyptic prophecy so that one could make appropriate preparations for Christ's imminent return. Broadsides, for example, like the one announcing Rev. Wm. B. Hayden's ten-part course explicating the book of Revelation (figure 1), were familiar parts of Protestant America, as were various explanatory maps that helped guide apocalyptic exegesis, like Lowman and Faber's "A Key to the Revelations" (figure 2).[39] One broadside even advertises the coming day of judgment by announcing it in the style of a playbill, with a description of the scenery, a list of the performers, and an act-by-act summary of events that culminates in an "oration by the SON OF GOD" (figure 3).[40] This publication uses dramatic conventions to capture the drama in Christ's expected return.

While antebellum Americans understandably regarded the apocalypse as an inherently dramatic category, its ubiquity rendered it a rather quotidian notion as well. The more ideas of apocalypse begin to populate the daily lives of antebellum Americans in the early decades of the nineteenth century, and the more frequently such notions become integrated into popular forms—in novels, poetry, paintings, and songs—the more commonplace and ordinary the

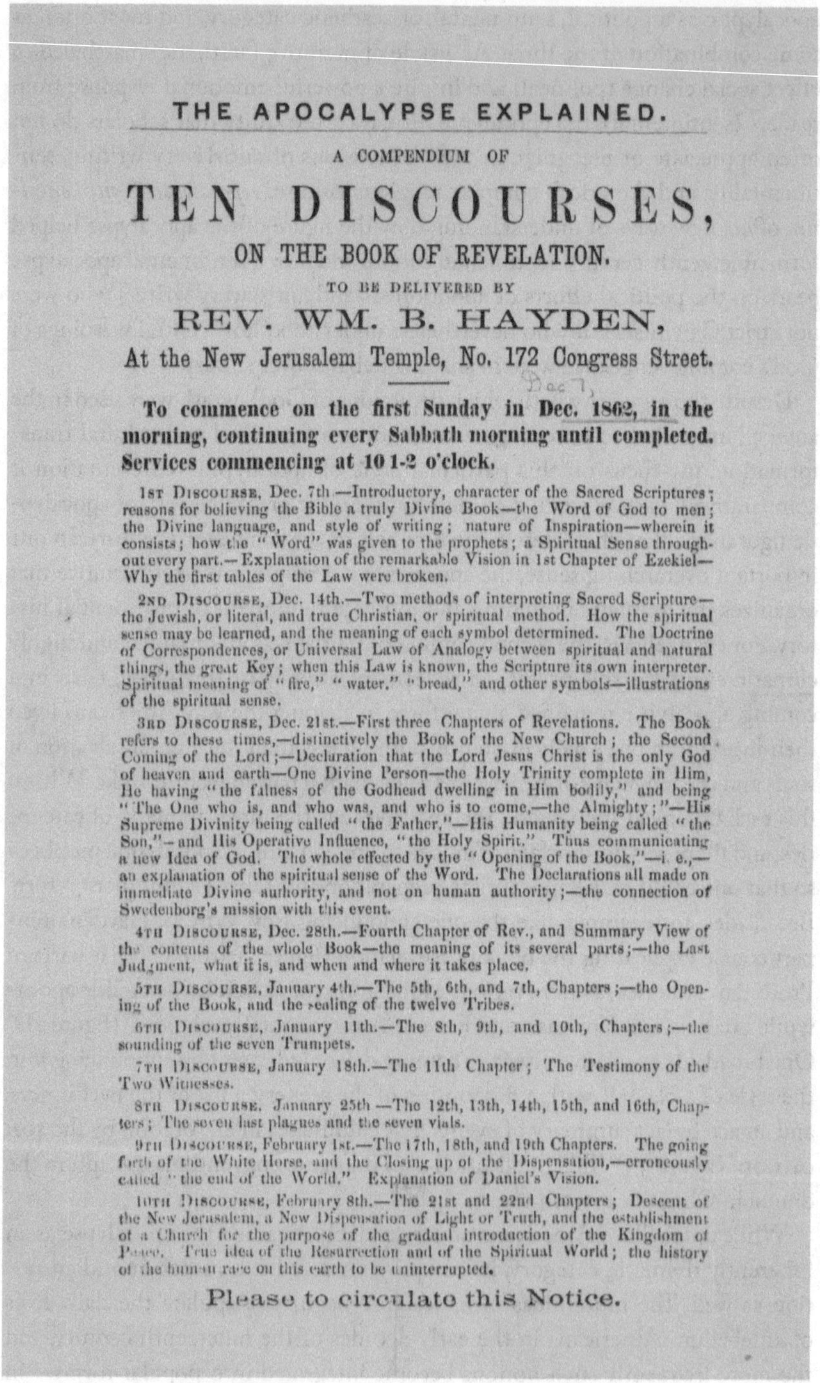

THE APOCALYPSE EXPLAINED.

A COMPENDIUM OF

TEN DISCOURSES,

ON THE BOOK OF REVELATION.

TO BE DELIVERED BY

REV. WM. B. HAYDEN,

At the New Jerusalem Temple, No. 172 Congress Street.

To commence on the first Sunday in Dec. 1862, in the morning, continuing every Sabbath morning until completed. Services commencing at 10 1-2 o'clock.

1ST DISCOURSE, Dec. 7th.—Introductory, character of the Sacred Scriptures; reasons for believing the Bible a truly Divine Book—the Word of God to men; the Divine language, and style of writing; nature of Inspiration—wherein it consists; how the "Word" was given to the prophets; a Spiritual Sense throughout every part.—Explanation of the remarkable Vision in 1st Chapter of Ezekiel—Why the first tables of the Law were broken.

2ND DISCOURSE, Dec. 14th.—Two methods of interpreting Sacred Scripture—the Jewish, or literal, and true Christian, or spiritual method. How the spiritual sense may be learned, and the meaning of each symbol determined. The Doctrine of Correspondences, or Universal Law of Analogy between spiritual and natural things, the great Key; when this Law is known, the Scripture its own interpreter. Spiritual meaning of "fire," "water," "bread," and other symbols—illustrations of the spiritual sense.

3RD DISCOURSE, Dec. 21st.—First three Chapters of Revelations. The Book refers to these times,—distinctively the Book of the New Church; the Second Coming of the Lord;—Declaration that the Lord Jesus Christ is the only God of heaven and earth—One Divine Person—the Holy Trinity complete in Him, He having "the fulness of the Godhead dwelling in Him bodily," and being "The One who is, and who was, and who is to come,—the Almighty;"—His Supreme Divinity being called "the Father,"—His Humanity being called "the Son,"—and His Operative Influence, "the Holy Spirit." Thus communicating a new Idea of God. The whole effected by the "Opening of the Book,"—i. e.,—an explanation of the spiritual sense of the Word. The Declarations all made on immediate Divine authority, and not on human authority;—the connection of Swedenborg's mission with this event.

4TH DISCOURSE, Dec. 28th.—Fourth Chapter of Rev., and Summary View of the contents of the whole Book—the meaning of its several parts;—the Last Judgment, what it is, and when and where it takes place.

5TH DISCOURSE, January 4th.—The 5th, 6th, and 7th, Chapters;—the Opening of the Book, and the sealing of the twelve Tribes.

6TH DISCOURSE, January 11th.—The 8th, 9th, and 10th, Chapters;—the sounding of the seven Trumpets.

7TH DISCOURSE, January 18th.—The 11th Chapter; The Testimony of the Two Witnesses.

8TH DISCOURSE, January 25th.—The 12th, 13th, 14th, 15th, and 16th, Chapters; The seven last plagues and the seven vials.

9TH DISCOURSE, February 1st.—The 17th, 18th, and 19th Chapters. The going forth of the White Horse, and the Closing up of the Dispensation,—erroneously called "the end of the World." Explanation of Daniel's Vision.

10TH DISCOURSE, February 8th.—The 21st and 22nd Chapters; Descent of the New Jerusalem, a New Dispensation of Light or Truth, and the establishment of a Church for the purpose of the gradual introduction of the Kingdom of Peace. True idea of the Resurrection and of the Spiritual World; the history of the human race on this earth to be uninterrupted.

Please to circulate this Notice.

Figure 1. "The Apocalypse Explained: A Compendium of Ten Discourses on the Book of Revelation." American Antiquarian Society.

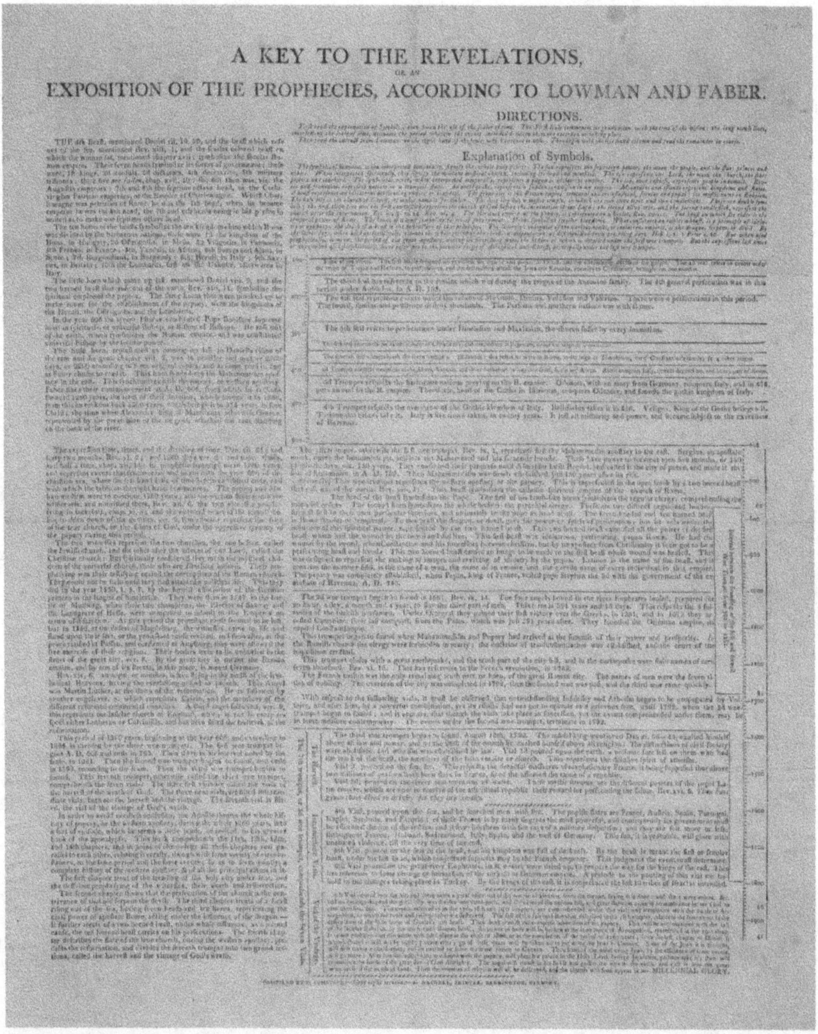

A KEY TO THE REVELATIONS,
OR AN
EXPOSITION OF THE PROPHECIES, ACCORDING TO LOWMAN AND FABER.

DIRECTIONS.

Explanation of Symbols.

Figure 2. "A Key to the Revelations, or an Exposition of the Prophecies, According to Lowman and Faber." American Antiquarian Society.

BY COMMAND OF THE

KING OF KINGS,

AND AT THE DESIRE OF ALL WHO LOVE HIS APPEARING.

AT THE

Theatre of the *Univerſe,*

ON THE EVE OF TIME, WILL BE PERFORMED, THE

GREAT ASSIZE, OR

Day of Judgment.

(RECOMMENDED TO THE INHABITANTS OF BOSTON.)

THE SCENERY, which is now actually preparing, will not only ſurpaſs every thing that has yet been ſeen; but will infinitely exceed the utmoſt ſtretch of human conception. There will be a juſt repreſentation of all the Inhabitants of the world, in their various and proper colours; and their cuſtoms and manners will be ſo exactly and ſo minutely delineated, that the moſt ſecret thoughts will be diſcovered.

THIS THEATRE will be laid out after a new plan, and will conſiſt of Pit and Gallery only: And, contrary to all others, the Gallery is fitted up for the reception of people of high (or heavenly) birth; and the Pit for thoſe of low (or earthly) rank. N. B. The Gallery is very ſpacious, and the Pit without bottom.

To prevent inconvenience, there are ſeparate doors for admitting the company; and they are ſo different that none can miſs them who are not totally blind. The Door which opens into the Gallery is very narrow, and the ſteps up to it are ſomewhat difficult; for which reaſon there are ſeldom many people about it. But the Door that gives entrance into the Pit is very wide, and very commodious; which cauſes ſuch numbers to flock to it, that it is generally crowded. N. B. The ſtrait Door leads towards the right hand, and the broad one to the left.

IT will be in vain for one in a tinſelled coat and borrowed language, to perſonate one of high Birth, in order to get admittance into the upper places; for there is one of wonderful and deep penetration, who will ſearch and examine every individual. And all who cannot pronounce Shiboleth in the language of Canaan, or has not received a white ſtone and new name; or cannot prove a clear title to a certain portion of the land of Promiſe, muſt be turned in at the left hand door.

THE PRINCIPAL PERFORMERS are deſcribed in 2 Theſſ. iv. 6. 2 Theſſ. i. 7. 8. 9. Matth. xxv. 30. 31. and xxv. 31. 32. Daniel vii. 9. 10. Jude 14. 15. Rev. xx. 12—15, &c. But as there are ſome people much better acquainted with the contents of a PLAY BILL, than the Word of God, it may not be amiſs to tranſcribe a verſe or two for their peruſal.

"The Lord Jeſus ſhall be revealed from heaven with his mighty angels, in flaming fire, taking vengeance on them that obey not the goſpel, but to be glorified in his ſaints. A fiery ſtream iſſued and came forth from before him: Thouſand thouſands miniſtered unto him, and ten thouſand times ten thouſand ſtood before him: The judgment was ſet, and the books were opened. And whoſoever was not found written in the book of life, was caſt into the lake of fire."

ACT FIRST of this GRAND and SOLEMN PIECE,

Will be opened by the *ARCH-ANGEL* with the Sound of a Trumpet.

ACT SECOND,

Will be a PROCESSION of SAINTS in White, with GOLDEN HARPS, accompanied with Shouts of Joy and Songs of Praiſe.

ACT THIRD,

Will be an Aſſemblage of all the Unregenerate. The MUSIC will conſiſt chiefly of Cries, accompanied with Weeping, Wailing, Mourning, Lamentation, and Woe.

TO CONCLUDE WITH AN ORATION, BY THE

SON OF GOD.

IT is written in the xxvth of Matthew, from the 34th verſe to the end of the chapter; but for the ſake of thoſe who ſeldom read the ſcriptures I ſhall here tranſcribe two verſes: "Then ſhall the King ſay to them on his right hand, Come, ye bleſſed of my Father, inherit the kingdom prepared for you from the foundation of the world; then ſhall he ſay alſo to them on the left hand, Depart from me, ye curſed, into everlaſting, prepared for the devil and his angels."

After which the CURTAIN will drop.

THEN! O to tell!
Some rais'd on high, and others doom'd to hell!
Theſe praiſe the Lamb, and ſing redeeming love,
Lodg'd in his boſom, all his goodneſs prove,
While thoſe who trampled under foot his grace,
Are baniſh'd now forever from his face.
Divided thus a gulph is fix'd between,
And EVERLASTING cloſes up the ſcene.

TICKETS for the PIT, at the eaſy purchaſe of following the vain pomps and vanities of the faſhionable World, and the deſires and amuſements of the fleſh. To be had at every fleſh-pleaſing aſſembly. Romans viii. 13.

TICKETS for the GALLERY, at no leſs rate than being converted, forſaking all, denying ſelf, taking up the Croſs, and following Chriſt in the regeneration. To be had no where but in the Word of God, and where the Word appointeth.

N. B. No Money will be taken at the door. Nor will any Tickets give admittance into the GALLERY but thoſe ſealed by the Holy Ghoſt, with Emanuel's ſignet.

Thus will I do unto thee, O Iſrael: And becauſe I will do thus unto thee, prepare to meet thy God, O Iſrael. Amos iv. 12.

Figure 3. "By the Command of the King of Kings." American Antiquarian Society.

apocalypse becomes and the more consumable it is as something other than a prediction for the end of the world. Canonical authors like Nathaniel Hawthorne, Edgar Allan Poe, and Herman Melville frequently engaged discourses of apocalypse to construct their fictional narratives, as did many popular (if understudied) authors of the period.[41] Painters like Thomas Cole and Asher Durand portrayed on large canvases what poets like Rufus Dawes, James Gates Percival, and Sarah J. Hale depicted lyrically: landscapes of vast and unremitting devastation.[42] The apocalypse even makes an appearance in a popular drinking song from the midcentury (figure 4).[43] So while it is treated as a theological category on the one hand, the antebellum apocalypse also operates as a popular and even playful aesthetic category on the other. Indeed, for some nineteenth-century Americans, the apocalypse was a form of entertainment.

The fact that it could appear rather ordinary and familiar within various entertainment media does not negate the apocalypse's capacity to inspire great fear. How it functioned and the types of responses it generated depended on the specific form the apocalypse took within a given context. The manner in which a minister communicated apocalyptic theology in a sermon and its purposes therein were often quite different from how it manifested and operated in novels (though, of course, they could be quite similar as well). Likewise, just as a political exhortation from an abolitionist differed from a landscape painting, so did the accounts of apocalypse produced within these respective discourses. While I have chosen to investigate how a very particular type of apocalyptic representation functioned within the genre of abolitionist sentimentality, the apocalypse was, by the nineteenth century, a radically versatile and polymorphous conceptual category that could be accommodated to the exigencies of theological debate while at the same time serving as a central aesthetic category within visual or written works of art. By foregrounding those depictions of apocalypse that emphasized God's wrath and judgment as a political instrument to challenge slavery, I want to emphasize one especially vital context in which the apocalypse performed important cultural work, even as this context was itself surrounded by many other political, aesthetic, and religious contexts in which alternative accounts of the apocalypse were being represented and consumed.

Apocalypse and Violence

Writers for whom apocalyptic theology constituted a fundamental component of their antislavery agenda were able to accomplish two distinct aims simultaneously. First, they inscribed a narrative of providential history with which everyone was familiar, one that linked one's actions on earth to the possible

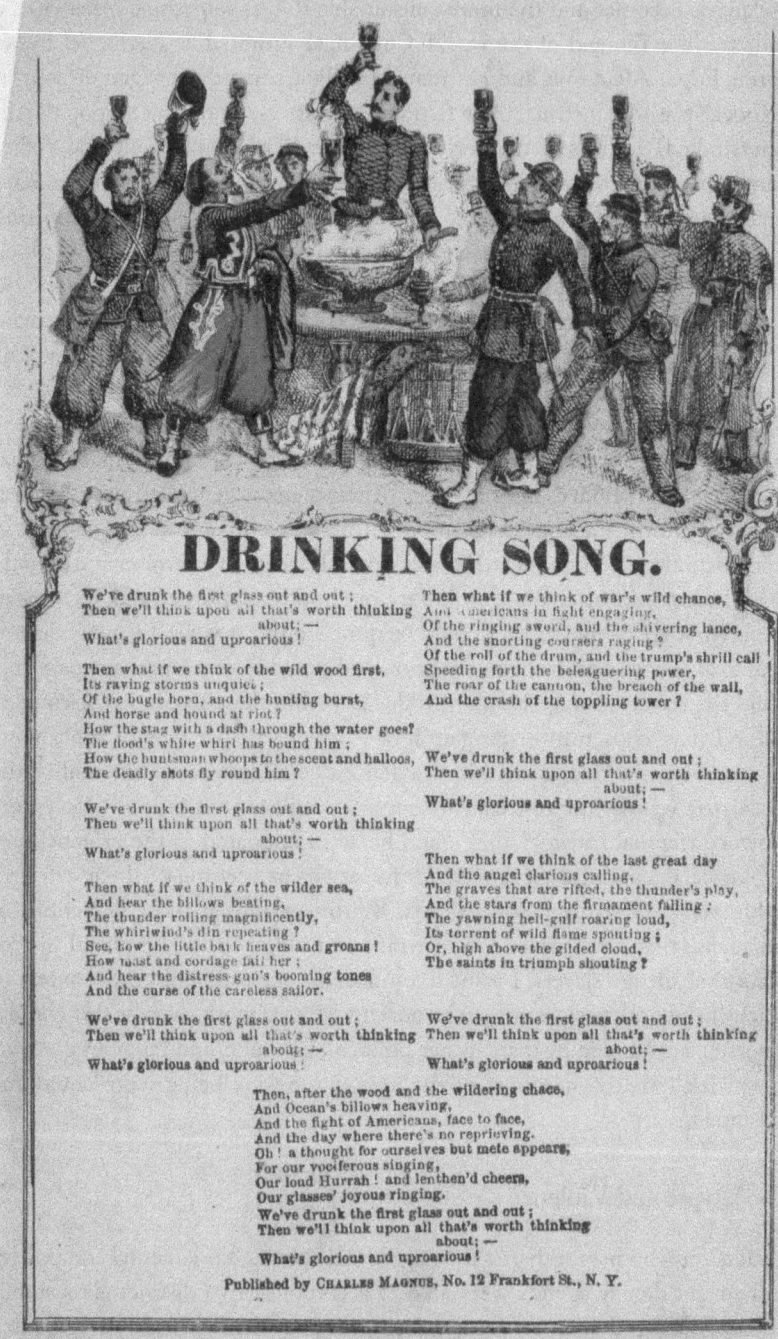

Figure 4. "Drinking Song." American Antiquarian Society.

fulfillment of God's earthly kingdom. This rhetorical maneuver immediately infused the claims they were making with a sense of urgency and importance because they were ostensibly offering a call to action (i.e., ending slavery) that was consistent with God's divine plan.[44] Second, and perhaps more subtly, warnings of apocalyptic retribution allowed these writers to express fantasies of brutal violence against slaveholders merely by tapping into a preexisting cultural idiom. Indeed, abolitionist sentimentality was a staging ground for meditations on violence as a response to slavery, even though many of the most prominent abolitionists, particularly the Garrisonians, proclaimed an antiviolence position. Because these fantasies were typically couched in a widely shared and culturally accepted apocalyptic syntax, they were seldom scorned by the targets of these threats as the deeply hostile sentiments that they, in fact, were. In addition to the violence they underwrote, these fantasies were simultaneously meant to energize a sympathetic response toward slaves and thus operate as the very engine of sentimentality that I map in this book. Apocalypse, then, along with being a motivating force behind the sentimental, is a charged euphemism for violence, especially violence inflicted on slaveholders for their cruelty toward slaves and their sins against God. Depictions of violence within the apocalyptic sentimental tradition typically come in one of two forms. In one version, readers are presented with a wrathful and transcendent deity who prepares to inflict retributive violence, a view that aligns with prevailing nineteenth-century religious notions of a just and angry God. In the other version, however, it is not the Christian God who exacts retribution against slaveholding sinners. It is the slave. The account of apocalypse that is constructed in these instances acts as a highly racialized code for black insurrectionary violence. *Apocalyptic Sentimentalism* charts this shift in signification, where apocalyptic theology becomes a cipher for insurrectionary violence, and the panic over the possibility of slave violence becomes itself a sentimental mode.

The scholarship on fictional as well as historical examples of slave resistance is as vast and diverse as the forms such resistance took in the nineteenth century.[45] There has been a tendency, however, for scholars to situate violent resistance to slavery in a revolutionary framework, so that acts of antislavery violence committed by black (and sometimes white) Americans fall within America's revolutionary genealogy, beginning with its campaign against British colonial rule. As Larry Reynolds has argued, "Throughout the nineteenth century, the American Revolution provided the most prevalent model for justifying violent resistance to established authority," especially slavery.[46] Indeed, ideas regarding the slaves' revolutionary agency have been a particular fixation among critics for at least the past forty years, with historians and literary scholars sympathizing with, and sometimes supporting, violent revolt "as the most extreme form of legitimate resistance against racist dehumanization and oppression."[47] Fighting to secure universal rights, rebellious slaves mirror some of the most cherished values modern liberal critics hold: individual independence, self-determination, and a commitment to universal equality. Slave violence becomes, within this scholarly view, a rational expression of Enlightenment-era desires to perfect the human spirit and universalize liberty and equality—the two foundational rights of liberal democracy. Regarding violence as an expression of a black revolutionary spirit, critics have normalized and avowed it as a necessary stage in the development and expansion of human freedom. And they have been justified in emphasizing black resistance within a liberal-revolutionary frame, given the abundance of examples from the nineteenth century of antislavery struggle that were described precisely in the liberal terminology that still holds sway within modern criticism. Perhaps no example is more representative of this liberal-revolutionary tradition than *The Heroic Slave* (1853), Frederick Douglass's only work of fiction. Its protagonist, Madison Washington (who is based on the real-life rebellious mutineer of the same name), liberates himself and his fellow slaves by orchestrating the takeover of a slave ship and sailing it into the British colony of Nassau where slavery has already been abolished. A paragon of ingenuity and masculine prowess, Washington represents the quintessential black revolutionary and is widely revered, even by those whites whom Washington overtakes onboard the *Creole*. Like his fictionalized protagonist, Douglass himself has come to symbolize the fundamental characteristics of liberal selfhood and is often used by scholars as the measure against which all forms of nineteenth-century black agency are assessed. He becomes the model of black manhood because he embodies the promise and the fulfillment of America's revolutionary history.[48]

Apocalyptic Sentimentalism considers accounts of violent resistance that do not neatly conform to the prevailing revolutionary framework. Focusing on how representations of apocalypse constitute a symbolic vehicle for challenging slavery, I argue that these depictions of resistance should be read as examples of religious violence, not political revolution. Literary critics and historians tend to collapse these two notions, treating theologically motivated violence as a cooperative but nevertheless subordinate ally in the service of revolution.[49] Because of their preference for liberal readings of nineteenth-century resistance, they fail to notice some of the crucial ways that revolutionary violence and religious violence differ or may even conflict. Rather than simply repeat this conflation, I consider some forms of religious violence that do indeed aim to further democratic ends; I also examine others that are more invested not in securing rights and expanding political liberties but in bloodshed, vengeance, and, most importantly, terrorizing the antebellum slaveholding community. In these examples, violence is not used to remake the political landscape so that it is more equitable and just. Rather, it is a strategy to hasten the end, an end that is often achieved with the killing of slaveholders and white Americans who support slavery. I term this form of religious force "messianic" to distinguish it from the revolutionary tradition and to signal that this type of violent expression cannot always be easily accommodated to a liberal, secular, post-Enlightenment worldview. Moreover, the violent actors I consider do not conform to modern scholarly assumptions about black revolutionary resistance—autonomy and rational self-determination being chief among them. Indeed, these perpetrators of religious violence willingly occupy a self-abnegating, self-subordinating state of radical dependency—traits that are typically decried as the hallmarks of slavery and the opposite of liberal selfhood. Within the accounts that I examine, it is the slaves' dependency and submission to a higher spiritual power that ends up being the very source of their strength, a fact that might explain why scholars have avoided exploring the religious contours of these examples, as they do not conform to modern expectations about autonomy and empowerment. I treat the messianic, then, as a theory of power and a crucial component of apocalyptic sentimentalism. First, it serves as an important alternative to revolutionary forms of black resistance, which I have described above. Second, it is a strategy for inciting action. The figures who exemplify messianic force are meant to inspire others to act against slaveholders and defenders of various forms of injustice. They may be drawn within a messianic frame that privileges submission over willful self-determination, but they are still embodiments of violence, making them a crucial component of a sentimental strategy that is all about threatening violence to incite a response. Finally, the messianic is an account of power rooted in Christianity, and its origins in the period's shared religious tradition make it difficult for nineteenth-century Americans to reject or disparage the account of violent power the messianic model conveys without also disparaging the faith on which it is based. Indeed, reformers and fictional characters who are represented within a messianic frame are meant to be seen as faithful, sympathetic Christians, not as bloodthirsty radicals. Rather than marshal the discourse of revolution that was admittedly well established in the antebellum period, the authors and actors I examine find greater emancipatory potential in a Christian tradition that requires total submission before an omnipotent God as a precondition to garnering greater personal power.[50]

Previous critics have identified undercurrents of violence running through the sentimental tradition. From Richard Brodhead's exploration of corporal punishment in educational and domestic literature, to the "tender violence" that Laura Wexler argues characterizes an American sentimental culture that both colludes in and then masks its complicity in violent acts, critics have detailed the many ways sentimentality imagines, promotes, and justifies violent aggression directed at women, blacks, children, the poor, and colonized others.[51] Marianne Noble's examination of masochistic fantasies of female empowerment within sentimental fiction has been the most influential study of violence within the antebellum sentimental tradition. Noble partly roots masochistic impulses in Protestant theology, arguing that "evangelical Protestantism plants an important seed associating love with punishment, domination, and/or cruelty," even if it does not "in and of itself link that love with eroticism."[52] Similarly grounded in Protestant beliefs, the representations of the apocalypse that I consider were often used obliquely to express fantasies of violence. One wonders, in light of Noble's analysis, how much the apocalyptic contributes to the masochistic pleasures generated by certain forms of sentimental narration. Such a consideration might receive further clarification from Michael Apter's work on the psychological dimensions of excitement and how danger can evolve into feelings of exhilaration when a potential threat is avoided or dispelled.[53] In *Apocalyptic Sentimentalism*, however, I pursue a line of inquiry that is distinct from these scholarly works by interrogating examples of religious violence that are used to challenge the racial structures which organized antebellum society. Despite the unease that ideas of religious violence engender in the contemporary moment, I choose in this study to confront how a certain reading of apocalyptic theology in the nineteenth century legitimated violent expression and vindicated acts of violence when they inevitably occurred.[54] Continuing to emphasize revolution, as many scholars often do, risks overlooking this crucial dimension of antislavery discourse, one rooted in religious belief in a God for whom vengeance was a natural reflex. Notwithstanding modern commitments to liberal norms, it is important to recognize that some antebellum forms of resistance did not emphasize personal independence, nor were they secular in the way most revolutionary accounts implicitly are. It is equally essential to consider that while some examples of messianic resistance that I consider in this book collaborate with the liberal-revolutionary model and thus can be read in tandem with it, not all of them do. Indeed, in some instances of messianic violence, individual freedom and rational autonomy are not the goals at all. Terror and bloodshed are enacted not to achieve some greater universal good, but instead to generate even more terror and bloodshed. I dedicate a portion of this study to thinking about the implications of this dynamic and how it fundamentally shaped (and was shaped by) nineteenth-century abolitionist sentimentality.

Terror and Terrorism

This phenomenon I have been describing, where theology is invoked in order to inspire terror and to legitimize acts of violence by claiming that they are ordained by God, has its modern-day equivalent. Given that our contemporary moment is marked by a global politics of terror, it may be challenging for Americans living in a post-9/11 world to regard terror as anything other than a threat to and violation of the rights intrinsic to a liberal democratic society. In *Apocalyptic Sentimentalism*, I explore a political movement—abolition—that most modern Americans hold in very high regard precisely for championing the nation's democratic values. And yet for some abolitionists, terror and democracy were not inimical; rather, the latter was in deep need of the former, especially when an institution like slavery subverted the philosophies and endangered the institutions that gave a political democracy like America its definition and purpose. While I am not arguing that modern-day terrorism and nineteenth-century abolition are the same, I do want to suggest that both share a common rhetorical style insofar as each believes in the efficaciousness of terror as a political tactic. It is worth keeping this parallel in mind, if only to establish a more comprehensive understanding of the uses of terror, both in the first half of the nineteenth century as well as today.[55]

One might understandably ask how terror in one context could have such a dramatically different meaning and effect in another. The reason is that terror is not a prepolitical category; its significance does not antecede its representation or deployment. Rather, terror is a deeply historical notion that must be understood within the constraints of the specific moment in which it is arrayed. We may regard the implementation of terror within nineteenth-century abolition as necessary to achieving a greater good—the manumission of slaves, for example—even as we recoil at the terroristic violence committed by groups like Al Qaeda.[56] Terror, in short, is neither inherently good nor bad. As challenging as it may be in our current geopolitical climate, we should refrain from making metaphysical claims about terror (i.e., "it is evil" or "it is irrational" or "it is antidemocratic" or "it is un-American") and instead examine the strategies of implementation and the consequences that unfold when terror is used in a given political or cultural context. Because 150 years separate us from nineteenth-century slavery, we can more easily study abolitionists' terror-based arguments without having the same immediate and visceral response we might have when we encounter contemporary acts of terrorism and the rhetoric that accompanies them. This, in turn, might allow us to cultivate a less reactionary and more thoughtful response to modern acts of terror. Such an approach might also help us identify and examine more fully those moments when the United States produces its own versions of political and ideological terror.[57]

Because fear operates as such a powerful organizing sentiment in each text I consider, and because the strategic deployment of apocalyptic terror is so central to the political and ethical interventions each undertakes, I focus on foundational narratives within a style of nineteenth-century sentimentality animated by an evangelical fervor that emphasizes fear as an essential affective dimension of moral reform. In order to dramatize the way imbrications of love and fear become constitutive of a nineteenth-century sentimental economy, I consider authors who are firmly established within the canon of sentimental fiction (like Harriet Beecher Stowe) alongside those who decidedly are not (like David Walker). The chapters in this book proceed chronologically and are meant to illustrate the emergence and unfolding of a tradition of sentimental representation in which depictions of God's vengeance function as a necessary goad for love, and love, when it is fully realized, comes to express itself as a form of vengeance and violence that can be read as sentimental. For example, an inchoate apocalyptic sentimentality plays a small but nevertheless meaningful role at very important moments in David's Walker's highly inflammatory *Appeal to the Coloured Citizens of the World*. By the 1850s, however, apocalyptic sentimentalism is organizing whole scenes of *Uncle Tom's Cabin* as well as the entire narrative structure of *Dred*, so that chapters in Stowe's second work of antislavery fiction which emphasize the importance of love are immediately followed by chapters foreboding God's impending wrath. On the eve of the Civil War, apocalyptic sentimentalism helps organize a widespread cultural response to John Brown and his raid on Harpers Ferry, Virginia, with many antislavery reformers arguing that Brown's violence, both in Kansas and in Virginia, was ultimately an expression of—and inspired by—his deep love for slaves. In structuring the book as I do, my point is not to suggest that earlier authors necessarily have a direct influence on later ones (although they sometimes do); rather, the authors I consider serve as signposts marking the stages of apocalyptic sentimentalism's development. I examine these figures principally to challenge some of the prevailing assumptions about the operations of sentimentality in the nineteenth century and to demonstrate that terror is a foundational affect within the sentimental tradition.

In part 1, I investigate the ideological origins of apocalyptic sentimentalism within antislavery thought, beginning with David Walker and Nat Turner, two figures rarely, if ever, associated with the nineteenth-century culture of sentiment. I open with Walker's *Appeal* and Turner's *Confessions* because these texts exert a powerful influence on how apocalyptic sentimentality will be understood by later sentimental thinkers and writers. Walker's *Appeal*, in particular, is infamous for repeatedly threatening Southern whites with a wrathful God who exacts retribution for the sin of holding slaves, a point few readers miss. What has gone unnoticed, however, are the ways in which Walker attempts to generate a sympathetic response in his readers, calling for Americans to reform their hearts and learn to feel compassion for slaves. In his *Appeal*, pleas for sympathy and expressions of apocalypse often exist side by side without being fully yoked together. The *Appeal* constitutes one of the earliest instances of a work of antislavery writing where an author uses wrath as a possible stimulus for love. Walker's *Appeal* serves in this study as an occasion to explore a moment before apocalyptic sentimentalism fully develops as a modality but when its central elements are present. And while there are no expressions of love in Turner's *Confessions*, thus making Turner's project markedly different from Walker's rather than an extension of it, his prison statement to Thomas Gray is essential to the development of apocalyptic sentimentalism in two related ways. First, Turner enacts the violence Walker spoke of only two years earlier, and he describes his rebellion not as an act of revolution but as apocalyptic retribution. Second, Turner's confession provides a form of expression for later writers like Harriet Beecher Stowe, for whom insurrectionary panic becomes a sentimental mode and who represent warnings of God's vengeance as a euphemism for black violence against slaveholders.

We see for the first time in part 1 the development of messianic force, a formation that occurs most notably in Walker's *Appeal* and Turner's *Confessions* but is also enlarged by Maria Stewart in her writings and lectures. Both Walker and Turner represent an empowered rebellious black subject through a seemingly counterintuitive act of self-abnegation and submission to higher authority. While Stewart also marshals a discourse of messianic power, she does so in order to authorize the public presence of a black female orator. A close friend of David Walker who began publishing and lecturing not long after Turner's insurrection in 1831, Maria Stewart's work embodies and expands the conceptual innovations of Walker's *Appeal* and the incendiary display of slave violence presented by Turner in his *Confessions*. Attacking slavery with the same zeal as Walker and Turner, Stewart also challenges the subservient position black women have been forced to occupy within a marginalized but nevertheless patriarchal black culture. Speaking in Boston in front of audiences composed of both men and women, Stewart transgresses cultural norms regarding proper feminine speech, most notably by warning of God's impending vengeance for the cruelties inflicted on blacks and black women in particular. Indeed, reading Stewart alongside David Walker, we can see how both authors contravene gendered protocols governing antebellum speech acts: Walker, at certain key moments, turns to a discourse of love to augment the potency of his condemnation of slavery, while Stewart marshals the fire-and-brimstone rhetoric of apocalyptic prophesy to authorize her pleas for social justice. The barrier separating what were understood at the time to be masculine and feminine forms of speech is more permeable within apocalyptic sentimentalism, as evinced by Walker's *Appeal* and Stewart's public lectures. Stewart also makes an important early contribution to the "domestication" of apocalypse, so that apocalyptic rhetoric and representation become acceptable modes of discourse not only from the pulpit or at the lectern, but on the home front as well. By foregrounding Walker, Turner, and Stewart in the opening chapters of this book, I argue that apocalyptic sentimentalism is a racialized structure that is deeply informed by early black literary representation as well as influenced by a white, bourgeois, European philosophical aesthetic.

In part 2 of *Apocalyptic Sentimentalism*, I consider the most famous and influential of the antislavery sentimentalists: Harriet Beecher Stowe, a writer whose fiction has become virtually synonymous with the sentimental tradition precisely for how it emphasizes sympathetic love as its principal affect. Jane Tompkins's view of *Uncle Tom's Cabin* represents an almost universally shared opinion among critics who read this novel in terms of its successful joining of sentimentality to an antislavery politics. What makes *Uncle Tom's Cabin* such a meaningful cultural intervention, in Tompkins's analysis, is Stowe's equation of social power with loving mothers, a view that most critics have reiterated, even when they chastise Stowe for failing to imagine a more comprehensive and pragmatic antislavery or feminist politics. It is against this tradition that I read *Uncle Tom's Cabin* in chapter 3. While I agree that Stowe does privilege love, and while I support the view that Stowe is indeed the paradigmatic sentimental writer of the nineteenth century, I nevertheless maintain that Stowe does not possess absolute confidence in the power of love to transform a nation of readers into vehement opponents of slavery. Love, in Stowe's view, is powerful and absolutely necessary, but it is not autogenic. While Stowe insists on nurturing a loving disposition, and while she repeatedly depicts fictional characters who demonstrate great love, neither approach will guarantee that such a loving spirit will emerge from among her readers. To compensate for love's inability to convert readers on its own into ardent abolitionists, Stowe repeatedly warns of a coming day of wrath when sinners in America will have to answer for their moral shortcomings. Indeed, if there is a nineteenth-century novel that theorizes the logic of apocalyptic sentimentalism and adapts it as a device for fictional narration, it is *Uncle Tom's Cabin*. Stowe fuses the discourses of apocalypse and sympathy in a way that Walker and Stewart never fully do. While most modern readers emphasize Stowe's critical stance against Calvinism (especially as it was embodied by her father, Lyman Beecher), I argue that this scholarly perspective has been overstated. Stowe mobilizes an inextricable economy of terror to bolster the power of love, especially when characters (and readers) are more sympathetic toward the slaveholding system than they are toward America's slaves. Rather than merely call for love or represent scenes that depict the loving and merciful Jesus of liberalized Protestantism, Stowe returns again and again to the prospect of a wrathful God exacting retribution against hardened sinners, and it is this dynamic, where terror is the necessary incentive to and goad for love, that constitutes the structure of this quintessential sentimental text.

Scholars have often questioned the efficacy and challenged the conspicuous limitations of an antislavery politics predicated on sentimentality, and Stowe has not been spared such criticisms. Her portrayal of Uncle Tom as a submissive and self-sacrificing protagonist as well as her decision to relocate the major surviving black characters of the novel to Africa are just two instances when a so-called sentimental politics has not seemed to accord with the principles of an inclusive democratic society. If Stowe's "political" solutions seem limited and impractical in *Uncle Tom's Cabin*, they become highly radicalized in *Dred*, Stowe's second antislavery novel. One dramatic difference is that in *Dred*, Stowe earnestly considers and appears at times to even promote the possibility of slave violence as an acceptable response to slavery. In this novel, it is not the threat of God's wrath that white Southerners need to worry about; it is Dred's. Like Nat Turner, who assumed the prerogative of God when he decided to exact theologically sanctioned vengeance against white Southerners, Dred is represented in this work of antislavery fiction precisely as the incarnation of God's apocalyptic retribution. In this way, Dred not only further dramatizes the synecdochic connection between prophecies of apocalypse and slave insurrection, but he constitutes one of the principal sentimental agents of the narrative. While many readers of *Dred* regard this novel as a failed work of sentimental fiction for how it foregrounds insurrectionary violence as a legitimate challenge to slavery, I argue that insurrectionary violence, constructed through an apocalyptic idiom, constitutes one of the foremost sentimental characteristics of this narrative. Within this framework, Dred himself must be seen not as a threat to or subversion of Stowe's sentimental politics but as a deeply sentimental character. The violence that Dred forebodes and the terror that he engenders within the Southern community is foundational to the novel's sentimental logic. If apocalyptic sentimentalism is a form of narration marked by a suspended threat, "Dred" is the name Stowe gives to this threat. And insofar as the interactions between love and vengeance/violence organize most of the narrative, *Dred* is more sentimental than *Uncle Tom's Cabin*, not less.

The incarnational logic of *Dred* further develops the idea of messianic force that I introduce in part 1, most notably in the way Stowe abandons the view that apocalyptic retribution must originate as a transcendental event. In place of this more conventional understanding of theological vengeance, Stowe locates the possibility of retribution with her black male protagonist. In revising traditional end-times theology where Christ returns to pass his final judgment, Stowe also rewrites her previous portrayal of a black male hero. As the protagonist of *Uncle Tom's Cabin*, Tom exists in a state of passive nonresistance, willing to surrender his body as an act of absolute devotion to God. Indeed, Uncle Tom's physical body is a votive offering for the redemption of humankind, and it is precisely for this reason that so many readers of *Uncle Tom's Cabin* have maligned Stowe for promoting such a limited and apolitical solution to slavery, one that requires the death of a slave rather than his incorporation as a free citizen. With Dred, however, the black male body is a heavenly instrument. Dred's material body is literally the apocalypse made flesh. Rather than portray an obedient Christian who faithfully represents a loving and merciful Jesus, Stowe invents a dangerous hero who dramatizes Christ in all his wrath and fury. It is also in *Dred* where we see Nat Turner's influence on Stowe's sentimental imagination. The violence and terror that Turner portrays in his *Confessions* become, in Stowe's hands, an archive within which to further theorize antislavery sentiment. Stowe appends excerpts from Turner's *Confessions* not to distance herself from sentimentality or because she has failed to devise a proper response to slavery but to affirm, once and for all, the absolute necessity of terror and vengeance within a sentimental antislavery politics.

Of course, like Tom, Dred is murdered near the end of the narrative. But Dred's death, I show, serves a different purpose than did Tom's, both aesthetically and politically. What is perhaps most surprising is that with Dred's death, Stowe, rather than renouncing vengeance, firmly establishes it in the novel's sentimental economy. What might initially seem counterintuitive is, in fact, necessary to the development of apocalyptic sentimentalism. That is, Stowe's abiding commitment to retribution is affirmed with the death of her eponymous hero. It is also with Dred's death that Stowe is able to examine the possibility of establishing a multiracial democracy, something she did not do in *Uncle Tom's Cabin*. In order to illustrate just how central ideas of wrath and vengeance are to this novel, and to explore how Stowe reconciles the apparent tension between the novel's aim to fictionalize a multiracial democracy with its depiction of the kind of retributive violence Dred plans to enact, I contrast *Dred* with the foremost antivengeance and antisentimental novel of the antebellum period: *Moby-Dick*. Melville examines the consequences of vengeance, ultimately disavowing it as a thoroughly destructive impulse. Five years after the publication of *Moby-Dick*, Stowe rescues vengeance from the sinking *Pequod* and sets it loose on the dry land of North Carolina. In so doing, she asserts that vengeance is neither irrational nor the expression of a mad mind but an essential instrument with which to combat race-based slavery.

Apocalyptic sentimentalism functions in Harriet Beecher Stowe's antislavery fiction as an organizing principle, not just of occasional scenes, as it did in Walker's *Appeal* and Stewart's lectures, but of the entire narrative structure. Indeed, Stowe's fiction reveals an enlargement in the influence apocalyptic sentimentalism has, and on the eve of the Civil War, it actually extends beyond the literary narrative, helping to shape a cultural response to John Brown and his raid on Harpers Ferry. In part 3, I consider Northern responses to John Brown's raid, especially the surprising ways in which Brown is constructed in highly sentimental terms, deserving of great love and sympathy for his actions on behalf of black slaves. Most modern-day accounts of Brown describe him as a revolutionary hero, but for many antislavery reformers, Brown exemplified

Christian love and was motivated by a deep sense of compassion for America's most marginalized populations. The reason, I argue, that many defenders of Brown could regard his actions at Harpers Ferry as examples of his deep love and thus describe their own affection for him in similarly loving terms was a firmly embedded sentimental discourse in which expressions of love and acts of violence were closely correlated and sometimes regarded as interchangeable. By 1859, when Brown led the raid on the federal arsenal, ideas of vengeance had become so deeply enfolded within a sentimental epistemology that Brown's supporters could describe, without a shred of irony or contradiction, his violent insurgency as a properly loving act toward slaves. In a very real sense, then, it is sentimentalism itself that made John Brown possible.

With John Brown, however, there comes a reversal in the sentimental structure that I chart for most of the book. Rather than threats of vengeance being used as a motivating source for love and a meaningful response to slavery, it is John Brown's love that precedes and is the catalyst behind the violent acts he commits, a view he reiterates throughout his letters from prison. In turn, these violent acts are read by many of his supporters as clear expressions of Brown's sympathetic affection for slaves. Much like the example of PAULUS with which I opened this book, where God's vengeance is understood to be a clear indication of his love for the oppressed, John Brown's violence in Virginia (and in Kansas) is seen to be the true sign of his loving heart and the reason he can be so easily regarded by supporters as a sentimental figure.

At the same time that John Brown constitutes the apotheosis of apocalyptic sentimentalism, his actions also precipitated the erosion of this discourse as well, as some supporters struggled to balance his violent acts with his loving words. The effect of the actual physical violence was to displace the suspended threat of apocalyptic vengeance. In contrast to those supporters who regarded Brown's raid as an example of his love, other defenders of Brown began to separate his caring heart from his violent impulses, lauding the former and minimizing or disclaiming the latter. I analyze a range of letters written about and lectures delivered on behalf of Brown while he remained in prison following his trial as well as after his execution. While some insist that Brown's insurgency was an expression of sympathetic love for slaves, others emphatically reject violence as an epiphenomenon of his deep and abiding love. I expand the scholarly archive to include statements by Brown's children, especially his son Salmon Brown, that describe him as a family man and loving father while almost entirely avoiding a discussion of the bloodshed he was responsible for. Rather than locating Brown on the field of battle or nearing the gallows, which is where critics typically place him, these statements by Salmon Brown situate his father by the hearth, singing to his children and caring for his wife. After Brown, the pleas for love and fantasies of violence that were entangled within the discourse of apocalyptic sentimentalism are no longer so readily accommodated within nineteenth-century American culture.

As one can see from the above description, I have chosen to examine mainly Northern antislavery writing as particularly fertile terrain for the study of apocalyptic sentimentalism, but I do not want to give the impression that this tradition was solely a Northern phenomenon. Southern writers who challenged antislavery views at times also employed some of the same conventions Northern writers were employing. Mary H. Eastman, for example, rebutted Harriet Beecher Stowe's attack on Southern plantation culture with *Aunt Phillis's Cabin, or, Southern Life as It Is*, a scathing adaptation and parody of Stowe's international best-seller. Eastman concludes her novel by echoing Stowe's famous interrogative: "*What* can any individual do?" and she responds by repudiating Northern inclinations to meddle in Southern affairs: "Christian men and women should find enough to occupy them in their families, and in an undoubted sphere of duty." The people of the South, Eastman argues throughout the novel, have done a more than sufficient job of caring for their slaves. "Let the people of the North," she concludes, "take care of their own poor."[58] In these final passages from the novel, Eastman returns to some of the emblematic sentimental tropes of Stowe's novel, namely, the need among citizens to concentrate on family and to care for those less fortunate. Eastman's sentimental response to the national conflict over slavery mirrors Stowe's. And just like Stowe, Eastman concludes with words of wrath to underscore and incentivize her ostensible commitment to love. "Let each remember," Eastman writes in the final lines of the novel, "the great and awful day when they must render a final account to their Creator, their Redeemer, and their Judge."[59] Eastman's deployment of this sentimental trope not only indicates its geographical ubiquity in the antebellum period, it also underscores that apocalyptic sentimentality is not inherently antislavery or proslavery, progressive or conservative. It is a politically neutral configuration that is marshaled in the service of various and at times competing ideological positions.

If John Brown signaled the decline of apocalyptic sentimentalism, the Civil War was its death knell. With the onset of the Civil War, the style of sentimentality I chart in this book is no longer possible; apocalyptic sentimentalism, having played such an important role in the debates leading up to this conflict, comes to an end. It is Abraham Lincoln who announces the end of apocalyptic sentimentalism, with the Second Inaugural serving as its obituary. I close this book with a coda exploring the dénouement of this rhetorical mode with a look at Lincoln's inaugural speech, a text that invokes apocalyptic sentimentality even as it calls for new forms of discourse that are meant to heal the nation rather than divide it further. Despite its diminishment during the war and especially in its immediate aftermath, apocalyptic sentimentality does not disappear for good. For the remainder of the coda, I briefly examine three modern illustrations of apocalyptic sentimentalism. As in the nineteenth century, this sentimental structure is a formative part of America's political discourse and its artistic culture. The three examples I consider—one from a political pundit, one from the environmental movement, and one from a novel—all expand upon and revise the tradition of apocalyptic sentimentalism that first emerged in the antebellum period. What is perhaps most surprising about the uses of apocalyptic sentimentalism in post-9/11 America is how terror itself has been so thoroughly incorporated into our own political and entertainment imaginations.

I aim in this study to illustrate how one of America's foundational conceptual categories, the apocalypse, formed an essential facet of the nineteenth century's sentimental aesthetics, and how this sentimental aesthetics was, in turn, deployed within one of the great reform movements in this nation's history. How citizens of the antebellum period came to think about and debate questions of democratic rights, race, personhood, and liberty depended, in no small way, on this most dramatic and foundational of religious categories. And the nineteenth-century literary tradition, itself a staging ground on which these conflicts were often fought, was equally shaped by, and gave shape to, diverse representations of apocalypse that are essential to the larger fictional and political narratives that comprise its canon. Indeed, given its recurring presence throughout the American literary tradition—from Puritan writing to romanticism, sentimentalism to science and postmodern fiction—the apocalypse, as I see it, is not incidental to this tradition but rather one of the major engines of American literary and cultural history.

PART I

Black Abolition and the Ideological Roots of Apocalyptic Sentimentalism

CHAPTER 1

David Walker, Nat Turner, and the Logic of Sentimental Terror

> The first step of the earthquake, which is ultimately to shake down the fabric of oppression, leaving not one stone upon another, has been made. The first drops of blood, which are but the prelude to a deluge from the gathering clouds, have fallen. The first flash of the lightning, which is to smite and consume, has been felt. The first wailings of a bereavement, which is to clothe the earth in sackcloth, have broken upon our ears.
> —William Lloyd Garrison, "The Insurrectionist," (1831)

The ascendancy of love as the defining characteristic of sentimental fiction marked a crucial moment in literary criticism, for it announced a departure from critics' earlier reading of the nineteenth-century canon as being dominated by the more "serious" works of male writers like Emerson, Melville, and Hawthorne. In order for modern scholars to claim that a formidable feminist presence existed within the American Renaissance, however, they first had to separate the sentimental tradition from nineteenth-century Calvinism, which previous generations of critics had equated with patriarchal power. Thus, they detached Calvinism's severe brand of evangelical theology, which stressed the judgment of God, from a feminized sentimental philosophy that emphasized salvation through motherly love.[1] As a result, the prevailing scholarly view currently understands love to be the revolutionary impulse behind nineteenth-century sentimental reform, and critics use "sympathy" and "sympathetic identification" as shorthand for this process whereby love and compassion result from an affective bond formed across racial and class lines.[2]

These accounts that see sympathy and love as the inevitable outcomes of sentimental narration often suggest, through a subtle but unmistakable tautology, that these outcomes are, at the same time, *produced by* representations of sympathy and love, treating sympathy and love as both an effect *and* a cause within a given work of sentimental fiction. In most sentimental narratives, argues Glenn

35

Hendler, "the motivating force behind the character's actions is the subordination of the protagonist's self in a sympathetic identification with an other."[3] According to Hendler, sympathetic identification, which is what sentimental fiction seeks to produce, is concomitantly the force that precedes the appearance of sympathy and that retroactively (and paradoxically) activates sympathetic identification in a particular character (and, the sentimental writer hopes, in the reader as well). Sympathy, in this view, is the outcome and origin of itself. Cindy Weinstein offers a similar formulation in an analysis of *Uncle Tom's Cabin*, stating that tears are "the traditional evidence for sympathetic feeling and the primary mode of eliciting sympathy in Stowe's novel."[4] For Weinstein, tears—the external signs of internal sympathy—are also what create sympathy in others. When a character weeps, he or she inspires other characters to weep, which may move the reader to shed a tear as well.

Arguments like the ones Hendler and Weinstein make are founded on the widely shared assumption that quintessential sentimental scenes will inevitably produce quintessential sentimental responses, so that representations of compassion will, in turn, arouse compassion in the reader, sympathy will invoke sympathy, love will generate even more love. These views comprehend sympathy and love to be autotelic, where affective bonds between persons are created and sustained merely by the presentation of sympathy and love within a sentimental narrative. Because many scholars writing on the sentimental tradition hold these same views, they often overlook instances when an autotelic logic breaks down, when sympathetic love is not the source of itself and some other catalyst is needed to assure its activation. When love could not be depended on as a guaranteed effect, nineteenth-century authors often turned to fear to stimulate readers into nurturing an affectionate heart. And within antebellum evangelical culture, biblical prophecies of God's apocalyptic retribution provided writers with a powerful lexicon through which to generate this fearful response, suggesting that the fear inspired by a coming day of wrath was essential to the very operations of sentimentality within these works.

While expressions of love and warnings of retribution appear together with some frequency, specifically within the highly charged reform setting of Northern abolition, critics rarely regard this deployment of politicized terror to be a sentimental gesture. Gregg Camfield, for example, regards the Scottish Common Sense tradition, which stressed "moral sense" and sympathy as primary ways of establishing intersubjective relations, as the epistemological source of nineteenth-century American sentimentalism. And because the Scottish Enlightenment developed, at least in part, in opposition to Calvinist doctrine, something like apocalyptic fear cannot be seen as part of the grammar of sentimental narration.[5] Camfield's view is one that critics presumably share, given that none has described terror as a sentimental affect. What Camfield's argument misses, however, is the fact that nineteenth-century sentimental sympathy was profoundly invigorated by the evangelical enthusiasm of the Second Great Awakening. Despite challenges to Calvinist theology leveled throughout the early part of the nineteenth century by more moderate religious denominations, representations of apocalypse—often constructed through fire-and-brimstone warnings of retribution and judgment—nevertheless remained and proliferated across denominational lines. This was especially true within abolition, where the apocalypse was deployed as a political category (and not merely a theological one) that antislavery radicals used to inspire a properly Christian response from their audiences: sympathize with and learn to love America's slaves or else suffer God's wrath.

In this chapter, I examine one of the first antislavery writers that brings together calls for love with threats of divine vengeance. Throughout his *Appeal to the Coloured Citizens of the World*, David Walker repeatedly (and notoriously) details the apocalyptic consequences of slavery, with God exacting vengeance against brutal slaveholders. While Walker frequently underscores the penalty of slaveholding, he also at several key moments pleas for white readers to nurture compassion for the slave so that America can become a nation of racial harmony rather than discord. For Walker, creating sympathy and declaring God's vengeance are both essential components of his antislavery critique, and these discourses often exist side by side in his argument. Walker, however, ultimately stresses vengeance more emphatically than he does love. As a result, readers, rather than having a sympathetic response to the *Appeal*, are horrified by it instead. Despite its failed attempt to instill greater sympathy, Walker's *Appeal* assembles the basic elements of an inchoate apocalyptic sentimentalism by bringing together discourses of sympathy and vengeance. In this way, the *Appeal* helps establish some of the foundational narrative structures and tropes of antislavery sentimentality and thus serves as an instructive model for how to read fear as a sentimental mode in the antebellum period.[6] Walker marshals the affects of love and terror and portends catastrophic consequences for America's slaveholders, even as he outlines a theory of sympathy that might save the nation from ruin. Radicalized within the African Methodist Episcopal Church of Charleston, South Carolina, in the era of Denmark Vesey, David Walker begins to illustrate how abolitionist sentimentality, although traditionally viewed as a love-based, oftentimes melodramatic, domestic ideology, nevertheless had a ruthless and vengeful streak running through it, a streak that is not ancillary or accidental but constitutive of its very makeup.[7]

In addition, I briefly consider Nat Turner's *Confessions* for its enactment of a politics of terror that Walker's *Appeal* merely threatened. Unlike Walker, Turner expresses no desire to reconcile with white enslavers and displays no interest in the possibility of interracial sympathy. For this reason, Turner stands in contrast to David Walker's project rather than as its expression (as it is usually imagined). However, Turner's confession serves as a crucial bridge linking Walker to later writers like Maria Stewart, Lydia Maria Child, and especially Harriet Beecher Stowe. Following his insurrection in Southampton County, Virginia, Turner comes to stand as the very symbol of religious violence, a form of violence that surprisingly becomes sentimentalized throughout the antebellum period. Turner represents his rebellious actions to Thomas Gray through an apocalyptic idiom, and it is this discursive mode that writers like Stowe will incorporate in sentimental works of antislavery fiction. In *Dred*, for example, slave insurrection becomes part of a sentimental strategy, so that the panic produced by the threat of rebellion emboldens sentimental pleas for love. Constructing slave violence within an apocalyptic frame, Turner's discourse further joins insurrection to apocalyptic theology, where the latter is often used as a euphemistic stand-in for the former. This literary shorthand, of which Turner is the representative figure, will be deployed again and again in the years leading up to the Civil War. Turner should be read, then, in the way antebellum Americans read him: as the fulfillment of Walker's prophesy (even if Turner had no knowledge of Walker's *Appeal*) and as an agent of wrath terrorizing the slaveholding South.

By discounting the fiery evangelical context in which American sentimentalism developed, scholars have framed it as a discourse rooted in a European bourgeois aesthetic. They have similarly mischaracterized the forms of violence that appear in texts like Walker's *Appeal* and Turner's *Confessions*, choosing to treat them as representations of revolutionary agency rather than as religiously motivated. It is this misreading that I explore in considerable detail in the final section of the chapter. It is critical to see these examples of violence as stemming from a religious rather than secular discourse for two important reasons. First, Walker and Turner articulate a notion of power that is not predicated on a liberal-revolutionary model, one in which the perpetrators of these violent acts possess a self-determining rational agency. Instead, each text unfolds a theory of force that requires self-abnegation and a state of dependency on a transcendental deity, and these traits conflict with the belief in a secular liberal autonomous will, a move that offers a more problematic, but potentially more powerful, expression of selfhood. It is in this section that I begin to outline some of the important distinctions between revolutionary and religious violence by showing that the descriptions of power Walker and Turner provide are fundamentally different from the prevailing norms of liberal discourse. Second, these examples of theological violence catalyze sentimentality by supporting pleas for sympathy and love. It is religious violence, often presented within an apocalyptic context (rather than a secular revolutionary one), that undergirds the structure of sentimentality I examine throughout this book.

David Walker and the Sentimentality of Terror

"But why are the Americans so very fearfully terrified respecting my Book?"[8] This question, posed by David Walker about his *Appeal*, will no doubt strike modern readers as disingenuous, given what we know about the effects his work had throughout the South. Once the *Appeal* began circulating, officials arrested anyone who possessed copies of the document. Laws were enacted quarantining Northern black sailors in order to prevent them from disseminating Walker's polemic or any other literature thought to agitate slaves or endanger the autonomy of the planter class. Southern authorities were in such a state of agitation, in fact, that prohibitions against black literacy were reinvigorated and earnestly enforced.[9] As one writer in *The North Star* put it, "This little book produced more commotion among slaveholders than any volume of its size that was ever issued from an American press."[10] Indeed, the *Appeal* was the most incendiary attack against slavery in the antebellum period, and it achieved this status by constructing a rhetoric of terror that portended bloody insurrection and linked ideas of slave rebellion with prophecies of God's apocalyptic retribution. "Perhaps," warns Walker in a paradigmatic example of this linkage, "they will laugh at or make light of this; but I tell you Americans ! that unless you speedily alter your course, *you* and your *Country are gone! ! ! ! !* For God Almighty will tear up the very face of the earth! ! !" (*A* 39; original emphasis). Warnings such as this one pervade the *Appeal* and inflamed the anxieties of Southerners, many of whom would have remembered Gabriel Prosser's and Denmark Vesey's thwarted but nevertheless alarming attempts at insurrection and wondered if similar rebellions were being organized in which slaves would ultimately succeed in killing their masters.

Despite the *Appeal*'s apparent fixation on the penalties whites will incur if slavery continues, and notwithstanding Walker's abiding rage at the injustices free and enslaved blacks are made to endure, Walker's project aspires not merely to hasten the destruction of white America but to fundamentally reimagine interracial relations in the antebellum period. To this end, Walker's plea seeks to establish a form of sympathetic connection between his white audience and slaves, one that might catalyze a change in or even a dismantling of the slave system, and he relies throughout the *Appeal* on what will become by midcentury a classic strategy for sentimental writers: Walker addresses his readers' hearts. He announces to his audience early in the *Appeal* that, with God's help, he will "open [their] hearts to understand and believe the truth" (1) of the slave's degradation and the need for Southerners to relinquish their slaveholding practices. "I appeal to every man of feeling," says Walker (10), suggesting that moral reform begins with feeling right, a view that Harriet Beecher Stowe will codify twenty years later in *Uncle Tom's Cabin*. Walker reasons that a man who witnesses firsthand the slave's burden, provided he is "not a tyrant, but has the feelings of a human being, who can feel for a fellow creature," will surely "see enough to make his very heart bleed" (21). The bleeding heart is a sympathetic heart, and redressing slavery begins for Walker as it will begin for so many antislavery reformers who adopt sentimental conventions: with appeals to emotion and calls for the reformation of the heart.

Walker believes that white and black Americans can learn to live together harmoniously, provided a proper affective bond between them can be constituted. Indeed, his ultimate goal in the *Appeal* is a racially integrated nation in which blacks enjoy the same respect and rights as citizens that whites enjoy. "Treat us like men," says Walker, "and there is no danger but we will all live in peace and happiness together.... Treat us then like men, and we will be your friends" (*A* 70). Given the *Appeal*'s angry tone, it is possible to overlook Walker's reconciliatory vision, where racial segregation and acrimony are overcome in favor of amity between all citizens, regardless of skin color. Walker remains emphatic, though, in his desire for unity, assuring readers that any misgivings they might have are unfounded and underscoring interraciality as a necessary national ethos as well as a real political possibility. "And there is not a doubt in my mind," Walker states, "but that the whole of the past will be sunk into oblivion, and we yet, under God, will become a united and happy people. The whites may say it is impossible, but remember that nothing is impossible with God" (70). Notwithstanding the hardships they have suffered under slavery, black Americans will surrender the past in order to realize a more promising future. It could be said, then, that the aim of the *Appeal* is nothing less than the creation of a racially heterogeneous but nevertheless unified nation-state that is sanctioned by God and federated by feeling, with each citizen affectively associated with every other citizen.

Even as he unfolds this vision in which a compassionate white audience feels for black slaves, and this sentimental solidarity, in turn, leads to national unity, Walker faces a problem, one that antislavery reformers and sentimental writers throughout the 1840s and 1850s would continue to face: that is, white Americans are simply not feeling for or sympathizing with slaves, regardless of how pitiable or deplorable the slaves' circumstances might be. Calling for sympathy or representing scenes that are meant to elicit a compassionate response from white readers is not necessarily going to achieve the desired effect. Walker explicitly engages the failure of white Americans to sympathize with slaves and their willingness to take the slaves' wretchedness as a fact of nature and a reflection of God's will. "But the Americans," says Walker, "having introduced slavery among them, their hearts have become almost seared, as with an hot iron, and God has nearly given them up to believe a lie in preference to the truth! ! !" (*A* 43). Instead of enabling whites to bond with and learn to care for black slaves, white hearts have been hardened by slavery and have thus lost their capacity to feel. Walker cannot simply appeal to the hearts of white readers when these hearts no longer perform their primary function as symbolic repositories of emotion and agents of sympathetic identification. It is typically at these moments when Walker imagines the failure of white sympathy that he also expresses his deep rage for white Americans and articulates some of his most emphatic calls for divine retribution, such as this one, which immediately follows the preceding passage:

> And I am awfully afraid that pride, prejudice, avarice and blood, will, before long prove the final ruin of this happy republic, or land of *liberty!!!!* ... Will the Lord suffer this people to go on much longer, taking his holy name in vain? Will he not stop them, PREACHERS and all? O Americans! O Americans! ! I call God—I call angels—I call men, to witness, that your DESTRUCTION *is at hand*, and will be speedily consummated unless you REPENT. (43; original emphases)

Warnings of God's vengeance like this one can be found throughout the *Appeal* and underscore the limits of white sympathy. It is the inability or unwillingness of white Americans to sympathize with blacks that inspires in Walker such fury and ultimately compels him to express his desperation and anger in apocalyptic terms. Walker struggles to establish a sympathetic connection across racial lines even as he condemns whites for their hardened hearts. And it is the repeated pairing of love and vengeance which suggests that this pattern is not precisely random; rather, there is emerging in the *Appeal* an incipient strategy for inspiring sympathy in those who fail to feel compassion for slaves. Indeed, Walker's *Appeal* is the first significant piece of antislavery discourse in which terror and love are at times linked in this way. These two impulses seem to be at odds with one another but Walker starts to position them side by side so that the former might serve as an incitement to the latter. What may seem counterintuitive to modern readers is precisely what Walker is beginning to apprehend: love is not an absolute or self-sufficient emotion but might instead require a threat to actuate its power. Hearts do not necessarily sympathize on their own but instead require some reason to feel. Walker's *Appeal* outlines how the threat of God's retributive wrath, and the fear that this threat engenders, might be used to motivate whites to feel and perhaps even learn to care for black slaves. His argument is predicated on a sympathetic connection rooted in deeply felt emotion; but unlike scholarly claims that understand love and sympathy to be autogenic, Walker positions fear as a necessary inspiration for sympathetic affection. America can only achieve a multiracial union when whites are bonded by sympathy to their black brethren, and this sympathetic connection, Walker suggests, may only be established if it is energized by the fear of divine vengeance. What the *Appeal* illustrates is that antislavery reform will need some corrective measure to activate white sympathy and to calibrate these sympathies with their proper object, and it will find this measure in the threat of God's vengeance.

Walker initiates what will become a more common trend of inscribing the apocalyptic in both theological and sentimental registers, combining established religious ideas regarding God's judgment with emergent sentimental ones. Indeed, fire-and-brimstone rhetoric and representations of retribution and judgment—familiar early-nineteenth-century conceptions of apocalypse that helped form a powerful epistemology within the Second Great Awakening's evangelical culture—are designed to inspire an emotional response in the reader, and it is on the level of affect that the sentimental and the apocalyptic converge. Walker's repeated use of violent and bloody imagery is grounded in the highly charged political and cultural climate in which his antislavery sensibilities developed. His participation in the AME Church in Charleston and his probable involvement in the Denmark Vesey plot no doubt made a formative impression on Walker's thinking about violent rebellion.[11] Like Vesey, Walker's notions of insurrection are based on Scripture and modeled on those passages from the Bible that portray God smiting unregenerate sinners.[12] Walker invokes the apocalyptic not merely to challenge the institution of slavery but to inspire terror in his audience, appealing to a wrathful divinity that has promised to mete out punishment. Unlike America's Declaration of Independence, which authorizes citizens to use violence to replace a tyrannical form of government with a benevolent one, Walker does not imagine the reconfiguration through violence of America's democratic foundations. Instead, the violence he portrays in the *Appeal* appears to play out a fantasy of eradicating whites as a just punishment for failing to discontinue their slaveholding practices.

Walker's *Appeal* exemplifies the emergent structure of sentimental persuasion that I examine throughout this book. Representations of God's wrath typically follow soon after pleas for love, reminding readers that there are consequences if they fail to cultivate a loving heart. (As I discuss in chapter 5, this sequence is inverted in the responses to John Brown.) And one finds throughout the *Appeal* lamentations about a lack of love in whites immediately followed by threats of God's wrath. One emotional economy bolsters the other. "I hope that the Americans may hear," pleads Walker, "but I am afraid that they have done us so much injury, and are so firm in the belief that our Creator made us to be an inheritance to them for ever, *that their hearts will be hardened, so that their destruction may be sure*" (*A* 40; emphasis mine). Hardened hearts are poor conductors of sympathy, and instead of merely depicting scenes of the slaves' sorrow, as if images of a suffering slave could somehow guarantee a sympathetic response, Walker reminds his readers of the destructive consequences that will ensue if they do not reform their sentiments. "This language," Walker continues, "perhaps is too harsh for the American's delicate ears. But Oh Americans! Americans! ! I warn you in the name of the Lord, (whether you will hear, or forbear,) to repent and reform, or you are ruined! ! !" (40). Fear resuscitates unresponsive hearts and is targeted at those Americans who exist furthest outside the bonds of sympathy and compassion. "For I declare to you," says Walker, "that there are some on this continent of America, who will never be able to repent. God will surely destroy them, to show you his disapprobation of the murders they and you have inflicted on us" (69). Acknowledging the problem of readers who are disinclined to feel compassion for slaves and who consequentially must be provoked into penitence, Walker sketches an antislavery approach in which inspiring readers to "feel right" entails first making them afraid so that they may avoid the apocalyptic repercussions that in his *Appeal* seem so inevitable.

And it is precisely the inevitability of apocalypse/insurrection that makes Walker's *Appeal* such a terrifying indictment of slavery. It is for this same reason that Walker fails to elicit any sympathy from his readers. The *Appeal* embodies the essential features of apocalyptic sentimentalism without yoking together calls for sympathy and warnings of retribution into a consolidated antislavery discourse. It is, in some sense, too apocalyptic. Given how emphatically Walker renders his threats (the capital letters, the frequent use of exclamation points, etc.), there is a sense that it is almost too late, that the nation is precipitously close to the edge and that what Walker really desires is to give America a shove into bloodshed and torment. It is typically at this moment that scholars retreat from rather than pursue the full implications of the *Appeal*'s argument, claiming Walker as a revolutionary in order to circumvent the disturbing possibility that he is championing an antislavery response founded on terror and religious violence that does not accord with American liberal ideals. Robert Levine, for instance, avoids the reading of Walker I am offering here. Acknowledging that the *Appeal* ends with an enthusiastic call for "black vengeance," Levine nevertheless claims that Walker's ideas of violence are fundamentally informed by his reading of the Declaration of Independence. Levine highlights the fact that Walker marshals the declaration as part of his critique of the nation's hypocrisy, but he overlooks Walker's references to America's founding document as "*your* Declaration of Independence" and "*your* language" and "*their* Declaration" (107, 110; emphases mine). Walker suggests, in other words, that he does not share a common language of freedom with white Americans, nor do his ideas of liberty and resistance originate from the same ideological source. And why should they? America has already had one revolution, and it did nothing to improve the lives of its slaves. Given the failure of America's revolutionary history as it bears on slavery, it stands to reason that Walker would adopt an alternative worldview in order to theorize new modes of resistance. In fact, as I have been arguing, Walker is much more indebted to the emancipatory potential of radical Christianity than he is to the Declaration of Independence, a point that is missed when apocalypse and revolution are treated as synonyms or when the theological is so thoroughly subsumed by the revolutionary that it is barely distinguishable from its privileged counterpart. I address this dilemma more fully in the last section of this chapter.[13]

Walker's *Appeal* ominously portends a coming day of wrath, and the seemingly prophetic quality of Walker's words is fulfilled with Nat Turner's insurrection in 1831 and the subsequent publication of his *Confessions*. Turner represents the incarnated threat that Walker prophesied only two years earlier. And by articulating an affiliation between apocalyptic prophecy and violent responses to slavery, Turner's *Confessions* constitutes an important companion text to Walker's *Appeal*, even if it refuses any pleas for sympathy and love. Indeed, what makes the historical moment in which the *Appeal* and *Confessions* appear so powerful is the combined statement on apocalyptic fear that each makes. Turner's *Confessions* also connects the African American tradition of apocalyptic representation in the early nineteenth century to Harriet Beecher Stowe (whom I treat in part 2 of this book), given that Stowe will directly engage with and make use of the historical problem of Turner in her fiction. The theological terror in Turner's *Confessions* is equally a part of Stowe's intellectual and aesthetic itineraries; she is always threatening God's judgment, always prophesying apocalyptic destruction. In the following section, I examine Turner's fusion of apocalyptic prophecy to acts of slave rebellion and foreshadow how this linkage will help shape later works of sentimentality.

The Sentiments of Nat Turner

While recounting to Thomas Gray the events that took place beginning on August 21, 1831, Nat Turner indicates that inspiring widespread panic among Southerners was one of the chief aims of the rebellion. "'Twas my object," says Turner, "to carry terror and devastation wherever we went."[14] It is important that Turner never mentions as his objective the reorganization of America's democratic institutions, the emancipation of other slaves, or even his own manumission.[15] The insurgency was less about transforming the social order or achieving personal liberty than about acting on Turner's desire to "strike terror to the inhabitants" (*C* 51) of Southampton County, Virginia.[16] Indeed, the portrait of Nat Turner that emerges from the *Confessions*, underscoring his unquenchable "thirst for blood," did succeed in terrorizing the planter class with the image of a slave who might, at any moment, kill his master while he sleeps.[17]

Like Walker, Turner constructs his insurrection as an apocalyptic event, thus augmenting the terror for an already horrified Southern readership, given what they already knew from newspaper reports of the revolt. "For as the blood of Christ had been shed on this earth," says Turner, "and had ascended to heaven for the salvation of sinners, and was now returning to earth again in the form of dew ... it was plain to me that the Saviour was about to lay down the yoke he had borne for the sins of men, and the great day of judgment was at hand" (*C* 47). Here, Turner establishes an equivalence between divine judgment and slave insurrection that resembles Walker's descriptions in the *Appeal*. In so doing, Turner further develops this bourgeoning conceptual linkage where slave rebellion acts as a metonym for apocalyptic retribution. Unlike Walker, who only imagines some of the possible forms a slave revolt might take, Turner is able to follow his own apocalyptic threat with gruesome details of the events that took place under his leadership. Turner describes how Mrs. Travis (Turner's mistress) "shared the same fate" of her husband, both of whom were killed with an axe by one of Turner's fellow insurgents. Turner and the other rebels subsequently murder Mrs. Reese "in her bed, while sleeping." Mrs. Reese's son wakes, Turner continues, "but it was only to sleep the sleep of death" (49). Further carnage ensues, and by the time the Virginia militia reaches Southampton County and quells the rebellion, Turner and his band have killed some sixty whites, more than half of them women and children.

Of all the murders Turner commits during his so-called work of death (*C* 48), the one that would have been the most shocking for genteel white audiences would have been the killing of Travis's infant child "sleeping in a cradle" who, Turner says, was almost "forgotten" by the rebels who "had left the house and gone some distance" but who returned to murder the baby (49). The idea of Turner's men callously disposing of a sleeping infant would have been especially horrifying for an antebellum culture that invested enormous symbolic significance in images of dying children who in death could help redeem those they left behind. Nineteenth-century stories are populated by children who fulfill such a role and whose dying helps enact a teleology of Christian salvation for the living.[18] Turner's narrative violates this tradition. Rather than redemption and the promise of a forgiving God, Turner gives his readers vengeance; rather than love, he gives them a God who seeks retribution on the unholy, even those as seemingly innocent as a sleeping child. The dying infant in Turner's *Confessions* is divested of its salvific force.

This depiction of the murdered child in the *Confessions* constitutes the first "panel" of a literary triptych that I would like to construct throughout the progression of this book (the next two panels appear in chapters 3 and 5). The image I mention above is not only a highly antisentimental one, but one that reproduces and augments pervasive stereotypes about the violent black male figure. It does nothing to foster the sense that slaves are beings with whom

Americans should sympathize. To the contrary, it assures white Americans that blacks, and especially black men, are not to be trusted (and thus, implicitly, should be kept in fetters) because they harbor hostile intentions toward even the most ostensibly innocent members of the white community. This dynamic, in which an adult male interacts with a child to dramatize some important insight about interracial interaction, will recur at several crucial moments in the development of apocalyptic sentimentalism; these dyads operate as useful indices for measuring the evolution of this tradition. The scene of the rebellious slave murdering the infant in the crib suggests that, while the structure of apocalyptic sentimentalism is beginning to emerge, most noticeably in the writing of David Walker, it is at a very early stage in its development.[19] Even as Walker is trying to imagine a loving bond that can be formed by interracial collaboration, Turner reminds readers that interpersonal relations between blacks and whites are still overwhelmingly defined by a violent antipathy. In light of Turner's insurrection, Walker's hope for a possible peaceful resolution will for now have to remain unfulfilled.

If inspiring terror in the surrounding communities was one of Turner's principal aims, contemporary responses to the revolt suggest that he hit his mark. In a letter to the *Richmond Whig* dated September 1831, one writer said that "indiscriminate carnage" was Turner's "watchword."[20] Another writer explains that Turner was a "dreamer of dreams, and a would be Prophet" who "used all the arts familiar to such pretenders, to deceive, delude, and overawe" the minds of Southamptoners.[21] According to Henry "Box" Brown, who was living in Richmond at the time of Turner's revolt, "the slaveholder lives in constant dread of such an event" following Turner's "successful" insurrection. "The rustling of '—the lightest leaf, / That quivers to the passing breeze,' fills his timid soul with visions of flowing blood and burning dwellings; and as the loud thunder of heaven rolls over his head, and the vivid lightning flashes across his pale face, straightway his imagination conjures up terrible scenes of the loud roaring of an enemy's cannon, and the fierce yells of an infuriated slave population, rushing to vengeance."[22] Brown elegantly captures the abiding sense of doom that followed the rebellion and subsequent publication of Turner's account of it. In the spirit of Turner's confession, one Northern paper, the *New York Morning Courier and Enquirer*, painted the events in Southampton as a dreaded apocalyptic moment: "[T]he hellish plot . . . was to be the day of judgment. . . . With the morning commenced the butchery—a 'black sun' arose in the east with a vengeance!—a day of judgment came upon the heads of 64 innocent men, women, and children. The sentence of the judge and the blow of the executioner fell at once on the helpless victims of fanatic fury!" Even as he claims that these were "helpless victims" of some grisly plot, this newspaper writer acknowledges that the events in Southampton on this "day of judgment" had providential meaning.²³ Like this writer, witnesses throughout the South appear to have recognized that this was no mere rebellion but instead a sign of God's wrath and omen of greater woes to come. The sense of insurrectionary panic inspired by Turner and his coconspirators was so great that the Virginia legislature, as well as various Southern presses, briefly discussed the feasibility of manumitting slaves before ultimately deciding to place even greater restrictions on the slaves and free blacks living within the state.²⁴

While Turner did not emancipate any slaves, this was never his stated goal.²⁵ In addition to engendering a deep sense of terror in those who protected and enabled slavery, Turner also unwittingly provided subsequent writers with a powerful rhetorical construction for contesting slavery by linking acts of insurrection with prophesies of God's apocalyptic retribution—an ideological formulation that will recur with increasing frequency over the course of the antebellum period. Such figurations of slave insurrection / divine retribution will also be marshaled to galvanize a loving and sympathetic link between whites and enslaved blacks, even if Turner's text itself is entirely devoid of love. For these reasons, I locate Turner neither fully outside of apocalyptic sentimentality nor fully within it. Rather, Turner is a kind of connective tissue that fastens the early discourse of Walker to later antislavery writings.

Messianic Violence

Scholarly readings of the *Appeal* and *Confessions* must inevitably account for each text's deeply divisive and highly inflammatory language, and critics often treat these meditations on theological wrath as a metonym for revolutionary black resistance. Gene Andrew Jarrett, Robert Levine, and Jeremy Engles have all recently contended that Walker's theory of slave resistance aligns with what Maggie Sale has succinctly identified as the "trope of revolutionary struggle."²⁶ Walker's emphatic critique of Jefferson's racialist views in *Notes on the State of Virginia* and his co-optation of the Declaration of Independence only further underscore his apparent investment in revolutionary modes of critique. Walker's engagement with Jefferson's ideas on freedom, ideas that form the bedrock of American liberal society, suggest that he is deliberately locating himself within a genealogy of revolution that traces back to the nation's founding.²⁷ And while scholars have done a convincing job of describing the religious underpinnings of Turner's insurrection, he is still often thought of in terms similar to Walker: that is, as an early black revolutionary who uses his understanding of prophecy to justify his engagement in revolutionary resistance to slavery.²⁸ Indeed, as Eric J. Sundquist has argued, "African American writers such as [Frederick] Douglass, [Martin] Delany, [David] Walker, William Wells Brown, and Harriet Jacobs" were deeply invested in strategies for resisting enslavement and "had been quick to link slavery [and slave resistance] to its complex revolutionary heritage."²⁹ Critics continue to read Walker and Turner specifically, and nineteenth-century arguments supporting slave insurrection more generally, as signs that antebellum black Americans were revolutionaries insofar as they opposed institutions that violated rights intrinsic to nature and guaranteed by God, confirming, in Wendell Phillips's words, that "colored men" like Walker and Turner are "patriotic—though denied a country:—and all show a wish, on their part, to prove themselves men, in a land whose laws refuse to recognise their manhood."³⁰ The story of America's revolutionary origins remains a favorite among modern critics as a way to frame how the most subversive abolitionists justified violence as a chief mechanism for emancipating Negro slaves.³¹

When scholars deploy the "revolutionary" as an explanatory category, they invoke, either implicitly or explicitly, a set of ideological associations for which the term "revolution" serves as a stand-in: specifically, liberal rights, democratic citizenship, and the inherent and universal equality of all persons. Scholars have been able to affirm Walker and Turner by normalizing the violence they promote, claiming that they are "revolutionary" in the modern understanding of this notion. By making violence revolutionary and not apocalyptic or merely retributive, critics temper Walker's and Turner's incendiary presence by placing them in a tradition in which violence was necessary to preserve the self-evident freedoms of every individual. Anyone who fights for these rights, including Negro slaves, is identified as a revolutionary, so that revolutionary violence is understood to be a rational phenomenon and indicator of the Enlightenment push toward the perfectibility of the human spirit. Revolutionary violence, then, is not destabilizing or destructive in these views, but normative and constructive of a world where all persons enjoy the rights and privileges of citizenship. Given that most slaves presumably desired freedom and equality, and in light of scholarly interest in the forms of nineteenth-century slave resistance, it makes sense that modern critics would apply a revolutionary framework to interpret acts of violent resistance. As a result of their fixation on the revolutionary, however, scholars have incorrectly described the manner in which Walker and Turner represent violent agency in their texts, treating it as a willful act of revolution rather than the religious insurgency that it was.³²

I propose an alternative paradigm—the "messianic"—that exemplifies how the violence Walker and Turner construct is predicated on and enabled by ideas of a vengeful God. Messianic violence functions in these texts as a powerful framework for imagining a potent black presence in the U.S., and it is through the revised category of the apocalyptic that fantasies of black power (perhaps the first meaningful instance in which an ideology of "black power" is articulated in the American context) get played out. By invoking the apocalyptic to underwrite this mode of power and to certify acts of slave revolt, Walker and

Turner aim to discourage white readers from simply explaining away insurrectionary violence as the predictable expression of putatively barbaric Negro slaves. But the structure of power expressed in each text is curiously paradoxical insofar as it is instantiated only when the slave submits himself fully to a sovereign God. The insurgent is only made "free," in other words, through a seemingly counterintuitive act of self-abnegation and self-subjection, a surprising tactic given, first, that the *Appeal* and *Confessions* appear to be about self-reliant acts of violence and, second, that abnegation and subjection are two traits of enslavement that mark the slave's disempowerment and exclusion from antebellum discourses of rights and personhood. As a theory of violent resistance via abnegation and subjection, however, the messianic is coordinated with antebellum notions of self-reliance based on abnegation (as exemplified in the writings of Ralph Waldo Emerson) and prefigures postmodern theories of identity formation via subjection (embodied in the writing of Judith Butler, among others), with Walker and Turner offering ideas of rebellion that challenge assumptions about revolutionary resistance and overlap with, but ultimately remain distinct from, nineteenth-century *and* contemporary ideas regarding the spiritual foundation and discursive production of the self.

The *Appeal* and *Confessions* were such incendiary documents because readers understood that in foreboding divine vengeance as a response to slavery, Walker and Turner were also foretelling slave insurrection, equating slave rebellion with apocalyptic retribution, and aligning the figure of the insurrectionist with a wrathful God. Imbuing the slave rebel with a divine purpose, as Walker and Turner both did, was one strategy to empower the slave to act on behalf of other slaves and to legitimize the violence a slave might use to achieve his desired end. Linking the rebellious slave to a wrathful God, in other words, was one way of making him more than just a rebellious slave, more than just a degraded man. Consider, to begin, the note that precedes the preamble of Walker's argument, in which he writes that "the day of our redemption from abject wretchedness draweth near, when we shall be enabled, in the most extended sense of the word, to stretch forth our hands to the LORD OUR GOD, but there must be a willingness on our part, for GOD to do these things for us" (*A* 1; original emphasis). While this passage conveys Walker's hope that blacks will be delivered from bondage, it is not so clear who the redeemer in this passage actually is—or, in other words, precisely where agency originates. Walker employs the passive voice to claim that black male slaves will be *enabled* by God to liberate themselves, but that they will have to be willing, in an active sense, before God agrees "to do these things for us." The slaves' "willingness" must, according to Walker's account, precede God's authorization to act, and yet when the slave is finally authorized, it is not the slave who acts at all, but God. Walker's argument about violent resistance is markedly different from the revolutionary manhood modern readers have come to associate with writers like Frederick Douglass or his semifictional protagonist from *The Heroic Slave*, Madison Washington. If we keep Madison Washington in mind as the exemplar of a nineteenth-century black revolutionary hero, we can see just how different Walker's and Turner's construction of resistance is. Indeed, both Walker's *Appeal* and Turner's *Confessions* outline an alternative model of forceful resistance that will inform and be developed by the figures I explore throughout the rest of this book.

I begin with Walker, who repeatedly subordinates the will of black men to the will of God, privileging the agency of God above all others.[33] "Remember," says Walker, "also to lay humble at the feet of our Lord and Master Jesus Christ.... Never make an attempt to gain our freedom or *natural right*, from under our cruel oppressors and murderers, until you see your way clear" (*A* 11; original emphasis). Walker places the black slave prostrate before God, prone and passive, while God removes oppressive slaveholders from the nation. The slave's liberation, Walker suggests, and his claim to rights, will ultimately depend on divine intervention. "For be assured," Walker announces, "that Jesus Christ the King of heaven and of earth who is the God of justice and of armies, will surely go before you.... He will remove" (12). Black slaves act only if God acts before them, clearing the path to freedom; they acquire agency by waiting patiently, letting God battle in their stead for a time.

Evoking God as the source of slaves' authority to act entails depriving them of the agency they desire, so that self-determination paradoxically involves remaining in a state of dependence. Walker explains that "God rules in the armies of heaven and among the inhabitants of the earth" (*A* 3), waiting for the proper moment to strike oppressors. In the revolt as Walker describes it, Christ will lead and the slaves will compose his army. At the moment of battle, however, Christ himself does not enter the fight but offers the slaves someone to lead in his place. "Beloved brethren" says Walker, "—here let me tell you, and believe it, that the Lord our God ... will give you a Hannibal" (20). God will send a leader like the African commander of antiquity who will fight alongside America's slaves and on God's behalf. "The person whom God shall give you," Walker continues, "give him your support and let him go his length, and behold in him the salvation of your God. God will indeed, deliver you through him from your deplorable and wretched condition under the Christians of America" (20). This divinely ordained commander constitutes the promise of salvation. Part secular agent of deliverance and part divinely conscripted marionette performing as God's stand-in, this Hannibal is an instrument who both acts and is acted upon, aggressively resisting slavery precisely by remaining receptive to God's will. And it is "through" this leader that God will liberate America's slaves, who are themselves charged with supporting this general. Strength comes to the slave who willingly subjugates himself to Hannibal and, by extension, subjects himself to God.

While Walker's theory of subjection might seem like a misguided approach to imbuing the rebellious slave with power, especially given that subjection is what enslaved blacks were trying to escape, this framework is not without its historical correspondences, especially in the early American context.[34] Both Jonathan Edwards and Ralph Waldo Emerson, for example, elaborated models of selfhood predicated on disavowal, so that some of the earliest literary notions of discrete personhood were characterized by a subordination of the self to a more powerful spiritual force. Aspiring to cultivate the "soul of a true Christian," Edwards writes that he desired, above all things, "to lie low before God; and in the dust; that I might be nothing, and that God might be all; that I might become as a little child." In dedicating himself to God, Edwards is "giving up myself, and all that I had to God; to be for the future in no respect my own; to act as one that had no right to himself, in any respect."[35] Edwards experiences a passionate subjection to God, stating that "I love to think of coming to Christ, to receive salvation of him, poor in spirit, and quite empty of self ... cut entirely off from my own root."[36] The closer one comes to Christ, according to Edwards's formulation, the less individuated one is. "I felt," concludes Edwards, "an ardency of soul to be, what I know not otherwise how to express, than to be emptied and annihilated; to lie in the dust, and to be full of Christ alone."[37] For Edwards, personal holiness requires a displacement of the egocentric self so that God becomes the source of agency and guarantor of deliverance. This early Protestant view of the self is structurally analogous to Ralph Waldo Emerson's model of self-reliance that is founded on abnegation, a willful subordination of the self to the "ever-blessed ONE."[38] Emerson's writing marks the inauguration of what he once described as the "age of the first person singular," with self-reliance becoming a predominant model of selfhood in the antebellum period, one that will be adopted (and revised) by later black antislavery writers such as Frederick Douglass and William Wells Brown.[39] While writers like Douglass will employ self-reliance to describe how the subject achieves independent manhood by gaining mastery over the self,[40] Emerson's is a model of self-abnegated selfhood in which the self acquires power by relinquishing rather than superficially mastering itself. Power, according to Emerson, is intensified through a disavowal rather than a consolidation of self, a submission to an immanent and immeasurable divine unity that underwrites all being.[41] Self-reliance in this case requires the subordination of the superficial self to the true Self, an immutable self that Emerson calls the "aboriginal Self."[42]

These early articulations of subjection as a characteristic of subjectivization, or the process of self-making, are part of a long tradition in the American context where the self is imagined outside the parameters of the liberal tradition. Exemplifying postmodern concepts of the self, for example, Judith Butler has argued that "subordination proves central to the becoming of the subject. As the condition of becoming a subject, subordination implies being in a mandatory submission."[43] For Butler, the subject is constituted through a discourse that precedes its formation and that it never chooses but that is nevertheless essential to the subject becoming intelligible; subjection, in short, is what "initiates and sustains our agency."[44] It is in the act of exerting itself upon the subject from the outside that discourse calls the subject into social existence, giving subjection its dual nature as an oppressive as well as productive force.[45] Within this view, subjection is a precondition of subjectivity, so that "one is dependent on power for one's very formation, and that formation is impossible without dependency."[46]

While we can locate Walker's theory of the self on this long historical continuum that has understood subjection to be a constitutive aspect of social existence, Walker does not merely reproduce Edwardsian or Emersonian notions of abnegation or postmodern views on the inextricability of subordination in the production of the subject. Unlike Emerson, whose target is not slavery but the model of divinity offered by Calvinists and whose version of divinity is entirely benign as a result, Walker calls for a dependency on a retributive God of the apocalypse as the very grounding of empowered black resilience. And the form of subordination that Walker describes is something the slave must choose if he is to be free, an option that is unavailable within Butler's poststructuralist view. For Walker, the slave deliberately subordinates himself to God in order to escape his subjection under slavery. He exchanges one form of subjugation for another, but these forms are not equivalent. If slavery is the principal discourse that instantiates the social and psychic life of the slave, then it is the slave's subjection to a transcendent deity, one that exists outside of discourse and immanent notions of power, that begins to counteract subjection within slavery.[47]

These types of transfers in power, where the locus of action appears to vacillate between God and the slave, run throughout the *Appeal* and derive from an understanding of violence that is thoroughly theological and that is rooted in notions of a God who exacts retribution against those who have transgressed his law. Whereas the revolutionary self is understood to be an autonomous being who fights to reclaim and protect inherent natural rights, the violent messianic agent as it is portrayed by Walker is subordinated to a transcendental divinity that promises to act on behalf of black Americans, and this subjugation, in turn, constitutes the source of the black subject's power. Indeed, the paradox of messianic force in the *Appeal* is that authority is garnered by the slave through his subjugation to God, and not just any God, but a vengeful one.

This vision of violence that Walker presents dramatically differs from a natural rights–based account of revolutionary agency that continues as the scholarly default setting. In being subjected *to* God, the slave becomes a subject *of* God, and it is precisely in this privileged station as one of God's subjects that the black insurrectionist is transformed from a degraded being into an agent white Americans must not only take seriously as a man but must also fear, given the apocalyptic contours of his agency.

It is within this subordinated but nevertheless proximate relationship to a wrathful God that Walker is able to begin articulating what this form of black power might look like. As Walker argues, man is made in "the image of his God," and "though he may be subjected to the most wretched condition upon earth, yet the spirit and feeling which constitute the creature, man, can never be entirely erased from his breast, because the God who made him after his own image, planted it in his heart; he cannot get rid of it" (*A* 61). What God is, man will become, though in less amplified form, and whites, knowing "that they have done us so much injury," are "afraid that we, being men, and not brutes, will retaliate, and woe will be to them," for "some of them will have enough of us by and by—their stomachs shall run over with us" (61–62). Black rebels, according to Walker, are made in the image of God, and what is the image of God in the *Appeal* other than an agent of biblical fury? Within the logic of Walker's argument, then, the rebellious slave is not so much revolutionary as he is apocalyptic, meting out wrath and vengeance toward enslavers. What appears to be merely inflammatory rhetoric is, in fact, Walker's careful attempt to theorize a form of violent power within a religious framework:

> For, if we lay aside abject servility, and be determined to act like men, and not brutes—the murderers among the whites would be afraid to show their cruel heads.... But remember, Americans, that as miserable, wretched, degraded, and abject as you have made us in preceding, and in this generation, to support you and your families, that some of you, (whites) on the continent of America, will yet curse the day that you ever were born. You want slaves, and want us for your slaves! ! ! My colour will yet, root some of you out of the very face of the earth! ! ! ! ! ! (62, 72)

Created in the image of a God who will surely redress the nation's sins, black slaves shed their brutishness and consolidate their manhood by performing the very act God means to carry out in his final judgment. The violence that Walker imagines in the *Appeal* is "messianic" because it corresponds to the scriptural warnings of Christ's own vengeance and judgment. The messianic insurrectionist is engendered in a subordinate but inseparable relation to God, and whether he does it under, alongside of, or with God's "crushing arm of power," the prone and prostrate slave is, through his subjection, simultaneously an empowered slave who participates in theological acts of destruction.

If Walker foretells the appearance of a messianic black savior who will deliver slaves out of bondage, Turner constitutes himself as the figure Walker imagines in his *Appeal;* he is the Christ-like agent who is called by God to right the wrongs of slavery and whose violence is imitative of apocalyptic prophecy.[48] Turner mobilizes his fellow slaves to exact vengeance against slaveholders "by the communion of the Spirit whose revelations I often communicated to them," aiming "to prepare them for my purpose, by telling them something was about to happen that would terminate in fulfilling the great promise that had been made to me" (*C* 46). Insurrectionary violence is both Turner's plan ("my purpose") and God's pledge ("the great promise"). Insofar as Turner is empowered to act precisely by being subject to God's purpose, the locus of agency remains ambiguous, and this ambiguity is necessary to how he imagines his strength and legitimates his role as a conspirator of rebellion. Turner certifies his sense of purpose through messianic self-representation, internalizing the apocalypse so that it becomes both scriptural promise *and* psychic state. Describing his rebellion as an extension of eschatological prophecy, Turner recounts an incident when he "discovered drops of blood on the corn as though it were dew from heaven" as well as "hieroglyphic characters" on the leaves of trees "and numbers, with the forms of men in different attitudes, portrayed in blood, and representing the figures I had seen before in the heavens" (47).[49] These signs prefigure the fast-approaching day of judgment, when the South will be held accountable for its sins. An emissary of God's message, Turner is the subject of enunciation who, in giving expression to God's desire, confirms his importance in God's plan. He receives these signs because he is meant to play a central part in the eradication of sin and the dénouement of history.[50]

Turner's transfiguration from passive prophet to the embodiment of messianic power is consolidated in one especially dramatic vision where he "saw white spirits and black spirits engaged in battle, and the sun was darkened—the thunder rolled in the Heavens, and blood flowed in streams—and I heard a voice saying, 'Such is your luck, such you are called to see, and let it come rough or smooth, you must surely bare [*sic*] it'" (*C* 46). Peals of thunder, streams of blood, the sun darkening, and an epic contest between light and dark forces signal that an apocalypse is at hand. No mere insurrectionist, Turner is ushering in messianic devastation. Interpellated into this mode of existence by a divine calling, Turner works vigorously "to obtain true holiness before the day of judgment should appear" (47). Turner locates insurrection within a teleology culminating in judgment and the end of history as he mediates the word of God, receiving its signs and giving voice to its meanings. He also suggests that he is the one charged with the colossal task of bearing the burden that comes with being an instrument of devastation. When the voice implores him to "bare it," it calls Turner into a new mode of existence. He is transubstantiated from a prophet of destruction into an agent of apocalyptic doom. In a later vision, Turner explains that he "heard a loud noise in the heavens, and the Spirit instantly appeared to me and said the Serpent was loosened, and Christ had laid down the yoke he had borne for the sins of men, and that *I should take it on and fight against the Serpent*, for the time was fast approaching when the first should be last and the last should be first" (47–48; emphasis mine). Here, Turner is no longer simply a co-agent with God, hastening apocalyptic devastation to slave owners, nor is he merely haunted by phantasms of the coming day of wrath. He *is* the day of wrath. Turner rewrites the book of Revelation so that the serpent is no longer Satan but the slaveholder, and Turner, not Christ, is its persecutor. It is Turner who fights the serpent, Turner who makes the last first. The prerogative that was once God's, the Spirit enjoins "that [Turner] should take it on" as the redeemer of his people and God's surrogate on earth, an agent of messianic violence whose intervention is designed to dismantle the nation's most insidious institution. What Walker threatened in the *Appeal*, Turner takes to its logical conclusion. And whereas Walker offers his readers a way out, promising reconciliation if whites will simply liberate their slaves, Turner provides no such consolation. "And," explains Turner, "by signs in the heavens ... it would make known to me when I should commence the great work" (48). Chosen by God as his privileged messenger, favored by the Lord as his divinely ordained workman, Turner will usher in the apocalypse. Far from the heroes of America's revolutionary past who were later revered in antislavery discourses as protectors of natural rights and guarantors of freedom, Turner is out for blood. He displays little interest in defending his actions to his white audience and instead works merely to increase their horror.

David Walker's representation of religious violence does not negate the fact that what he ultimately desires is that all blacks be treated like beings who possess the natural rights ostensibly inherent in all men, rights espoused by America's forebears and enshrined in the nation's charter.[51] Indeed, it is precisely for this reason that scholars often locate Walker in a revolutionary tradition. However, the violence Walker imagines is about punishing whites, not about expanding the scope of inclusiveness. Violence as Walker presents it in the *Appeal* is the ultimate penalty for white America's failure to regard blacks as equal. In 1829 Walker would have had no reason to believe that white Americans would willingly assign such rights to black Americans. If the liberal theories and natural rights that Walker evokes throughout the *Appeal* are to be made available to blacks, it will only happen in response to the dire warning in Walker's condemnation of slavery. Citizenship becomes possible for black Americans only insofar as it is regarded as an expedient alternative to the messianic threat, which serves as an incentive for white Americans to free their slaves and extend to them rights as free men. But Walker's account of violence should not be located primarily within America's revolutionary genealogy, first because it is not a way for blacks to prove their worth and claim the rights that have been denied them; it is instead an act of vengeance for the injustices they have suffered. Second, rebellious force as Walker presents it in the *Appeal* does not conform to a liberal-revolutionary model to the extent that it requires voluntary submission to a power that is not ultimately one's own. And third, slave violence is comprehended to be the fulfillment of apocalyptic prophecy, not part of the unfolding of a secular history of ever-expanding freedom.

And while Nat Turner is, in some sense, an obvious extension of Walker, Turner entirely refuses to adopt the lexicon of white liberal citizenship; he makes no gesture toward the lofty ideals on which the nation was ostensibly founded. Turner's confession therefore differs from Walker's *Appeal* to the extent that it offers no alternative to the messianic threat and the terror that such a threat was meant to provoke; nor does it demonstrate any regard for abiding by normative codes of personhood. Turner is the instantiation of a mode of freedom that neither depends on nor seeks state sanction or approval from white Americans. Turner's self-portrait exceeds the limits (and limitations) of liberal egalitarianism. Depicting himself within a messianic frame, Turner avoids co-opting white bourgeois norms altogether, rooting his insurrectionary identity in a radical revision of apocalyptic theology.[52]

Given the inflammatory content of the *Appeal* and *Confessions*, then, why would masters ever agree to set their slaves free? Indeed, Walker and Turner unwittingly make the slaveholders' argument for them, giving slaveholders reason enough to keep these potentially violent slaves, with their insatiable "thirst for blood," in chains. This rhetorical dilemma is one that many antebellum antislavery writers, black and white alike, found themselves confronting as many of them struggled to articulate carefully an account of Negro selfhood that deserved emancipation without at the same time undermining their political efforts to free slaves. To be sure, Walker and Turner inscribe an empowered black subject that contests notions of racial inferiority but, in so doing, run the risk of energizing the resolve of white slaveholders who could only recoil at the vision of black violence they represent.[53] But the choice between representing a strong black presence that resists being reduced to assumptions about Negro inferiority and depicting an account of black personhood that meets white liberal standards for civic recognition is a false one. The problem that marks antebellum culture is that free and enslaved Negroes are precisely *not* recognized as persons according to prevailing nineteenth-century standards and are thus precluded from full civic recognition, regardless of how much they embody normative white values. Black writers, in particular, faced a predicament in appropriating theories of natural rights and liberal notions of the self, given that these discourses provided the exclusionary logic for whites to police the boundaries between black and white culture and maintain the subordinate status of black Americans.[54] In constructing an alternative model of black resistance, Walker and Turner might circumvent this impasse, but they nevertheless put on display a radical notion of black force that slaveholders were unlikely to see as deserving freedom. Despite some of the entanglements that it creates, however, messianism, as it is represented in the *Appeal* and *Confessions*, should be understood within the political and discursive constraints of antebellum culture, with Walker and Turner constituting two of the first prominent black figures to assert a unique voice in opposition to the logic of race-based slavery.

The tradition of apocalyptic sentimentalism that I am charting in this book requires us to think about the forms of violence that energize it; incitements to fear are manufactured by way of a theological prophecy that many antebellum Americans found to be quite real and quite terrifying. For this reason, I have spent considerable time in this chapter making a careful distinction between revolutionary and theological violence. Of course, there are instances when religious and revolutionary discourses cooperate to form a powerful statement about selfhood and freedom. There are other instances, however, like the ones I examine in this study, that less seamlessly integrate religion and revolution. In such cases, sometimes violence will be the work of God, other times it will be the purview of rebellious slaves. In all cases, warnings of retribution are articulated within an apocalyptic frame, and it is out of this frame that antislavery writers ultimately hoped to engender a loving response in their audience in order to avoid divine punishment. The sentimental as it appears in the texts I explore is a consequence or by-product of these appeals to divine vengeance, which is itself firmly rooted in the evangelical theology of antebellum Christianity.

The nascent sentimental configuration in which threats of apocalyptic destruction are used to motivate sympathetic connections will surface throughout the antislavery discourses of the antebellum period. Writers as varied in their aesthetic and political sensibilities as William Lloyd Garrison, Harriet Beecher Stowe, and Martin Delany will develop the sentimental model I describe in this chapter, accompanying calls for love with terrifying images of God's vengeance, using fear of God's wrath as a sentimental support system for sympathy and compassion. Sentimental culture is often thought to be a middle-class construct, and literary sentimentalism a style that blossomed among white midcentury bourgeois women. Reading Walker on the threshold of this blossoming helps us frame and explain the emotional dynamism of his argument. Such a perspective should also help us revise our views about the racial and class origins of American sentimentalism so that we begin to see its emergence rooted in white *and* black forms of representation.⁵⁵ As an early example of apocalyptic sentimentalism, Walker's *Appeal* expands the category of the sentimental and should be read alongside lesser-known but no less important black writers who share aspects of Walker's approach, such as Maria Stewart, Jarena Lee, and Rebecca Cox Jackson, as well as more well-known sentimentalists like Harriet Beecher Stowe. Indeed, by establishing Walker's foundational presence, and by recognizing that a rhetorical style present in Walker's *Appeal* will continue to reappear in diverse styles of antislavery sentimentality, we are forced to reassess what we mean when we deploy the term "sentimentalism," beginning with our ideas about sentimentalism's relationship to evangelical theology.

In the next chapter, I examine Maria Stewart's public lectures and private writings as they expand upon the sentimental logic she inherits from her reading of Walker's *Appeal*. Unlike Walker, however, Stewart launches a critique that is far more attentive to the overlapping constraints of race and gender. Stewart also begins to shift the logic of apocalyptic utterances, treating what had just a few years earlier been a decidedly public expression (typically announced from the pulpit or lectern) to a domestic category. In Stewart's writing and lectures, the apocalypse finds a home.

CHAPTER 2

"The Wrath of the Lamb"

*Maria W. Stewart and the
Domestication of Apocalypse*

God is all love.
—Maria Stewart, *"An Address Delivered Before the Afric-American
Female Intelligence Society of America,"* 1832

When the world shall be on fire, and the elements shall pass away with a great noise, and the heavens shall be rolled together as a scroll; when death, and hell, and the sea shall deliver up the dead that are in them, and all nations, kindreds, tongues, and people shall be arrayed before the awful bar of God, and the books shall be opened; then, then, if we have not the pure and undefiled religion of Jesus, wo, wo, wo, will be unto us! Better for us that we had never been born; better for us that a mill-stone were hanged about our necks, and that we were cast into the depths of the sea.
—Maria Stewart, *Meditation XI,* 1879

In her earliest political essay, *Religion and the Pure Principles of Morality, the Sure Foundation on Which We Must Build*, which was published in the *Liberator* in 1831, Maria W. Stewart explores the entangled issues of religious belief, antislavery reform, and women's rights that would come to characterize the thought of so many antebellum women reformers. An impassioned plea for the expansion of political liberties that would afford America's most dispossessed—black women—the ability to chart their own course, the essay is a singular document insofar as it is the first major political statement made by a black woman in America at a time when few spaces existed for a statement such as this one to be articulated. At the end of the essay's first section, Stewart makes what will be the first of many controversial claims that marked her brief but important career. Stating that she believes firmly "that the God in whom I trust is able to protect me from the rage and malice of mine enemies," Stewart nevertheless accepts that if her enemies "rise up" against her, "and if there is no other way for me to escape," then God may "take me to himself, as he did *the most noble, fearless, and undaunted David Walker.*"[1] Stewart upholds Walker—the radical abolitionist and author of *The Appeal*—as an emblem of righteousness, favored by God and steadfast in his fight against racial injustice. In a document that purports to expound on the "pure principles of morality," Stewart singles out Walker as a key example of Christian faithfulness and a source of comfort and encouragement as she begins her own very public campaign against racial oppression and patriarchal authority.

For a black woman seeking a public audience in 1831, Stewart's ideological alignment with Walker was a potentially risky gesture.[2] A colleague and close friend of Walker's, Stewart was deeply engaged in his antislavery critique, especially as it was outlined in the *Appeal*. At a time when many were blaming Walker for the insurrectionary panic his writing ostensibly inspired, Stewart claims him as an ally and mentor.[3] By frequently enlisting Walker, and by organizing her own lectures in a style that recalled Walker's discourse, Stewart deliberately positions herself within a tradition that he helps to inaugurate. This chapter explores Stewart's strategy of adapting and revising Walker's language of sentimental terror in order to challenge black women's subjection to the dual oppressions of racism and patriarchy. By representing stern warnings of theological vengeance in order to generate greater Christian love and compassion, Stewart fully engages with Walker's religious rhetoric in a way that further shapes as well as indexes the emergent sentimental discourse of love and fear; Stewart brings this entanglement to the domestic space and harnesses its affective strength to bolster her pro-woman, antislavery arguments, a move that would ripple through the antebellum period. It might seem to modern readers that in transgressing established nineteenth-century norms governing "proper" feminine speech—that is, Stewart seeks a public audience composed of both men and women, she often invokes gruesome images of divine violence and bloodshed in her lectures, and she even considers the potential need for slave insurrection—Stewart is adopting a set of argumentative tactics that fundamentally oppose nineteenth-century sentimental conventions. But the tradition of apocalyptic sentimentalism that I explore in this book and that Stewart helps to develop explodes the gender divide that ostensibly organized masculine and feminine speech in the antebellum period. Reading Stewart as an early pioneer of apocalyptic sentimentalism suggests that gendered spheres and the modes of discourse that characterize them, with fire and brimstone defining the masculine sphere, love and sentiment marking the feminine, are blended and then deployed to create a sentimental tradition that cannot be cleansed of fiery speech.[4] By foregrounding love *and* threatening God's vengeance together, Stewart contributes to what I call the domestication of apocalyptic terror. I use "domesticate" in two different but related ways. On one hand, Stewart cultivates and naturalizes the apocalypse as an essential aspect of her thought, where feminine speech and warnings of vengeance go hand in hand. On the other, domesticating the apocalypse means bringing the apocalypse quite literally into the home. Even though Stewart's lectures are public, she writes about the domestic concerns of black Americans and demonstrates that the apocalyptic can be deployed from *within* the home to describe the political importance *of* the home, especially for black women.

Despite growing interest in Stewart as an abolitionist and early black feminist, scholars have erased the deep links between domesticity and God's vengeance that were such an elemental part of her thought and work. Lora Romero, for example, considers "what vocabulary antebellum African American women had for articulating the [political] presence they desired in this complex national household." "How," in a patriarchal culture, "would an African American woman—committed equally to both black nationalism and women's participation in that enterprise—make her resistance recognizable?"[5] While Romero quite rightly argues that Stewart fashions a "politicized version of domesticity to license her intrusion into a male-dominated arena," she makes no mention of how the apocalyptic thrust of Stewart's discourse contributes to the politicization of the home; nor does she consider how Stewart's sentimental account of women's political resistance is deeply informed by her abiding belief in a God who implements justice through vengeance.[6]

Unlike Romero, Linda Grasso highlights Stewart's appropriation of God's wrath as a way to communicate her anger at the unjust hierarchies that organize American life in the 1830s. Grasso describes this anger as a "patriarchal God persona," however, and thus misses how Stewart challenges the very gender divide that Grasso herself ends up reifying.[7] "Stewart creates a new kind of discourse," argues Grasso, "one that incorporates both a female-gendered and a male-gendered sensibility. This fusion allows her to participate in both worlds simultaneously: she can appropriate the stance of an angry, patriarchal God while still viewing the world from a female perspective."[8] Grasso appears to recognize the fundamental interrelation between Stewart's wrath and her "moral emotionalism" but ultimately segregates them, treating the masculine and the feminine as hypostatized and essentially distinct categories.[9] The domestic politics that Stewart advocates is, in Grasso's view, separate from the masculine apocalyptic persona she frequently deploys and ultimately abandons. According to Grasso, Stewart was eventually "unable to reconcile a militant, antagonistic, angry-God public stance that was gendered male, and a placating, forgiving, Jesus-style humility that was gendered female." At the end of her brief career, argues Grasso, Stewart "retreats from the stance of a vengeful, punishing god, and replaces it with a forgiving and self-sacrificing posture that makes her reentry into secular womanhood socially acceptable."[10] Grasso's argument maintains a division that critics of Stewart's writing widely share, with the maternal/domestic standing separate from rather than being dependent on and thoroughly infused with the apocalyptic.

My reading of Stewart recovers and returns the apocalypse to the domestic—the space where sentimental love is commonly located. Stewart's potency as a speaker and reformer depends on the interactions between two powerfully linked discourses of vengeance and domesticity, discourses that Stewart brings together rather than separates. In the first section of this chapter, I examine Stewart's construction of an ideation of womanhood that does not neatly square with scholars' understanding of conventional nineteenth-century femininity. As someone whose writing and elocutionary performances invoke God's wrath and imply the need for antislavery violence, Stewart comports herself in very untraditional ways, thus placing her in a genealogy of other "untraditional" female writers and reformers like the Grimkes, Margaret Fuller, and Fanny Fern. In her capacity as a lecturer, Stewart further develops the rhetoric of apocalyptic sentimentalism that Walker's *Appeal* began to adumbrate shortly before Stewart takes the public stage. Whereas Walker primarily emphasized God's vengeance with the occasional plea for sympathy, Stewart strikes a greater balance by foregrounding the primacy of love, a love that is emboldened by the promise of a coming day of wrath. Stewart unsettles conventional gender binaries not only by speaking in a language that transgresses established norms, but also by championing forms of black female empowerment that upset ideas of a self-determining, autonomous, rational self.

I turn next to Stewart's critiques of the way race and gender are used to establish regimes of oppression that inevitably inflict the greatest amount of harm on black women. Stewart launches scathing condemnations of black men, often with them in the very room she is lecturing in. She indicts the luxuries that patriarchal structures afford free black men, and she censures her male listeners for shirking their duties to their families and the larger black community. Stewart expends considerable energy trying to reinvigorate some of the authority that patriarchy is supposed to afford her male listeners. Indeed, the irony of Stewart's argument is that she insists black men be more authoritative, not less—a provocative claim for an early black feminist to advance. Stewart understands, however, that it will be nearly impossible to uplift all black Americans without the efforts of assertive black men. And while Stewart directs much of her ire at free black men, she does not spare women from her critical gaze, scorning them when they fail to protect and provide for their families and challenging them to participate in their own uplift. Thus, while Stewart shares with Walker many of the same critiques of racial injustice, she performs a far more nuanced examination of gender than Walker offers in his *Appeal*, demonstrating that black men like Walker who rightly attacked slavery often failed to account for the unique position antebellum black women were in. These men, in fact, contributed to the subjugation of black women, a point Stewart repeatedly makes in her speeches, even as she continues to laud Walker and integrate his rhetorical tactics.

Stewart's examination of gender, as well as her engagement with members of the black community in and around Boston, is what makes her project strikingly different from Walker's. Stewart's lectures are not, in the end, about challenging slavery, despite her obvious contempt for the institution and empathy for those blacks shackled within it. Rather, Stewart interrogates forms of oppression within racially stratified Northern communities. And unlike Walker, who directs a bourgeoning apocalyptic sentimentalism at white readers, Stewart primarily targets black Americans. This suggests, first, that African American apocalyptic rhetoric is not meant solely for those whites most responsible for race-based slavery but instead can be a mechanism for black leaders to critique the failings they saw within black America itself. More importantly, Stewart's targeting of other blacks reveals that the will to challenge structures of oppression is not produced by the mere fact of being oppressed. Racial uplift itself requires an incentive. Despite how frustrated many Northern blacks were with their social and economic circumstances and how desperate they may have been for relief, desperation and frustration do not by themselves generate a desire to incite change, a reality that Stewart is forced to confront. It is precisely for this reason that Stewart warns them of the apocalyptic consequences of remaining complacent. She is not threatening violence toward white America as much as she is trying to inspire sympathy among African Americans; she seeks to construct them as a group, a polity, a community rather than separate identities (i.e., slave vs. free). Uplift, as a political project and a cultural ethos, requires a transcendental source of encouragement. Stewart articulates the venture of racial improvement within a framework of apocalyptic sentimentality because she recognizes that terror may be necessary to motivate blacks to work on their own behalf and on the behalf of all black Americans.[11]

I conclude this chapter by looking at three texts from the 1840s—a popular domestic manual written by Catherine Beecher and two works of short fiction by Lydia Maria Child—in order to show how contemporaneous sentimental traditions were examining the often overlapping issues of domesticity and slavery, and in notably different ways. While Maria Stewart refashions the apocalypse into a domestic category, Catherine Beecher emphasizes the domestic space as the privileged site of the millennium in which Americans can work to hasten the second coming of Christ. She does not recognize the domestic space as a potential site of turmoil the way Lydia Maria Child does, however.

Indeed, in the two works of short fiction by Child that I examine—"The Black Saxons" and "Slavery's Pleasant Homes"—Child identifies the home as a place of slave violence rather than one of millennial promise. In Child's narratives, brutal violence shatters the tranquility of the domestic space, though the culture of violence that slavery engenders is never framed as an apocalyptic event. Stewart, Beecher, and Child epitomize the way antebellum women writers from diverse backgrounds marshaled sentimental discourses to challenge some of the nation's most invidious cultural practices. I, however, underscore some crucial differences among them as a way to distinguish the apocalyptic sentimental tradition that Stewart develops from other sentimental traditions and to make clear how Stewart (and to a lesser degree Beecher) exemplifies the extent to which modern scholars have segregated the apocalyptic from the domestic.

"Shall it be a woman?": Constructing a Public Self

Maria Stewart was the first African American woman to engage in political exhortations before an audience composed of both men and women, and her presence in antebellum Boston augured a shift in the expressive style of some women within the public domain. The manner in which she announced herself as a speaking subject is an essential component of her public identity, and this construction, in turn, ultimately shapes the nascent sentimentalism of her discourse. In a lecture at Franklin Hall, Stewart describes the moment when her existence was transformed from a private to a decidedly public one: "Methinks I heard a spiritual interrogation—'Who shall go forward, and take off the reproach that is cast upon the people of color? Shall it be a woman?' And my heart made this reply—'If it is thy will, be it even so, Lord Jesus!'"[12] Stewart's political life is constituted through a religious interpellation, with God calling her to intervene in the service of other black Americans. In claiming that she was called by God, Stewart unsettles the patriarchal order by contending that God is imbuing a woman with the authority to act on his behalf. What was once the entitlement of men is now the privilege of a woman, and a black woman no less. Stewart's political agency is powerful precisely insofar as it is configured by a higher power. "Be not offended," Stewart states in a later lecture, as if anticipating her audience's possible response to her audacious claims, "because I tell you the truth; for I believe that God has fired my soul with a holy zeal for his cause."[13] Stewart's credibility as a speaker is predicated not simply on the authority of her own mind but on a divine power that animates her soul and bolsters the veracity of her words. Stewart reminds her listeners that her lectures and the injustices they address are the manifestations of a divine plan. If they find Stewart's critiques offensive and her style unladylike, then they place themselves in direct opposition to God's will.

While it is important to credit Stewart with being the first public political activist among black women, it is equally important to recognize that she emerges from a larger cultural context in which white female preachers were launching very public critiques that focused on America's various moral shortcomings and urgent need to repent.[14] Like Stewart, these women also encountered intense criticism and scorn for crossing long-established boundaries separating the public existence of men from the private lives of women. In particular, these preachers contravened gender norms by warning of God's impending wrath, an oratorical style that had historically been the purview of male ministers. As Catherine Brekus has explained, antebellum female preachers like Abigail Roberts, Rachel Thompson, Salome Lincoln, and Nancy Towle "mixed [their] stern demands for repentance with maternal words of affection."[15] Their rhetoric combined the fiery patriarchal tone of the jeremiad with gentle caring words that symbolized a "feminine" ethos. Some female preachers in the antebellum period, says Brekus, imaged themselves "as warriors as well as nurturers."[16] Instead of abiding by cultural assumptions that assigned aggressive, often vengeful language to the masculine domain and loving, tender words to the feminine, many female preachers in this period combined the two to create a hybrid discourse in which the so-called feminine and masculine, the loving and vengeful, were inseparably enmeshed.[17] "Perhaps other nineteenth-century Christians, especially those of a more liberal bent, found these images contradictory," Brekus concludes, "but female preachers saw God's mercy and his anger as simply two different manifestations of his love for his children."[18] Despite the fact that she is not a preacher herself, Stewart's body of work should be considered within this milieu of the antebellum female preacher. Moreover, as a black woman entering into the most fraught and divisive debate of the antebellum period, Stewart runs a risk far greater than even some of these white female preachers, many of whom operated in counternormative ways but would not have been targeted because of their race as Stewart was. Finally, Stewart was far more critical of patriarchal structures than her white counterparts; whereas Stewart regularly challenged the hegemonic status of men (both white and black), many of these white female preachers left these structures untouched and sometimes even defended them.[19] Notwithstanding these important differences, Stewart is instrumental in shaping a tradition in which women authorize themselves as speaking subjects by adapting the apocalyptic rhetoric of Protestant ministerial traditions and combining it with repeated calls for compassion and mercy.

It is the ferocity of Stewart's hybrid discourse that marks the tradition she helps to fashion, and like the white female preachers mentioned above, Stewart's language is often deeply militaristic. "I have indeed found," she writes in her first meditation, "that the Christian life is a life of warfare."[20] Religious faith does not merely provide comfort; instead, it requires a dangerous engagement with a hostile and unjust world, a reality about which Stewart remains acutely aware. "I have enlisted in the holy warfare," she tells members of the Afric-American Female Intelligence Society of America, "and Jesus is my captain; and the Lord's battle I mean to fight, until my voice expire in death. I expect to be hated of all men, and persecuted even unto death, for righteousness and the truth's sake" (52).[21] No mere preacher, Stewart is a soldier in a Christian army fighting under Jesus's command. Her dedication to "the truth" and willingness to be reviled by her community and inevitably die in the service of her faith approaches a fanatic intensity. Stewart articulates this account of herself to an audience of women, perhaps to conscript them to skirmish alongside her. For many in her audience, this would have been the first time they heard another woman speaking as Stewart does. She fashions herself as one who has "promised to fight under Christ's banner against the world, the flesh, and the devil, and to be His faithful soldier and follower until my life's end."[22] Stewart is a holy warrior, not a genteel lady, and Boston is a kind of battleground on which she could lose her life as she believes David Walker lost his.[23] It is through the frame of religious violence that Stewart is able to imagine the possibility of agency for black women, even if possessing agency ultimately leads to death. Unfriendly whites "would drive us to a strange land," Stewart acknowledges in her lecture at the African Masonic Hall. "But before I go, the bayonet shall pierce me through" (64). Stewart models for her audience a new and formidable style of female black power, but one that brings with it its own set of hazards. By displaying herself in a warlike manner, Stewart destabilizes the limits of normative womanhood and attempts to inspire other black women to do the same.

In moments like these, Stewart's Christianity is far from the compassionate and domesticated religion modern readers often associate with the nineteenth-century woman's sphere. Indeed, from the very beginning of her public discourse, the vengeance/love–male/female dichotomies were disrupted by Stewart. The ferocity and militarism in Stewart's language refuse antebellum compulsory norms requiring female discourse to be properly "feminine"; that is, to avoid the kinds of topics and rhetorical modes that Stewart marshals in her lectures.[24] This defiance is further augmented by Stewart's use of apocalyptic rhetoric and imagery, especially in her warnings to sinful Americans of God's impending vengeance. Stewart describes Christ descending "in the clouds of heaven, surrounded by ten thousand of his saints and angels." In such a moment, it "shall be very tempestuous round about him" and then "shall the King separate the righteous from the wicked, as a shepherd divideth the sheep from the goats. . . . Then, says Christ, shall be weeping and wailing, and gnashing of teeth, when ye shall see Abraham and the prophets, sitting in the kingdom of heaven, and ye yourselves thrust out" (FIS 51). David Walker's influence is clearly visible in passages this like one, as is Stewart's engagement with Northern Baptist theology.[25] For Stewart, retribution is as fundamental to Christianity as mercy, and she often reminds her audience of the consequences of backsliding. "O, how will they feel in that day," she remarks, lamenting that religion has become unpopular, even among professed followers of Christ, "to see their skirts filled with the blood of souls? Will not their eye-balls start from their sockets to see sinners who have stumbled into hell over them? and will not their hearts be rent in twain to hear them in anguish condemn them?"[26] The penalty sinners pay for their transgressions is a severe one, and Stewart intensifies the exigency of her moral claims by marshaling a discourse whose chief purpose in antebellum America was to inspire terror. Stewart represents an account of Christianity that sees retribution as foundational to the meaning of Christ; she also exemplifies that antebellum men are not in sole possession of the language of vengeance, that the apocalyptic can be part of the political arsenal of female orators like Stewart.

Considering how assertive Stewart is in the public sphere, and given her use of violent and oftentimes gory theological imagery to construct her public self, it may seem counterintuitive for modern readers to find Stewart simultaneously evacuating power from herself and other black women. After listing some of the women throughout history who have been leaders and had a meaningful social impact, for instance, Stewart writes the following:

> If such women as are here described have once existed, be no longer astonished then, my brethren and friends, that God at this eventful period should raise up your own females to strive, by their example both in public and private, to assist those who are endeavoring to stop the strong current of prejudice that flows so profusely against us at present. No longer ridicule their efforts, it will be counted for sin. For God makes use of feeble means sometimes, to bring about his most exalted purposes.[27]

This passage might initially read as an expression of strength couched in Christian humility, but it signifies a far more complex and subtle insight about the nature of female empowerment in Stewart's writing. While Stewart calls for and often asserts a strong capacity on the part of women to act as self-determining beings, she also suggests that the source of their power derives from a transcendent God who acts on their behalf, who, in short, makes their strength possible. Uplift comes in the form of outside support, not as an act of self-determination. In the passages previously cited above, Stewart imagines "woman" as discrete, autonomous, and resilient; here, she is feeble but no less exalted for her feebleness. Her frailty, in other words, is not a weakness; nor does it simply confirm the assumptions of white Americans and many black men. To the contrary, her authority is constituted by her dependency on God; her identity is a means, not an end, and her subordination is precisely the source of her power.[28]

What we see in Stewart's representation of a thoroughly politicized female presence is a structure of messianic force, an empowered selfhood that is achieved through an act of self-abnegation which we see in Walker and Turner as well. "I am but a feeble instrument," Stewart says. "I am but one particle of the small dust of the earth" (*Religion* 31). Stewart's warrior mentality in other passages is submerged here under a sense of her own insignificance. She is an object waiting passively for another to use, a role that she not only accepts but encourages others to follow: "O, then, let us bow before the Lord our God, with all our hearts, and humble our very souls in the dust before him" (*Religion* 35). Stewart's Christianity provides her with a sense of comfort, but it demands that she relinquish her ego. At a moment in history when African Americans are seeking to affirm their worth, Stewart is pleading with her audience to abandon the self and remain prostrate before God.

Despite their seeming incongruity, the self as warrior and the self as insignificant are not antagonist models of power but instead inform and energize each other throughout the course of Stewart's writing. Being dependent on another can be empowering, particularly within a religious framework. This is why African American writers, male and female, at times theorize power in this period as a state of dependency on God. Stewart often derives authority, not simply from her sense of personal autonomy, but from the idea that God works through her. "I believe," she says, "that for wise and holy purposes, best known to himself, [God] hath unloosed my tongue, and put his word into my mouth, in order to confound and put all those to shame that have rose up against me. For he hath clothed my face with steel, and lined my forehead with brass. He hath put his testimony within me, and engraven his seal on my forehead [Revelation 9:4]. And with these weapons I have indeed set the fiends of earth and hell at defiance" (FA 67–68). If this passage were found in Walker's *Appeal*, we could be sure that the fiends of earth and hell referred to white slaveholders. But the case is not so simple with Stewart, who was as critical of black men and the power they exercised over black women as she was of white domination. Within this language of subordination, Stewart is able to encode a possible critique not simply of white hegemonic authority but of black masculine authority as well, something male listeners might have overlooked but like-minded female audience members could have detected. Stewart uses the seal of Revelation to further certify her importance; the concluding book of the New Testament is, in this context, a corporeal sign of who Stewart is and not simply a prophecy of what is to come. The apocalypse marks her body and colors her words. Such a seal serves as a talisman against the reductive and highly sexualized gaze of men, black and white, who see the black female body as something to be exploited and dominated. Stewart offers a religious model of authority whereby dependence becomes a position of strength; transgression is achieved through submission.

Notwithstanding its apparent power, Stewart's use of the messianic brings with it considerable risk. As I mentioned in chapter 1, there is a danger in promoting self-abnegation as a challenge to racial oppression. This danger, however, is augmented when a woman arrays a strategy of self-submission against patriarchy as well. In advocating absolute submission to God (the transcendental Patriarch), Stewart comes perilously close to reaffirming a set of cultural assumptions that were already in place and that greatly limited the cultural spheres women were permitted to occupy. These spheres shrink exponentially when these women are also black. Stewart's writings on self-abnegation, then, not only "confirm" racial hierarchies, they solidify gendered ones as well. Consider her views on the importance of subordination in her pedagogical writings on Christian education for children. Lamenting the failure of many parents to teach their children "the first lessons of piety and obedience," Stewart writes: "Hence arises want of respect and reverence for their Spiritual pastors, ministers and teachers, and those whom God has placed in authority over them. They are not taught to order themselves lowly and reverently to all their betters. They are not taught to rise up before the hoary head and honor grey hairs."[29] In Stewart's view, education is not meant to foster independence, nor should it lead to the formation of a freethinking individual. Rather, children should know their place within God's plan, which is decidedly hierarchical. Stewart genuinely sees this as an empowering framework, but what, we should ask, might it mean for a little black girl in the 1830s to be educated in the Christian mandates of submission? Can a viable model of freedom be nurtured among black youth in antebellum America when the expectation is, from the very start, that they obey? Braving these very real risks, Stewart inhabits an impossible reality with no good solutions, something she surely realized. And thus she deploys two different tactics simultaneously. One is to appropriate the fiery ministerial discourse of American Protestantism to embolden and amplify the black female voice; the other is to encourage black women in particular to depend wholly on a just God. This latter model does have some strategic benefits. Male listeners might be more inclined to hear the language of submission and subordination and feel less threatened by what Stewart is also proposing about new forms of womanhood and female discourse. Conversely, like-minded women might hear in Stewart's subtle critiques the very combination that is at play: power requires both a strong sense of individuated selfhood as well as a willingness to submit to a higher empowering authority. In whatever form it takes, power, for Stewart, ultimately requires being dependent on something other than black men.

This structure of action and passivity that characterizes Stewart's ideas on power also informs her most explicit mention of slave insurrection. Stewart uses her discourse on possible rebellion as an occasion to include women in the fight for independence, consequently revising one of the major conceptual shortcomings of Walker's *Appeal*. For Walker, violent slave resistance was entirely the province of black men; the ultimate liberation of "helpless" black women was, in Walker's view, predicated on the willingness and ability of black men to intervene on their behalf. In Stewart's updated account, we find black women fully engaged in the battle for independence: "But many powerful sons and daughters of Africa will shortly arise, who will put down vice and immorality among us, and declare by Him that sitteth upon the throne that they will have their rights; and if refused, I am afraid they will spread horror and devastation around . . . and when our cries shall have reached the ears of the Most High, it will be a tremendous day for the people of this land; for strong is the hand of the Lord God Almighty."[30] Stewart imagines a moment when black Americans actively rise up to meet their oppressors and claim their rights. Yet it is God who authorizes the claiming of these rights, so that what black Americans achieve has, in some sense, already been determined for them. Stewart continues, arguing that when the sons and daughters of Africa secure their rights, it will be through violent rebellion. These same black Americans cry to heaven for deliverance, however, and what makes this coming day glorious is not that blacks earn their freedom on their own, but that the strong hand of God finally sets them free. Like David Walker's account in the *Appeal*, Stewart's description exposes her secular wish to see black Americans acting independently, and her Christian view that human achievement is not possible without the permission and assistance of God. Unlike in Walker's view, where women are chastised for being weak and submissive, women are a fundamental part of Stewart's emancipatory vision. It is sons *and* daughters—men *and* women—who rise up. Women are on the frontlines of the antislavery movement; instead of leaving them powerless and in need of protection by men, as Walker does, Stewart presents women as the principal agents of liberation because they are often favored by God over men, a claim she repeatedly makes. And by embedding the possibility of black female violence in a messianic idiom, where it is God who fights on behalf of submissive slaves, Stewart shrewdly negotiates a patriarchal culture in which the idea of women engaging in violent acts of rebellion, or of promoting such notions in a public address, was seldom tolerated.

By foregrounding her account of the messianic, I do not mean to suggest that Stewart does not desire the freedoms and rights of citizenship or that she derogates the importance of self-reliance. She says repeatedly that the souls of black Americans "are fired with the same love of liberty and independence" as whites, and that "it is high time" for African Americans "to promote ourselves by some meritorious acts"[31] and be "recorded on the bright annals of fame" (*Religion* 40, 35). But Stewart uses preexisting religious forms to invent a new theory of force for black women, one characterized by an apparent contradiction where a militant female speaker (embodied by Stewart herself) who strikes with a fiery apocalyptic tongue also obediently submits herself to a transcendent religious power. It is the latter trait that scholars often miss because Stewart's model does not conform to uninterrogated assumptions about the self-evident superiority of self-reliant individualism. Stewart's account demonstrates that nineteenth-century strategies of freedom were configured in various ways, even through the ostensibly counterintuitive gesture of self-subjection. This latter messianic formulation is visible in other nineteenth-century black writers like Jarena Lee and even Martin Delany. It is within the larger frame of a growing apocalyptic sentimentalism that such a view of power—one that displays autonomy and strength while promoting submission—becomes intelligible, in part because the apocalypse is the central organizing principle within Stewart's thinking about agency and freedom. Ideas of an apocalyptic God form an essential foundation on which to locate messianic resistance. At the same time, Stewart uses the apocalypse as a key figure to inspire sentimental bonds between black Americans that might generate among them a more enthusiastic spirit of reform and resistance. Within the context of this emergent female-centric speaking position, Stewart develops and deploys a rhetoric of apocalyptic sentimentalism to contest the forms of oppression she finds most objectionable. What is perhaps most striking about Stewart's critiques is not merely her use of apocalyptic sentimentality but how she targets fellow black Americans with this discourse in order to arouse them to live righteously and dedicate themselves to the work of improving conditions for all black Americans.

Apocalyptic Sentimentalism and Racial Uplift

Despite how her use of an aggressive apocalyptic discourse challenges modern assumptions about the gendered deployment of doomsday theology in the antebellum period, Stewart is not just another angry preacher. Rather, Stewart uses her public addresses to develop a structure of sentiment in which her threats of God's wrathful vengeance come to bolster moral pleas for love; Stewart's emphasis on the wrathful and militant dimension of her public persona is balanced by her frequent displays of love, and it is the interaction between militancy and love, wrath and mercy, that often characterizes her political rhetoric. She remarks to the women in her audience, for example, that "at times I have felt ready to exclaim, O that my head were waters, and mine eyes a fountain of tears, that I might weep day and night [Jeremiah 9:1], for the transgressions of the daughters of my people" (*Religion* 30). Stewart turns to a prophetic book from the Hebrew Bible, one that is often cited for its warnings of God's retribution, to express deep sorrow over the failure of black women to live righteously. She is candid about her intention as a speaker and reformer, which, she explains to her audience, is to "express my sentiments before you" (28), and her tears are signs of the compassion she feels for the community of black women living in America. And this very public presentation of emotion is meant to generate similar feelings in her listeners. Stewart explains that she has "merely written the *meditations of my heart* as far as my imagination led; and have presented them before you in order to *arouse you to exertion*, and to *enforce upon your minds* the great necessity of turning your attention to knowledge and improvement" (28; emphases mine). Stewart displays her sentiments in such a public manner not simply so her audience will know that her heart is in the right place, but because she wants her exhibition of affect to promote action on the part of her listeners. Emotion can be a catalytic agent, in other words, and Stewart emotes before her audience in hopes that they might be moved to care for their spiritual well-being and work toward their own uplift.

These gestures—the expression of deep emotion, the copious tears, references to the heart, calls to action—will become some of the foundational tropes of nineteenth-century abolitionist sentimentality. Stewart's lectures and writings develop an emergent form of argumentation that is rooted in deeply felt emotion and meant to produce in listeners a sympathetic response that will encourage them to act morally. Yet as we have seen, this primary register of affect runs parallel to—and, indeed, intersects with—the equally strong register of fear stemming from her repeated warnings of a possible apocalypse. The account of Christianity that Stewart develops in the course of her activism underscores that religion is, for her, a force to be embraced because of its purity and goodness, but a force that nevertheless requires terror in order to be a real influence in the lives of Americans. "Religion is pure;" writes Stewart, "it is ever new; it is beautiful; it is all that is worth living for; it is worth dying for. O, could I but see the church built up in the most holy faith; could I but see men spiritually minded, walking in the fear of God, not given to filthy lucre" but "fervent in spirit, serving the Lord" (*Religion* 33). The purity and beauty of Christianity are not tainted by fear but instead are constituted by it. Fear is what guarantees religious perfection because it is only when one exists in a state of fear that one is living as a proper Christian:

> The day is coming, my friends, and I rejoice in that day, when the secrets of all hearts shall be manifested before saints and angels, men and devils. It will be a great

day of joy and rejoicing to the humble followers of Christ, but a day of terror and dismay to hypocrites and unbelievers.... The dead that are in Christ shall be raised first. Blessed is he that shall have a part in the first resurrection. Ah, methinks I hear the finally impenitent crying, "Rocks and mountains! fall upon us, and hide us from the wrath of the Lamb, and from him that sitteth upon the throne [Revelation 6:16]!" (FIS 50)

The significance of a coming apocalypse depends on one's moral standing. If one has lived righteously, then one is awarded everlasting life. If one has failed to repent for one's sins—if one remains in a degenerate state—the penalty is severe. As Stewart describes it here, the apocalypse is a category that possesses opposite meanings simultaneously, a point that is captured in the ostensibly paradoxical and evocative phrase "the wrath of the Lamb," which Stewart takes from Revelation. The lamb, a metaphor for Christ, evokes the gentleness and compassion that is associated with the God of the New Testament and the "feminine" sensibilities of the sentimental. But this God does not simply dispense mercy; he is not merely a loving and forgiving God. Rather, he is a lamb that is capable of inflicting wrath and vengeance on those most deserving. This apparent contradiction is, in Stewart's work, and in so much antebellum writing, no contradiction at all.

Stewart brings this burgeoning logic, where calls for love are supported by threats of God's fiery wrath, to bear within her wide-reaching reformist agendas. Beginning with one of the most pressing concerns for the whole of black America, Stewart addresses the problem of slavery and white Americans' unwillingness to sympathize with the slaves' miserable state. After praising the achievements of white Americans, who have thrived "in arts and sciences, and in polite literature," and whose "highest aim is to excel in political, moral and religious improvement," Stewart grieves "how very few are there among them that bestow one thought upon the benighted sons and daughters of Africa, who have enriched the soils of America with their tears and blood: few to promote their cause, none to encourage their talents" (*Religion* 34–35). While Stewart freely acknowledges that white Americans consistently aspire to the highest virtues, she nevertheless condemns them for failing to show any concern for the well-being of the slave. Whites may cultivate their talents, but they suffer from a constitutive emotional defect, and most are incapable of nurturing feelings of compassion toward the enslaved. And compassion is what Stewart aims to induce. "O, ye southern slaveholders! We will no longer curse you for your wrongs; but we will implore the Almighty to soften your hard hearts towards our brethren" (CFE 43–44). By softening their hearts, Stewart is hoping that the Christian God will make slaveholders more likely to sympathize with and feel affection for the slave, and a change in feeling might facilitate a new form of interaction in which slaveholders, instead of adding to the slave's burden, aim to alleviate it.

Rather than describe the biblical God dispensing the kind of mercy she would like to see in slaveholders, however, Stewart, in the very next paragraph, brings in a God of wrath. "What has caused the downfall of nations, kings and empires?" Stewart asks. "Sin, that abominable thing which God hates. Why has the Almighty commissioned the destroying angels to execute the fierceness of his anger upon the inhabitants of the earth? Because they have made light of the name of the Lord, and forgotten the rock of their salvation [2 Samuel 22:47]" (CFE 44). Here, Stewart calls for love but soon after portrays vengeance. Instead of simply relying on the idea of Christian love, Stewart turns to God's vengeance as a possible stimulus to move slaveholders away from slavery and closer to the slaves, and thus closer to God, who, Stewart implies, will eventually intercede on the slaves' behalf. Stewart positions America within a lineage of fallen empires and corrupt nations, suggesting that it is next in line to perish if it does not address its shameful practices. Speaking to black Americans about their impending deliverance, Stewart embeds a similar threat:

> My brethren, sheath your swords, and calm your angry passions. Stand still and know that the Lord he is God. Vengeance is his, and he will repay.[32] It is a long lane that has no turn. America has risen to her meridian. When you begin to thrive, she will begin to fall. God hath raised you up a Walker and a Garrison. Though Walker sleeps, yet he lives, and his name shall be had in everlasting remembrance.... Then fret not yourselves because of evil doers. Fret not yourselves because of the men who bring wicked devices to pass; for they shall be cut down as the grass, and wither as the green herb. (*Religion* 40)

Stewart provides consolation to black Americans by ensuring them that God will seek retaliation against their oppressors and soon free them from bondage. Not only will the Christian God exact vengeance, but he has also placed in America his surrogates—David Walker and William Lloyd Garrison—who symbolize this threat for southerners and who work on God's behalf. Walker here enjoys a kind of resurrected status, having already died but living on in the *Appeal* as the foremost ideologue of insurrection.[33]

Stewart shares with Walker a deep frustration over the obstinacy of white Americans, and much like Walker before her, she repeatedly pairs ideas of Christian love and divine wrath to encourage unfeeling whites to express greater compassion. White Americans are not her only target, however; in fact, Stewart confronts black Americans more frequently than she does whites in order to engender in them a commitment to community building and to motivate them to engage in the kind of activist reform that she believes they have been too unwilling or too afraid to undertake. While Walker criticizes other blacks, his primary aim was to unsettle a widely shared and highly ossified white perspective on the naturalness and therefore immutability of slavery. Stewart, however, aims a substantial part of her critique at other blacks because she believes that uplift can only begin when it is generated from within a coherent black community. And while it is often black women on whose behalf Stewart tirelessly works, it is just as often that Stewart censures these women within an apocalyptic frame.

FREE BLACK WOMEN

Early in *Religion and the Pure Principles of Morality*, Stewart makes her first plea to women in her audience by positioning them as the potential purveyors of Christian goodness and virtue. She challenges antebellum norms by suggesting that black women possess the moral authority on which a just nation could be built.

> O virtue! How sacred is thy name! How pure are thy principles! Who can find a virtuous woman? . . . Blessed is the man who shall call her his wife; yea, happy is the child who shall call her mother. O woman, woman, would thou only strive to excel in merit and virtue; would thou only store thy mind with useful knowledge, great would be thine influence. Do you say you are too far advanced in life now to begin? You are not too far advanced to instil these principles into the minds of your tender infants. Let them by no means be neglected. (*Religion* 31–32)

Stewart's exhortation prefigures what will become a common refrain among sentimentalists who see women as the true paragons of Christian morality: it is the responsibility of women to nurture themselves as moral beings so that they may imbue their husbands and children with a fortified Christian ethic, ensuring the stability and goodness of not only their families but the nation as well. While Stewart does not specify that she is addressing black women in particular, such an audience can be inferred based on the political task she has undertaken, and this gesture subtly unsettles the genealogy of sentimentality that descends through a largely white middle-class aesthetic. Stewart stresses the maternal obligations of black women in order to invest them with power and establish for them a mission that is achievable within the otherwise limited scope of the domestic space.

This long passage that extols the virtues of black womanhood takes a surprising turn, however. After Stewart implores women to uphold and transmit goodness to their children, she writes: "Discharge your duty faithfully, in every point of view: leave the event with God. So shall your skirts become clear of their blood [Jeremiah 2:34]" (*Religion* 32). This description of bloodstained skirts that follows Stewart's call for virtuous women and moral mothers suggests that while black women have the potential to model for their husbands and children how to live according to Christian ideals, this is an obligation they do not currently fulfill. And the price for shirking their duties, as Stewart warns, is paid in the blood of the family members these women fail to protect. This passage is especially evocative given the era in which Stewart is working. Perhaps husbands and children are cut down by a vengeful God who rebukes them for failing to live according to the moral principles mothers and wives were supposed to instill. Or perhaps they are the victims of racial violence against which only a strong Christian faith could protect them. Regardless of the cause, Stewart warns of violence and bloodshed precisely as a way to provoke black women to take up the moral cause for which Stewart herself is currently fighting.

While Stewart decries the forms of tyranny blacks are subjected to within a white racist culture, she nevertheless maintains that it is not just white racists who perpetuate the subjugation of free and enslaved blacks. According to Stewart, free blacks, and here black women, possess the power to alleviate their own suffering, but they have failed to do so because they lack sympathy for other blacks. A skilled diagnostician of overlapping racial and gendered forms of oppression, Stewart reports on an ailment that surely was surprising even to her: whites *and* blacks suffer from the same affliction—the absence of a loving heart. "O, ye daughters of Africa," Stewart proclaims to the black women composing her audience. "What examples have ye set before the rising generation? What foundation have ye laid for generations yet unborn? Where are our *union and love?* And where is our *sympathy*, that *weeps at another's woe*, and hides the faults we see?" (*Religion* 30–31; emphases mine). If blacks are going to have a future in America, Stewart suggests, then it will be under the guidance of black mothers who thus far have failed to nurture a sympathetic heart and therefore have done nothing to diminish the suffering of other blacks. In Stewart's view, a view that midcentury sentimentalists will similarly promote, the burden rests on mothers who must lay the moral foundation that might allow future generations to thrive in a nation rigidly divided along racial and gendered lines. Stewart understands that being subjected to various forms of domination does not necessarily create in victims a desire to resist them. She recognizes that many black women are unwilling to fight back because of the dangers inherent in confronting coercive and cruel systems of power. For these reasons, Stewart does not simply plead for black women to be loving and sympathetic, nor does she simply assume that her listeners, who may be complacent, fearful, or both, will heed her response without any additional provocation. She seeks to generate intraracial sympathy by locating her critique of black women within a parental frame, and circumscribing this frame within the larger frame of apocalyptic prophecy. "Where is the parent," Stewart inquires, "who is conscious of having faithfully discharged [her] duty, and at the last awful day of account, shall be able to say, here, Lord, is thy poor, unworthy servant, and the children thou hast given me?" (31). If there is a sphere that black women can productively inhabit and influence, Stewart asserts, it is the home. She emphasizes the importance of motherly duties by warning that God will harshly judge women who fail at them. Stewart uses such threats to foster a domestic ideology in which black women care for, love, and weep over the suffering of those in their charge.

When emphasizing black female domesticity, Stewart returns to an account of womanhood that conforms to traditional, normative (white) standards of nineteenth-century femininity. This model of womanhood circulates and interacts with two previous models I have used to characterize Stewart, one in which she speaks in an emboldened, apocalyptically inflected idiom, the other where she embodies a submissive, messianic style of female empowerment. While it is the linkage between these three different but related modes of being that forms the core of female agency and empowerment in Stewart's writing, she often emphasizes this third model, focusing on the act of mothering for its universally understood importance within antebellum sentimental culture. Stewart frequently foregrounds the vital work black women can accomplish as caregivers within the home, remarking, "O, ye mothers, what a responsibility rests on you! You have souls committed to your charge, and God will require a strict account of you. It is you that must create in the minds of your little girls and boys a thirst for knowledge, the love of virtue, the abhorrence of vice, and the cultivation of a pure heart" (*Religion* 35). By modeling this view of femininity on the example set by white, middle-class women, Stewart contributes to a conservative understanding of womanhood in which mothers are located in the home and remain focused on nourishing the well-being and virtue of their family members. "The American ladies," explains Stewart, "have the honor conferred on them, that by prudence and economy in their domestic concerns, and their unwearied attention in forming the minds and manners of their children, they laid the foundation of their becoming what they are now" (*Religion* 37). White women, in other words, have set an example that black women should aspire to imitate—"as far as they are worthy of imitation" (37), Stewart adds a bit derisively, lest anyone assume she does not hold white women partially accountable for the condition of black Americans. Nevertheless, Stewart implores black women to follow the example established by white women and attend to their domestic responsibilities with care. In so doing, they may begin to receive the same kind of praise and respect that is bestowed on their white counterparts: "Let each one strive to excel in good housewifery, knowing that prudence and economy are the road to wealth. Let us not say we know this, or we know that, and practise nothing; but let us practice what we do know" (37–38). For Stewart, domestic economy provides the context in which black women can elevate their status. Being traditional can, in Stewart's view, constitute the most radical tactic of all.[34]

Notwithstanding her occasional reliance on mainstream codes of housewifery, Stewart's account of domestic management cannot be reduced to a simple mimetic task in which black women merely copy white bourgeois matrons. For Stewart, the daily act of mothering is inflected by apocalyptic history, so that what mothers teach in the home bears directly on issues of salvation and the chance for everlasting life. There is an urgency surrounding the particular style of mothering women choose to adopt. Consider, as just one example, Stewart's description of the proper administration of discipline. "Lying is one of the grand characteristics of children;" she writes, "and if all liars are to have their part in the lake that burns with fire and brimstone, what a fearful doom awaits many" (TT 160). It is not surprising that Stewart would counsel mothers to reprimand lying children. What might seem strange, however, is that she would invoke an apocalyptic image to underscore the consequences of lying. Stewart's views on mothering a child, and her understanding of the consequences of that child's dishonesty, are shaped by a Christian outlook in which liars sin against God and are consequently punished with everlasting damnation. Stewart's ideal loving mother is motivated by a fear that her children might one day receive God's disapproving judgment. Severity and love are part of a complementary formation, both informed by apocalyptic prophecy, and both constituting a necessary part of child rearing. "Thus," says Stewart, "many for want of being early taught the fear of God, and self-government of temper at home, in after-life become the authors of their own misery and the misery of those around them" (160). Proper mothering prepares children for eternity; reared improperly, these children grow into adults who live in sin and endanger the welfare of those around them. Mothers are, in Stewart's view, the true disciplinarians, and it is the apocalyptic that forms the religious underpinning of her pedagogical theory. "Spare not for their crying;" Stewart commands, for "thou shalt beat them with a rod, and they shall not die [Proverbs 23:13]; and thou shalt save their souls from hell. When you correct them, do it in the fear of God, and for their own good.... It is no use to say you can't do this, or you can't do that; you will not tell your Maker so, when you meet him at the great day of account" (*Religion* 36). Mothers should be motivated by the same incentive as their children and see their actions against the backdrop of a coming day of wrath when they will have to explain why they failed to discipline their children. Mothers, moreover, are encouraged to replicate God's severity in rearing their offspring. They are to their children what God is to humanity: a potential source of love *and* constant threat of punishment.

As one of the first African Americans to redefine established ideas about black womanhood, Stewart generates a complicated set of claims whereby to be black and a woman in the 1830s meant at times prophesying vengeance, at other times relinquishing power and subordinating oneself to a transcendent authority, and still at other times aspiring to white middle-class respectability. And while each of these models appears to be antagonistic with the others, they are far more cooperative than contradictory. The prophetic sensibility can (and oftentimes must) emerge from the domestic sphere and organize its daily operations. It can also originate from an empowered and self-determining speaking subject or from a prostrate self in a state of messianic abnegation. Stewart's account is a messy one, to be sure, but it should be seen as evolving from within and helping to develop and expand the tradition of apocalyptic sentimentality. Stewart targets black women with a rhetoric of apocalyptic sentimentalism to inspire new ways of inhabiting an already restrictive cultural context even as she imagines new categories of existence for black women that deny those restrictions. I want to turn next to Stewart's critique of free black men, whom she claims impose and maintain many of the constraints she is so fiercely contesting. Indeed, it is at black men that Stewart directs some of her harshest criticisms.

FREE BLACK MEN

If free black women in Stewart's view too often fail in their role as mothers and nurturers, black men just as often fail in their duties as men to stand in defense of free and enslaved blacks. "I would ask," says Stewart, in a lecture delivered to an audience composed of black men, "is it blindness of mind, or stupidity of soul, or the want of education that has caused our men who are 60 or 70 years of age, never to let their voices be heard, nor their hands be raised in behalf of their color? Or has it been for the fear of offending the whites?" (MH 57). In one concise statement, Stewart attacks black men at two principal levels on which nineteenth-century masculinity was consolidated: the rational mind and the potent body. Black men, Stewart seems to suggest, neither possess the intellectual acuity to articulate a challenge to white oppression, nor the physical prowess to defend black Americans and fight for greater freedoms. To the contrary, free black men have, according to Stewart, timidly accommodated white Americans by remaining silent and have therefore permitted their own oppression. The men she addresses in the above passage have had a lifetime to stand up against slavery but have failed to act in any meaningful way to enlarge the scope of freedom for black Americans. That a northern black woman makes this public critique at all would have been startling, even among black audiences; that Stewart expresses it directly to the black men she is condemning demonstrates just how incendiary her discourse was. "African rights and liberty," complains Stewart, "is a subject that ought to fire the breast of every free man of color in these United States, and excite in his bosom a lively, deep, decided and heart-felt interest" (56). Like free black women, who have thus far lacked the determination to fulfill their chief purpose as good Christian mothers, free black men remain passionless and mute over an issue that should animate the greatest emotional response—namely, their liberty. It is their lethargy that Stewart is attempting to counteract:

> I am sensible that there are many highly intelligent men of color in these United States, in the force of whose arguments, doubtless, I should discover my inferiority; but if they are blessed with wit and talent, friends and fortune, why have they not made themselves men of eminence, by striving to take all the reproach that is cast upon the people of color, and in endeavoring to alleviate the woes of their brethren in bondage? Talk, without effort, is nothing; you are abundantly capable, gentlemen, of making yourselves men of distinction; and this gross neglect, on your part, causes my blood to boil within me. Here is the grand cause which hinders the rise and progress of people of color. It is their want of laudable ambition and requisite courage. (57–58)

Stewart's critique is thoroughly gendered, manipulating masculine anxieties about being seen as soft, weak, and effeminate. If black men do possess capacities for reasoned thought and physical resistance, Stewart argues, they are too cowardly or complacent to display them. As a result, Stewart is forced to do a man's work, which she models for black men right before their eyes. If they will not speak with effort, then she will; if they will not elevate their status and the status of all blacks to a position of distinction, then she must; if they will not rage at the humiliations all blacks are made to suffer, then she will speak with wrath against white power and disdain for all who feebly submit to it. "Had those men among us who had an opportunity, turned their attention as assiduously to mental and moral improvement as they have to gambling and dancing, I might have remained quietly at home and they stood contending in my place," she says in the same Masonic Hall address (60). Stewart claims that her public existence and dramatic breach of social protocol are only due to the failure of black men to lead with conviction. At the same time that she tries to call black men to action, Stewart models for the women in her audience and for those who read her words a new kind of feminine strength that confronts patriarchy and condemns publicly all forms of oppression.

And it is a politics of incitement that will remain a challenge for Stewart and for many of the abolitionist writers who will follow her. How does one inspire others to act in the face of injustice when there appears to be little incentive and even less hope of success? If free black men do not become agitated over concerns with their liberty, then what could possibly motivate them? How, in Stewart's words, does one "fire the breast" of complacent individuals so that they develop a "heart-felt interest" and zeal for the kinds of political concerns Stewart is addressing? Stewart aims to stir black men the same way she aimed to inspire in whites greater sympathy toward blacks and the way she sought to invigorate in black women a greater domestic sensibility so that they might lay a moral foundation for generations of black youth to come. Says Stewart: "You have a right to rejoice, and to let your hearts cheer you in the days of your youth; yet remember that for all these things God will bring you into judgment" (MH 60). Here, God's judgment constitutes perhaps the only impetus in Stewart's view that might compel black men to renounce their frivolity and appreciate the urgency of Stewart's plea. Once again, Stewart frames the actions of these men—who continually fail to sympathize not only with one another but with the women they are supposed to protect—within a prophetic structure. Stewart desires an emotional response from them, and when she does not get one, she attempts to manufacture one by situating their actions within the context of God's imminent judgment. While this argument may ultimately reify norms governing masculine and feminine roles, where men are charged with protecting and providing for women (a view explicitly promoted by David Walker), Stewart decides she must run this necessary risk if she is going to move black men out of their complacency. Stewart, moreover, never simply reproduces gender norms in an artless or programmatic way. Even if black men come to see themselves as patriarchs as a result of Stewart's argument, they may nonetheless have to contend with a new kind of black woman who deploys multiple tactics to resist the more oppressive forms of black masculine authority and asserts a more authoritative and empowered presence both within the domestic sphere and, as with Stewart, perhaps even outside of it.

Throughout her brief career as a lecturer and activist, Stewart often reminded her audiences of the importance of establishing sympathetic relations and the steep cost of failing to do so. Warnings of vengeance functioned for Stewart as a kind of last-resort strategy for generating intersubjective connections rooted in a love that was itself inspired by fear. Even in her farewell address, Stewart outlines a structure of affect that will come to play a more formative role within later abolitionist discourses, and she once again directs this rhetoric at other blacks rather than at slaveholders and defenders of slavery. "Long will the kind sympathy of some much loved friend," says Stewart, "be written on the tablet of my memory, especially those kind individuals who have stood by me like pitying angels, and befriended me when in the midst of difficulty; many blessings rest on them. Gratitude is all the tribute I can offer. A rich reward awaits them" (FA 72). Here, Stewart discreetly chastises her detractors by suggesting that no reward awaits them in the next life. Salvation is reserved for those who expressed sufficient sympathy for Stewart and the cause she championed. Indeed, at this point, one can begin to predict the consequences of neglecting to cultivate loving ties with others:

> To my unconverted friends, one and all, I would say, shortly this frail tenement of mine will be dissolved and lie mouldering in ruins. O, solemn thought! Yet why should I revolt, for it is the glorious hope of a blessed immortality, beyond the grave, that has supported me thus far through this vale of tears. Who among you will strive to meet me at the right hand of Christ? For the great day of retribution is fast approaching, and who shall be able to abide his coming? You are forming characters for eternity. As you live so will you die; as death leaves you, so judgment will find you. (FA 72–73)

With her own finitude in mind, Stewart considers the implications of her religious faith and the faith of those who have not fully embraced a Christian ethic. Always abiding by her conscience, Stewart can approach her death confident that eternal life awaits her. For those black women who have not committed themselves fully to their domestic obligations, and those black men who are preoccupied with trivial enjoyments rather than working for the freedom and uplift of their race, however, a far more terrible end looms. In Stewart's view, black Americans in the North were as in need of the threat and promise contained within Stewart's sentimental rhetoric as were white slaveholders in the South. She uniquely appropriates a discourse that she directs at free blacks so that they will, in turn, initiate their own emancipatory politics.

By incorporating the apocalyptic in her writings and speeches, Stewart used an ostensibly masculinist rhetorical form and turned it against white racist authority. Even though many nineteenth-century Americans would have thought it inelegant for Stewart to incorporate the kinds of images that populate her lectures, and while modern scholars have replicated nineteenth-century assumptions by maintaining that fire-and-brimstone rhetoric was solely a patriarchal phenomenon, female lecturers and preachers like Stewart commonly embraced apocalyptic theology and the power it commanded among antebellum audiences. Indeed, Stewart complicates the binary that has characterized the scholarly tradition since Ann Douglas, which has posited a fierce, patriarchal Christianity on one side and a softer, irenic feminine theology on the other.[35] This gendered opposition only partially explains how female-centric public discourse during the antebellum period was organized.

As she advanced her complex and far-reaching reform agenda, Maria Stewart often operated within the two affective registers of love and fear. Indeed, her deployment of these registers not only further developed the tradition of apocalyptic sentimentalism; it also provides modern readers with an occasion to reflect on David Walker as a nascent sentimental writer. Readers of the *Appeal* who become understandably distracted by Walker's inflammatory language often miss the fact that his warnings of God's vengeance / slave violence have the underlying goal of generating greater compassion from his white readers.

Walker's apocalyptic plea for reformed hearts prefigures Stewart's elocutionary style, and the sentimental structure of Stewart's lectures and private writings serves as a sign and reminder of the bourgeoning sentimentality within Walker's *Appeal*. Stewart, in short, takes Walker seriously as a rhetorician; it is not his exaggerated manner that compels Stewart, but his recognition that stern warnings and loving sentiments are needed equally and must work together to organize a challenge to slavery.

Stewart also domesticates the category of the apocalypse so that it can be deployed by women in order to address the unique concerns that black women face in antebellum America. Because Stewart spoke daringly about issues of race and gender to her audiences and often used the discourse of apocalyptic retribution to do so, the apocalypse can no longer be seen solely as a signifier of masculine authority. Stewart was able to generate a powerful argument on behalf of black women, not by encouraging them to leave the home, but by locating the domestic space in a religious framework where the apocalypse is both an inducement for free black mothers to establish loving families and a source of power for black women living within patriarchy. These claims, along with Stewart's scathing critiques of free black men and white men and women, made her a decidedly controversial figure in the early 1830s. Stewart's language, while deeply loving, is too often linked with visions of apocalyptic doom to have the influence on her audiences she was hoping for. Indeed, Stewart was such a subversive presence that she was essentially forced out of Boston in 1833. And while she continued to work as an abolitionist and teacher in New York and Baltimore before finally settling in Washington, D.C., Stewart made an indelible mark on the tradition of apocalyptic sentimentalism by taking apocalypse out of the heavens and nestling it in the home front.

Domesticating Apocalypse, Sentimentalizing Insurrection

Maria Stewart is not the only figure at this time challenging established notions of race and gender as they play out within the domestic sphere; nor is she the only writer who utilizes the apocalyptic to articulate these challenges. Stewart *is* the only one who combines these frameworks in such a powerful way to express their linkage and to develop a style of antislavery sentimentality that understands domesticity and apocalypticism to be deeply and inseparably connected. In this final section, I want to explore briefly the work of two notable antebellum reformers—Catharine Beecher and Lydia Maria Child—in order to illustrate how their representations of the domestic space and slavery, while powerful, constitute a different account of sentimentalism than the one Stewart portrays. Reading Beecher and Child alongside Stewart, I underscore the various sentimentalities that were in circulation at this time; I also show how Stewart helps innovate a unique sentimental model that will be powerfully revised and redeployed in the years leading up to the Civil War.

I have been exploring throughout this chapter the domestication of the apocalypse, an idea that will be important for thinking about later sentimental works because, within much of the period's sentimental fiction, the sentimental and the domestic are inseparably yoked. And it will be from within the domestic space that representations of apocalypse will occur, so that the apocalyptic genuinely becomes a domestic, and not simply a domesticated, category. Catherine Beecher's *A Treatise on Domestic Economy* (1843) is one such example in which she elaborates the virtues of domestic upkeep and explains why women should be attentive to the organization and management of the home. Near the end of the first chapter, Beecher writes the following:

> It thus appears, that the sublime and elevating anticipations which have filled the mind and heart of the religious world, have become so far developed, that philosophers and statesmen are perceiving the signs, and are predicting the approach, of the same grand consummation. There is a day advancing, "by seers predicted, and by poets sung," where the curse of selfishness shall be removed; when "scenes surpassing fable, and yet true," shall be realized; when all nations shall rejoice and be made blessed, under those benevolent influences, which the Messiah came to establish on earth.[36]

Why, in a domestic manual, would Beecher ruminate on God's second coming if she did not perceive a direct link between the proper management of the home and the fulfillment of providential history? The domestic space is, in Beecher's view, *the* space in which apocalyptic prophecy plays itself out; the fate of the world is decided not in churches or statehouses but in the parlors of American women's homes. She goes on to explain that "this is the Country, which the Disposer of events designs shall go forth as the cynosure of nations, to guide them to the light and blessedness of that day" (36). Adopting the long-standing idea that America was a covenantal nation, a "city on the hill," chosen by God to exemplify and impart the virtues of Christianity to the world, Beecher's remarks underscore the link home has to nation, and nation has to the world. If America is going to be a marker of religious progress and a source of hope to all other nations, this ethos will need to be first nurtured in the domestic space.

And "the part to be enacted by American women, in this great moral enterprise," Beecher continues, "is the point to which special attention should here be directed":

> The success of democratic institutions, as is conceded by all, depends upon the intellectual and moral character of the mass of the people.... It is equally conceded, that the formation of the moral and intellectual character of the young is commit-

ted mainly to the female hand. The mother forms the character of the future man; the sister bends the fibres that are hereafter to be the forest tree; the wife sways the heart, whose energies may turn for good or for evil the destinies of a nation. Let the women of a country be made virtuous and intelligent, and the men will certainly be the same. The proper education of a man decides the welfare of an individual; but educate a woman, and the interests of a whole family are secured. (*T* 36–37)

Like Stewart, who asserted that the development of a moral country begins with proper mothering in the domestic space, Beecher positions women and mothers as the principal agents to shape the minds and hearts of their offspring. Women must be educated because they form the basis of a moral family and ethical nation. Because they wield such influence over their children and husbands, and because their children and husbands will inevitably exit the domestic space in order to make their way in the world, a mother's power extends far beyond the walls of the home. Indeed, women are not only preparing their husbands and children to lead a moral existence; they are the catalysts who hasten the second coming of the biblical Messiah. It is women's labor, says Beecher, that is fundamental to the "regeneration of the Earth" (37). Beecher's elevation of women is grounded in a postmillennialist worldview. The "regeneration of the Earth" references Revelation 21:20, where the speaker explains that he saw "a new heaven and a new earth, for the first heaven and the first earth had passed away." Women, then, are endowed with the capacity to construct a new and more perfect reality, like "the building of a glorious temple, whose base shall be coextensive with the bounds of the earth, whose summit shall pierce the skies, whose splendor shall beam on all lands; and those who hew the lowliest stone, as much as those who carve the highest capital, will be equally honored, when its top-stone shall be laid, with new rejoicings of the morning stars, and shoutings of the sons of God" (38).[37] Women who fulfill their domestic obligations in the home do not simply contribute to the spiritual prosperity of their spouses and children. Their actions as wives and mothers are implicated in the fate of human salvation itself.

Beecher earnestly addresses apocalyptic prophecy in the very first chapter of the manual. In other words, her millennialist preoccupations are not secondary to the issue of domestic upkeep but rather primary and inseparably related to the work women do in the home. And in elevating the importance of domestic economy, Beecher privileges women not simply as the purveyors of virtue but as agents who, through meticulous housekeeping, lay the ground for the return of Christ. Unlike Stewart's rhetoric, Beecher's treatise does not invoke the more fiery elements of premillennial thinking, in part because Beecher speaks from a position of relative privilege, where racial oppression and economic scarcity are not pressing factors as they were for Stewart and other early black activists. And while both authors invest mothers with the authority to construct communities and ultimately build nations, Stewart understands the black family to be in far greater peril than Beecher does the white family because of the racial and economic constraints that circumscribe the black family to a far greater degree than they do the household represented in Beecher's *Treatise*. Beecher articulates the apocalyptic as a domestic category, but she ignores how an apocalyptic domesticity is inflected by race. Within Beecher's sentimental economy, the domestic and the apocalyptic belong together, with race segregated and kept from view.

While Beecher neglects instances when race shapes the contours of nineteenth-century domesticity, Lydia Maria Child confronts this issue directly in two works of short fiction that she published a decade after Stewart stopped lecturing and within two years of Beecher's *Treatise*. "The Black Saxons" (1841) and "Slavery's Pleasant Homes" (1843) are narratives that investigate the intersection of slavery and the domestic space. Unlike Beecher's *Treatise*, these narratives are not "apocalyptic"—that is, there are no explicit references to judgment, retribution, or the second coming. They are nevertheless produced in a context in which figures like David Walker, Nat Turner, and Maria Stewart have already used apocalypse as shorthand for insurrection; moreover, Child's stories foreshadow Stowe's use of insurrectionary panic as a sentimental mode in her antislavery fiction. In what follows, we see Child narrativize insurrection's entry into the home; slavery and domesticity come together in Child's sentimental account, but without any of the millennialist rhetoric of Beecher and Stewart. Stowe's aesthetic approach will be to unify all these strategies, sustaining the link between insurrection and apocalyptic retribution and bringing this threat to bear on the American home front.

In the very first paragraph of "The Black Saxons," Child establishes what will be one of the principal preoccupations of this narrative; that is, the convergence of slave insurrection with domesticity. The story opens with Mr. Duncan, the story's protagonist, reading a "volume of the History of the Norman Conquest" in his "elegantly furnished parlor" near Charleston, South Carolina. Most antebellum readers would have immediately associated Charleston with Denmark Vesey's 1822 slave rebellion. Even though Vesey's was a failed revolt, it inspired widespread panic throughout the slaveholding South. Child invokes this history as part of the setting in which we find Duncan reading another history, this one about the Norman invasion of England. The depiction of a character reading is one of the quintessential symbols of Victorian domesticity, so it is significant that antebellum readers first come upon Duncan in the act of reading because such an act would have invoked the bourgeois assumptions and norms associated with the reading subject (leisure, comfort, wealth, etc.). Reading about the Norman conquest, Duncan expresses his sympathies with the "slaves" in England who were subject to the tyranny of the Normans. "And so that bold and beautiful race became slaves!"[38] Duncan reflects. And after a long rumination about the Normans' dominion over the Saxons, Duncan thinks, "Troubled must be the sleep of those who rule a conquered nation!" (21). In this early moment in the narrative, Duncan identifies with and expresses sympathy for his enslaved ancestors, the Saxons, who "tamely submitted to their lot, till their free, bright beauty passed under the heavy cloud of animal dulness, and the contemptuous Norman epithet of 'base Saxon churls' was but too significantly true" (20).

It is while reading about a moment of enslavement from long ago that Duncan is forced to reflect on the South's present situation with regard to its slaves. As "these thoughts [about the Norman conquest] were passing through his mind" (BS 21), one of Duncan's own slaves interrupts to ask if he can attend a nearby Methodist meeting, to which Duncan agrees. Within a short period of time, in fact, all of Duncan's slaves ask if they can attend the meeting, and he accedes to each request. What appears at first to be a benign appeal—these slaves are merely seeking a religious education—is, in fact, a coded reference to a more troubled reality that bears on the South, for Southern blacks, some quite notable, were radicalized via black Methodist theology (including David Walker and Denmark Vesey). That these slaves are seeking to attend a Methodist meeting is a signal to careful readers that their aims might not be as innocent as Duncan first assumes. At the moment that Duncan realizes all his slaves have left his house for the meeting, moreover, he connects two seemingly unrelated rumors that have been circulating: first, that the British were "near the coast, and about to land in Charleston" (suggesting that the story is set during the American Revolution); and second, that a fugitive slave named Big-boned Dick "was suspected of holding a rendezvous for runaways in the swampy depths of some dark forest" (23). For the first time, Duncan has the idea that his slaves, and other slaves from the surrounding community, may be planning to join the English when they attack at Charleston and take up arms against their masters. The illusion of safety within the domestic space is shattered by the possibility of insurrection. Duncan's slaves, who appear to be obedient and servile, may, in fact, be plotting against his life. At the very least, the fear of this possibility has arisen to disturb what had been for Duncan a rather pleasant and genteel lifestyle.

While the home front in this tale is, on one hand, a site of potential hazard, it is also a possible space of transformation. Duncan quickly realizes that his "republican sympathies" and the "system entailed upon him by his ancestors were obviously out of joint with each other" (BS 24). His commitment to the value of personal liberty is incommensurable and irreconcilable with the practice of holding slaves. The enslavement of the English by the French, the fact that he is a slaveholder, and the threat of his own slaves revolting, endangering him and his comfortable way of life, are ideas that constellate to convince him that "his sympathies were right, and his practice wrong" (25). Child brings her protagonist to the edge of reform, pushing the idea that it may indeed be possible for a member of the planter class to change his mind about the morality of slavery and even consider manumitting his slaves. Duncan stops short of emancipating his slaves, however, largely because, as one who entertains the notion of freedom for slaves, he would be alone among his slaveholding peers. Instead of abiding by his principles, the "admonitions of awakened conscience gradually gave place to considerations of personal safety, and plans for ascertaining the real extent of his danger" (25). Duncan plans to follow his slaves to the site of the next meeting and uncover their plot; he chooses, that is, to protect his life of leisure rather than live by his beliefs and follow through on liberating his property.

Having Duncan make this particular decision, while disappointing to modern readers, allows Child the opportunity to explore the possible repercussions of failing to free the slaves. For once Duncan begins to worry about his own safety and the possibility of insurrection, a deep panic sets in, one that Child concedes often grips the entire South when they entertain ideas of rebellion. On the following morning, for instance, when Duncan rides into the city, "[h]e endeavored to conceal anxiety under a cheerful brow; for he was afraid to ask counsel, even of his most familiar friends, in a community so prone to be blinded by insane fury under the excitement of such suspicion" (27). Child both acknowledges the South's predilection to panic and tries to amp up such feelings by charting her protagonist's increasing sense of foreboding. Duncan rides on horseback from plantation to plantation, inquiring of the slaves about the Methodist meeting and whether it was an edifying one. Recognizing that all of the slaves in the surrounding area attended this meeting, Duncan decides to acquire "a complete suit of negro clothes, and a black mask well fitted to his face" (27) in order to infiltrate the next meeting. In contrast to the opening scene in which we find him living a life of carefree leisure, Child depicts Duncan in this scene earnestly seeking the truth about his surrounding conditions and whether he, along with the entire slaveholding South, will need to take precautions against a slave revolt.

On the appointed night of the next Methodist meeting, Duncan distributes passes to all his slaves and, donning his disguise, follows them at a distance. As he approaches the designated area for the gathering—"one of those swamp islands, so common at the South, insulated by a broad, deep belt of water, and effectually screened from the main-land by a luxuriant growth of forest trees"— Duncan spies a tree that had been cut down to use as a bridge, "and over this dusky forms were swarming, like ants into their new made nest" (BS 28). This ominous image of the gathering masses inspires in Duncan a trepidation that is exacerbated once the purpose of the meeting is made clear. "When we had our last meeting," says one slave presiding over the meeting, "we all concluded it was best for to join the British.... And now, boys, if the British land here in Caroliny, what shall we do with our masters?" (30–31). Duncan's suspicions were right all along: the slaves were using these Methodist meetings as an opportunity to discuss not simply if they should join the British, but whether they should dispose of their masters once the British came ashore. Whatever sense of safety and comfort Duncan (and the South) enjoyed has been eradicated by the prospect that his very own slaves might kill him when they revolt.

As the slaves in attendance begin to speak, a variety of views emerge about how these slaves regard their masters and what should be done with them. "Ravish wives and daughters before their eyes," asserts one slave, "as they have done to *us*. Hunt them with hounds, as they have hunted *us*. Shoot them down with rifles, as they have shot *us*. Throw their carcasses to the crows . . . and then let the Devil take them where they never rake up fire o' nights" (BS 31; original emphases). This slave embodies an eye-for-an-eye perspective shared by many at the gathering. His call for retribution, however, is answered by "an aged black man" who pleads for compassion "because the blessed Jesus always talked of mercy" (31). He implores that these slaves forgive their oppressors: "let us love our enemies; let us pray for them" (32). A lively debate ensues at the conclusion of the old slave's statement, with some slaves "crying out vehemently for the blood of the white men, others maintaining that the old man's doctrine was right" (33). The debate that Child rehearses here increases the drama of the narrative by delaying the slaves' decision on how they should deal with their masters. And the conflict between those who support violence and those who refuse it foreshadows another famous example from Harriet Beecher Stowe's novel *Dred*, in which characters choose either to ally themselves with Dred and his endorsement of bloodshed, or with Milly and her calls for compassion and forgiveness.

Ultimately, the slaves decide that if the British land, "they would take their freedom without murdering their masters," a compromise that inspires gratitude in Duncan but which causes a few in attendance to leave "in a wrathful mood, muttering curses deep" (BS 42). While Child stops short of depicting a rebellion or of representing these slaves agreeing collectively to murder their masters if the British attack, the threat of insurrection nevertheless influences Duncan (and, if Child's narrative succeeds, her readers as well), who begins to recognize that the spirit that animates the slaves' desire to rebel is the same spirit that animated the "Robin Hoods, and Wat Tylers" to resist the tyranny of their French oppressors.[39] "Was the place I saw to-night," Duncan wonders, "in such wild and fearful beauty, like the haunts of the *Saxon* Robin Hood? . . . And who shall calculate what even such hopeless endeavors may do for the future freedom of their race?" (43; original emphasis). Duncan begins to sympathize with the slaves—these "black Saxons"—because they resemble his ancestors who suffered under and fought against a similar kind of cruelty. And while the assembly of black rebels engenders fear in the white interloper, it also sows the seeds for a cross-racial understanding that is larger than Duncan's personal interests. He understands the slaves' motives, even if he does not agree with or explicitly support them. In fact, while Duncan recognizes similarities between the peasant Saxons and the plotting slaves, this does not lead "to the emancipation of his bondmen; but they did prevent his revealing a secret, which would have brought hundreds to an immediate and violent death" (43). Though Duncan does not actively enable an insurrection, he gives his tacit permission by not informing the authorities. No John Brown, Duncan's decision makes him a race traitor nevertheless.

Interestingly enough, "The Black Saxons" exemplifies the logic of apocalyptic sentimentalism in several key ways, even if the violence and love are muted when compared to what has come before and what will come after. The potential violence that Child forebodes, while terrifying, is more "ordinary" insofar as it is not configured as an apocalyptic event. This threat is still meant to inspire dread in the reader as it does in Duncan. What is crucial, moreover, is that the violence Child is threatening is not just violence against whites, but also the terrible violence Duncan knows will be unleashed against blacks should he make his knowledge more widely known. Duncan decides to keep his awareness of the conspiring slaves to himself because his heart has been brought into greater sympathy with blacks; he now identifies with them through the Saxons in his domestic reading. The primary reason violence never unfolds in the narrative, in short, is because of Duncan's own softened and enlightened heart. Whereas Stewart derided whites for their inability to feel compassion for free and enslaved black Americans, Child's fictional narrative suggests what is possible and perhaps even necessary to alleviate mounting tensions over slavery. That is, a compassionate white man willing to protect the welfare of slaves.

While Child threatens slave violence without depicting it in "The Black Saxons," she takes her argument to its logical conclusion in "Slavery's Pleasant Homes," a story published in 1843, only two years after "The Black Saxons" appeared in print. As in her previous tale, much of the action in "Slavery's Pleasant Homes" occurs in the domestic space, where a sense of harmony between the slaves and their white masters appears to exist. In the opening lines, the reader learns about Frederic Dalcho's return from New Orleans with his new bride, Marion, and her two slaves, Rosa and Mars. This event arouses "great demonstrations of joy among the slaves of the establishment,—dancing, shouting, clapping of hands, and eager invocations of blessing on the heads of 'massa and missis.'"[40] This image of a harmonious household is quickly challenged when readers learn that such expressions of affection and joy on the part of the slaves are not necessarily spontaneous or genuine. The slaves know that "he who manifested [the] most zeal was likely to get the largest coin, or the brightest handkerchief" (147). This passage can be read in one of three ways: the master knows that he must purchase the affection of his slaves (their favor is not something they would offer him freely), or the slaves manipulate the master by exchanging public displays of "love" for payment, or it is some combination of the two. Whichever it may be, what is clear is that Child is raising the idea of domestic harmony and troubling that idea in the same breath to prepare readers for even greater domestic disturbances.

Indeed, Child furthers the notion that a congenial home is incongruent with the practices of slaveholding. The epigraph of this narrative reflects this notion: "Thy home may be lovely, but round it I hear / The crack of the whip, and the footsteps of fear" (S 147). These lines begin to expose the truth about domestic relations in the context of slavery. The slave fears the whip, marking the home as a space in which coercive and brutal tactics of subordination are regularly deployed. Female slaves in particular have reasons to be fearful. Soon after they return from New Orleans, Frederic develops an "unholy fire" for Marion's slave, Rosa. Frederic's desire inevitably culminates in Rosa's rape, underscoring what Harriet Jacobs describes as the particular injustice perpetrated against slave women.[41] In fact, Frederic's slave and Rosa's husband, George, is a quadroon and Frederic's biological sibling, so that George himself is the probable product of a rape by Frederic's father of one of his slaves. Frederic's violation of Rosa spotlights this especially insidious aspect of slaveholding culture. The Dalcho home not only bears the marks of sexual violence against slave women; it reveals that Southern families themselves are constituted precisely by way of this violation.

Along with being a concise technique to foreground the violence slaves, and especially slave women, must suffer, the epigraph also suggests that the home is itself becoming a space of fear in which everyone is a potential victim, including whites. The innovation of this story is that it transforms the home from a site in which only slaves suffer violence into one in which violence is democratized. Four days after Rosa is murdered by Frederic for obstinately disobeying his orders not to see her husband, readers overhear George as he hides in a nearby forest. "Shall I escape now and forever?" he asks, "or shall I first—" (S 156–57). George silences himself before he completes the thought, but the gap is pregnant with meaning. What George hesitates to announce is the introduction of slave violence into the white domestic space. The violence that has been so endemic to slave life is about to enter white homes.[42] Later that evening, Marion asks a slave girl to locate her husband, who has not yet retired to bed. The slave girl returns, "pallid and frightened," with the news: "Oh, mistress, he is dead! . . . there is a dagger through his heart" (157). Readers discover that the "dagger found in Frederic Dalcho's heart was the one he had himself been accustomed to wear. He lay upon the sofa, with an open book beside him, as if he had fallen asleep reading" (158). Frederic is not only murdered with his own dagger, itself a symbol of the power he once wielded in the home that has now been usurped and turned upon him, he is also killed while reading. What was only threatened in "The Black Saxons" is seen through to completion in "Slavery's Pleasant Homes." The domestic space is thoroughly transformed into a space of violence, so thorough, in fact, that Southern slave masters are becoming the victims of violence and not merely its perpetrators.

While George would seem like the obvious culprit, another of Marion's slaves named Mars is found guilty. A dropped handkerchief discovered near the body belonging to Mars and the disappearance of a sum of money in the desk drawer are evidence used to convict him of murder and theft. On the day that Mars is supposed to be executed, "slaves from miles around were assembled, to take warning by his awful punishment" (S 159). Moments before the execution, however, we are allowed to overhear George's thoughts. "The *theft* I did not commit; but if I take all the blame, they can do no more than hang me." After "confessing" his crimes to the reader, George makes the truth known to all in attendance. "Mars is innocent," he proclaims. "I murdered [my master]—for he killed my wife, and hell was in his bosom" (159; original emphasis). At this, the narrative voice interposes to relay the rest of the relevant details: "No voice praised him for the generous confession. They kicked him and cursed him; and hung up, like a dog or a wolf, a man of nobler soul than any of them all" (160). We learn that subsequent to his hanging, George was excoriated in Southern newspapers and denounced in Northern ones. He was not even mentioned by name, only identified as Mr. Dalcho's slave. While the newspapers deliver a predictable characterization of George, the narrator praises him for his integrity, suggesting a subtle but radical development in the politics of antislavery narratives. That is, while most in the South and many in the North decry acts of slave violence, there are those within American society, including the narrator (and maybe even the white author of this story), who can conceive of violence against slaveholders as both just and an expression of an honorable, virtuous soul. The man who murders his slave master, in other words, should be lauded for his heroism, not hanged for his alleged crime. I will return to this perspective again in chapter 5 when I examine Child's response to John Brown and his insurgency at Harpers Ferry.

Even though the action takes place offstage—readers do not witness George murdering Frederic firsthand—Child nevertheless presents a scenario that is meant to inspire dread in the hearts of white masters. George breaks laws that prohibit slaves from beating and killing masters. And he performs this violent act within the home of his master, so that white domesticity becomes a location equated with insurrection. What Child does not do, and what Harriet Beecher

Stowe will do in *Dred*, is augment this terror by conjoining slave insurrection with apocalyptic retribution, suggesting, like David Walker and Nat Turner before her, that a murderous slave is a manifestation of God's wrathful vengeance.

When read together, the work of Maria Stewart, Catherine Beecher, and Lydia Maria Child illustrates the various and often uneven ways in which sentimental accounts will understand the home and its intersections with slavery, violence, and apocalyptic vengeance. Along with constructing the apocalypse as a domestic category, Stewart and Beecher foreground women as principal agents within the home who possess the transformative power to reconfigure the social order as a more just and equitable arrangement. Beecher, however, makes no mention of emancipation or how American homes are racially (and therefore economically) inflected. Child, however, like Stewart, is preoccupied with the racial contours of domesticity and sees the domestic space as a possible arena of radical, and sometimes violent, transformation—though she never locates transformation, especially violent slave rebellion, within the framework of apocalyptic history as Stewart sometimes does. And even though she writes some years before Child and Beecher and produces a comparatively small body of work, Stewart begins to show how all of these moving parts might conspire together to form a powerful antislavery agenda. Most importantly, Stewart's account combines the apocalyptic and the domestic to generate a distinctive sentimental model, a model that critics have long neglected and one that will become especially prominent in the 1850s.

In the next two chapters, I consider how the various approaches initiated by Stewart, Beecher, and Child are unified and systematized by Harriet Beecher Stowe. What Stewart, Beecher, Child, and other authors were developing throughout the 1830s and 1840s, Stowe fully incorporates into the sentimental logic of her antislavery fiction. It is in Stowe's fiction that the related issues of domestic and antislavery reform, together with calls for Christian compassion and threats of apocalyptic retribution, fully and dramatically cohere, suggesting that Stowe's ideas regarding sentimentality are coextensive with what I am calling apocalyptic sentimentalism, where the love that is central to Stowe's antislavery fiction is supported by the equally essential threat of God's retributive wrath.

PART 2

Salvation through Motherly Vengeance

The Sentimentality of Harriet Beecher Stowe

CHAPTER 3

Uncle Tom's Cabin and the Fictionalization of Apocalyptic Sentimentalism

> I wrote [*Uncle Tom's Cabin*] because as a woman, as a mother I was oppressed & broken-hearted, with the sorrows & injustice I saw, because as a Christian I felt the dishonor to Christianity—because as a lover of my country I trembled at the coming day of wrath.
> —Harriet Beecher Stowe, letter to Lord Denman, *1853*

The quintessence of nineteenth-century sentimental fiction, *Uncle Tom's Cabin* is a novel that predicates its antislavery politics on the belief that each reader can learn to sympathize with and ultimately come to love America's slaves. For Stowe, doing good starts with feeling right, and white Americans must cultivate a loving and sympathetic bond with Negro slaves in order to guarantee slavery's demise. Indeed, ideas of love form the core of this novel and were, by the 1850s, at the very heart of nineteenth-century sentimentality. And it is precisely because love is central to *Uncle Tom's Cabin* that the novel's concluding remark seems so incongruous with the logic of sentimentalism that Stowe appears to have meticulously unfolded for her readers:

> O, Church of Christ, read the signs of the times! . . . [E]very time that you pray that the kingdom of Christ may come, can you forget that prophecy associates, in dread fellowship, the *day of vengeance* with the year of his redeemed? . . . Both North and South have been guilty before God; and the *Christian church* has a heavy account to answer. Not by combining together, to protect injustice and cruelty, and making a common capital of sin, is this Union to be saved,—but by repentance, justice and mercy; for, not surer is the eternal law by which the millstone sinks in the ocean, than that stronger law, by which injustice and cruelty shall bring on nations the wrath of Almighty God![1]

Along with encouraging readers to weep over the sorrows of the slave, Stowe exhorts them to remain mindful of and even fear the possible apocalyptic consequences they might suffer because of their sins. She supplements sympathy and love—the putative emotional grounding of sentimentalism—with a discourse of judgment, inviting her readers to ruminate on God's wrath and the destruction that befalls a people who fail to uphold the theological imperatives of justice and mercy.

Stowe's threatening language in the novel's closing passage raises a question about the politics of love in *Uncle Tom's Cabin* that readers have thus far failed to ask: why would Stowe, who enjoins her readers to "see to it that *they feel right*" (*U* 632; original emphasis), and who relies so heavily on sympathy and love to transform the hearts of the novel's characters and of its readers, conclude by invoking a terrifying image of God's apocalyptic retribution? While modern readers might find depictions of a vengeful God out of place in a novel that is dedicated to the revolutionary power of love, nineteenth-century readers immersed in a setting where warnings of divine wrath were pervasive would have recognized that images of retribution could appear alongside representations of sympathy and love. Rather than seeing her plea for love on one hand and her warning of apocalypse on the other as existing in tension, Stowe's contemporaries would have understood that these two categories are yoked together in a fundamental way. As I argue in this chapter, Stowe evokes familiar nineteenth-century conceptions of apocalypse in *Uncle Tom's Cabin* and reinscribes them within a novelistic framework, exemplifying the strategy of "apocalyptic sentimentalism" where imbrications of love and fear constitute the sentimental structure of this representative sentimental text. What David Walker and Maria Stewart begin to develop with their styles of political rhetoric, Stowe incorporates as a fictional mode, translating apocalyptic sentimentality across genres so that it becomes a key feature of her literary aesthetic. Combining the discourses of early black polemicists with her education in the Scottish Enlightenment and the Presbyterian faith that she inherits from her father, Lyman Beecher, Stowe sustains an abiding fidelity to sympathetic love as the moral force of antislavery reform.[2] Stowe also returns again and again to the threat of a wrathful God who chastens sinners, and this recursion is an essential trait of the novel's sentimental politics.

If sentimentalism has constituted one of the prevailing conceptual frameworks contemporary scholars have used to map cultural and aesthetic trends in the United States since the late eighteenth century, *Uncle Tom's Cabin* has served as the operational blueprint for sentimental narration. While modern readers widely recognize *Uncle Tom's Cabin* as the sentimental *urtext*, they have overlooked the symbiotic pairing of love and fear in Stowe's novel, choosing instead to read them individually and antagonistically rather than in a reciprocal relation. As a consequence, scholarly accounts of sentimentalism that mark *Uncle Tom's Cabin* as the paradigmatic novelistic expression of this tradition but that nevertheless minimize or overlook the apocalyptic dimension of the novel are themselves based on a fundamental misreading of the sentimental as it is embodied in Stowe's writing. Jane Tompkins's influential analysis is a case in point for the kind of scholarly account that sees love and fear working in separate emotional spheres rather than inhabiting the same affective space. While Tompkins identifies the fears that arise from the threat of a possible apocalypse, claiming that Stowe's novel "is a jeremiad in the fullest and truest sense," her argument never classifies fear as constitutive to the makeup of sentimentalism as Stowe envisions it.[3] In order to highlight Stowe's feminism and make a claim for the powerful shaping influence women writers had within the American Renaissance, Tompkins ultimately has to privilege love over fear as the chief affective register of the novel and the surest sign of the supremacy of motherly influence. As a result, the oscillation in Stowe's novel between fear and love, and what this relation means for literary sentimentalism, is left unexplored in an otherwise influential and probing analysis. Tompkins's assertion that *Uncle Tom's Cabin* is the "*summa theologica* of nineteenth-century America's religion of domesticity" because it retells "the culture's favorite story about itself—the story of salvation through motherly love" has now come to stand as the canonical view, with love emerging from and sustained by virtuous mothers.[4] Dawn Coleman treats Stowe's apocalypticism, for example, as an error that needs to be corrected, a superficial gesture that distracts readers from Stowe's more sincere and authentic discourse of sympathy and love. Coleman ultimately prefers a domesticated and properly feminine version of Stowe—"a little lady with a pen" rather than an angry preacher, "a symbolic mother to *all* of her readers" instead of a prophet warning of the end of days.[5] Like Tompkins and Coleman, Joshua Bellin focuses on the fear the novel prominently displays, arguing that *Uncle Tom's Cabin* "both arises from the apocalyptic fears of the time and makes the most of them, offering a reassuring alternative to apocalypse, even if that alternative is predicated on apocalypse." Even though he maintains that the apocalypse "offers readers the opportunity to judge themselves and to decide whose side they are on, the right side or the wrong," Bellin's argument fails to locate fear in the sentimental tradition or see it as a necessary companion to love.[6]

Along with Tompkins, Coleman, and Bellin, most readers continue to assume that Stowe's injunction to "feel right" is exclusively a call to love or compassion rather than an incitement to appreciate and fear a coming apocalypse. But Stowe understands that she cannot depend on the spontaneous generation of love, even among those who may read about the slaves' deplorable circumstances in a novel like *Uncle Tom's Cabin*. Thus, Stowe uses fear to activate sympathy, a move that scholarly accounts have missed because they have fixated almost exclusively on the transformative force of love. They have been so invested in love that they have created a circular account of the sentimental in which the representation of a so-called sentimental scene is itself adequate to produce sympathy, proceeding, in short, as if sympathy can invoke sympathy. Love is not the autonomous force for Stowe that modern readers assume it to be.[7] Rather than constructing an autotelic account of sympathetic love, Stowe instead uses the fear of an impending apocalypse to personalize and invest the sentimental with greater power. It is the threat of God's retributive wrath and the terror that this threat engenders which guarantees Stowe's confidence in the efficacy of sympathy. Fear, Stowe often suggests, is what ultimately impels characters (and readers) to sympathize with and love slaves.[8]

I read *Uncle Tom's Cabin* in this chapter for the way Stowe aestheticizes the logic of apocalyptic sentimentality within a work of fiction. Rooted as it is in the fiery vernaculars of early black political expression and Protestant apocalyptic theology, Stowe narrativizes these discourses, so that calls for love and warnings of vengeance mediate as well as organize the interactions between the novel's characters as well as the reader's encounter with the narrative itself. I carefully uncover the sentimental structure of this novel for four important reasons. First, *Uncle Tom's Cabin* is the masterpiece of nineteenth-century sentimentality, and as such, I want to clarify precisely how sympathy operates within the narrative, something I do not believe scholars have explained fully. Second, as the *urtext* and lens through which the larger culture of sentiment is often read, my revised reading might allow us to consider how foundational terror is to nineteenth-century sentimental culture. Third, my analysis allows us to examine how early black apocalyptic representation may have influenced Stowe's thinking about sentimentality, and it is this influence that needs to be put into conversation with Stowe's training in the Scottish Enlightenment and her critical relationship to Edwardsian theology. Finally, clarifying how vengeance and terror function within the sentimentality of *Uncle Tom's Cabin* will enable me to better illustrate how Stowe employs and further develops this structure of sentiment in her second important work of antislavery fiction, *Dred*. By the 1850s, apocalyptic sentimentalism is a more established construct than it was in earlier decades, exerting a greater degree of influence. While an inchoate apocalyptic sentimentalism marked specific moments in the writings of David Walker and Maria Stewart, for instance, it was still in its embryonic form and thus had a more episodic presence in these respective texts. In *Uncle Tom's Cabin*, however, Stowe uses the configuration of apocalyptic sentimentality as the primary structuring principle of the narrative. Rather than appearing irregularly, apocalyptic sentimentalism frames many of the scenes throughout the whole of Stowe's novel. Its formal expansion from sporadic moments to the entire narrative signals the maturation of this tradition, an ongoing development that will continue up until the Civil War. It also exemplifies one of the innovations of fictionalizing apocalyptic sentimentality, so that the apocalypse becomes a defining aspect of the novel's sentimental architecture. In *Uncle Tom's Cabin*, fear inspires love when there is a shortage of love, and love sentimentalizes the apocalypse as primarily a *felt* experience, a dimension of affect that together with sympathetic love helps to shape the novel's aesthetic and its antislavery politics.

In addition to constituting an essential dimension within this paradigmatic work of sentimental fiction, the novel's apocalypticism is the primary shaping influence for the colonization solution that Stowe proposes and that leads to all the major surviving black characters emigrating to Liberia. Rather than offering an antislavery politics that represents ex-slaves as integrated citizens of the United States (a politics that most critics have understandably vilified Stowe for failing to advocate), Stowe unfolds an apocalyptic vision of Christ's second coming that takes the place of a secular program of racial integration. The overriding concern in the novel is with the fulfillment of a very particular religious worldview, one in which Christ reigns on earth. For Stowe, abolition and the reorganization of the domestic space are merely two possible vehicles for arriving at the telos of providential history, one that culminates with the earthly installment of Christ's heavenly kingdom. This fulfillment of history exists at the heart of *Uncle Tom's Cabin*'s eschatology. Moreover, Stowe reiterates throughout the novel that the true sign of the apocalypse is the conversion of Negro heathens, both in America and in Africa. Thus, her black characters return to Africa because Africa is God's next covenantal nation, and American slaves, along with Africans, will be God's chosen people whom he will continue to protect, provided they uphold their covenantal obligations. The colonizationist ending, in other words, is inextricably bound up with the novel's apocalyptic logic. Stowe's concern is not, finally, with worldly politics but instead with the question of how to abide by the covenant and achieve everlasting life—how, in other words, to make it through the apocalypse. The removal of black characters from the national landscape is perfectly consistent with and a logical (if unsettling) extension of apocalyptic sentimentalism.

Fictionalizing the Sentimental Apocalypse

Stowe's literary strategy draws upon a variety of rhetorical and religious discourses that she inherits and combines into a powerful argument against slavery. The polemical style of Walker and Stewart, Lyman Beecher's Calvinism, and Stowe's own education in the Scottish Enlightenment and appreciation for increasingly liberal forms of Protestantism all contribute to the sentimental construction of *Uncle Tom's Cabin*.[9] Even though Stowe attempted throughout her life to adopt a softer version of her father's more severe brand of Calvinism, which she felt emphasized the judgment of God rather than Christ's love and the possibility for universal salvation, she nevertheless continued to embrace the notion that Christ would one day return triumphantly to pass judgment.[10] Her dispute with Calvinism and her education in the Scottish Enlightenment, in other words, do not necessarily translate into a wholesale rejection of her belief in an apocalyptic end to history.[11] Stowe's fiction in the early to mid-1850s often embodies a conservative Puritanism; her theology has at its center a Christ who, while loving, will bring apocalyptic retribution upon unregenerate sinners nonetheless. As she explains as late as 1879 in a letter to her son, Charles: "If Christ meant nothing by his terribly plain words—or meant that everybody eventually and somehow or other would come out right—then his preaching, life and death was without point. God is love—salvation free—the spirit and the bride say come—but *come* you must or be lost."[12]

Stowe's decision to augment love with fear as she does in *Uncle Tom's Cabin* was driven, in part, by some of the political developments in the early 1850s which suggested that sympathy was waning and America was becoming less compassionate toward its slaves, not more so. The ratification of the Fugitive Slave Law, for example, which partly inspired her to write *Uncle Tom's Cabin*, also confirmed that even ostensibly virtuous Northerners were willing to condone, and often collude, in the practice of returning escaped slaves to their Southern masters. Stowe recognizes, in other words, that her most outwardly moral readers—"Christian men" from the North—may not share her views on slavery and may, in fact, help perpetuate slavery by remaining unwilling to feel compassion for America's slaves.[13] Stowe requires a safeguard to ensure that sympathy will be effective in reforming the hearts and minds of her readers, and she deploys the apocalypse in order to intensify her readers' experience of sympathetic love precisely because love is not an automatic or guaranteed response. "For what hope," Stowe asks, "what help, what salvation can there be for those who cannot be reached by [Christ's] love? If they have seen and hated both him and his Father—what remains?"[14] In *Uncle Tom's Cabin*, what remains is terror. The sympathetic bond of love that circumscribes the community and sustains its existence is itself circumscribed and motivated by the fear of a coming apocalypse.

The religious aim of *Uncle Tom's Cabin*, with individuals choosing Christ in order to be saved, is most powerfully dramatized through the character of Augustine St. Clare. It is also with St. Clare that Stowe illustrates for her readers that a sentimental approach to slavery requires an apocalyptic supplement to achieve sympathetic bonds among slaveholders and their slaves. Although St. Clare endeavors to act with benevolent virtue, he does not always fully appreciate the evil of his slaveholding practices until he is given a powerful incentive to discontinue them. Initially, St. Clare attempts to cultivate a sympathetic relation with his slaves and rejects owning "a great gang of seven hundred, whom I could not know personally, or feel any individual interest in" (*U* 325). Even with his munificent approach to slaveholding, however, St. Clare recognizes that slavery is inherently evil, no matter how generous the slave master is. He also acknowledges that justice for the slave might soon be implemented through a momentous change:

> One thing is certain,—that there is a mustering among the masses, the world over; and there is a *dies irae* coming on, sooner or later. The same thing is working in Europe, in England, and in this country. My mother used to tell me of a millennium that was coming, when Christ should reign, and all men should be free and happy.... Sometimes I think all this sighing, and groaning, and stirring among the dry bones foretells what she used to tell me was coming. But who may abide the day of His appearing? (330–31)

While he perfunctorily recollects his mother's musings on the approaching day of wrath, St. Clare has removed the threat that a vision like this often contains. He presents a peaceful, postmillennialist image of a day when men are happy and free without any of the fire and brimstone that attend such an event. As a result, St. Clare does not regard himself as a likely target of God's vengeance. This nostalgic presentation of apocalypse temporarily fails to intensify the bond of sympathy that connects St. Clare to his slaves, and this weakened bond, in turn, cannot move him to emancipate the slaves for whom he claims to care so deeply. Unable to feel the dread of an impending judgment, St. Clare imagines a mere abstraction and thus cannot see how his mother's revelation pertains directly to him. Even when he begins to consider the possible repercussions of holding slaves, as he does after the passing of Eva, he continues at moments to echo what his mother once told him, enthusiastically stating, "What a sublime conception is that of a last judgment! ... a righting of all the wrongs of ages!—a solving of all moral problems, by an unanswerable wisdom! It is, indeed, a wonderful image" (445). Romanticizing his mother's notion of justice, St. Clare overlooks how terrifying this vision should be for a slaveholding sinner like himself. Ophelia St. Clare, however, appreciates the awfulness of his rumination on divine justice. Her cousin may describe it as a "sublime conception," but Ophelia knows it "is a fearful one," to be sure (445).

What begins as an abstract conception of apocalypse finally becomes a personal one for St. Clare. He recognizes his responsibility in perpetuating injustice and ultimately rejects the practice of slaveholding. His conversion occurs soon after Eva's death, but it is not her passing that underpins his renouncement of slavery. Even though the scene in which Eva dies, "the epitome of Victorian sentimentalism,"[15] might facilitate the conversions of Ophelia and Topsy, it does not possess the requisite force to transform St. Clare from a slaveholder to a proper Christian. Few critics who describe Eva as the emblem of love have questioned precisely why her death does not have the same effect on St. Clare as it does on Ophelia and Topsy, and none has convincingly explained what ultimately causes his conversion.[16] It is, in fact, only after reading apocalyptic passages from the Bible that describe the unjust being cursed "into everlasting fire" (*U* 442) that St. Clare finally realizes that he is just like those sinners who are suffering God's torment. "These folks," he remarks, "that get such hard measure seem to have been doing just what I have,—living good, easy, respectable lives; and not troubling themselves to inquire how many of their brethren were hungry or athirst, or sick, or in prison" (443). The fear of suffering this same fate is what finally softens St. Clare's heart enough for him to recognize how objectionable his own slaveholding practices are. He realizes that he possesses "that kind of benevolence which consists in lying on a sofa, and cursing the church and clergy for not being martyrs and confessors" (446), and decides it is better to act against injustice than to allow such examples of cruelty to continue. Although he is killed before he can free his slaves, his death does not minimize the importance of his conversion for Stowe. St. Clare has reformed his heart and saved his soul, which, according to the novel's religious worldview, must be the highest priority of each individual. Having atoned for his past sins, St. Clare enters heaven not in a state of sin but in a state of grace and remarks that he is "coming HOME, at last!" (452). The fear of everlasting damnation is what effects St. Clare's conversion and subsequent salvation, something that the death of his daughter—his "beloved child" (421)—could not accomplish on its own.

It is this kind of logic—this choice between "heaven and the flames"—that James Baldwin rejects as "medieval morality." Baldwin loathes conversions from fear, as they signify, in his view, the "dishonesty" of sentimentality and underscore the sentimentalist's "inability to feel." Baldwin is right that if white readers are moved by *Uncle Tom's Cabin*, it is not because Stowe engages in any meaningful introspection or considers what "moved her people to such deeds" as holding slaves.[17] Rather, Stowe is counting on her readers' desire for self-preservation, of evading God's vengeance; their fear of immolation is what inclines them to act differently toward slaves. It is a tactical gesture on Stowe's part, one that, for Baldwin, might be appropriate for political pamphlets but certainly not novels. What Baldwin does not recognize, however, is that Stowe is as suspicious of her audience as Baldwin is. She understands that her readers possess, in Baldwin's apt phrase, an "arid heart" and might remain inactive, even if she succeeds in convincing them that slavery is wrong. Their fear of damnation is all that is left to move them against the slave system. Whereas Baldwin reads Stowe's turn to God's vengeance as a cop-out and a marker of the sentimentalist's "violent inhumanity," Stowe deploys God's vengeance as the last desperate measure to restore humanity to white Americans.[18]

St. Clare's transformation is significant not only because it further underscores the importance of apocalyptic fear within the novel's sentimental structure, but also because his decision to abandon his slaveholding practices originates in a textual encounter. St. Clare represents Stowe's ideal reader, responding to biblical passages the way Stowe wishes her own readers will respond to *Uncle Tom's Cabin*. The Bible converts St. Clare from a sinner to a Christian, and *Uncle Tom's Cabin*, Stowe hoped, would transform America from an unjust nation to a just and equitable one. And the novel would accomplish this through a specific form of sentimental education, where ideas of love are ignited by threats of God's judgment. Indeed, of particular importance is the fact that at the moment of St. Clare's epiphany, he is reading passages that detail Christ's judgment and retributive wrath. Instead of having him absorbed in passages that portray a gentle and forgiving God, or a God that proselytizes the loving of one's neighbor, Stowe presents St. Clare engaged with Christ in all of his biblical fury. Like St. Clare, who is reformed by the fire-and-brimstone passages of Scripture, Stowe's readers would be converted by her own representations of apocalypse. Their salvation depended, not just on their surety of Christ's love, but also on their fear of his impending vengeance.

While St. Clare's conversion is one of the most instructive examples of how the threat of judgment inspires sympathetic love, it is not this benevolent Southern plantation master who ultimately poses the biggest obstacle to achieving a community of free citizens cohered by Christian affection. It is instead the slave trader who remains most resistant to sympathetic influence and who stands as the greatest challenge to sympathy's usefulness as a political strategy. He refuses to recognize the interior life of the slave and thus appears impervious to sympathy's penetrating force. In the novel's opening scene, we meet a slave trader who "when critically examined, did not seem, strictly speaking, to come under the species" of a gentleman (*U* 3). Stowe immediately invites the reader to scrutinize the slave trader Haley, to evaluate and judge his humanity, for the trader's questionable humanity is a concern to which the novel repeatedly returns. Her description of Haley signals his obsession with material possession, an obsession that the novel generalizes onto all traders. Haley has "commonplace features, and that swaggering air of pretension which marks a low man who is trying to elbow his way upward in the world" (3). His ambition for and indulgence in worldly success and pleasure are symbolized by his ostentatious dress and accoutrements. Haley's "blue neckerchief, bedropped gayly with yellow spots, and arranged with a flaunting tie" is "quite in keeping with the general air of the man." His hands are "plentifully bedecked with rings" and he wears "a heavy gold watch-chain, with a bundle of seals of portentous size, and a great variety of colors, attached to it,—which, in the ardor of conversation, he was in the habit of flourishing and jingling with evident satisfaction" (3). In her objectification of Haley, Stowe mimics Haley's objectification of the slave. He is simply a material object consumed with consuming the material world; he is a body, out of touch with his own humanity, who trades in other bodies. When Mr. Shelby observes that Tom is "a good, steady, sensible, pious fellow" who "got religion at a camp-meeting, four years ago," Haley sees Tom's propensity for religion as a "valeyable thing" that will make him a more attractive commodity for potential buyers (4–5). Rather than seeing the slave's religiosity to be proof of his soul and a marker of his humanity, Haley is all surface, focusing exclusively on the surplus value garnered from the slave's material body.

If sympathy possesses sufficient force on its own, then Haley would merely need to be exposed to the sorrows of a slave in order for his heart to be transformed. But Stowe highlights the problem of the slave trader who does not feel sympathy even though he sees "sentimental" scenes unfold all around him. He bears witness to the suffering of others but feels no compassion, thus existing outside the sympathetic bond of love. As Haley oversees the transport of slaves and other cargo on an Ohio passenger boat, for instance, the ship provides the setting for a brief reunion between a slave woman and her husband before he is sold downriver. This temporary and tearful reunion, however, is a tale that "needs not to be told," for it is all too common. In other words, incidents that should evoke sympathetic reactions are ubiquitous but go unnoticed by the trader (and, Stowe hints, by the reader). A nearby gentleman reproaches Haley for breaking apart a loving family. "My friend," the young man asks, "how can you, how dare you, carry on a trade like this? . . . Here I am, rejoicing in my heart that I am going home to my wife and child; and the same bell which is a signal to carry me onward towards them will part this poor man and his wife forever. Depend upon it, God will bring you into judgment for this" (*U* 178). By sympathizing with the slave couple's burden, this young passenger does what Haley cannot. It is because of his own familial relations and his mindfulness of God's vengeful wrath that he can mourn over what these slaves are denied. But Haley remains unmoved, and thus the traveler must amplify the consequences of such callousness by suggesting that Haley will one day suffer God's fury. The narrative voice underscores this point: "Patience! patience! ye whose hearts swell indignant at wrongs like these. Not one throb of anguish, not one tear of the oppressed, is forgotten by the Man of Sorrows, the Lord of Glory. . . . Bear thou, like him, in patience, and labor in love; for such as he is God, 'the year of his redeemed *shall* come'" (187; original emphasis). This scene of the slaves' hardships and many others like it are unable to produce in the trader a sufficiently sympathetic response; in this case, sympathy cannot activate itself. If Haley is going to appreciate the pathos of a slave family's separation, he is first going to have to feel the terror of being the subject of Christ's judgment. He is, in other words, going to have to dread an impending apocalypse. Terror is a prerequisite for sympathy, and it is precisely during this representative sentimental moment that the apocalypse is not only invoked but required, if sympathy is going to work at all.

The reality, of course, is that apocalyptic sentimentality might not work, either, to move the trader to discontinue his trade—but, Stowe suggests, it might still influence the reader. While the narrative indicts those characters like Haley who are most clearly implicated in sustaining America's slave system, Stowe does not allow her readers to become cozy in their sense of righteous indignation at the actions of the trader: "But who, sir, makes the trader? Who is most to blame? The enlightened, cultivated, intelligent man, who supports the system of which the trader is the inevitable result, or the poor trader himself? You make the public sentiment that calls for his trade, that debauches and depraves him, till he feels no shame in it; and in what are you better than he? Are you educated and he ignorant, you high and he low, you refined and he coarse, you talented and he simple?" (*U* 189). This passage, which is ostensibly directed at the bystanders on the passenger boat, also resembles one of Stowe's many direct addresses to her readers, subtly subverting their naïve and faulty sense of self-assurance. With this sudden rhetorical movement, the critical focus shifts away from Haley and is fixed onto the reader who objectifies the slave and whose complicity with and endorsement of chattel slavery actually produces and legitimizes the trader's employment. With all of his or her refinement, learning, and proper rearing, it is the reader who may be unable to sympathize with the slave's burden and, instead, actually contributes to it. In this context, Stowe diverts the threat of apocalypse away from the trader and directs it instead at her audience. "In the day of a future Judgment," Stowe writes, "these very considerations may make it more tolerable for him than for you" (189). It is not enough for Stowe's audience simply to read this scene with Haley and the slave couple. In order to recognize their culpability in the injustices the slave suffers, Stowe's readers must first be reminded of the consequences of either participating in, or simply permitting, such acts of injustice to go unredressed. Stowe invokes an apocalyptic warning to incite a sympathetic connection between characters and readers who refuse or are unable to foster a suitable emotional bond. In fact, it takes Eliza Harris, a slave, to demonstrate how this lesson should be incorporated. When she discovers that Tom Loker has been injured in a fight, she remarks, "O, I hope he isn't killed! . . . Because, after death comes the judgment" (285). Eliza's connection to Loker is a sympathetic one, but the reason she feels sympathy for Loker is that she has considered the grave consequences of his actions. Her compassion for Loker is produced by her belief that God punishes the wicked and that Loker might soon be held accountable for his sins.

While Stowe emphasizes numerous "negative" models of apocalyptic sentimentalism in the form of characters who fail to conjoin love and fear in a harmonious relation that leads to Christian virtue, she also provides several examples of those who, like Eliza, embody apocalyptic sentimentality precisely in the way they incorporate the lessons of Christian love and apocalyptic prophecy to shape a moral existence. If Haley fails to understand the logic of apocalyptic sentimentalism, Eva and Tom are its foremost practitioners. Two paragons of virtue who approach perfection in their capacities to sympathize and love, Tom and Eva spend their time reading from the book of Revelation, and the parts of Scripture that delight Eva most are "the Revelations and the Prophecies" (*U* 368). She reads aloud to Tom directly from the concluding book of the New Testament, repeating that "I saw a sea of glass, mingled with fire" (369). Just because one has achieved a pure and sympathetic disposition—as Eva and Tom both have—does not mean one cannot return to the source of that sympathy in order to reinvigorate its force. For Stowe, as long as one remains emotionally engaged with apocalyptic prophecy, one will continue to love the nation's slaves, and this sentimental symbiosis of love and fear is embodied in her most dependable Christians, Tom and Eva. Indeed, their love of humanity sustains the fear of judgment, keeping God's wrath in view as the consequence of failing to abide by the theological injunctions of mercy and love exemplified by Christ and expressed in his teachings. And fear of apocalypse feeds their love, augmenting its intensity and expanding its scope.

The relationship between Tom and Eva constitutes the second "panel" of the literary triptych that I began describing in chapter 1. By way of the pair's interaction, Stowe revises the horrific scene readers first encountered in Turner's *Confessions* in which two of Turner's conspirators return to the Travis residence to kill the white infant sleeping in its crib. In stark contrast to that scene, Stowe portrays Tom and Eva as deeply loving beings who see themselves as perfect equals.[19] The murderous adult black male of Turner's *Confessions* is transformed in *Uncle Tom's Cabin* into a supremely loving being and model Christian. The category of the adult black male, according to Tom's portrait in this novel, is no longer a threatening figure with vengeful intentions and a "thirst for blood." In fact, both Tom and Eva are invested with salvific power; both, in other words, model for readers the path to righteousness and salvation. They embody the interplay between the Gospels and the book of Revelation; that is, they have incorporated into their Christian living the lessons of God's love and the need for his vengeance as a guarantor of that love and a punishment for those who fail to achieve a compassionate heart. Read as a political allegory, however, and as a marker for the development of apocalyptic sentimentalism, this dyad fails to dramatize an interracial sociality capable of destroying an institution like slavery. It is insufficient, although a laudable effort on Stowe's part, that this relationship is between an adult black male and a white child. While Eva has moral force in the novel, the scope of her authority as a political symbol is limited by her youth (despite Stowe's privileging of Eva's authority above all others). In other words, if Tom and Eva represent an idealized interracial union—a portrait of racial egalitarianism between whites and blacks—this idealized portrait is undermined by the fact that Eva is a child and Tom is childlike. While it may be a charming depiction for genteel white readers and a decidedly sentimental maneuver for Stowe to construct such an idealized friendship between a loving male slave and a knowing, virtuous child, the institution of slavery and the politics of race are nevertheless transacted among adults, especially white men. Any attempt to symbolize an ideal interracial bond must necessarily involve a benevolent, sympathetic, loving white man, for white men constitute the greatest impediments to slaves seeking freedom, obstacles that even Eva cannot surpass, despite her angelic nature. The final literary panel that I examine in this book will have to enact a displacement of the white child in favor of an adult white male, for it is the white male that holds political authority in antebellum America and thus symbolizes the promise of legal emancipation and not just religious salvation. It is the adult white male who needs to interact with and show deep compassion for Negro slaves.

Even after her death, Eva continues to play a central role in unfolding the novel's sentimental logic and its challenge to the hard-hearted slaveholder, this time the infamous Simon Legree. In a pivotal scene near the end of the novel, Sambo hands Legree a piece of paper that he has confiscated from Tom containing a silver dollar and a curl of Eva's hair that she gave to Tom before she died. When this curl of hair wraps itself around Legree's finger, Legree recoils with horror at its touch "as if it burned him" (*U* 528). This seemingly banal incident reminds Legree of how he betrayed his mother when he was younger, choosing to drink alcohol and swear and remain "wilder and more brutal than ever" rather than listen to her entreaties to renounce "a life of sin." Right before his mother's death, she sends him a locket of her own hair with the message that she "blest and forgave him" (530). Eva's hair triggers these memories for Legree, who has violated the sentimental mandate and fallen far from the "bosom of his mother" into an ignominious life of sin, tyranny, and unruliness.

Eva's hair inspires in Legree a surprising amount of terror, given how this hardened slave master epitomizes unremitting cruelty. "There is a dread, unhallowed necromancy of evil," Stowe writes, "that turns things sweetest and holiest to phantoms of horror and affright. That pale, loving mother,—her dying prayers, her forgiving love,—wrought in that demoniac heart of sin only as a damning sentence, bringing with it a fearful looking for of judgment and fiery indignation" (*U* 530). What was meant to be an emblem of love is, for Legree, an omen of his inevitable judgment at the hands of an angry God. In reminding Legree of his original sin against his mother, the curl of hair also evokes for the reader Eva's own commitment to apocalyptic theology as a foundational part of Christian morality. To ensure that her readers make this connection, Stowe describes Legree's fear in apocalyptic terms; he trembles as he meditates on "everlasting fires" (530). Stowe uses Legree's fears as an occasion to articulate the operative logic of apocalyptic sentimentalism: "Ye who have wondered to hear, in the same evangel, that God is love, and that God is a consuming fire, see ye not how, to the soul resolved in evil, perfect love is the most fearful torture, the seal and sentence of the direst despair?" (531). Stowe not only explains to her readers that the Christian God is simultaneously a God of love and vengeance, she also points out what may be one of the most ironic outcomes of apocalyptic sentimentality; that is, the purest expressions of love inspire in the unrepentant the most acute feelings of fear.[20]

It is also in this scene that Stowe's investment in apocalyptic theology converges and cooperates with her deployment of gothic conventions, suggesting an underlying compatibility between these two discourses that are both deeply invested in producing terror, despite the differences in idiom.[21] In describing the effect Eva's hair has on Legree, for example, Stowe refers to the "necromancy of evil" (*U* 530), which transforms objects of love into sources of deep dread. Legree, moreover, dreams in characteristically gothic fashion of his "pale mother rising by his bedside" as if she is a ghostly apparition haunting his sleep, causing the "cold sweat" to "roll down his face." Such nightmares cause Legree to "spring from his bed in horror" (531). Cassie contributes to his fright by singing to Legree from the shadows in a "strange and ghostlike" voice that echoed in the "dreary old house." And the words Cassie sings are these: "O there'll be mourning, mourning, mourning, / O there'll be mourning, at the judgment-seat of Christ!" (531). These haunting sounds are charged with references to judgment, and these threats of judgment amplify the nightmarish quality of Cassie's gothic libretto, leaving Legree with "large drops of sweat . . . on his forehead" and his heart beating "thick with fear" (532). By joining the apocalyptic to the gothic, Stowe may be suggesting that neither is sufficient on its own to convert a sinner like Legree (who may be the most notorious villain in nineteenth-century American fiction). Perhaps in rare instances like this one, fear, which is supposed to catalyze love, must *itself* be motivated by even more fear. In her confrontation with Legree, in other words, Stowe approaches the theoretical limits of what even apocalyptic prophecy can do to inspire terror. It, like love, is neither self-generative nor guaranteed to work; as improbable as it may seem, even the threat of God's wrath might require some additional discourse to activate it. Modern readers are here reminded not to make the same mistake that we have already made regarding love and assume that fear is autotelic, even if it appears to be. Stowe, in quite dramatic fashion, reaches the imaginative impasse of apocalyptic sentimentalism: there is nothing left to inspire fear except more fear; the absolute foundation of apocalyptic sentimentalism is ultimately without foundation. Fear is just as tenuous, contingent, and chancy as love. And if the apocalyptic and the gothic together fail to convince of the evils of slaveholding, then what is left but the coercive measures of violent force, a possibility that Stowe will entertain in *Dred* as she enfolds the mutually constitutive threats of insurrectionary violence and God's wrath into the sentimental structure of the narrative.[22]

Just as Stowe uses Eva (and Eva's hair) to further the argument about the necessity of fear in establishing a loving Christian heart, she also uses Tom throughout *Uncle Tom's Cabin* to typify her sentimental model and remind readers that sympathy grows out of an appreciation of God's wrathful nature. Tom, for example, admonishes Jake and Andy when he overhears them wishing that Haley would experience the kind of eternal punishment sinners are bound to endure when they fail to measure up at judgment. "Chil'en!" Tom rebukes, "I'm afeard you don't know what ye're sayin'... it's awful to think on't. You oughtenter wish that ar to any human crittur" (*U* 78). Of all possible punishments, damnation is the most dreadful, and while Andy pleads that "we wouldn't to anybody but the soul-drivers" (78), Tom understands that judgment is too terrible a thing to wish on any sinner. In fact, it is precisely the fear that Tom feels for Haley's fate that motivates him to silence Jake rather than support his sentiments. Tom experiences a sympathetic connection to Haley because he knows that Haley's day of doom fast approaches. The prospect of suffering an outcome similar to Haley's (as remote as that possibility may be) is what helps Tom remain a good and loving Christian. This is the sentimental structure—a structure in which love and compassion are kept in check by fear—that the novel repeatedly employs to encourage its characters and readers to cultivate a bond of sympathy which can prolong the community and protect its members from sin.

In the final chapter of the novel, titled "Concluding Remarks," we read the novel's most consolidated statement on apocalyptic sentimentalism. The governing question of the narrative vis-à-vis slavery is recast one last time—"what can any individual do?"—and the novel's response is unequivocal: "they can see to it that *they feel right*. An atmosphere of sympathetic influence encircles every human being; and the man or woman who *feels* strongly, healthily and justly, on the great interests of humanity, is a constant benefactor to the human race. See, then, to your sympathies in this matter!" (*U* 632; original emphases). In this final imploration, the novel emphatically underscores the necessity of "right feeling" if the nation is going to expiate its sins. Proper atonement requires that one's sympathies be "in harmony with the sympathies of Christ" (632).

If feeling right were simply a matter of feeling love—if, in other words, all communities were like the Hallidays' Quaker household, perfect in their compassion for slaves—then Stowe could stop here, for threats of God's vengeance would be superfluous. The Hallidays, however, are the standard against which all other communities come up short. Stowe must turn, then, one final time to the threat of Christ's retribution, for if the nation does not attend to its sympathies, it "will have reason to tremble, when it remembers that the fate of nations is in the hands of One who is very pitiful, and of tender compassion" (*U* 633). Americans live "in an age of the world when nations are trembling and convulsed," and one must wonder, "is America safe?" For "[every] nation that carries in its bosom great and unredressed injustice has in it the elements of this last convulsion" (636). And this "last convulsion" is a dreadful one, indeed: "'for that day shall burn as an oven: and he shall appear as a swift witness against those that oppress the hireling in his wages, the widow and the fatherless, and that *turn aside the stranger in his right:* and he shall break in pieces the oppressor'" (637; original emphasis). That such a conclusive warning should come immediately after Stowe encourages her readers to see to it that they feel right suggests that sympathy has power in the novel but may not be the source of its own power. The apocalypse, rather, provides the foundation on which sympathetic love rests. If hearts cannot be softened by the sorrows of the slave, perhaps they can be provoked by the fear of suffering God's wrath. "Nothing," Stowe observes, "in human language can be conceived more terrible than these last denunciations of the rejected Lord and Lover of the chosen race."[23] Sentimentalism as it is represented here is structured by the co-relation of love and fear; feeling right means feeling both emotions equally. Indeed, to have sympathies that are in harmony with Christ's, readers must first appreciate that the Christ of *Uncle Tom's Cabin* is the Christ of the Gospels *and* the book of Revelation; he is simultaneously a god of love *and* vengeance, mercy *and* retribution. Just as these two dimensions exist in the Bible, so they appear in Stowe's novel in order to make certain that her readers are adequately afraid, so that they remain thoroughly loving.

This final warning in *Uncle Tom's Cabin* bears a striking resemblance to a sermon delivered by Lyman Beecher titled "A Reformation of Morals Practicable and Indispensable." Beecher, like Stowe, cautions that "it will soon be too late" to satisfactorily reform the national landscape, for "the time is short."[24] He goes on to announce that

> never, since the earth stood, has it been so fearful a thing for nations to fall into the hands of the living God. The day of vengeance is in his heart, the day of judgment has come; the great earthquake which sinks Babylon is shaking the nations, and the waves of the mighty commotion are dashing upon every shore.... Is this a time to run upon his neck and the thick bosses of his buckler, when the nations are drinking blood, and fainting, and passing away in his wrath? Is this a time to throw away the shield of faith when his arrows are drunk with the blood of the slain?[25]

In the final gesture of this paradigmatic sentimental novel, Stowe turns not just to apocalyptic vengeance but to one of the earliest "sources" of her faith: her father, the figure from whom she is allegedly distancing herself and who symbolizes a sterner theological system of an earlier time. If last words matter, then it is significant that in the final words of *Uncle Tom's Cabin*, Lyman Beecher is brought to bear on the sentimental aesthetic of the novel, and Calvinism is given a privileged place within the account of sentimentality this book articulates, suggesting, once again, that Stowe's theory of the sentimental does not work in contrast with Calvinist notions of vengeance and wrath but rather requires such notions—set within a new framework—for its very intelligibility.

Colonization and Apocalyptic Sentimentalism

The sentimental structure of *Uncle Tom's Cabin*, based on the mutually reinforcing emotional economies of sympathetic love and fear, has larger implications in terms of how Stowe aims to "resolve" America's slavery dilemma. In an especially salient passage in the novel that prefigures her dramatic turn away from America and toward Africa as God's chosen nation, Stowe writes:

> If ever Africa shall show an elevated and cultivated race,—and come it must, some time, her turn to figure in the great drama of human improvement,—life will awake there with a gorgeousness and splendor of which our cold western tribes faintly have conceived; ... and the Negro race, no longer despised and trodden down, will, perhaps, show forth some of the latest and most magnificent revelations of human life.... In all these they will exhibit the highest form of the peculiarly *Christian life*, and, perhaps, as God chasteneth whom he loveth, he hath chosen poor Africa in the furnace of affliction, to make her *the highest and noblest in that kingdom which he will set up*, when every other kingdom has been tried, and failed; for the first shall be last, and the last first. (*U* 256–57; second emphasis mine)

This formulation illustrates how the novel's eschatology posits Africa as the world's next covenantal nation, one whose greatness will reach its culmination when Christ installs his kingdom on earth. All nations that were once charged with the colossal task of establishing the New Jerusalem have failed, explains Stowe, and now it is Africa's turn to take center stage in this drama of providential history. The installation of Christ's kingdom is precisely the apocalyptic event that readers must take seriously, for within the novel's account of a divinely ordered existence, the apocalypse is a central organizing principle, one that marks humanity's liberation from sin and the establishment of a righteous order. The Christianization of Africa, in other words, becomes a powerful sign of the impending apocalypse. Stowe advocates colonization not because she necessarily desires monochromatic national spaces (even if this ends up being the unfortunate consequence), as many readers have suggested, but because the conversion of Africans that follows colonization is the primary signal that the apocalypse will soon arrive. *Uncle Tom's Cabin* asserts that the successful conversion of blacks is what will set in motion the second coming of Christ, and within this religious vision, members of the Church of Christ in England, America, and Europe, as well as in Africa and elsewhere, are brought to judgment. For Stowe, the drama of history comes to an end with Christ's reign on earth, as the righteous of all nations achieve everlasting life and the unregenerate suffer eternal damnation. The surviving black characters who leave America to work as missionaries in Africa do so in order to prepare for and even to set in motion events that will lead to the apocalyptic dénouement of history.

Because the religious logic of the novel maintains that the apocalypse follows the successful Christianization of Negroes, *Uncle Tom's Cabin* spends considerable time elaborating the importance of conversion for its black characters, and apocalyptic sentimentalism is designed to facilitate such a conversion. Indeed, the emotionality of *Uncle Tom's Cabin* is, in the short term, meant to inspire white readers to reform their hearts and learn to love and work to free black slaves. In the long term, however, the aim of apocalyptic sentimentalism is, for Stowe, to save souls and guarantee everlasting life by nurturing in all readers an inviolable Christian faith. And Stowe suggests that it is when Negroes become fully Christian that Christ will install his earthly kingdom, an event to which all faithful Christians can look forward.

The most famous discourse on conversion in the narrative comes, of course, from Eva. Wondering whether there is "any way to have all slaves made free?" (*U* 393), Eva suggests that salvation, not abolition, is the chief vehicle for slaves to achieve emancipation. And in order to guarantee the freedom and justice that come with everlasting life with God, these slaves must embrace Christianity. On her deathbed, she gathers together Augustine St. Clare's slaves for one final sermon. "I want to speak to you about your souls," she says. "Many of you, I am afraid, are very careless. You are thinking only about this world. I want you to remember that there is a beautiful world, where Jesus is. I am going there, and you can go there. It is for you, as much as me.... Try all to do the best you can; pray every day; ask Him to help you, and get the Bible read to you whenever you can; and I think I shall see you all in heaven" (410–11). In her last moments on earth, Eva asks these slaves to consider the state of their souls rather than the status of their enslaved bodies. The concern that is foremost on her mind as she prepares for her own death is whether or not her father's slaves will achieve everlasting life with her in a multiracial heaven.

Many slaves who are not present to hear Eva's sermon nevertheless possess a proper sentimental sensibility, so much so that they begin to desire their own apocalyptic finales because they know that the apocalypse brings everlasting life for devout followers of Christ. When Master George reads from the book of Revelation to the slaves in Tom's cabin, for instance, he is repeatedly "interrupted by such exclamations as 'The *sakes* now!' 'Only hear that!' 'Jest think on't!' 'Is all that a comin' sure enough?'" (*U* 43). These slaves welcome Christ's second coming because his return will deliver them from worldly bondage. Unlike the trader who must dread apocalyptic death, slaves look forward to it because they will be granted God's grace. They even sing the praises of the apocalypse: "O, I'm going to glory,—won't you come along with me? / Don't you see the angels beck'ning, and a calling me away? / Don't you see the golden city and the everlasting day?" (42). Within the religious framework of *Uncle Tom's Cabin*, it is the apocalypse that guarantees freedom and justice for these slaves and ensures their triumph over earthly oppression. This example of slaves eagerly anticipating Christ's second coming as an event that will deliver them from bondage also suggests that not all religious works in this period adhere exclusively to either a premillennial or postmillennial model. When Stowe needs to engage an unsympathetic character or reader in order to incite a change in heart, she often represents God's judgment within a premillennialist framework, underscoring his punishing wrath. Confirming, as she does in the above example, the slaves' righteousness and inevitable salvation requires that Stowe deploy a postmillennial discourse, one that rewards religious devotion and guarantees everlasting life.[26]

The Christianization of George Harris exemplifies the sentimental realignment that is such a central part of the novel's eschatological design. As he plans his escape to the North, Eliza enjoins him to place his trust in God. "I an't a Christian like you, Eliza," Harris replies, "I can't trust in God" (*U* 26). Harris loves his wife but his love is not situated within the necessary religious framework to ensure his salvation. By the end of the narrative, however, we discover that he plans to emigrate to Liberia and learn that he has accepted Christianity. It is Eliza whose "gentler spirit ever restores" him and keeps before his eyes "the Christian calling and mission of our race" (617). Now that he is a Christian, Harris can recognize that the "development of Africa is to be essentially a Christian one" (616). Not only does he acknowledge that Africa is meant to be a Christian continent, but he also remarks that Africans are destined to inherit God's kingdom. "As a Christian," he says, "I look for another era to arise" that will supplant the Anglo-Saxon era that has gone before. "On its borders I trust we stand; and the throes that now convulse the nations are, to my hope, but the birthpangs of an hour of universal peace and brotherhood" (616). Echoing the apocalyptic language of Lyman Beecher, who sermonized that the "great earthquake" is "shaking the nations" (10), and prefiguring the novel's concluding jeremiad, when Stowe herself warns that America is living in an age "when nations are trembling and convulsed," George Harris is signaling that the apocalypse—the triumphal fulfillment of history—is fast approaching. The hour of universal peace and brotherhood that Harris prophesies is also the event that begins when Christ installs his heavenly kingdom on earth. The novel locates this kingdom not in England, and certainly not in America, but in Africa.

At the conclusion of the narrative, we witness all the major living black characters leaving America to work as missionaries in Africa. The problem, as Timothy Powell explains, is that the conclusion of *Uncle Tom's Cabin* "reads like the literary realization of the American Colonization Society's mission to 'promote and execute a plan for colonizing . . . the free people of color residing in [America to] Africa.'" "Given the racist subtext of so much of ACS rhetoric," Powell continues, "it must be asked whether part of the 'cultural work' of [*Uncle Tom's Cabin*] is to enact the discursive exile of the free black community from the United States."[27] Shirley Samuels holds a related view, arguing that Stowe "cannot imagine a nation *not* based on race." Stowe's understanding of national belonging is thoroughly racialized, a view that many antebellum Americans held; thus, her black characters must return to Africa so that national spaces can be consolidated along racial lines.[28] Richard Yarborough perhaps best sums up scholarly frustration with Stowe's ending: "Stowe's tragic failure of imagination," says Yarborough, "prevented her from envisioning blacks (free or slave, mulatto or full-blood) as viable members of American society, so she deports the most aggressive, intelligent, 'acceptable' ones to Africa to fill the same role there that she assigns to women in the United States."[29] Amy Kaplan takes Yarborough's argument one step further, insisting that "[t]he idea of African colonization does not simply emerge at the end as a racist failure of Stowe's political imagination; rather, colonization underwrites the racial politics of the domestic imagination." *Uncle Tom's Cabin*, in Kaplan's view, is implicated in and motivated by America's expansionist impulses, illustrating how the nation's imagined home fronts were "intimately bound" to the ideological administrations of empire.[30]

Critical objections to the ending of *Uncle Tom's Cabin* have been powerful precisely because colonization appears to violate the fundamental tenets of justice that the Constitution and Declaration of Independence are supposed to uphold, tenets that recognize the inherent worth and natural equality of each human being. For Stowe, however, the proper function of colonization far eclipses the consequences of its apparently racist underpinnings; while colonization might facilitate the formation of racially homogenous nations, this is a side effect of what Stowe perceives to be colonization's much more primary and urgent purpose. Namely, colonization is, first and foremost, a necessary step in hastening the end of days; the conversion of Africa is the final stage in the unfolding of providential history, and once Negroes are fully Christianized,

God will return in all his majesty. Stowe sends missionaries in order to promote the conversion of Africa, and she epitomizes the urgency of black conversion by dramatically rendering Africa's place within the teleology and fulfillment of God's divine design. As the narrative voice apostrophizes, "And this, oh Africa! latest called of nations,—called to the crown of thorns, the scourge, the bloody sweat, the cross of agony,—this is to be *thy* victory; *by this shalt thou reign with Christ when his kingdom shall come on earth*" (*U* 564; second emphasis mine). It is the moment when Christ erects his earthly kingdom that the novel enthusiastically presages. And when the kingdom of Christ comes—when the apocalypse, which has until now remained imminent, finally arrives—Africa, the next great covenantal nation, will be prepared to receive it. Within the framework of apocalyptic sentimentalism, colonization is the process by which Africa's status as the world's next great Christian land is firmly secured.

This analysis of the novel's colonizationist ending reconceives many of the critical readings of Stowe's solution to slavery, readings that invariably malign Stowe for her perceived inability or flagrant unwillingness to incorporate blacks as political subjects. Because contemporary readers do not share many of the racist assumptions that prevented nineteenth-century Americans from imagining a racially integrated nation, the ending of *Uncle Tom's Cabin* and its promotion of black emigration appear troubling at best, shortsighted and racist at worst. It is true that Stowe problematically assumes Africa to be a continent of heathens in need of Christianity. And while she understood the conversion of Africa to be a sign of the second coming of Christ, Stowe does not portray whites engaging in missionary work in Africa, leading to a troubling racial homogeneity within the geographical spaces of America and Africa. Stowe, however, sends exclusively black missionaries to Africa rather than white ones because Africa is where Negroes (both native Africans and former black slaves from America) will fulfill their covenantal obligations. The Negro's "place," Stowe suggests, is not in America because America is no longer a divinely commissioned nation. Because *Uncle Tom's Cabin* is a conversion narrative that is principally about saving souls and readying Christians for the forthcoming apocalypse, Stowe inscribes colonization as not only *a* viable option for American slaves, but *the* option. For Stowe, there is nothing politically regressive about being chosen by God to inherit the earth (even if contemporary scholars do not share this view). From her Christian point of view, in fact, this is the most radical antislavery gesture of all. Rather than offering a secular political program for achieving justice that involves integrating ex-slaves into a corrupt nation and providing them full status as citizens, the novel posits them as God's elect. Stowe's religious worldview and her antislavery politics are imbricated, and while scholars may be justified in deriding Stowe for the way her novel ends, they nonetheless minimize this very important point. Justice for Stowe is not the worldly justice of liberal citizenship, nor is it being imbued with certain inalienable rights. It is eternal life with God.[31]

George Fredrickson speaks for many critics when he disparages Stowe's religious perspective as "romantic racialism," which he defines as "an image of the Negro that could be construed as flattering or laudatory in the context of some currently accepted ideals of human behavior and sensibility."[32] But this perspective only appears "romantic" if it is viewed with our contemporary liberal sensibility. Fredrickson's account, and others like it, tend to discount just how vital a role apocalypticism played in shaping Stowe's response to slavery specifically and the novel's understanding of politics more generally. Providential history is Stowe's master narrative, one that subsumes and supersedes all earthly and finite concerns, and the apocalypse is its central figure. Readers of Stowe consistently eschew the fact that the style of Christianity she embodies expects to see history fulfill itself in a blaze of apocalyptic glory. The abolition of slavery, the reorganization of the domestic space, the triumph of emotion over reason—these are all secondary concerns within the novel's messianic vision, epiphenomena to the phenomenon of the apocalypse, the event that marks the fulfillment of time and the end of injustice, when all will bear witness to a new heaven and a new earth. For Stowe, justice only becomes possible when it is divinely ordained, with Christ separating the righteous from the unrighteous, the wheat from the chaff. And within the hierarchy of the Christian church, Africa finds itself above all other nations, like England and America, that were once favored by God but have since failed to uphold their covenantal obligations. Stowe looks away from England, away from America, to find the next city on the hill, one that has yet to sin against God and that possesses the requisite virtue to shoulder the burden that comes with being a covenantal nation. She locates this city in what would have been for many readers the most unlikely of places. When Africa is successfully converted from a land of heathens to one of Christian faith, Stowe posits that this transformation will form the bedrock of Christ's church and will signal to the rest of the world to make preparations, for the apocalypse is at hand.

Apocalyptic Implications

Stowe's sentimentalism, with the mutually reinforcing affects of sympathetic love and fear, is not intended to distract readers from political realities or to create, through the "ostentatious parading of excessive and spurious emotion," as James Baldwin put it, a distorted portrait of the world they inhabit.[33] Rather, Stowe attempts to intensify her readers' experience of their social context, to bring into focus what might otherwise be vague or lack urgency, like the nation's response to slavery. Apocalyptic sentimentalism facilitates a critical engagement with America's moral shortcomings through the interplay of what for Stowe constituted the two fundamental emotional economies of human experience. This antislavery approach is no doubt informed by her reading of the Scottish Enlightenment and by sympathy's place within that philosophical system. And the legacy of Lyman Beecher's strict Calvinism lingers in Stowe's sentimental imagination, at least as it expresses itself in some of the early antislavery fiction she produces before the Civil War. Stowe's sentimental rhetoric, however, also displays traces of the antislavery approach marshaled by writers like David Walker and Maria Stewart. Indeed, the structure of sentiment in *Uncle Tom's Cabin* more closely resembles early black apocalyptic discourse than it does the Scottish Enlightenment or even the Protestant sermon. Whether or not Stowe read Walker or Stewart is less important than the fact that the discursive mode represented in Walker's *Appeal* and Stewart's lectures is part of an ever-expanding tradition that Stowe inherits and integrates into an antislavery sentimental aesthetic.

I have read *Uncle Tom's Cabin* in this chapter with a very specific goal in mind: to revise prevailing accounts of the novel's sentimental logic in order to amend how we think about Stowe's antislavery corpus as well as the larger culture of sentiment of which Stowe is part. If critics are going to continue to assert that Harriet Beecher Stowe is the representative author of nineteenth-century sentimentalism (and they should, because she is), they must discuss love and terror—that is, the primary emotional economies of her antislavery narratives—not as discrete and fundamentally oppositional formations but as an inseparable ensemble. Indeed, the novel was an extraordinary success and best-seller, I am arguing, precisely because of the apocalyptic tenor of the narrative. And its success is a sign of the way terror in the antebellum period was being generated from within forms of entertainment that antebellum audiences were eager to consume.

CHAPTER 4

"Can Fear of Fire Make Me Love?"

Dred *and the Incarnation of Apocalypse*

> It is remarkable that, in all ages, communities and individuals who have suffered under oppression have always fled for refuge to the Old Testament, and to the book of Revelation in the New.
> —Harriet Beecher Stowe, Dred: A Tale of the Great Dismal Swamp, *1856*

Shortly before one of the climatic scenes in *Uncle Tom's Cabin*—in which Tom receives a particularly severe beating at the hands of Simon Legree, a beating, in fact, that will end his life—readers are reassured that Tom's unshakable Christian faith will allow him to withstand the repeated blows of his master. They learn that "an inviolable sphere of peace encompassed the lowly heart of the oppressed one,—an ever present Saviour hallowed it as a temple," suggesting that Tom's spiritual well-being is protected, despite the pain he is about to feel in his body. "Past now the bleeding of earthly regrets; past its fluctuations of hope, and fear, and desire; the human will, bent, and bleeding, and struggling long, was now entirely merged in the Divine." Tom's former attachment to the material world is superseded by a newly established spiritual life, one that is indistinguishable from the Divine, thus ensuring that "life's uttermost woes fell from him unharming." Following this description, we learn that when Legree finally does beat Tom, "the blows fell now only on the outer man, and not, as before, on the heart."[1]

This account, though meant to highlight Tom's holiness, is nevertheless troubling for the way it subordinates Tom's material body as an unessential characteristic of his existence. Stowe, in trying to imagine a righteous slave empowered by his Christian faith, creates a strange scenario in which such a characterization leads her to minimize a slave's bodily existence, despite the fact that a slave's suffering was fundamentally an embodied reality. So incongruous is Stowe's construction of this scene that moments before he dies, Tom says to Master George Shelby, "[Legree] an't done me no real harm,—only opened the gate of the kingdom for me; that's all!" (*U* 595).[2] The brutal violence inflicted on Tom, while being a sure sign of slavery's wickedness, is also what ultimately hastens Tom's attainment of everlasting life. Passages like this are emblematic of a larger problem Stowe repeatedly encounters: the tension between religious orthodoxy's focus on the soul at the expense of the body, and the bodily suffering that is inherent to slavery, the representation of which seems key to producing sentimental reactions. Stowe's eschatology, while a powerful organizing force within *Uncle Tom's Cabin*'s antislavery sentimentality, is nevertheless limited insofar as it promotes the removal of the novel's major black characters in the service of fulfilling the larger religious mission to which Stowe's fiction remains ardently dedicated. George Harris, for example, returns to Africa to ensure it develops as a Christian land, and Africa's Christianization will, according to the novel's soteriology, lead to the second coming of Christ. And Tom—the very emblem of Christian devotion—must die in order to be free, and he does so willingly, even gratefully, in order to illustrate for Stowe's readers that true freedom is not worldly freedom but eternal life with God. What the novel stresses as possible strengths of George and Tom, many of her readers saw and see as severe limits. Rather than shaping a more inclusive and democratic national landscape in America, these characters are expelled from it instead.

In this chapter, I examine Stowe's second antislavery novel, *Dred* (1856), for the way she once again uses religious ideas to construct her black male protagonist, but this time to compensate for and correct some of the limitations I outline above. Whereas in *Uncle Tom's Cabin*, Tom expresses his religious faith through absolute servility, putting up no resistance to the overbearing slaveholder and instead accepting with unshakable Christian humility the trials God puts before him, in *Dred*, Stowe's male protagonist is a fully embodied presence prepared to confront slavery with the force of God's wrath. Stowe enacts this revision by taking a religious category that is essential to *Uncle Tom's Cabin*—the apocalypse—and reinscribing it within the black male body of her eponymous hero. What is initially a transcendental concept now has material reality in the form of Dred's physical presence in the Great Dismal Swamp of North Carolina. By incarnating the logic of apocalyptic prophecy in the black male figure, Stowe continues to rely on a religious notion to construct her protagonist, but with significant revision, and with different outcomes in mind. Namely, Stowe entertains black violence as a possible strategy for challenging slavery.

Stowe's audacious portrait of Dred is a reflection of a larger concern the novel raises about the representation of slaves within sentimental fiction as well as within the larger antislavery movement. While much of the emphasis within antislavery writing from this period was understandably placed on spotlighting the slave's humanity, so that critics who challenged slavery did so by characterizing the institution as a clear violation of the humanity that inhered in the black self, Stowe's novel expresses anxiety over whether such an approach can be sufficiently persuasive to weaken a practice as firmly embedded as slavery was. Does portraying black humanity, in other words, pose any real threat to slavery? In one important sense, the answer to this question in *Dred* is no. Stowe personifies the slave Harry Gordon, for example, as a representative of nineteenth-century masculine ideals, even as he is confined to the plantation. Harry displays great intelligence, industriousness, an abiding loyalty to family, and moral virtue—features that should make him a deeply sympathetic figure to readers. Rather than demonstrating the power these traits have to confirm Harry's humanity and thus unsettle the assumptions that informed chattel slavery, however, Stowe shows that the features which make Harry a laudable figure are what plantation slavery appropriates and turns against him. Stowe portrays Harry's family origins and his belief in the virtues of earnest labor as the very qualities that further enchain him as a slave when they should instead be clear indications of his right to live freely as a citizen within a democratic society. It is, I argue, precisely because familiar nineteenth-century norms like the ones Harry typifies fail to make the case for his freedom—thus exposing the limits of white sympathy—that Stowe invents Dred as a radical alternative, one that bolsters Harry's emasculated sense of self and whose agency is authorized not according to antebellum norms but by a prophetic calling to bring wrath and woe to the citizens of North Carolina. Stowe constructs Dred as the human incarnation of apocalyptic theology; as such, he poses a legitimate threat to Southern slavery that Harry's humanity never could.

I carefully chart Stowe's dramatic revision of apocalyptic prophecy to map the physical and spiritual topography of her titular character. I elaborate the novel's incarnational logic to show that Dred's personhood exists outside of recognizable nineteenth-century norms, underscoring the weariness Stowe may have felt with simply presenting an abstract notion of "black humanity" to answer slavery's more pernicious accounts of an inherent racial hierarchy.[3] Indeed, Stowe's treatment of theological vengeance in *Dred* is markedly different from its more conventional configuration in *Uncle Tom's Cabin*, where a wrathful God returns to punish those who have sinned against him. In *Dred*, the power of apocalyptic retribution is imbued in Dred; his physical presence in the swamp and his fiery speech work together to generate a whole new category of rebellious agent, one who seeks neither revolutionary transformation nor the acquisition of an autonomous will, but instead prepares to rain fire and brimstone upon slaveholding Southerners. This radical representation of Dred's messianic power, however, while exposing the limits and limitations of normative categories of the self, nevertheless endangers one of the major outcomes the novel aspires to imagine: a multiracial democratic society. Given Stowe's incendiary portrait of Dred and her commitment to democratic ideals, the novel raises the important question of whether or not a democracy can be achieved through acts of rebellious vengeance.

I explore Stowe's commitment to democratic principles in *Dred* by contrasting it with the premier antebellum jeremiad against vengeance: *Moby-Dick*. While both novels foreground protagonists who are motivated by vengeance, I demonstrate how Ahab's desire for vengeance against the white whale, rather than expanding democratic possibilities, ultimately destroys them instead. Conversely, Dred's ideas concerning vengeance end up being essential to how Stowe envisions a multiracial democracy. Indeed, not only do I illustrate in this section how Stowe's handling of Dred within the novel creates the possibility of a democracy to flourish, I also clarify how Stowe fashions Dred as a deeply sentimental character and an essential part of the novel's sentimental antislavery politics.

Slave Humanity and the Problem of Black Masculine Authority

If slavery is predicated on a logic of racial difference that understands African-descended persons to be innately inferior to Anglo-Europeans and therefore suited for enslavement, then part of the work of antislavery fiction begins with identifying the illogic in this premise and reconceiving black slaves as something other than a degraded set of beings. What made *Uncle Tom's Cabin* such a revolutionary novel was the way it challenged many of the assumptions held by white Americans about black inferiority. And yet, as I have suggested (and other scholars have illustrated in convincing detail), Stowe at times reenergizes some of these assumptions and ultimately draws some unsettling conclusions about black freedom, which she locates either in Africa or the afterlife. Given these unsatisfying resolutions in *Uncle Tom's Cabin*, one of the principal challenges for Stowe in *Dred* is in constructing slave characters who possess the kind of authority that cannot be undermined or co-opted by slavery and who, as a result of their various virtues, can be incorporated into the national imagined community. Writers working within the sentimental tradition commonly responded to this dilemma by generating slave characters who embody many of the traits privileged within liberal democratic society, confirming for readers that black Americans exemplify the features that white Americans cherish and thus are appropriate candidates for freedom and full citizenship. Given the sentimental aims of *Uncle Tom's Cabin*, it would seem that in *Dred*, Stowe would simply continue, in Philip Fisher's terms, to ascribe "full and complete humanity to classes of figures from whom it has been socially withheld."[4] That is, Stowe merely needs to produce a convincing enough portrait of the slave's humanity to persuade readers that slavery is a genuinely immoral institution.

Dred, however, questions whether the presentation of a slave with "full and complete humanity" is, in fact, a useful strategy to overturn long-established and deeply entrenched racial hierarchies. Indeed, at a moment when many antislavery reformers believed that slavery was attributable, in part, to a fundamental misrepresentation of blacks as inferior, arguing instead that blacks actually shared common traits and thus a common humanity with whites and therefore should be free, there exists in *Dred* an abiding uncertainty about whether depicting slaves according to dominant (and therefore white) norms will persuade readers that these persons should be integrated into democratic society. As much as Stowe aims in *Dred* to revise the imaginative shortcomings of *Uncle Tom's Cabin*, she nevertheless dramatizes how the norms privileged within white middle-class culture do not easily translate to the plantation, where they are inevitably perverted by slavery. Stowe's novel offers a powerful critique of antislavery strategies that insisted on a common humanity to achieve democratic ends, a strategy, that is, that depended on white sympathy at a moment when white sympathy was difficult to arouse. Because the notion of a shared humanity does little to improve the conditions for plantation slaves, the invention of Dred becomes necessary.

Before turning to Dred, I want to look in some detail at Stowe's depiction of Harry Gordon for how he embodies normative masculine attributes as well as how slavery undermines and even co-opts these attributes, so that Harry comes to support the very institution from which he is trying to free himself and his family. One of the most effective strategies Stowe initially uses to establish the personhood of Harry and the potential symmetries between white and black Americans is her representation of Harry's blood. Harry shares a bloodline with the Gordon family, a significant detail, given how a rhetoric of blood was deployed in the 1840s and 1850s to mark and naturalize racial boundaries and to bolster the notion of innate racial difference. For many engaged in early racialist debates, and especially for proponents of slavery, blood legitimized racial hierarchy. Leading intellectuals like Samuel Morton, George Gliddon, Josiah Nott, and, later, the Swiss biologist Louis Agassiz, who immigrated to the United States in 1846, used their latest scientific findings to, in George Fredrickson's words, "convince educated Americans that the Negro was not a blood brother to the whites."[5] Indeed, in the antebellum period, blood was commonly used as shorthand for marking racial essences. Somewhat surprisingly, then, Stowe depends on this logic to characterize Harry, whose identity can be traced internally to his amalgamated blood, which flows partly from his black mother and partly from his white master.[6]

Even as Stowe deploys a discourse of blood to reveal Harry's essential nature, she flips the prevailing logic by showing that Harry's amalgamated blood is one of the principal sources of his elevated status. Stowe, for example, draws Harry as an independent, self-reliant, caring sibling and husband and dedicated worker in order to allay and perhaps even counter cultural anxieties about miscegenation. What she only implied with George and Eliza Harris in *Uncle Tom's Cabin*, she states more deliberately with Harry: that is, mixed blood is not intellectually and morally debilitating, as many Americans believed; rather, as we see with Harry, it might even be the source of his superior character. By showing that Harry was born to parents of different races, and that amalgamated blood spurs rather than impedes Harry's growth, Stowe challenges the opinion that hybridized blood would ultimately lead to a degeneration of the human species.[7] As Werner Sollors explains, "In the nineteenth and the first half of the twentieth century the belief that Mulattoes were 'feeble' or unable to procreate among themselves, or that their children would be impaired in fertility, had so much political, scientific, and general intellectual support that it may be called the 'dominant opinion' of the period."[8] In opposition to this view, Stowe demonstrates that the only real difference between Harry and his white (nonslave) siblings is Harry's status as a slave. It is slavery that identifies Harry as "inferior" and thus prevents his being seen as exemplifying all the norms that white middle-class Americans ostensibly privilege (even surpassing his siblings, given Nina Gordon's initial self-indulgences and Tom Gordon's depraved moral character), not some biological debility stemming from bad blood.

Describing Harry's character as a product of his hematological composition, Stowe writes: "Harry was the son of his master, and inherited much of the temper and constitution of his father, tempered by the soft and genial temperament of the beautiful Eboe mulattress who was his mother."[9] Harry's talents and rational mind stem from his Anglo-Saxon lineage; his warmth and compassion—his sentimental side—he inherits from his African mother. Stowe depends on and deploys established gender stereotypes to make racialist claims about Harry. In Stowe's imagination, Harry's amalgamated blood creates in him a perfect blend of Western rationalism and African affection; his head and heart harmonize Harry into a full person. In addition to being well educated, Harry "had also accompanied his master as valet during the tour of Europe, and thus his opportunities of general observation had been still further enlarged, and that tact by which *those of the mixed blood* seem so peculiarly fitted to appreciate all the finer aspects of conventional life, had been called out and exercised" (38; emphasis mine). Because of his mixed blood, Stowe maintains, Harry's cosmopolitanism can be taken seriously by readers; his Anglo-Saxon and African origins make him intellectually receptive and emotionally sensitive to high culture, and thus mark him as a recognizable—and even ideal—person according to prevailing post-Enlightenment standards. Indeed, his blood and his uncommon rearing would make it "difficult in any circle to meet with a more agreeable and gentlemanly person" (38). With the exception of his skin color, Harry exemplifies all the characteristics that are regarded among cultured (white) individuals as signs of sophistication. Stowe depicts this equivalency between white and black identity to illustrate that possessing black blood does not disqualify one from the kingdom of culture but might make one better suited to be a coworker within it.[10] Ironically, then, it is Harry's refinement that persuades Colonel Gordon to keep Harry, his son, a slave. "A man so cultivated, he argued to himself, might find many avenues opened to him in freedom; might be tempted to leave the estate to other hands, and seek his own fortune" (38). Colonel Gordon recognizes what most white Americans would have rather repressed: that though he is legally a slave, Harry possesses enough talent to be capable of succeeding as a free man. Because Colonel Gordon does not want to lose Harry's services, however, especially for Nina's sake, he "resolved to leave him bound by an indissoluble tie for a term of years, trusting to his attachment to Nina to make this service tolerable" (38). And this indissoluble tie is the knowledge of his blood relation to Nina, his half-sister, which Colonel Gordon discloses to Harry before he dies. Blood unassailably binds Harry to Nina like few things could.

While blood suggests a biological filiation between slave and slaveholder, its power to equalize racial difference is appropriated and used against Harry to fasten him more firmly to the plantation. No sooner does Stowe introduce this structure of equivalence through blood than she exposes its fault lines. Harry's blood ultimately does nothing to challenge his status as a slave or change how he is perceived by white culture (many of whose members suspect he is a Gordon because of his physical resemblance to his master). Worse still, Harry Gordon's bloodline is at the root of his loyalty to Nina, who does not know she is a half-sibling to Harry and whom Harry feels obligated to look after because she is a blood relative. The Anglo-Saxon component of his amalgamated blood, rather than unsettling the racial hierarchy that structures the Gordon family, instead is an additional link in the manacle that binds Harry to Nina. And when Nina inadvertently questions Harry's love for her, Harry responds by saying, "Love you? You have always held my heart in your hand! That has been the clasp upon my chain! If it hadn't been for you, I should have fought my way to the north before now, or I would have found a grave on the road!" (*D* 146). Harry's sentimental regard for Nina, itself an alleged expression of his African blood (which is responsible for his "soft and genial temperament"), ends up being an impediment to freedom in addition to a sign of his virtue. Harry's love for his half-sister is assimilated by slavery and reconstituted as a supplemental piece of property that Nina possesses, ensuring Harry's enslaved status.

As implausible as it may be, even in a work of fiction, that a slave would demonstrate such fidelity to a sibling who owns him as property and who is unaware of her blood ties to him, Stowe uses Harry's dedication to Nina to imbue him with humanizing attributes and to cast him as a highly sympathetic character for the novel's readers.[11] Given the symbolic power of family ties within the larger culture of sentiment, Stowe presents Harry as unfailingly family oriented to shore up his admirable character. Because of his dedication to family, in fact, Harry decides to labor tirelessly for Nina when she encounters serious financial trouble. While modern readers might mistake Harry's misguided efforts as merely a superficial sign of his industriousness, nineteenth-century readers would have seen Harry as epitomizing the linked ideologies of hard work and free labor that were prominent, particularly in Northeastern states, during the latter part of the antebellum period. Though a cliché now, what we call "work ethic" powerfully informed how Americans in the late antebellum period understood the meaning of labor before the rise of industrial capitalism. For many, work constituted a virtuous act; the toil of the farmer, artisan, or merchant had a moral dimension, and this view would carry through to the end of the century and beyond. As Emerson declared in 1862, "a man coins himself into his labor; turns his day, his strength, his thought, his affection into some product which remains as the visible sign of his power."[12] To work was to imprint one's autonomy onto the world. It was a sign of one's independence and a manifestation of one's high moral standards. As Daniel Rodgers has succinctly put it, "To doubt the moral preeminence of work" during the antebellum period "was the act of a conscious heretic."[13] These assumptions surrounding the work ethic intersected with the free-labor ideologies that were circulating in mostly Northern states in the 1850s, so that "the dignity of labor" remained "a constant theme of antebellum northern culture and politics."[14] Such notions about the natural right of free labor formed an ideological foundation for the bourgeoning Republican Party, prompting William Evarts to announce: "Labor, gentlemen, we of the free States acknowledge to be the source of all our wealth, of all our progress, of all our dignity and value."[15]

That an act of labor could create value and was so often seen by nineteenth-century Americans as a source and sign of personal independence were ideas that resonated with Stowe, who often reflected on the need for meaningful labor in her fiction.[16] In *Dred*, she uses Harry's dedicated labor as a sign of his inherent dignity. If work is a sacred act because it "uncovers the soul of the worker," then Stowe's emphasis on Harry's labor is meant to reveal the truth about who he is.[17] Harry's propensity for hard work, in other words, communicates to the reader that he is more than just a slave. When Lisette, Harry's wife, asks him what he plans to do to resolve Nina's financial woes, Harry responds by saying, "I shall have to do what I've done two or three times before—take the money that I have saved, to pay these bills—our freedom-money, Lisette" (*D* 60).

Harry privileges Nina's economic security over his and Lisette's independence, so much so that he would sacrifice his own earnings to pay Nina's debts, something he has done several times already. Harry's selflessness is matched by Lisette's, who supports Harry's decision, saying, "O, well, then, don't worry! We can get it again, you know. Why, you know, Harry, you can make a good deal with your trade ... as for me, why, you know, my ironing, and my muslins, how celebrated they are. Come, don't worry one bit; we shall get on nicely" (60). The loyalty Harry and Lisette display toward Nina conveys two points at once. First, it demonstrates that slaves possess a selfless generosity that even slavery cannot expunge, making them potential candidates for civic membership. Second, this exchange underscores the resourcefulness of many slaves, like Harry and Lisette, who are confident they can recuperate their losses because they possess skills that the marketplace demands.[18]

Even as Stowe attempts to underscore the inherent loyalty and independence of Harry and Lisette, the scenario in which these characters find themselves further reveals the limited strategies of representation available to a white antislavery writer like Stowe who tries to reimagine black identity as something other than degraded or fundamentally different from white identity. Stowe constructs a multidimensional portrait of Harry and Lisette—only to show that their industriousness, generosity, and compassion, while commendable, do not alter their positions as slaves or pose any real danger to slavery. Importing the virtues of Northern labor and assigning them to plantation slaves neither extricates these slaves from their context nor transforms them from property into persons; indeed, Stowe's portrait of Harry and Lisette ends up emphasizing their unfailing loyalty to their masters—a peculiar relation indeed given that Stowe's ultimate aim is to make a case for black independence. In light of Nina's financial troubles, for instance, Harry worries about what might happen were Nina to take a husband. "I've seen trouble enough coming of marriages," Harry explains to Lisette, "and I was hoping, you see, that before that time came the money for my freedom would all be paid in, and I should be my own man" (*D* 60). Harry seeks financial independence so that he can purchase his freedom, but his loyalty to Nina and his concern for her financial situation frustrate his aspirations. "Just as the sum is almost made up," laments Harry, "I must pay out five hundred dollars of it, and that throws us back two or three years longer" (60). Harry might embody the dedication and industry of a Northern free laborer at a moment in antebellum history when free labor was a central part of the political and cultural discourse among many Northerners, but it is precisely these traits that lead him to sacrifice his own freedom for the long-term safety and comfort of his sister/mistress. "I was trusted with it," Harry says, referring to Nina's estate, "and trusted with her. She never has known, more than a child, where the money came from, or went to; and it shan't be said that I've brought the estate in debt, for the sake of getting my own liberty. *If I have one pride in life, it is to give it up to Miss Nina's husband in good order*" (63; emphasis mine). Harry's work ethic and commitment to family produce a fealty that makes him loyal not to himself or his wife but to slavery and to Nina (and her future husband). His financial contribution to cover Nina's debts leads Harry to collude in his own enslavement.[19]

Because defenders of slavery often enlisted a discourse of kinship to show that slavery was principally a familial institution in which slaves were cared for as members of the family, Stowe chooses to use the same discourse of family to dispute the so-called paternal benevolence of the plantation.[20] Because Harry is irrevocably tied to his sibling, he is not able to act with full autonomy and a sense of unfettered freedom, so that family in this context becomes another site of enslavement. Despite the way Harry nurtures—and sometimes displays—a sense of independence, the numerous binds in which he finds himself lead to a pervasive sense that he is not, nor will he ever be, fully recognized for the impressive man that he is. Notwithstanding his wish that "I should be my own man" (*D* 60), Harry remains dismayed that his potency as a man is constantly undermined by the realities of slavery: "I come just near enough to the condition of the white to look into it, to enjoy it, and want everything that I see. Then, the way I've been educated makes it worse. The fact is, that when the fathers of such as we feel any love for us, it isn't like the love they have for their white children" (63). Here, Harry recognizes that his identity and experiences are equivalent to those of white Americans. The novel represents the natural similitude between blacks and whites that most white Americans actively denied, suggesting that deep down, beneath shallow racial markers, slaves "look" the same, share the same values, possess the same inherent traits, and so should be treated the same as whites. What Stowe also shows, and what Harry fully appreciates, is that this correspondence might exist as a theory—slaves might embody many of the virtues that Anglo-Saxons claim make them rational and enlightened and thus superior—but chattel slavery prevents such truths from fully materializing or being recognized in black slaves. Stowe constructs a sympathetic slave in Harry, but sympathy only goes so far toward Harry's liberation; he is loved differently than whites, even by his own father. "If we show talent and smartness," says Harry to Lisette, "we hear some one say, aside, 'It's rather a pity, isn't it?' or, 'He is too smart for his place.' Then, we have all the family blood and the family pride; and what to do with it? I feel that I am a Gordon. I feel in my very heart that I'm like Colonel Gordon—I know I am" (*D* 63–64). Slavery violates Harry's deep sense of himself as a person (like the Gordons) deserving of all the civic rights and privileges that autonomous, self-determining beings are eligible to enjoy.

It is primarily with Harry that Stowe's novel highlights slavery's incommensurability with nineteenth-century norms, and it does this in two key ways. First, it demonstrates that as long as slavery exists as an institution, the kinds of virtues exemplified by Harry cannot be fully recognized, no matter how perfectly those virtues are realized in an enslaved person. Harry, then, will remain external to democratic society, even if he perfectly embodies the characteristics that normally entitle one to full participation in civic life as well as state recognition. Second, Stowe's portrait of Harry underscores an imaginative dilemma that is common to her first two antislavery novels. That is, how does Stowe construct a black male slave with whom white Americans will sympathize and whose authority can somehow exceed the constraints and co-optive measures of slavery? In *Uncle Tom's Cabin*, Tom and George Harris were able to "escape," but doing so required their displacement. In *Dred*, Harry privileges labor, has a perfect blend of European and African blood, is intellectually and aesthetically discerning, and has a thoroughly loving heart—that is, he epitomizes ideal white manhood in a post-Enlightenment sentimental culture—and yet he is not permitted to express fully the depths of his manhood and contributes to his own servitude instead. Simply portraying a perfectly constructed and praiseworthy slave, Stowe's novel seems to suggest, is itself not a solution, despite how ardently antislavery thinkers sought to reimagine the most harmful accounts of African and black identity. Harry may have resisted slavery's dehumanizing pressures on him, but what pressures does he put on slavery? He may be fully human, but how is his humanity the answer?

A possible solution to this dilemma is presented during a scene in which Harry laments his emasculated status as a slave. As he struggles in this disempowered state, unable to care for himself or his wife (and failing to protect his sister, Cora, whom Tom Gordon, Nina's brother, is attempting to claim as his slave), Harry concisely expresses what for him is the most debilitating effect of slavery. "I can do nothing!" he says. "I am not even a man!" (*D* 340). It is immediately after Harry utters this statement about slavery undermining his manhood that he encounters Dred, who marshals apocalyptic language to encourage Harry to engage in violent plots of insurrection against the very forces that have unmanned him. "I tell you, Harry," says Dred, "there's a seal been loosed—there's a vial poured out on the air; and the destroying angel standeth over Jerusalem, with his sword drawn" (341). The juxtaposition between Harry and Dred that is established just as Harry raises the problem of his disempowered manhood announces to the reader a new category of black selfhood, one that is meant to compensate for Harry's powerlessness and circumvent the strictures of slavery. With Dred, Stowe presents an alternative form of masculinity whose agency is authorized not according to the prevailing standards of normative manhood (hard work, self-reliance, capacity for reasoned thought, etc.) but by a religious calling to prophesy and help usher in God's apocalyptic vengeance against slaveholders. Dred is the novel's dramatic response to Harry's problem of being an autonomous man within a structure that demands his servility.

Dred and the Making of a New Man

In one of her more provocative descriptions of the animating force behind Dred's rebelliousness, Stowe constructs a scriptural analogy that not only helps explain his violent impulses but also gets at the heart of how readers should understand Dred's interior life. Stowe writes:

> As the mind, looking on the great volume of nature, sees there a reflection of its own internal passions, and seizes on that in it which sympathizes with itself,—as the fierce and savage soul delights in the roar of torrents, the thunder of avalanches, and the whirl of ocean-storms,—so is it in the great answering volume of revelation. There is something there for every phase of man's nature; and hence its endless vitality and stimulating force. Dred had heard read, in the secret meetings of conspirators, the wrathful denunciations of ancient prophets against oppression and injustice. He had read of kingdoms convulsed by plagues; of tempest, and pestilence, and locusts; of the sea cleft in twain, that an army of slaves might pass through, and of their pursuers whelmed in the returning waters. He had heard of prophets and deliverers, armed with supernatural powers, raised up for oppressed people. (*D* 210)

Educated in parables of vengeance, Dred's conception of justice is firmly rooted in biblical narratives where the meek and lowly smite their oppressors and unjust kingdoms are afflicted and toppled to the ground. These numerous tales from Scripture, in which seemingly superior forces of oppression are beaten back and destroyed while the righteous are set free, serve to reinforce Dred's belief that America's slaves will one day be liberated from their subjugated state and slaveholders judged and punished for their transgressions.

As it is configured in this passage, however, vengeance is not simply a form of biblical payback; it comes to signify an essential component of who Dred is, a point that Stowe begins to elaborate when she describes the Transcendentalist notion of the mind's correspondence to the natural world, where "the great volume of nature" reflects back to the onlooker, in a form of sympathy, the very structures of the self and all its "internal passions." For the Transcendentalist, one comes to know the self by coming to know the natural world; the self and nature are part and parcel of the same cosmic unity, and the structure of one is emblematic of the structure of the other. After quickly invoking this Transcendental analogy, Stowe invites readers to draw a similar analogy with Dred, except that it is not nature illuminating the structures of Dred's interior self but Scripture, and in particular, those biblical narratives that foreground violent retribution against the wicked. It is "in the great answering volume of revelation," Stowe suggests, that one recognizes what Dred fundamentally is: a "prophet" and "deliverer," "armed with supernatural powers, raised up for oppressed people." Stowe is making an ontological claim here: what Dred is at his core is not a self-reliant man or an autonomous being (the very fantasies of liberal thought) but vengeance incarnate. And we know this from the biblical passages he reads, the parables he cites, and the threats of vengeance that so thoroughly constitute his speech. The apocalypse is no longer simply an event that comes from outside of history in the form of an angry deity (as Stowe portrayed it in *Uncle Tom's Cabin*); it is embodied within Dred himself, who is an agent of God's wrath and "a sign unto this people of the terror of the Lord" (D 242).

This description could easily be misconstrued as Stowe's attempt to exaggerate Dred's power or merely embellish the threat he represents within this North Carolina community. But Stowe constructs Dred outside an economy of recognizable norms precisely to imbue him with a power that does not require him to be a victim of slavery (as it did Uncle Tom) or to conform to nineteenth-century masculine standards that ultimately shrink rather than enlarge a slave's sphere of liberty (as we saw with Harry). Stowe revises the religious category of apocalypse in order to construct an embodied threat, one that could unsettle the institution of slavery, if not destroy it altogether. Stowe tells us that Dred is a disciple of Nat Turner and son of Denmark Vesey, so that his ideological and biological genealogies mark him as a retributive threat with apocalyptic implications. He possesses a "herculean strength" that harkens back to the "old warrior prophets of the heroic ages" (D 198). As a child, he "received from his mother the name of Dred; a name not unusual among the slaves, and generally given to those of great physical force." Dred's bodily potency is as essential a trait as his intellectual precociousness, and "the impression seemed to prevail universally among the negroes that this child was born for extraordinary things" (208).[21] Like Nat Turner, who was also "intended for some great purpose," Dred is called to accomplish something astonishing.[22] Indeed, Dred's "unsubduable disposition" toward slavery "made him an object of dread among overseers" (209), and when a particularly severe slaveholder once tried to break him, "Dred struck him to the earth, a dead man" and "made his escape to the swamps, and was never afterwards heard of in civilized life" (209).[23] Hiding in the swamps, reappearing only to threaten white slaveholding culture with bloodshed or to conscript other slaves to fight alongside him at the coming day of insurrectionary vengeance, Dred—a decidedly human, fully embodied, religiously inspired insurgent—menaces the South as the very incarnation of apocalyptic terror.[24]

While Dred is not subjected to the cruelties of slavery in the same way as Harry and Uncle Tom, this does not therefore mean that he is an autonomous being. Dred is constructed according to the same structure of messianic dependence that we have seen in previous chapters. Dred, Stowe writes, appears to have been "seized and possessed . . . by the wrath of an avenging God," and this seizure is all-encompassing. "That part of the moral constitution, which exists in some degree in us all," Stowe writes, "which leads us to feel pain at the sight of injustice, and to desire retribution for cruelty and crime, seemed in him to have become an absorbing sentiment, as if he had been chosen by some higher power as the instrument of doom" (*D* 496–97). Stowe acknowledges that a desire for vengeance is a natural sentiment in most, but in Dred, it is a singular preoccupation and consequence of his status as God's surrogate on earth. Dred's subordination to and reliance on God is, in one sense, a characteristic he shares with Uncle Tom. Unlike Tom—although passiveness is regarded as a virtue in *Uncle Tom's Cabin*, it nevertheless renders him ineffective in the face of brutal slave masters—Dred's dependence on a wrathful God is a precondition for his spiritual resoluteness and physical might. And while Harry responds to the coercive strictures of slavery by insisting on greater self-reliance, Dred is a key component of the novel's critique of self-reliant individualism. As the narrator explains,

> The Bible divides men into two classes: those who trust in themselves, and those who trust in God. The one class walk by their own light, trust in their own strength, fight their own battles, and have no confidence otherwise. The other, not neglecting to use the wisdom and strength which God has given them, still trust in his wisdom and his strength to carry out the weakness of theirs. The one class go through life as orphans; the other have a Father. (408)

One does not, according to the novel, compensate for the failure of self-reliance with even more self-reliance. Rather, as this passage proposes, one places one's faith in the transcendental source of the individuated self. The self only achieves power when it foregoes its orphaned status and submits itself to the paternal care of God. Dred is the one character in the novel who does not possess an independent will. He is neither freethinking, nor does he enjoy sovereignty over himself. He will neither submit to nor be coerced by slavery. For precisely these reasons, he functions for Stowe as a legitimate challenge to America's culture of slavery.

The threat of Dred's physical presence is further supported by his words, and seldom does Dred utter a phrase that is not taken directly from Scripture. Indeed, the "one solitary companion" Dred brings with him when he absconds to the Great Dismal Swamp is "the Bible of his father" (*D* 210). The Bible is what nourishes Dred once he departs from civilization; it informs his thinking about justice, shapes his thoughts about rebellion, and provides a sense of comfort in the wilderness. And to Dred, the Bible "was not the messenger of peace and good-will, but the herald of woe and wrath!" (210). Indeed, Dred reads and quotes Bible passages so incessantly that it is at times impossible to discern where Dred-the-person ends and the biblical extracts begin. To the extent that it is constituted as a series of Scriptural citations, Dred's will is not his own. Stowe underscores the novel's messianic structure by creating a protagonist who depends on Scripture for virtually every thought that he thinks and every word that he says. The Bible is ventriloquized *through* Dred, especially the revelatory passages that portend God's apocalyptic retribution. "The word of the Lord is as a fire *shut up in my bones*," says Dred (242; emphasis mine). This simile is instructive of how readers should understand Dred's makeup; that is, biblical ideas of God's vengeance are so constitutive that they seem to take corporeal form in Dred's body. God's word shapes the skeletal structure of Dred's being, and it is this process, where divine word is transubstantiated into human flesh, that allows Stowe to endow the male black body with heavenly power. Dred is spiritual, but not ethereal; unlike Uncle Tom, who was otherworldly, Dred is fully of this world. The sum of Dred's parts—wrath, vengeance, physical might, rebellious violence, apocalypse incarnate—reveal what he is in homonymic form. He is dread, sent to North Carolina by a genteel sentimental writer to visit on its citizens what a retributive biblical God once visited on sinful nations.

And it is Dred's promise to inflict wide-scale devastation on slaveholders that begins to enliven none other than Harry. After one salient encounter with Dred, readers learn that "there was an uprising within" Harry, "vague, tumultuous, overpowering; dim instincts, heroic aspirations; the will to do, the soul to dare" (*D* 200). Harry begins to undergo an awakening as a result of his exchanges with Dred, and soon after conveys to Milly: "I'll have my revenge! Old Dred has been talking to me again, this morning. He always did stir me up so that I could hardly live; and I won't stand it any longer!" (201). When Milly tries to dissuade Harry from fighting, asserting that "Jerusalem above is *free*—is *free*, honey; so, don't you mind, now, what happens in *dis* yer time," Harry responds that "it don't answer to go to telling about a heavenly Jerusalem! We want something here" (201; original emphases). Several important details here are worth mentioning. To begin, Harry contemplates revenge because of Dred's influence. His sense of manhood is invigorated at the thought of seeking retribution for the injustices he has had to endure. If hard work and blood do not guarantee freedom and justice, then maybe violence will. In addition, Harry challenges Milly's suggestion to wait until the next life to obtain freedom. By stating that he wants freedom "here," Harry indicates that slaves should be able to achieve freedom in America, rather than in the afterlife or in Africa. And at a climactic moment in the narrative when Tom Gordon tries to claim Harry as his slave, Harry strikes his brother in retaliation, flees the house, gathers his wife, and absconds to the spot where on two separate occasions he encountered Dred (it should be noted that by this point in the narrative, Nina Gordon has already died from cholera).²⁵ And while the narrator indicates that Harry "had inherited the violent and fiery passions of his father," it takes Dred to activate them. And it is to Dred that Harry and Lisette flee and become by that same evening "tenants of the wild fastness in the centre of the swamp" (389).

Once he is safely harbored within the protection of the swamp, Harry writes a letter to Edward Clayton in which he poses the following question: "Mr. Clayton, if it were proper for your fathers to fight and shed blood for the oppression that came upon them, why isn't it right for us?" (*D* 435). Harry references in this letter the Declaration of Independence and the freedoms preserved within it, highlighting how the nation has failed to live up to its democratic ideals— ideals for which blacks are now willing to fight. Harry's devotion to democratic principles exposes a subtle but nevertheless meaningful tension between Harry's goals and Dred's. Indeed, as an initial compensation for Harry's unmanning within slavery, and as a powerful counterexample to those characters in *Uncle Tom's Cabin* who achieved liberty by either escaping to Africa or surrendering the body and entering God's kingdom after death, Dred is a powerful presence in the narrative and constitutes a bold reimagining of an empowered black self that evokes the theory of messianic power we saw in Walker's *Appeal* and Turner's *Confessions*. Because of his audacious depiction, however, Dred poses a problem for Harry (and for Stowe); namely, how can the vengeance he represents and promises to enact be reconciled with the novel's larger democratic aims? Dred's violence is not about achieving some multiracial society through revolutionary violence, as many scholars have argued; it is, rather, about hastening the end of white hegemony in America by murdering whites.²⁶ As Dred explains to a fellow conspirator: "When the Lord saith unto us, Smite, then we will smite! We will not torment them with the scourge and fire, nor defile their women, as they have done with ours! But we will slay them utterly, and consume them from off the face of the earth!" (460).²⁷ Dred's antidemocratic revenge fantasy exists in contrast with and endangers the novel's larger attempt to rewrite blacks as potential members of the American democratic polity. Stowe's messianic portrayal of Dred as being fundamentally dependent on a higher power—a portrayal that the novel seems to favor over a model of self-reliant manhood—also disrupts the liberal-revolutionary fantasy that persons can be free and self-determining. Given these frictions, it is reasonable to wonder if Stowe can rethink the outcomes of her black characters with Dred in the picture. In short, can a multiracial democratic society be achieved through, or simply accommodate, the promise of racial vengeance?

Before we examine how Stowe attempts to resolve this dilemma, it might be useful to consider briefly another important midcentury novel in which vengeance is the principal trait of the protagonist and the driving force of the narrative. As in Stowe's *Dred*, Herman Melville's *Moby-Dick* examines how vengeance might be deployed to outline an account of insuperable power. Like the character Dred, Ahab is motivated by a deep desire to exact vengeance, though in Melville's novel it is vengeance against Moby-Dick, the creature responsible for taking Ahab's leg and undermining his sense of manhood. Unlike *Dred*, however, *Moby-Dick* is a novel that highlights the dangers of vengeful acts and understands vengeance as a force that, rather than consolidating one's power, ultimately jeopardizes it instead. Melville's rejection of vengeance intersects with his disavowal of sentimentality as well.

Ahab's Vengeance

With a characteristically sardonic tone, Herman Melville writes in a letter to Nathaniel Hawthorne: "It seems an inconsistency to assert unconditional democracy in all things, and yet confess a dislike to all mankind—in the mass. But not so."[28] It is with this idea in mind that I consider Ahab's vengeance, for Melville constructs a protagonist who consolidates power, not through a commitment to democratic ideals, but by the expression of an inexorably undemocratic will whose sole aim is to hunt and eradicate Moby-Dick. Ahab derives power from an indomitable imperial consciousness, and vengeance is the chief expression of his domineering spirit. Indeed, if there is one force over which he has sovereignty in the novel, it is his will, which Ahab brings to bear on an equally sovereign, equally indomitable albino sperm whale. Describing Ahab's first appearance on the deck of the *Pequod*, Ishmael remarks: "There was an infinity of firmest fortitude, a determinate, unsurrenderable wilfulness, in the fixed and fearless, forward dedication of that glance."[29] Ahab is all will, and it requires a will such as his—with unbounded might and an uncontainable zeal that seems to surpass the limits of reason—to engage a foe with a seemingly insuperable, "unexampled, intelligent malignity" (199). Indeed, rather than deny that his passion to kill the whale verges on insanity, Ahab affirms it instead. "What I've dared," Ahab soliloquizes, "I've willed; and what I've willed, I'll do! They think me mad—Starbuck does; but I'm demoniac, I am madness maddened!" (183). The supremacy of an individuated will is recognized in *Moby-Dick* as a mind maddened by the need to exact vengeance against a likewise maddened whale that has already made Ahab its victim once before, of which the "barbaric white leg upon which he partly stood" (135) served to Ahab and to the novel's reader as a constant reminder.

Whereas Dred's legitimacy as a vengeful agent is established through religious notions of divine retribution, Ahab's power is legitimized through an imperialization of the self. Ahab is described by Ishmael as "supreme lord and dictator" onboard the *Pequod*, and his presence is so commanding that soon after his first appearance, he has rallied the crew, particularly the harpooneers, to "chase that white whale on both sides of land, and over all sides of earth, till he spouts black blood and rolls fin out" (*M* 177). So categorical is Ahab's command that even Starbuck desists his protest of the captain's motive, which is no longer about the economic gain a successful hunt might yield, especially of a sperm whale, but instead about satisfying a thirst for vengeance. It is the whale's violation of Ahab's empire of the self that Ahab seeks to redress, and it is his unchecked, imperial agency on the *Pequod* that makes such a quest possible. "My one cogged circle," Ahab reflects, "fits into all their various wheels, and they revolve" (183). Ahab is the prime mover onboard the *Pequod* with a seemingly unassailable sovereignty, and vengeance is the force that propels the captain's hunt and drives the narrative onward.

From these initial descriptions, we can draw some important distinctions between Ahab and Dred. Perhaps the most striking difference between the way Ahab's power is established compared with Dred's is that while Ahab's will serves as the engine for the *Pequod*'s pursuit of the whale, Dred's agency is marked by inactivity. Even as he sermonizes a fast-approaching day of wrath and warns that slaves will soon exact vengeance against slaveholders, Dred spends considerable time waiting for a sign from God that these events can begin. "Brethren," he tells his fellow conspirators, "the vision is sealed up, and the token is not yet come! . . . And there is silence in heaven for the space of half an hour! But hold yourselves in waiting, for the day cometh!" (*D* 460). A consequence of his messianic subjection to God (even as he is simultaneously a physical manifestation of the apocalyptic threat), Dred is forced to wait for a sign from the heavens that the bloodshed can begin. Unlike Ahab, who actively orchestrates the hunt, Dred is a passive instrument in the hands of God. The hallmark of Dred's rebellious spirit is, surprisingly, his persistence in "waiting for that sign from heaven which was to indicate when the day of grace was closed, and the day of judgment to begin" (499). *Moby-Dick* and *Dred*, then, offer dichotomous and radically divergent theories of power; whereas Ahab wills to the point of madness, Dred abides in a state of inertia. Like Ahab, whose will is unsurrenderable, fearless, and of the firmest fortitude, Dred possesses an equally "immovable firmness," but his fortitude is derived from being "an instrument of doom in a mightier hand" (447). While Dred's constant waiting is a sign of his steadfast faith, one might also infer that Stowe is justifiably hesitant to set Dred loose, even though she recognizes his necessity as a legitimate threat to slavery. Once Dred begins the work of killing whites, he could very well become, in the eyes of readers, a kind of blasphemous Frankensteinian monster that turns on its creator. For Captain Ahab, however, blasphemy is what is required to destroy the preternatural power of Moby-Dick. "I will wreak that hate upon him," Ahab says to Starbuck about the white whale. "Talk not to me of blasphemy, man; I'd strike the sun if it insulted me" (*M* 178).³⁰

Perhaps because of this obsession, there is with Ahab a pervading sense of inevitable destruction, no doubt attributable to his indomitable, imperious will; the path to his unavoidable annihilation seems "laid with iron rails, whereon [Ahab's] soul is grooved to run" (*M* 183). As Wai Chee Dimock has elegantly put it: Ahab "is a product of negative individualism. He too is a victim of his own fault, and an instrument of his own fate. *Moby-Dick*, then, is not just a story of doom, but the story of a particular kind of doom, self-chosen and self-inflicted."³¹ And in hunting the white whale, Ahab jeopardizes not only his own life, but the existence of the entire multinational crew onboard the *Pequod*. Ahab is, however, offered a final reprieve, a chance to renounce this mad pursuit in which he will surely write his own tragic fate. In a pivotal chapter titled "The Symphony," the final chapter before the three concluding chase sequences, this chance to escape a narrative that seems unalterable appears in a conversation between Ahab and Starbuck. What makes this scene pivotal is that it is the only time Ahab displays a sentimental disposition within his otherwise vengeful will, and this moment of sentimentality will link us directly back to Stowe. We first come upon Ahab looking woefully into the sea on an otherwise picturesque "clear steel-blue day" (*M* 589), and the "lovely aromas in that enchanted air did at last seem to dispel, for a moment, the cankerous thing in his soul" (590). An otherwise cruel "step-mother world" finally "threw affectionate arms round his stubborn neck, and did seem to joyously sob over him, as if over one, that however wilful and erring, she could yet find it in her heart to save and to bless." Nestled within the world's maternal embrace, "Ahab dropped a tear into the sea" (590). With Ahab's tear, Melville announces to his reader that we are indeed in the realm of the sentimental, and it is by creating a sentimental opening that Melville imagines a possible exit strategy for Ahab.³²

When Starbuck comes upon him, Ahab immediately pursues this newly laid course. "I think of this life I have led," Ahab remarks, and "the desolation of solitude it has been; the masoned, walled-town of a Captain's exclusiveness, which admits but small entrance to any sympathy from the green country without" (*M* 590). Whaling may have put Ahab in contact with cultures and nations far from America's shores, but his activity as captain is anathema to sympathy. He is a walled town, a fortified island lost at sea who cannot escape the barriers he has himself erected. Worse still is what taking to the sea required Ahab to leave behind on shore. He remains

> whole oceans away, from that young girl-wife I wedded past fifty, and sailed for Cape Horn the next day, leaving but one dent in my marriage pillow—wife?—

wife?—rather a widow with her husband alive! Aye, I widowed that poor girl when I married her, Starbuck; and then, the madness, the frenzy, the boiling blood and the smoking brow, with which, for a thousand lowerings old Ahab has furiously, foamingly chased his prey—more a demon than a man!—aye, aye! what a forty years' fool—fool—old fool, has old Ahab been! Why this strife of the chase? ... how the richer or better is Ahab now? (591)

Ahab has banished himself from the safety and tranquility of the domestic space. He exchanged a home, in which sympathy and affection are able to freely flow, for the lonely quarterdeck. This, Melville suggests, is an additional source of Ahab's madness. He has chosen vengeance over a life of sentimental love.

It is this life of love that Starbuck so nobly tries to give back. Ahab, for the moment, remains lost in mournful reveries of his family, asking Starbuck to "stand close," for "I see my wife and my child in thine eye" (*M* 591). He envisions a heart-wrenching scene with his family that is clearly an invention of his sentimental imagination but that nevertheless conveys the deep longing he has for them and the home they occupy. "I have seen them—," he reports, "some summer days in the morning. About this time—yes, it is noon nap now—the boy vivaciously wakes; sits up in bed; and his mother tells him of me, of cannibal old me; how I am abroad upon the deep, but will yet come back to dance him again" (592). It is in response to nostalgic thoughts such as these that Starbuck proposes a new option for Ahab. "Oh, my Captain! my Captain! noble soul! grand old heart.... [W]hy should any one give chase to that hated fish! Away with me! let us fly these deadly waters! let us home!" (591). Home is the alternative to the hunt. Starbuck then expresses a similar longing to see his own wife and child, conveying a sympathetic connection with Ahab over a shared sense of familial loss, and pleads with his captain, "let me alter the course!" (591).

As Melville has presented it here, then, it would appear that Ahab has a choice: vengeance or the sentimental, one or the other. The sentimental might save his life. He would not achieve his goal of killing the whale as he might by pursuing vengeance, but he would be free, with wife and child. At this crucial moment in the narrative, Melville brings together the foundational elements of apocalyptic sentimentalism; Ahab's vengeance confronts his sentimental longing for home and family. But rather than appreciating how these impulses might work together, Melville keeps them apart—indeed, he pits one against the other—and ultimately rejects both. In *Moby-Dick*, neither vengeance nor the sentimental is a viable option. The sentimental has insufficient power to placate Ahab's monomaniacal obsession with what the whale has come to symbolize for him; it instead paints a portrait of a false world, one that is organized around compassion and love when the world Ahab inhabits rages and hates. In contrast to Stowe, Melville possesses a conservative, hackneyed account of the sentimental that opposes love and vengeance. And Ahab's vengeance, as we know, while directed at the whale, literally turns on the *Pequod* and tragically sinks it. As Moby-Dick squares off with the ship, Ismael describes the whale: "Retribution, swift vengeance, eternal malice were in his whole aspect, and spite of all that mortal man could do, the solid white buttress of his forehead smote the ship's starboard bow, till men and timbers reeled" (*M* 622). Moby-Dick has always been a mirror to Ahab, and Ahab to Moby-Dick. In this encounter, the white whale meets Ahab's vengeance with a destructive vengeance of its own, splitting apart the ship's diverse crew. Vengeance, for Melville, is a purely destructive force that turns on its practitioners and harms those around them. If one might infer a moral from *Moby-Dick*, it is that democracy is anathema to vengeance, and vengeance is the greatest threat to democracy.[33]

It is this conclusion that Stowe rewrites in *Dred*. Unlike Melville, who emphasizes the inutility of sentimental discourse and who exposes the cataclysmic consequences of fulfilling one's vengeful desire, Stowe weaves vengeance into the sentimental to show that they are both necessary, indeed both required, if a vibrant democratic nation is to be achieved. Not only do vengeance and the sentimental coexist in *Dred*, they cooperate.

Dred and the Sentimental

Before we can examine how Stowe resolves the tension between vengeance and democracy that characterizes *Dred*, so that, rather than being in conflict, the latter actually depends on the former, we need to backtrack just a bit in order to see how Stowe develops a theory of sentimentality that revises her account in *Uncle Tom's Cabin* to include apocalyptic vengeance that is drawn in the figure of a black insurrectionist. For the first seventeen chapters, the novel portrays "ordinary" life in Canema, a pleasant and typically Southern plantation, and focuses specifically on Nina, a young white Southern heiress, and her romantic relationships, especially the one she entertains with Edward Clayton. Like Lydia Maria Child, who opened the two works of short fiction that I discussed in chapter 2 ("The Black Saxons" and "Slavery's Pleasant Homes") by highlighting the tranquility of Southern life, Stowe slowly unfolds her narrative by emphasizing the idyllic qualities of Canema. And like Child, who demonstrates just how endangered this tranquility actually is, Stowe shatters the illusion of serene plantation existence with the introduction of Dred in chapter 18. When Harry encounters Dred on the outskirts of the community, Stowe's readers realize two hundred pages into the narrative that Dred has been there the entire time. He lurks on the margins and in the swamp, waiting for the opportunity to exact vengeance on the white slaveholding South. The novel initially fantasizes white Southern life as easygoing and agreeable, but Dred explodes this fantasy.

Southern whites live under the threat that at any moment, Dred might perpetrate insurrectionary violence, annihilating "ordinary" life in the South. Harry's immediate recognition of Dred ("O, it is you, then, Dred!" [*D* 198]) confirms that Dred is always there, has always been there, threatening, waiting to strike. His presence, and the possibility of violence he symbolizes, circumscribe not only the narrative but the actual community in which readers find themselves embedded. Dred is not a presence that "finally arrives" in the eighteenth chapter; he instead prowls in the shadows as the events of the narrative unfold.

The panic engendered by Dred is itself part of the novel's sentimental mode. Rather than undermining the possibility of a sentimental politics, as many scholars have claimed, Dred's existence and his repeated warnings of a coming wrath (in the form of black insurrectionary violence) are required for Stowe's sentimental critique of slavery to manifest. When Dred proclaims that "the day of vengeance is in my heart" (*D* 459), Stowe subtly establishes the logic of insurrectionary sentiment. Dred's heart—the very symbol of love and the "site" of the sentimental—is, with Dred, filled with retribution. Fear, as I demonstrated in the previous chapter, has a central place in Stowe's sentimental aesthetic, and vengeance resides in the heart, alongside love. To underscore the transformative potential of insurrectionary terror, Dred invokes his ideological predecessor—Nat Turner—stating: "Nat Turner—they killed him; but the fear of him almost drove them to set free their slaves! . . . A little more fear, and they would have done it" (341). Dred reminds readers of the impact that Turner's insurrection had on Virginians, many of whom were so fearful that another insurrection like Turner's could occur that they debated whether or not to manumit their slaves. Dred references one of the most apocalyptic figures who in turn produces one of the most apocalyptic texts of the entire nineteenth century to frame his own actions as deserving the same fearful response from Southerners.[34] And by summoning Nat Turner as often as he does, Dred foreshadows the key role that Turner plays in Stowe's sentimental resolution of the novel. Indeed, as her most audacious gesture, Stowe will sentimentalize the legacy of Nat Turner.

Of course, what is missing from Dred's discourse is also what was missing from Nat Turner's confession: love. Because Dred is so loveless, readers have uniformly privileged Milly as the chief spokesperson for sentimentality in this otherwise "failed" sentimental novel. In fact, the most powerful piece of "evidence" readers use to discount Dred's importance in favor of Milly's is the scene in which she interrupts a meeting between Dred and his coconspirators and ultimately "dissuades" them from choosing violent insurrection. "If dere must come a day of vengeance," says Milly to those in attendance, "pray not to be in it! It's de Lord's strange work" (*D* 461). She implores them to reconsider, exclaiming, "O, brethren, dere's a better way. . . . Leave de vengeance to him. Vengeance is mine—I will repay, saith de Lord" (461, 462). To her injunctions against violence, Dred replies, "Woman, thy prayers have prevailed for this time! The hour is not yet come!" (462). Dred's apparent hesitation has led scholars like Joan Hedrick to conclude that Dred's "Old Testament militancy is stilled by the words of Milly" and Charles Foster to argue that Milly accomplishes the "conversion of Dred to Christian pacifism." Based on the supposed supremacy of Milly's moral persuasion, John Carlos Rowe has even asserted that she is the "fictional persona for Stowe herself."[35]

While it is understandable that critics would assume that Dred and Milly occupy antithetical positions, and that Stowe ultimately favors the latter over the former, I want to argue instead that these two characters actually work in concert to structure the sentimental foundation of this narrative. Dred's wrath and the fear that it produces is meant to incite an abiding commitment to compassion and forgiveness exemplified by Milly, and these two affective energies are more symbiotic than they are oppositional. Stowe favors neither Milly nor Dred, but instead constructs these characters to exemplify the biblical figure of Jesus, a being who is both loving and vengeful, capable of mercy and prepared to mete out punishment. In other words, Stowe does not use Milly and Dred to present two dichotomous paths, one leading to sympathy and love, the other to violence and retribution. Just because Dred concedes to Milly that the hour has not yet come does not mean that it will not come, only that Dred is willing to wait for a sign from God that the moment to insurrect has arrived. Once readers understand the affective dynamic that is created by the interaction between Dred and Milly, where the terror embodied by Dred is meant to goad the love espoused by Milly, they will more easily recognize and appreciate the countless examples throughout *Dred* where scenes foregrounding love and compassion run adjacent to and are motivated by moments that invoke wrath and woe.

It is worth noting that while most readers see Milly as the perfect expression of sentimental love, there was a time when she was far from the loving Christian most assume her to be. We see this alternative side of Milly, for example, when she tells the story of her son, Alfred's, murder at the hands of an overseer. After learning about Alfred's death, Milly wishes reprisal upon her slave mistress who traded Alfred away, stating "*You* killed him; his blood be on you and your chil'en! O, Lord God in heaven, hear me, and *render unto her double!*" (*D* 181; original emphases). Immediately following her rebuke, Milly is described as a "black marble Nemesis in a trance of wrath" (181). Nemesis, of course, is the Greek goddess of divine retribution, so that Milly has within her the trace of vengeance which precedes her transformation into a representative of Christian love. As she explains to Nina, "Dem was awful words, chile; but I was in Egypt den.... I had heard de sound of de trumpet, and de voice of words; but, chile, I hadn't seen de Lord" (181). It is only later that Milly comes to love and explains: "Now I see into it—that mystery of [God's] love to us, and how he overcomes and subdues all things by love; and I understand how 'perfect love casteth out fear'" (348). Fear, according to Milly's account, is superfluous when love is rendered perfect. The problem is love is rarely perfect, even for someone as thoroughly loving as Milly. Only when Milly finally expresses love for the woman who was responsible for her son's death can she say, as she does to Nina, "Chile, I overcome—I did so—I overcome by de blood of de *Lamb*—de Lamb!—Yes, de Lamb, chile!—'cause if he'd been a lion I could a kept in; 'twas de *Lamb* dat overcome" (183; original emphases). While it is Jesus' love and sacrifice that ultimately wins Milly over, Milly acknowledges that there are two powerful dimensions to Christ—the lion and the lamb—and these two dimensions have been at work within her. In this respect, Milly is surprisingly similar to Dred insofar as both identities are constructed on foundations of vengeance. The only difference is that Christ made Milly's love "perfect," which in turn cast out fear. It is this internal "conflict," which takes place within Milly, that gets externalized onto the narrative: the lion and the lamb, in some sense, are the novel's principal sentimental agents, the latter represented by Milly, the former by Dred.

That a discourse of apocalyptic sentimentalism organizes this narrative is best illustrated in a scene involving Nina Gordon and Edward Clayton in which Stowe appears to be explicitly delineating the logic of apocalyptic sentimentality that I have been examining throughout this book. At a large camp meeting near the Canema plantation, Nina and Edward listen to one of Father Bonnie's impassioned sermons. "I tell you the Lord is looking now down on you," Father Bonnie proclaims, "out of that moon! He is looking down in mercy! But, I tell you, he'll look down quite another way, one of these days! O, there'll be a time of wrath, by and by, if you don't repent!" With language emblematic of the jeremiadic tradition, Father Bonnie warns, "There's a judgment-day for you! O, sinner, what will become of you in that day? Never cry, Lord, Lord! Too late—too late, man! You wouldn't take mercy when it was offered, and now you shall have wrath!" (*D* 259). The terrifying threats contained in Father Bonnie's sermon inspire Nina to ask what is the foundational question regarding sentimentalism within the novel: "Can fear of fire make me love?" (261). For Nina, the question of whether fear is a necessary dimension of affect in the creation of a loving Christian heart is an urgent one in light of Father Bonnie's warning to sinners that they are running out of time. Clayton's response to Nina is telling: "If we may judge our Father by his voice in nature," Clayton explains, "he deems severity a necessary part of our training. Fire and hail, snow and vapor, stormy wind, fulfilling his word—all these have crushing regularity in their movements, which show that he is to be feared as well as loved" (261). If severity is indeed necessary to the development of a proper Christian, as Edward suggests, then no character better exemplifies the crushing regularity of God's movements than Dred. *Dred* insists on the necessary pairing of love and fear to form the novel's sentimental core. And Stowe uses the character of Dred to personify God's wrath and ensure that slaveholders in North Carolina remain adequately fearful of the repercussions of slaveholding.

Based on the way I have described him up until this point, it would appear that Dred serves two mutually exclusive functions. On one hand, Dred is central to the sentimentality of this novel, which is deeply invested in getting readers to *feel right* about slavery, and that means, in part, being afraid of a possible insurrectionary-apocalyptic threat. On the other hand, the violence Dred promises endangers the possibility of a more inclusive democratic nation. The novel promotes a sentimental response to slavery, but this response contains a very real and embodied form of vengeance in the figure of a rebellious slave. The novel also seeks a more inclusive multiracial democratic union, but as we learned from Ahab, vengeance sinks democracy. Indeed, given its rejection of revolutionary heroism, and as a follow-up to *Moby-Dick*, *Dred* examines whether it is possible for a sentimental rhetoric to energize a commitment to greater democratic inclusivity when that rhetoric is itself energized by a religiously zealous and wrathful black insurrectionist. Stowe suggests it is possible, but it requires a sacrifice first. Stowe must kill Dred in order to rescue the sentimental option *and* the democratic one.

We learn late in the novel that Dred is mortally wounded before he is able to strike a blow against slavery. He never leads his people out of bondage, and exits the novel as suddenly and as unexpectedly as he entered it. As the narrator reveals, "The DEATH of Dred fell like a night of despair on the hearts of the little fugitive circle in the swamps—on the hearts of multitudes in the surrounding plantations, who had regarded him as a prophet and a deliverer." In her description of Dred in death, Stowe reminds us of his embodiment, with his "splendid, athletic form," his "wild vitality," "powerful arm," and "trained and keen-seeing eye" (*D* 514). He was a source of encouragement for fellow fugitives because he possessed the requisite physical force to challenge the slave system. However, more important for the purpose of this discussion is what occurs after Dred's death. Following Dred's passing, readers learn that Edward and Anne Clayton buy land in western Canada and establish a township where they bring their freed slaves. This township thrives under the leadership of Harry, who arrives after he helps orchestrate the escape of many of the major slave characters from the narrative, including Lisette, Tiff, Milly, Hannibal, and others. Harry's labor as a freeman is now esteemed rather than denigrated under slavery, and as "one of the head men of the settlement," Harry "rapidly [acquires] property and consideration in the community" (544). Hannibal, one of Dred's coconspirators, also works on the Clayton property, and now with Dred gone, "instead of slaying men," he "is great in felling trees and clearing forests" (544). Milly also escapes, not to Canada, but to New York City where she lives in a "neat little tenement in one of the outer streets of New York, surrounded by about a dozen children, among whom were blacks, whites, and foreigners" (546). When Edward Clayton visits Milly and comments on the racial mix of the children, Milly comments, "I don't make no distinctions of color,—I don't believe in them. White chil'ren, when they 'have themselves, is jest as good as black, and I loves 'em jest as well" (546).

The resolutions proposed by *Dred* accomplish many important revisions to *Uncle Tom's Cabin*.[36] Most notably, none of the major black characters returns to Africa. Some of the fugitive slaves make a home in Canada (rather than in the U.S.), and Harry is valued and rewarded for his labor. While they may exist just outside of the U.S. national border, the former slaves living on the Clayton land nevertheless enjoy a form of civic life that was denied them on the plantation. With Dred's death, moreover, Hannibal's thirst for vengeance has been extinguished, so that he can be enfolded into a democratic community as one of its most productive members. Milly, however, lives in what we might call an embryonic multicultural democratic community *within* the U.S. territorial borders. Not only does her example dramatically rewrite the colonizationist ending of *Uncle Tom's Cabin* as well as her own claim about waiting for the afterlife to be free, but it makes a strong assertion for greater democratic inclusivity in Northern urban space. And it is the removal of Dred that makes these democratic options possible. So while Dred posed a formidable opposition to race-based slavery, his presence in the narrative, while necessary, is ultimately irreconcilable with its democratic agenda.

As I mentioned earlier, it is not simply the democratic option that Stowe is able to preserve by eliminating Dred. By killing her protagonist, Stowe also maintains the novel's sentimental structure as well. This likely seems counterintuitive, as the killing of Dred may look like Stowe's ultimate disavowal of a character who symbolized hope for America's slaves and who was an important instigator of terror, but who also posed a threat that in the end Stowe found to be untenable. Perhaps it is for this reason that some readers have criticized Stowe for failing to depict a slave revolt.[37] The problem, in other words, is that Stowe is unable to follow her own antislavery politics to their logical conclusion. She lacks the courage to depict a rebellion in which slaveholders finally suffer for their treatment of enslaved blacks. This view, however, misses the larger point. Stowe does not depict Dred and his coconspirators committing acts of violence because her challenge to slavery is a *sentimental* one, not one predicated on actual slave rebellion. By threatening insurrection throughout the narrative, and by linking insurrection to apocalyptic prophecy, Stowe aims to inspire fear in her readers, fear that will in turn motivate them to love Negro slaves and reject slaveholding. This is the sentimental structure of Stowe's political response.

If, however, she depicts Dred committing actual acts of violence—if she represents his coconspirators killing white people—then these slaves will become, in the eyes of white readers, insurgents that are undeserving of sympathetic love. Slaves will be seen not as worthy of compassion (which would be the proper sentimental response), but as a threat that needs to be removed, perhaps even preemptively. By representing insurrection and not simply threatening it, Stowe would, in effect, undermine the very sentimental response that she has been trying to foster all along, which entails shaping a nation of readers that loves as the figure of Christ did and thus rejects America's most immoral practice.[38] In Stowe's account, a multiracial democracy is only possible when insurrectionary violence is converted into a suspended threat. Apocalyptic sentimentalism is all about rebellion in suspension; it is a tactic to generate continuous feelings of love and fear. In contrast to Melville, Stowe incorporates vengeance into a larger sentimental strategy so that Dred's threat generates enough fear to inspire others to act with more compassion without Dred ultimately having to act on that threat. Dred is not meant to be a sympathetic figure but rather a catalyst for sympathy. In this respect, he fits into the novel's sentimental logic without himself being an object of sympathy.

In order to ensure that terror is continuously generated and that readers do not think that, with the death of Dred, the threat of insurrectionary vengeance has disappeared altogether, Stowe concludes the narrative by appending an excerpt of Nat Turner's *Confessions*. Stowe links the fictional characters in *Dred* with the historical actors who participated in the Southampton revolt. As Stowe remarks, "[One] of the principal conspirators" (*D* 551) in the Turner-led insurrection was a man named Dred, and if readers are to understand Stowe's fictional creation, they must first consider one of the historical sources on which she bases her protagonist. Dred's language parallels Turner's. As Turner says, "[On] the 12th of May, 1828, I heard a loud noise in the heavens, and the Spirit instantly appeared to me and said the Serpent was loosened, and Christ had laid down the yoke he had borne for the sins of men, and that I should take it on and fight against the Serpent, for the time was fast approaching when the first should be last and the last should be first" (*D* 557). Unlike Dred, Turner receives the sign from heaven that the bloodshed can begin, and his "object" from that moment on is "to carry terror and devastation wherever" he goes, and "neither age nor sex was to be spared—which was invariably adhered to" (558). Turner gets to do what Dred was never permitted: usher in the violence. Stowe appends Turner's *Confessions* precisely to underscore the point that Americans can expect real bloodshed, and not simply fictional warnings of it, if they fail to end slavery. Stowe requires Turner in order to pose a sentimental challenge against slavery, a move that has confounded modern readers who want to claim her as a paragon of love-based sentimentality and who have had to exclude Dred (and ignore Turner) as a product of her sentimental imagination in order to do so.

While she uses Turner to sustain the possibility of insurrectionary violence, Stowe refuses to portray it, even though she is not responsible for Turner's actions as she would be for Dred's. As in *Dred*, the violence is cleansed from Turner's confession. After the excerpt Stowe includes, Turner proceeds to describe the details of his violent rebellion through Southampton County. Just as he begins to address the acts in question, the narrative voice interposes, saying, "We will not go into the horrible details of the various massacres, but only make one or two extracts, to show the spirit and feelings of Turner" (*Dred* 558). While Stowe redacts Turner's account for the purposes of her narrative and excises the most violent parts, her readers would have been acutely aware of Turner's original statement, namely those passages from Turner's account that detail the killing of the Travises, especially the infant "sleeping in a cradle" (Greenberg 49). This is the outcome toward which America is headed, with Turner acting the part of God wreaking havoc within the slaveholding community.

As this novel makes evident, Nat Turner has a profound influence on the way Stowe constructs her second antislavery narrative. Indeed, Dred is, in some sense, modeled directly after Turner. They share similar origins and are both destined for remarkable achievements; they both exemplify a messianic structure of power; Dred is used as the inspiration for terror in this novel, and one of Nat Turner's primary goals was to terrorize the South. Given Dred's actions as an agent of terror, and in light of terror's fundamental place within Stowe's sentimental confrontation with slavery, I would even argue that Turner is partly responsible for determining Stowe's account of sentimentality, for it is really the legacy of Nat Turner that she sentimentalizes through her portrait of Dred. Turner is the bridge that links midcentury white bourgeois sentimentality with the incipient forms of black apocalyptic sentimentalism that I examined in part 1 of this book. And Stowe, the foremost sentimental writer of mid-nineteenth-century America, inherits this tradition and popularizes it as a powerful fictional form with which to dramatize the nation's need to disentangle itself from regimes of racial oppression.

While modern readers—and even some of Stowe's contemporaries—might justifiably point out the naïveté or ineffectual nature of Stowe's argument, we must nevertheless see her challenge to be a decidedly sentimental one in that it uses threats of violent reprisal to compel readers into nurturing a loving and sympathetic disposition. Between the death of Dred and the appearance of Turner lies a narrative space where reform can occur. That is, Dred's passing does not mean that Americans have nothing left to fear, because while Dred represents a fictional apocalypse, what is coming may be much worse and no longer imaginary. This recursive movement in history to Turner to anticipate what is coming in the future suggests that American history itself will continue to be marked by insurrectionary violence so long as the South continues to hold slaves. (In fact, the next important violent outburst is already in the making, as I show in the next chapter.) As much as Stowe may believe America is headed toward a terrible but just end, it is an end she would nevertheless prefer to avoid. Her sentimental response to slavery is meant to stave off the impending apocalypse, whereas figures like David Walker and Nat Turner suggested that apocalypse was exactly what was needed for America's sins to be purged.

Stowe's engagement with democratic and apocalyptic discourses in *Dred* also underscores an important amendment to the accounts of religious violence offered in Walker's *Appeal* and Turner's *Confessions:* a vibrant democracy depends, Stowe suggests, on the fantasy of apocalypse for its very existence. The apocalypse as Stowe outlines it in the novel is integrated into the logic of democracy and makes democracy possible by irrupting into history and threatening the end of democratic ideals and practices. The threat of religious violence, configured as it is in *Dred* through the linked discourses of apocalyptic vengeance and slave rebellion, is used to supplement and incite a nation's commitment to democratic ideals. The apocalypse is the event that could obliterate democratic history; as such, its deployment within the narrative frame works to encourage citizens to rededicate themselves to the ideals of democratic statehood. Indeed, Stowe takes the very models of antidemocratic insurrectionary violence promoted in the *Appeal* and *Confessions*—which envisioned the eradication of white Americans as punishment for their domination over free and enslaved blacks, thus endangering democratic principles—and she makes them part of a democratic-sentimental solution. Rescuing democracy from the corrosive effects of slavery requires more than a revolution, which only rearranges the parts, when what Stowe imagines in *Dred* could quite literally wipe the slate clean. The apocalypse matters as something to be avoided, and the best way to dodge an apocalyptic end is, as Stowe suggests in *Dred*, with the installation of multiracial democratic communities.

Stowe and Vengeful Sentiment

As I have demonstrated throughout this chapter, Stowe writes *Dred* as a revision to *Uncle Tom's Cabin* and makes important modifications, particularly with regard to imagining the site of freedom for her black characters as being partly in Canada, partly in the U.S. This is a better, but by no means perfect, account of what a multiracial North American landscape should look like when compared to what Stowe imagined in *Uncle Tom's Cabin*. With regard to her title characters, however, it may initially seem that what we encounter in *Dred* is something we have already seen in *Uncle Tom's Cabin;* that is, Stowe has created two black male protagonists that for different reasons are not ultimately meant for this world. These characters serve as sacrificial offerings, playing only a symbolic role, not a real, meaningful one, in the fight against slavery. Despite their similar outcomes, however, I would suggest that Dred has a life in the novel well beyond the moment of his death because he is enfolded into and energizes a sentimental structure that uses the fear of insurrectionary violence to stimulate readers into right action. Dred's death only marks the end of his material existence, while the threat he once embodied continues to have ideological and potentially political weight. This is the power of the novel's incarnational logic, of Stowe's decision to draw Dred as the physical manifestation of a retributive threat. The apocalypse, in short, was already here once, and it might come again.

The account of sentimentality that I have outlined in chapters 3 and 4 might continue to strike readers as jarring with the prevailing critical consensus of sentimentality within Stowe's early fiction. We must be careful, however, not to associate Stowe only with the (traditionally) feminine emotions of compassion and love, especially when there is ample evidence to unsettle this characterization. By expanding the sentimental paradigm to include vengeance and terror, readers might be able to appreciate the myriad ways antebellum sentimental culture is partly defined by the omnipresence of apocalyptic representation. Readers may also recognize that *Dred* is an expression not of black rage, as Ronald Walters has argued, but of white rage, and specifically Stowe's rage that the nation has made little headway in dissolving slavery since her comparatively measured apocalyptic statement in *Uncle Tom's Cabin*. And given how elaborately and emphatically Stowe draws the links between love, vengeance, insurrection, and democratic possibility, we should see *Dred* as more sentimental than *Uncle Tom's Cabin*, not less. Finally, readers can now regard Dred as I believe he should be regarded: as an emphatically sentimental character whose threat of violence is used to inspire those sympathetic to slavery to reorient their sympathies.

In the final chapter, I turn to a figure whose sympathies were never in need of reorientation. John Brown exemplified nineteenth-century sentimental sympathy, so much so that this sympathy moved him to fight, kill, and die on behalf of America's slaves. And it is sentimentality that enabled many antebellum Americans to see Brown's actions at Harpers Ferry not as an act of retributive vengeance, as one might reasonably think, but as an act of love.

PART 3

John Brown and the Legacy of Apocalyptic Sentimentalism

CHAPTER 5

Sentimental John Brown

> They who assert that, in this enterprise, [John Brown] was moved rather by hatred of the slaveholder than affection for the slave, do his memory most foul wrong. The love of his heart comprehended and encompassed both.... There never lived a man whose desire to promote human welfare and human happiness was more inextinguishable.... He desired society to be pure, free, unselfish—full of liberty and love.
> —*Richard Realf*, qtd. *in* Echoes of Harper's Ferry, *1860*

On the night of October 16, 1859, John Brown, accompanied by sixteen whites (including two of Brown's sons) and five blacks, famously took control of a federal arsenal at Harpers Ferry, Virginia. Brown hoped to spark an uprising among local slaves whom he would then lead into the nearby mountains. For two days, Brown and his men remained in the engine house of the armory, exchanging the occasional volley first with local militia, and then with a detachment of U.S. marines led by Colonel Robert E. Lee. On the morning of October 18, Lee's marines stormed the engine house, and within minutes Brown and his fellow raiders were captured. Seventeen men in all, including townspeople and a marine, were killed in the course of the Harpers Ferry affair. Ten of Brown's men, including his two sons, were killed; seven were captured (including Brown), and five escaped. On November 2 a jury found Brown guilty on three counts, and on the morning of December 2, 1859, Brown hanged for his crimes.[1]

As the meteor that signaled the coming Civil War, John Brown saw, perhaps more clearly than any of his contemporaries, that purging the land of slavery could only be accomplished with the spilling of blood—something Brown dedicated himself to, first in Kansas and later in Virginia. What is most striking about the contemporaneous response to the raid is how supporters of Brown repeatedly referred to him as a supremely loving and compassionate man, seeing the insurgency as an act of benevolence in the service of America's slaves. Most emphasized Brown's religious righteousness, underscoring that he was Christlike in his capacity to love and in his desire to deliver slaves from bondage. So great was the outpouring of sympathy for Brown that Governor Henry Wise of Virginia complained in a letter to Lydia Maria Child that Brown's insurgency was "a natural consequence of [Northern] sympathy, and the errors of that sympathy ought to make you doubt its virtue from the effect on his conduct."[2] Backers of Brown understood his violent acts to be expressions of his loving heart, and they celebrated his efforts by writing editorials, delivering addresses, and holding rallies on Brown's behalf while he waited in prison to be executed.

Most modern scholars share the view that violence was a necessary vehicle for eradicating slavery and thus often display sympathy toward Brown, arguing that he took necessary if unfortunate steps toward hastening slavery's demise. These critics regard Brown's violence as revolutionary in nature for aiming to expand political liberties to those deprived of the privileges of citizenship.[3] What makes Brown so remarkable (and laudable) within contemporary critical accounts is his deliberate self-martyring on behalf of America's slaves for the sake of racial equality at a time when even the most devout abolitionists were unwilling to make such a dramatic gesture.[4] In these readings, Brown's activities in Kansas and Virginia are signs not of his insane mind (as critics of Brown argued in the nineteenth century, a view some still hold today) but of his unmatched commitment to universal freedom.[5]

Despite the way modern scholars and nineteenth-century supporters exemplify a shared affection for Brown, critics today have avoided replicating, or even discussing, one of the most common strategies by which nineteenth-century defenders of Brown framed their support—namely, through a discourse of sentimentality. That Brown's contemporaries saw him as a deeply sentimental figure would not have been surprising at the time, but modern critics tend to read over or ignore this characterization. Consequently, none has fully explained precisely how Brown's acts of violence could have been read by a large segment of the antislavery community as a manifestation of his abiding love. Because the link between violence and love that was inextricable for antebellum Americans has been nearly forgotten by modern critics, the sentimental Brown, so often announced during the contemporaneous moment, is absent from most modern readings.

Two important exceptions are Franny Nudelman and Elizabeth Barnes, both of whom have examined in powerful yet divergent ways the eruption of sentimental discourses surrounding the figure of Brown. In a brilliant analysis, Nudelman argues that John Brown constitutes the "radical consequence" and "culmination" of calls for sympathy, but she stops short of arguing that Brown was inevitable, maintaining instead that "the production of sympathetic feeling can check or further violent practice."[6] In Nudelman's view, Brown's supporters saw his raid "as an example of sympathy put into practice" and "viewed the violence initiated and suffered by Brown as a model for further antislavery activism."[7] Barnes explores an alternative sentimental register and considers how Brown, as both agent and victim of violence, functions as a sacrificial figure meant to generate in whites a sense of the pain they inflict on black slaves. Brown "offers a dramatic example," Barnes argues, "not only of how the innocent may substitute for the guilty but of how the guilty may be spiritually corrected by learning sympathy for those they abuse."[8] The lesson Brown imparts, in Barnes's view, is that "through identification, the abuse of others is a punishment in itself."[9] With the execution of Brown, "white witnesses are asked to identify not only with black suffering through the sufferings of a white body like their own but also with the violent methods for which he dies.... Brown thus stands as a whipping boy for the sins of a white nation whose violence ... will come back to them in an inevitable, if unwelcome, identification with the 'tears and ... blood' of their victims" (Barnes quotes Rev. Henry Newhall's 1859 funeral oration for Brown here).[10] While these critical readings powerfully describe the operations of sympathy following Brown's raid, they do not explain fully how violence could have been so emphatically read as an act of sympathetic love by many of Brown's supporters. While Nudelman and Barnes are right to suggest that Brown extends himself in an act of sympathetic identification on behalf of slaves, not all abolitionist sentimentality would have led to the kind of violence in which Brown engages; in fact, much of the abolitionist discourses that promoted sympathy also decried violent measures within the antislavery struggle. For this reason, Brown's compassion for slaves, as well as his culture's avowal of him as a loving actor, are best explained within a sentimental tradition where violent fantasy had been an essential facet in the creation of sentimental sympathy.

In this final chapter, I return to nineteenth-century sentimental readings of John Brown in order to demonstrate that the logic of apocalyptic sentimentalism which I have described thus far was, by 1859, a firmly entrenched explanatory structure, one whose embeddedness allowed many Northern supporters to evaluate Brown according to a sentimental metric. Brown is the apotheosis of apocalyptic sentimentalism—the most successful rendition of this strategy—which allowed Brown to be seen by figures like Henry David Thoreau, Wendell Phillips, and Frederick Douglass as an embodiment of Christian love. The myriad warnings of theological vengeance that preceded the appearance of Brown and that were meant to inspire deep love are what helped prepare his defenders to see his violent undertaking at Harpers Ferry as a compassionate gesture. This argument, in which violence is seen as an expression of Brown's love, reorders the structure of affect that I have described in earlier chapters, where threats of violent retribution precede and are meant to produce love. With Brown, love precedes and motivates violence, which is then, in turn, read by his contemporaries as a sign of Brown's loving nature. The arguments I have outlined in the previous four chapters serve as a roadmap that leads unavoidably to Brown, who is not the radical alterity of abolitionist sentimentality but rather its inevitable result. In short, John Brown is the barely submerged, irrepressible fantasy of nineteenth-century abolitionist sentimentality.

As well as being the apogee of apocalyptic sentimentalism, John Brown nevertheless represented a crisis for it and was a sign of its impending collapse. The tension between ideas of vengeance and calls for love that this tradition encompassed could no longer stand once actual violence had been committed and had replaced a suspended apocalyptic threat. Antislavery writers used warnings of God's wrath, in other words, primarily as euphemisms for violence—divine vengeance was an idea through which writers could fantasize a violent challenge to slavery without having to explicitly promote acts of violence. With Brown, the imagined apocalypse gave way to real violence; apocalyptic sentimentalism was no longer a rhetorical construct but a reality. For this reason, some supporters, like Lydia Maria Child, who wanted to uphold Brown as an emblem of sympathetic affection, nonetheless struggled, at times frantically, to strike a balance between the love Brown epitomized and the violent acts he perpetrated. Whereas violence was for someone like Thoreau a true testament of Brown's loving heart, for Child it compromised Brown as the timely moral symbol Northern antislavery reformers desperately needed. In order to highlight Brown's loving nature, Child has to disentangle Brown's love for slaves from the violence he commits in his attempt to free them. Among many other effects, Brown's actions incited a heated debate within antebellum culture, as a whole, and antislavery advocates, in particular, over the question of what love is. By separating love and violence and subordinating the latter to the former, Child initiates a trend in which these two impulses will move further and further apart, so much so that Brown's sympathetic affection for slaves and his violent insurgency are no longer seen by modern critics as having once been entangled parts within a single sentimental economy.

In the sections that follow, I examine a diverse archive of letters and speeches in order to illustrate that John Brown marks the fulfillment of apocalyptic sentimentalism as well as its slow dénouement. I examine Brown's framing of his insurgency as a loving act and how his avid defenders, taking their cue directly from Brown, similarly see his raid on Harpers Ferry to be the quintessential sentimental expression. I also demonstrate how some defenders were uneasy about reading Brown's raid as evidence of his loving character and therefore emphasized Brown's affectionate heart while mostly ignoring his violent deeds. This practice of separating Brown's love from violence that begins in the midnineteenth century continues into the early part of the twentieth century, a of the most pernicious features of slavery and what ultimately injures young blacks the most. From his earliest recollections, Brown's thinking about race and his emphasis on family are closely correlated. Brown himself narrates the birth of his race consciousness in an autobiographical sketch that he writes in the third person. In it, he relays an incident from his childhood when he witnessed the beating of a slave boy, a "circumstance," he says, "that in the end made him a most *determined Abolitionist* : & led him to declare, *or Swear : Eternal war* with Slavery" (*M* 39; original emphases). Brown recounts in the sketch a brief period when he was staying with a U.S. marshal "who made a great pet of John : brought him to table with his first company ; & friends ; called their attention to every little smart thing he *said or did*." This same marshal owned a "negro boy" who was "badly clothed, poorly fed : *& lodged in cold weather*" (39; original emphasis). Brown displays deep affection for this slave, whom he describes as being "very active, inteligent, and good feeling ; & to whom John was under considerable obligation for numerous little acts of kindness" (39). For this reason, young Brown is horrified when this boy is "beaten before [Brown's] eyes with Iron Shovels or any other thing that came first to hand." This egregious example of violence inspires Brown to "reflect on the wretched, hopeless condition, of *Fatherless & Motherless* slave *children* : for such children have neither Fathers or Mothers to protect & provide for them" (39; original emphases). Brown articulates the brutality of the slave boy's experience in familial terms: what makes the slave's condition especially tragic for Brown is that he has no parents to intervene in or offer consolation for his suffering. Of the many ways he could represent slavery in this particular moment, Brown chooses to characterize it as a theft of the solace that comes with belonging to a family. It is the loss of father and mother as a source of love and protection that makes slavery such an unconscionable system, and this loss was on Brown's mind when he penned this particular scene. Indeed, earlier in the very same paragraph, Brown describes the experience of losing his own mother when he was only eight years old, a loss he describes as "complete and permanent." And while Brown's father remarried, John Brown "continued to pine after his own Mother for years" (39). The proximity of these two passages dramatizes the intimate connection between Brown's feelings of familial loss and his compassionate response to the slave's dilemma. Because he must live without his own mother, Brown can identify with this slave boy on whose family slavery has inflicted a more sinister violation. Brown embodies an ideal sentimental disposition: his sympathetic nature is constituted through a sense of shared suffering. Within this account and others like it, Brown at once shrinks the world and expands the family, closing the distance between blacks and whites.[15]

Brown's sympathetic disposition, itself rooted in a nurturing domestic sphere, contributes to his understanding and explanation of his actions at Harpers

Ferry. Following his capture, Brown repeatedly asserts that his activities were motivated by a deep sense of sympathy toward the slave, and he attributes his sympathetic sensibilities not just to a sense of localized family but also to the congruent religious instruction he received early in his life, which continues to shape his thinking about morality and justice. Brown's love of family translates into an ever-expanding family, dovetailing with a religious worldview that demands one see others as part of one's immediate concern. At the center of Brown's religious beliefs is the Golden Rule, a maxim that he emphasizes during his interrogation following his raid. Brown is asked by one of his interrogators, "Upon what principle do you justify your acts?" and Brown responds, "Upon the Golden Rule. I pity the poor in bondage that have none to help them: that is why I am here; not to gratify any personal animosity, revenge, or vindictive spirit. It is my sympathy with the oppressed and the wronged, that are as good as you and as precious in the sight of God" (*M* 125). The Golden Rule encourages universal sympathy and allows Brown to defend his actions, not as examples of bloodlust, but as a manifestation of his compassion for beings in need of help. Brown understands himself to be a good Christian, giving succor to the poor; his views on slavery and his opposition to the slave system, he contends, are consistent with biblical values promoting sympathy and love. Later in the interview, Brown further clarifies this point, saying that he "respect[s] the rights of the poorest and weakest of colored people ... just as much as I do those of the most wealthy and powerful.... We expected no reward except the satisfaction of endeavoring to do for those in distress and greatly oppressed as we would be done by. The cry of distress of the oppressed is my reason, and the only thing that prompted me to come here" (126). Brown merely acts in the service of religiously driven democratic principles, privileging egalitarian values over hierarchical ones. These democratic ideals are grounded in a theological imperative mandating that citizens "do for those in distress and greatly oppressed as we would be done by." The Golden Rule, then, is an incitement to and justification for Brown's activities in Virginia and Kansas before that. He is "moved," as Realf puts it in the passage that opens this chapter, to alleviate the sorrow that the slave conveys through cries of distress that everyone else ignores, and while his actions are perceived by his detractors to be immoral and possible evidence of his insanity, Brown sees them in accordance with the teachings of Christ.

Brown consistently rejects the notion that his actions at the federal armory were motivated by vengeance, and when a reporter asks him for any final thought at the end of his interrogation, he repeats his central claim: "I have nothing to say, only that I claim to be here in carrying out a measure I believe perfectly justifiable, and not to act the part of an incendiary or ruffian, but to aid those suffering great wrong" (*M* 127). His actions are defensible, suggests

Brown, because they stem from an abiding commitment to black slaves and an affective connection he has been nurturing since his youth. His motives are pure, in other words, and thus justify his means. Brown's logic here explains why he decides to participate in a violent attack when a writer like Stowe would only warn of one. Brown sees himself acting lovingly for a just cause, and his discourse begins to illustrate a shift in the rhetoric of apocalyptic sentimentality. Brown states that his violent response to slavery was itself *motivated by* his love for slaves, so that love precedes and generates the act of violence rather than the other way around. As sectionalist tensions mount and the imagined violence we saw with Walker, Stewart, and Stowe begins to morph into actual violence (and in this case, violence committed by a white Northerner rather than an enslaved black), the logic of apocalyptic sentimentality no longer follows familiar forms. The parts shift position; the structure becomes unstable, matching the increasing instability of the nation.

The messianic thread also undergoes revision with Brown, an additional sign that the architecture of apocalyptic sentimentalism is being redrafted. Having disclaimed any vengeful intent, Brown nevertheless mobilizes the messianic discourse that previous authors have deployed in their construction of a submissive but retributive force. When an interrogator inquires if Brown considers himself to be "an instrument in the hands of Providence," Brown succinctly replies, "I do" (*M* 125). Elaborating on the messianic construct, Brown writes to a friend a letter from prison, stating: "You know that Christ once armed Peter. So also in my case I think he put a sword into my hand, and there continued it so long as he saw best, and then kindly took it from me" (139). While Brown appears to be contradicting himself, rejecting vengeful impulses even as he asserts that he is a violent instrument in God's hands, he is transforming the messianic discourse to establish that he is in fact an instrument of love, not retribution. Brown is indeed armed, but with a loving heart that expresses itself in occasional outbursts of violence. In contrast to versions from previous chapters, Brown's power is predicated on a loving God rather than a vengeful one. The messianic structure of dependence is essential for Brown to imagine the source of his power, but he has modified this category so that his reliance on a loving God is the very thing that inspires his violent insurgency.[16]

Given Brown's emphasis on the intersection of familial devotion and interracial sympathy, his prison letters to friends and family should be read not just as vehicles by which he establishes his status as martyr, as some critics have claimed, but rather as a discourse in which Brown foregrounded his loving sentiments for America's slaves and promoted a politics of violent love that, he suggests, is essential to antislavery reform.[17] In these letters, Brown reveals himself as the very model of a loving citizen and compassionate Christian whose so-called radicalism is the natural effect of having spent a life cultivating an affectionate heart. As he awaits sentencing in a Charleston prison, Brown writes to his family in a letter dated October 31, 1859: "Never forget the poor nor think any thing you bestow on them to be lost to you even though they may be as *black* as Ebedmelch, the Ethiopian eunuch one to whom Phillip preached Christ" (*M* 138; original emphasis). Even from within his prison walls, Brown remains focused on the slave, encouraging his family to continue to care for and give to those in need, recognizing that slaves like Ebed-Melech are favored by God.[18] "Be sure to entertain strangers," Brown continues and, citing Hebrews 13:3, states, "Remember them that are in bonds as bound with them" (138). Brown reminds his family that their duty is to those whose circumstances are worse than their own; he also underscores their linked relation to the slave. So long as Americans continue to hold slaves, Brown urges his loved ones, the family is obligated to work for their emancipation and to regard them as members of an extended family just as Brown does. By demanding that his family care for the needs of slaves on the plantation rather than his in the jail cell, Brown represents himself as someone who, even in the most trying of times, nurtures a selfless and compassionate disposition toward those who have suffered even greater transgressions. Such a view subtly implies that whatever violence Brown may be responsible for should nevertheless be seen as a sign of his selfless commitment to God's laws and an expression of his loving devotion to slaves.[19]

The supremacy of love in John Brown's religious imagination gets its fullest articulation in the final letter he writes to his family just two days before his execution. His last prison letter is a prescription for sustaining a sympathetic heart and has, at its core, a powerful ethic of Christian love. Indeed, this last letter may serve as Brown's philosophical manifesto as he elaborates the fundamental ideas that have informed his stance on slavery. Brown begins by expressing a sense of peace at having done God's will, even though his day at the gallows is fast approaching. "I am waiting the hour of my public *murder* with great composure of mind, & cheerfulness," Brown writes, "feeling the strongest assurance that in no other possible way could I be used to so much advance the cause of God; & of humanity" (*M* 157; original emphasis). Brown asserts here that he has been a means through which a providential purpose could be achieved. His actions have been for the glory of God and humanity and as a result are a source of profound consolation. Brown goes on to articulate the ideological underpinnings of his thought, making explicit the logic of Christian living that he has embraced and that he mandates for the rest of his family. "I beseech you *every one*," Brown says, "to make the bible your *dayly & Nightly study;* with a *childlike honest, candid, teachable spirit:* out of love and respect for your Husband; & Father" (158; original emphases). Brown remains an ardent teacher and devout follower of Christ. Rather than seek pity or lament his impending fate, he implores his family to express their love for him by strengthening their relationship to God. Even in his final days, Brown's concern is with the welfare of his family members, whose spiritual life he aims to safeguard by encouraging in them greater religious commitment.

This final letter fully reveals the family-oriented, sympathetic soil from which John Brown emerged, and it is this ethos of sympathy that he desires to pass on to his surviving family members. Brown's writings also illustrate important structural shifts that take place when the standard order of apocalyptic sentimentalism is reversed. In the former economy, the fantasy of violence against the slaveholder from an outside source (i.e., a wrathful God) is channeled into love toward slaves, which neatly sublimates the threat but does not ultimately lead to actual violence. This structure breaks down with Brown, who represents a loving ideal but who also destroys the structure of containment in the process and unleashes its violence. When the economy works in reverse, and love explodes outward into violence, the threat is far from recontained. Rather than stopping violence, Brown ignites it (with, of course, the ultimate and ironic promise that, in the end, the violence would stop the violence). For Brown, a moral family and a just nation are only possible when the sympathy its members feel is powerful enough to engender action, perhaps even violent action, to protect its most vulnerable populations. When he implores his children to nurture a loving disposition, then, he is not asking them to be passive and meek. To the contrary, in Brown's view love is a violent weapon with which to strike at tyranny. By adopting love, Brown's children—and, implicitly, anyone who supports Brown's efforts—become dangerous citizens who privilege a moral order over social stability and who will fight and perhaps even kill to ensure that God's laws are enforced. Brown entreats his family "to love *the whole remnant or our once great family*: 'with a pure *heart fervently*,'" and as I have suggested, Brown's conception of family expands beyond his biological kin. "Nothing can so tend to make life a blessing," Brown continues, "as the consciousness that you *love: & are beloved:* & 'love ye the stranger' *still*" (*M* 158; original emphases). Brown urges that just as his children love one another, so must their love also be directed toward those strangers whom God commands to receive love as well. Love, for Brown, is the ethical condition of engagement and should govern how one exists in the world.

These many statements about love also have embedded within them a call to arms if the object of that love is suffering under oppression. The Golden Rule and other biblical passages frequently cited by Brown are powerful because they include a mandate to act with force in order to redress wrongdoing. By the time of his execution, Brown had been characterized in any number of ways, favorable and unfavorable: as a lunatic, zealot, and agent of the Republican Party as well as a martyr and revolutionary. Brown, however, portrays himself as a loving

Christian. With this final letter, the brief narrative of John Brown constructed here has come full circle. In it, issues of family, violent Christian sympathy, social justice, and racial equality—all obsessions of Brown's throughout his fight against slavery—come together in his most consolidated political statement on abolition.

Loving Responses

In the six weeks that John Brown was imprisoned, he generated more than one hundred "private" letters, most of which were published in newspapers throughout the North, with many of them containing the sentiments about love that I outline above.[20] The sentimental logic that operated within Brown's interaction with his family as well as in his thinking about violent rebellion translated into the public response to Brown, where many supporters, following his lead, lauded Brown as the very emblem of Christian compassion. They saw his insurgency at Harpers Ferry precisely as a sign of his sympathetic nature rather than as a destructive fanaticism that could endanger the antislavery cause. Henry David Thoreau was one of the first to announce his support for Brown, proclaiming that "No man has appeared in America as yet who loved his fellow man so well, and treated him so tenderly."[21] Brown's rebellion is, in Thoreau's view, an act of caring, and because he was so willing to love the slave, Brown emerges a singular figure in American history. For this reason, Thoreau insists that his contemporaries "can at least express [their] sympathy with, and admiration of, him and his companions."[22] And radical abolitionists and ministers did just that. Charles Henry Langston unequivocally stated, "I cannot deny that I feel ... the very deepest sympathy with the Immortal John Brown in his heroic and daring efforts to free the slaves."[23] What makes Brown a sympathetic figure, observes Langston, is that his actions were in concert with the teachings of Scripture. "Did not Capt. Brown act in consonance with these Biblical principles and injunctions [expressed in the Golden Rule]?" asks Langston. "His actions then are only the results of his faithfulness to the plain teaching of the word of God."[24] Brown's religious righteousness, rather than being undermined by his insurrection, is confirmed by it instead, a view that many Northern supporters shared and celebrated. As Brown awaited execution in his prison cell, rallies were held throughout the North in support of him. Expressions of sympathy for Brown became so abundant that Theodore Parker wrote from Rome in late December 1859: "I confess I am surprised to find love for the man, admiration for his conduct, and sympathy with his object, so widespread in the North, especially in New England, and more particularly in dear, good, old Boston!"[25] Ralph Waldo Emerson, though, was not at all surprised at the public's reaction and even exaggerated the outpouring of support for Brown: "I am not a little surprised at the easy effrontery with which political gentlemen, in and out of Congress, take it upon them to say that there are not a thousand men in the North who sympathize with Brown. It would be far safer and nearer the truth to say that all people, in proportion to their sensibility and self-respect, sympathize with him."[26] Along with being the personification of love, Brown is, in Emerson's view, a mirror that reflects back to his sympathetic onlookers an image of their own goodness and virtue. One's respectable judgment and sense of self-worth develop in direct proportion to the love one feels for Brown. Loving John Brown is, Emerson suggests, a prerequisite for being a good person.

The catharsis these supporters of Brown exhibit is emblematic of a similarly ecstatic response that runs throughout Northern antislavery culture. The frustration and rage that had accumulated over decades of unsuccessful attempts to undo slavery—political, artistic, and religious failures all—are finally cathected to Brown. This deep affective investment in Brown is one way that certain abolitionists purged these failures, and sentimentalism provided convenient, ready-made channels for these powerful emotions to circulate. Antislavery polemicists who often brimmed with fury but stopped short of calling for violence were able to glorify Brown because he embodied principled Christian ideals. And those who had always employed but had grown weary of futile political tactics were able to embrace Brown as a salvific figure for having struck at the very heart of slavery, even if Brown's raid was not technically successful. In both of these cases, Brown was a symbol around which radical abolitionists could rally and over whom they could indulge feelings of ecstatic triumphalism, feelings that were often expressed in sentimental terms. Sympathy for Brown marks the culmination of antislavery sentiment; it would have been virtually impossible even for members of the radical antislavery contingent to avow Brown if divine vengeance (as a euphemism for violence) and love were viewed (and felt) as entirely exclusive of each other. By the late 1850s, this highly Christianized sentimental culture was thoroughly familiar with these economies existing in a mutually dependent state. These discourses, and the relationship between them, are foundational if one is to understand why many Northern abolitionists responded to Brown as they did. Writers like David Walker, Maria Stewart, and Harriet Beecher Stowe developed a tradition in which love and vengeance could be seen as highly compatible and co-formative. These fantasies of retribution are literalized with Brown, and many within Northern antebellum culture are able to interpret these acts as expressions of love precisely because apocalyptic sentimentality had provided a vocabulary to accomplish this bold conceptual task. Indeed, because of the maturity of this tradition in the 1850s, the same abolitionists who had not been able or willing to express sympathy for the writings of David Walker and the actions of Nat Turner were now able to enthusiastically support Brown's raid on Harpers Ferry.[27]

LOVE WITHOUT VIOLENCE

In light of the enthusiastic support John Brown received from many of his defenders who understood his raid to be an act of loving violence, I read him as the fulfillment of apocalyptic sentimentalism. There was, however, an equally large number of supporters who were troubled by Brown's violence and who exhibited greater difficulty reconciling his violent acts with his loving words. The warning of God's apocalyptic vengeance that is so central to the logic of apocalyptic sentimentalism and that allowed writers to fantasize violence without promoting or depicting it outright disappears with Brown; the suspended threat collapses and the violence is actualized. No figure better illustrates this struggle than Lydia Maria Child. A committed Garrisonian and pacifist, Child nevertheless comes to regard Brown as an emblem of Christian righteousness but stops short of condoning his violent means. Child brackets violence in her discussions about Brown in order to focus on his moral character and her deep affection for him. Rather than reject Brown wholesale for engaging in acts of brutality, she emphasizes his loving nature and tries to separate out his insurgency. Child does not see Brown's rebellion as constituting a compassionate gesture the way Thoreau and Emerson do, but neither does violence disqualify Brown as an object of sympathy and affection. Brown's raid unsettles established assumptions about the meaning of love itself; whereas Thoreau and Emerson (and much of antebellum culture) see Brown's love and his violence to be perfectly compatible and even coextensive, Child and many of Brown's critics hold a competing belief in which any act of violence is ultimately incongruous with an ostensibly loving nature. Child embodies a more traditional sentimentalism in which love and sympathy oppose violence, in contrast to the radical apocalyptic sentimental tradition characterized by a figure like Thoreau. While her affectionate language for Brown seems at times to belie her expressed disapproval of his methods, Child struggles with and ultimately rejects incorporating actual violence into a sentimental framework, separating the two so that she can praise Brown's character while condemning his rebellion.

Throughout much of her correspondence, Child tries to maintain a difficult balance that both objects to Brown's violence and wholeheartedly embraces his integrity and virtue. "I cannot sympathize with the method you chose to advance the cause of freedom," she writes in a letter to Brown in prison. "But I honor your generous intentions, I admire your courage, moral and physical, I reverence you for the humanity which tempered your zeal, I sympathize with your cruel bereavements, your sufferings, and your wrongs. In brief, I love you and bless you" (*L* 324). Child aims here to uphold a distinction between the violence Brown employs and the principles he embodies, privileging the latter over the former.[28] She downplays the violence at Harpers Ferry and concentrates instead on "the sympathy you early manifested for the poor and the abused. Verily, God gave you a great heart!" (327). What makes Brown a laudable figure in Child's eyes is the sympathizing heart he possesses. In a letter to Peter and Susan Lesley, Child confirms, "I am astonished at the extent and degree of sympathy manifested for the brave old martyr.... To all outward appearance, all is defeat and ruin. Yet in reality what a glorious success! He is cursed, and scoffed at, and spit upon. Yet how the best intellects, and the largest hearts of the land, delight to do him honor!" (329). Rather than seeing violence itself as a form of sympathy, as others have done, Child positions Brown himself as the object of sympathetic affection. As such, Child can laud the man while marginalizing or even ignoring the violence he committed in Kansas and in Virginia, thus tenuously upholding her nonviolent principles even as she praises one who has transgressed these ideals.

Child is able to express her love for Brown with such unconditional language—language that would otherwise seem to contradict the nonviolent philosophy to which she adheres—only because she has adjusted the sentimental metric by which she evaluates Brown. "Thousands of hearts are throbbing with sympathy as warm as mine," Child writes. "I think of you night and day, bleeding in prison, surrounded by hostile faces, sustained only by trust in God, and your own strong heart. I long to nurse you, to speak to you sisterly words of sympathy and consolation" (*L* 324). Wishing to provide some form of comfort to the ailing Brown, Child figures herself as a sibling and caregiver and focuses her attention on the traits that make Brown a highly sympathetic figure—his trust in God, his strong heart, etc. She represents herself in traditionally feminine terms as a support for masculine authority in order to foreground a less incendiary sentimental dynamic than what is in play in Charles Henry Langston's and Henry David Thoreau's categorical embrace of Brown's violence. Child is so moved by Brown that she remarks in a letter to Thaddeus Hyatt, "I should like to have every form of [Brown's] likeness that can be devised, and have no corner of my dwelling without a memorial of him." Child longs to externalize her private thoughts of Brown, so that images of the "brave, self-sacrificing, noble old man" (328) that populate her mind will also occupy every corner of her home. As she articulates in a letter to a friend in November 1859, "He is my last thought at night, my first in the morning" (330). Here, Child revises the calculus of apocalyptic sentimentalism in order to accommodate her desire to embrace Brown and the virtue he exemplifies while rejecting his violent measures. She relies on an alternative view of the sentimental, where Brown's sympathy for slaves evokes sympathy in Child, leaving Brown's violence entirely out of the equation. Child rejects a theory of sentimentality that requires actual violence because she sees it as being inimical to and subversive of the power of sentimentality.

Child's sentimental attachment to John Brown is in a different—though no less exuberant—register than other allies who were more willing to see his raid as an act of sympathetic love. While she states that Brown is "mistaken in his efforts" and "made a grievous mistake" by attacking Harpers Ferry (*L* 325, 336), Child's letters nonetheless expose some understandable confusion over how she is supposed to make sense of a figure like Brown who exemplifies impulses that, for her, are finally irreconcilable. In expressing sympathy for Brown, Child disentangles love and violence, so that one is no longer an expression of the other. She characterizes Brown as a figure deserving of sympathetic attachment rather than a figure whose violent acts are themselves forms of sympathy.[29] It is worth remembering here the two short tales Child penned in the early 1840s that I examined at the end of chapter 2: "The Black Saxons" (1841) and "Slavery's Pleasant Homes" (1843), each of which ponders the possibility of slave insurrection and how such forms of revolt endanger the stability of white Southern domesticity. In "The Black Saxons," Child depicts a large group of slaves discussing the possibility of violent resistance, though she stops short of representing a massive rebellion in the tale; and while George, the protagonist in "Slavery's Pleasant Homes," does kill his master, he does so only after the slave master murders George's wife. The narrative voice praises him for his integrity, but George is ultimately executed for his crime and his corpse put on display for all slaves to witness. These two stories suggest that fantasies of violence were part of Child's antislavery imagination, even if this violence existed in a highly controlled form where she presents the possibility of violence only to manage the threat and mollify the terror such threats induce. With this in mind, it is fair to say that Brown is, in some sense, the return of Child's repressed; he forces her to engage her own fantasies of violence as well as confront the limits of nonviolent resistance. She writes the following to Garrison:

> Instead of blaming him for carrying out his own convictions by means we cannot sanction, it would be far more profitable for us to inquire of ourselves whether we, who believe in a "more excellent way," have carried our convictions into practice, as faithfully as he did *his*. *We* believe in *moral influence* as a cure for the diseases of society. Have we exerted it as constantly and as strenuously as we ought against the giant wrong, that is making wreck of all the free institutions our fathers handed down to us as a sacred legacy?[30]

Child attempts in this passage to redirect focus away from Brown's raid, underscoring instead his convictions and motivations without mentioning his actions, perhaps because she understands that the more Brown's violence is emphasized, the harder she will have to work to continue loving him. While Child ultimately abides by her pacifist convictions and rejects violent means, she nevertheless ends this letter to Garrison with one final reference to Brown: "The Recording Angel will blot out [Brown's] error with a tear, because it was committed with an honest heart."[31] The angel charged by God to witness and document history will, according to Child, sympathize with Brown and shed the obligatory tear that signifies right feeling because the angel will see what Child, deep down, suspects but refuses to acknowledge: that John Brown's violence at Harpers Ferry was indeed an act of love.

The work that Child begins of disconnecting love and violence continues following Brown's death. This move can be seen, among other places, in artistic renditions of Brown in which his violence and his sentimental disposition are rarely portrayed in the same image. Brown's insurgency and his loving devotion to slaves, in other words, are less frequently understood to be mutually constitutive aspects of his antislavery agenda, and this separation foreshadows the further decline of apocalyptic sentimentalism as a coherent tradition. No image more perfectly captures Brown as an icon of love without any violent urges than the one of him kissing the little black child on his way to the gallows, a fictional event that was first "reported" in the *New York Tribune* and was repeatedly depicted in poems, paintings, and orations celebrating Brown's heroism. On December 5, 1859, the *Tribune* reported what allegedly transpired when Brown exited his jail cell and headed to the gallows. "As he stepped out of door," recounts the newspaper entry, "a black woman, with her little child in her arms, stood near his way.... He stopped for a moment in his course, stooped over, and with the tenderness of one whose love is as broad as the brotherhood of man, kissed [the child] affectionately" (*M* 163–64). Despite the fabricated nature of this report—civilians were not permitted to attend the execution— it had a powerful influence in shaping public perception of Brown as well as subsequent representations of him. The article refers to Brown's tenderness and affection, qualities that are confirmed not by his actions at Harpers Ferry but by his willingness to kiss a member of the "despised race for whose emancipation and elevation to the dignity of children of God he was about to lay down his life" (163–64). Brown's love is communicated in conventional ways; kisses take the place of rifles and pikes. Brown is retained as a sentimental figure, but the violence that is a foundational part of other sentimental depictions of Brown which are being generated at this time has, in the *Tribune*'s portrait, been removed from view.

Various aesthetic representations of Brown produced in the weeks and months following his execution took up this image of him kissing the black child and emphasized his compassion for slaves while obscuring or ignoring his at times brutal tactics. In December 1859 the poet John Greenleaf Whittier published a controversial poem titled "Brown of Osawatomie" in the *New York Independent* that tries to reconcile Brown's loving heart, which Whittier lauds, with his violent acts, which Whittier decries. Whittier's poem describes, with some ambivalence, Brown's violent deeds, but concludes: "That kiss, from all its guilty means, / Redeemed the good intent."[32] Whittier's account subtly challenges the views espoused by writers like Thoreau and Emerson for whom Brown's deeds were a perfect reflection of his moral character. For Whittier, Brown's intent may have been noble, but his actions were unchristian, and it takes a paternal kiss to expiate his terrible actions at Harpers Ferry. A Quaker and pacifist, Whittier refuses to avow Brown's acts of violence, though he was able to regard the interracial affection displayed toward the slave child as an act of atonement and a marker of Brown's regenerated heart.[33] Whittier's poetic representation of Brown was deeply influential in guiding public perception of him as a compassionate and heroic man. In fact, numerous paintings that foregrounded the kiss were inspired by Whittier's poem, the most famous nineteenth-century examples being works by Louis Ransom, Thomas Noble, and Thomas Hovenden, all of which draw Brown as a benevolent patriarch who is best remembered for loving slaves, not for the deeds to which this love ultimately led.[34]

It comes as no surprise that Lydia Maria Child returns to Brown in 1866 with a short poem titled "John Brown and the Colored Child" in order to accomplish what she could not so easily do in 1859. Well after Brown's execution and the end of the Civil War, Child is now able to praise Brown's deeply sympathetic nature without equivocation because she, with the help of the *Tribune* article, has successfully removed violence from her sentimental understanding of him. This portrait of Brown kissing the black child is, in Child's view and in the view of so many defenders of Brown, the paradigmatic image that best captures his achievement. Child writes:

> The old man met no friendly eye,
> When last he looked on earth and sky;
> But one small child, with timid air,
> Was gazing on his hoary hair.
>
> As that dark brow to his upturned,
> The tender heart within him yearned;
> And, fondly stooping o'er her face,
> He kissed her for her injured race. (*M* 169–70)

Child's poem succinctly captures the antagonism toward Brown experienced by white onlookers (many of whom admitted to admiring his courage and steadfastness as he approached the gallows) as well as the interracial bond that exists between Brown and black slaves.[35] For his critics, Brown is the consummate race traitor, forsaking his Anglo-Saxon lineage to go "forth to die" for the sake of the slave. However, it is Brown's willingness to sacrifice himself, in Child's view, that makes him heroic. Once again, the idea of Brown's tender heart is emphasized, linking Child's poem to the article from the *Tribune*. Brown deliberately subverts firmly established racial hierarchies, stooping to kiss the child, a gesture that performatively enacts an equalization of social status among blacks and whites. About this kiss, Child writes: "But Jesus smiled that sight to see, / And said, 'He did it unto *me*'" (*M* 170; original emphasis). Brown's final imagined political act is, in fact, a deeply sentimental one; as readers envision Brown kissing the black child, they are assured of Brown's favor in God's eyes. "Who loves the poor doth love the Lord" (170), writes Child, and none love the poor as much as Brown, who, Christ-like, chose to die for the sake of the slaves and the entire nation.

This portrayal of John Brown kissing the Negro child is the final image in the triptych I have been outlining throughout this book, a literary "paneling" that acts as a signpost for the development of apocalyptic sentimentalism. Brown kissing the black child revises the scenes in *Uncle Tom's Cabin* where Tom and Eva demonstrate their love for each other, itself a revision of the scene from Nat Turner's *Confessions* in which members of Turner's band of insurrectionists summarily murder the white infant in the crib. In contrast to the scenes in *Uncle Tom's Cabin* in which Eva, the icon of nineteenth-century sentimentality, repeatedly expresses love toward Tom, a love that Tom reciprocates (at the horror of Ophelia), we have, in this equally fictional scene involving Brown, a fully grown and less-than-innocent white adult male kissing a young black child. Such a scene has been the symbolic goal of abolitionist sentimentality all along, exemplified by the *New York Tribune*–inspired renditions of Brown. For abolitionist sentimentality to work, white men must be willing to kiss and to love black children if slavery is ever to be undone without force. Indeed, this final panel further separates Brown's love from his violence by rewriting him as the fantasy of a peaceful solution. It is not enough for an innocent, angelic child like Eva to be willing to love an adult male slave, despite the affection nineteenth-century readers felt for her. This final transfiguration of the adult/child dyad is accomplished in what is perhaps the most unlikely of contexts where "weird John Brown"[36] is ultimately understood to be the sentimental (nonviolent) man par excellence. And while the discourse of apocalyptic sentimentalism helped to prepare antebellum Americans to understand Brown as an emblem of Christian compassion by showing how the seemingly antagonistic impulses of love and violence/vengeance were inseparably entangled, this discourse is beginning to erode as Brown's violence is overshadowed by a kiss.

I am not, of course, suggesting that representations emphasizing a violent John Brown are not generated in the years immediately following his execution or that such representations will not multiply in the decades to come. To the contrary, these versions of Brown will pervade the iconographic landscape, exemplified by Jacob Lawrence's gouache paintings of Brown and John Steuart Curry's famous mural in the Kansas statehouse (see figure 5).[37] Such versions of Brown purge his loving qualities as effectively as the pictures I have considered purge his violent ones. The very contradictions in these images themselves signal a destabilization in the tradition of apocalyptic sentimentalism, initiated by Brown himself, where it becomes increasingly difficult to emphasize the compatibility of love and violence. This transformation in the discourse helps explain why scholars now tend not to speak about Brown in sentimental terms—they have, that is, lost the framework by which to see expressions of love and acts of violence as indices of each other. Critics such as Paul Finkelman, Evan Carton, and Zoe Trodd tend to frame Brown as a martyr or revolutionary, and they use these categories to explain Brown's religious motivations (martyr) and his use of violence (revolution). But they have removed such notions from the sentimental framework of which Brown's violence and religiosity were initially a part and which made Brown so meaningful for initial supporters of the raid.

DOMESTICATING JOHN BROWN

As representations of John Brown continued to proliferate, describing him in a wide variety of ways—as a revolutionary, a martyr, a religious zealot, a madman, a criminal—it was Salmon Brown, John Brown's son, who, in the early twentieth century, insisted that his father be remembered as a caring patriarch. Salmon characterizes John Brown as a supremely loving father, retroactively providing "evidence" that the *Tribune*'s portrait of Brown, while factually untrue, nevertheless captured his moral essence. Salmon extends the work Child initiated years earlier of trying to sanitize the violence from the cultural memory of John Brown. Salmon Brown's description of his father's presence in the domestic space illustrates how sentimental depictions of Brown are beginning to oppose accounts that underscore his violence (regardless of whether these views are positive or negative); views that were once compatible in 1859 are, by 1913, seen as strongly antagonistic.

Reflecting on his father's influence, Salmon recasts John Brown as a decidedly private man in order to deemphasize his violent acts. For members of his immediate family, Brown's commitment to the home constituted one of his principal and most praiseworthy traits, despite his supervising the death and dismemberment of proslavery men in Kansas or daring to attack a federal armory in a maneuver that left seventeen dead. "Perhaps the most striking characteristic of my father," Salmon remarks, "as his children knew him, was his faith in God, his faith in family, and his sense of equity" (*M* 66). Salmon is careful to underscore the difference between cultural accounts of John Brown and the private man Salmon and his siblings knew as their father. John Brown was

Figure 5. *Tragic Prelude*, by John Steuart Curry. Kansas State Historical Society.

neither revolutionary nor villainous in his domestic comportment but rather someone who displayed devotion to his faith and love for his family. "He was stern when need be," Salmon continues, "but sympathetic and just always" (66). For Salmon, John Brown was first and foremost a caring parent, a view he repeatedly emphasizes, as in the following remark in which he describes a typical evening shared between Brown and his children. "Father would sit in front of a lively fire," explains Salmon, "and take up us children one, two, or three at a time, and sing until bedtime. We all loved to hear him sing as well as to talk of the conditions in the country, over which he seemed worried. A favorite song with father and us children was 'Blow Ye the Trumpet, Blow'" (67). Salmon locates his father next to one of the emblematic images of nineteenth-century domesticity—the hearth—to emphasize John Brown's dedication to his family. He is not a detached patriarch who leaves childrearing to his wife. Instead, he is deeply engaged with his children, educating them in matters of state and providing them religious instruction through song and entertainment.

This favorite song of Brown's deserves a few additional remarks. "Blow Ye the Trumpet, Blow" was a popular hymn written by Charles Wesley, a prolific hymnist who, with his brother John, founded the Methodist Church. At the heart of this hymn is a vision of Christ's second coming, an idea captured in the refrain "The year of jubilee is come! / The year of jubilee is come! / Return, ye ransomed sinners, home!" John Brown's abiding faith in apocalyptic prophecy is not ancillary to his paternal demeanor but central to it. The time he shares with children has, at its center, this Wesley hymn; and this hymn has, at its center, ideas about the apocalyptic end-time. In this reflection, domestic economy and apocalyptic prophecy converge just as they have in previous chapters. However, unlike Maria Stewart and many antebellum Americans who believed that a proper pedagogical approach to childrearing entailed inspiring in them a healthy fear of God, Salmon Brown presents a coming apocalypse with none of the accompanying terror; the violent end of history is shorn of violence. Just as Salmon presents the apocalypse as a day of jubilee without any of God's wrath, so he emphasizes John Brown's love without any of his violent inclinations. Rewriting the narrative of Brown, in other words, begins with revising the apocalyptic narrative of which he was initially a part. Rather than enfolding Brown's violence into his loving nature, Salmon excludes it altogether.

By emphasizing his father's domestic life, Salmon Brown constructs John Brown as a thoroughly historical figure who defies iconicity as revolutionary or insurrectionist. Though he is commenting fifty years after his father's raid on Harpers Ferry, Salmon marshals a rhetoric of domesticity that was axiomatic within antebellum culture, all the while muting the violent, apocalyptically inflected accounts of domesticity that I have examined throughout this book. "Blood has always been thick in the Brown family," remarks Salmon. "Family ties were firm, and the tendency has been strong to 'stick together'" (*M* 68). This devotion to family was an idea modeled by John Brown, who demonstrated a tireless commitment to his kin, a point that Salmon remembers with some fondness: "I first noticed this family trait in my father's case when he would go to grandfather's bed—after he became old—and tuck the covers about him as a mother would do with her children" (68). So devoted was John Brown to his family that he acted toward them with the kind of compassion ostensibly typified by mothers, who, in the 1850s, were the presumed nurturers and purveyors of domestic virtue. Salmon Brown initiates a transgendering of his father from a radical abolitionist and violent insurgent into a loving matron and idealized republican mother, a transformation he further develops in the following remarkable passage:

> Despite his relentless sternness, and underlying it, cropping through in his later years, when paternalism of necessity gave way to comradeship, there ran in John Brown's nature a strain of intense tenderness. Suffering in himself he bore without a murmur; but every fiber of his being was wrung by the suffering of others. It brought out the woman in him, the John Brown little known to history, who sat around the great open fireplace at night with his children in his arms and sang them to sleep; who rose on the coldest night and paced the floor with a collicky child, while his wife, worn by childbearing and childrearing, lay in bed asleep; and who was ever the nurse in sickness, watchful, tireless, tender, allowing no one to lift the burden of the night watch from him. During a protracted illness of my mother he hovered over her night and day, sleeping for a fortnight only at intervals in his chair, unrelieved of his clothes, afraid to go to bed lest he oversleep. (69)

Beneath his Puritanical severity is a deep and abiding tenderness that Brown regularly displays toward his family. Brown is intensely affected by the suffering of others, which makes him a supremely caring father (and made him an ideal abolitionist, a connection that Salmon Brown refrains from drawing, lest he remind readers of the lengths his father was willing to go to help slaves) who is willing to act tirelessly to aid those he cares for most. Like the *Tribune* and Lydia Maria Child, Salmon highlights John Brown's tender sensibility and thus contributes to his womaning; as "nurse," Brown fulfills a role typically associated with the feminine sphere. This image of a highly domesticated Brown serves as an interesting contrast to the more well-known iconographic depictions, like John Steuart Curry's painting of Brown, larger than life, arms outstretched, Bible in one hand, rifle in the other, with blazing, almost lunatic eyes. The love that John Brown embodies from his son's perspective is severed from the violence captured in Curry's portrait. It is Salmon Brown's account of his father that will be lost to most twentieth- and twenty-first-century readers who tend to miss or discount the loving, sympathetic, and self-sacrificing Brown; they forget about the sentimental John Brown. At the same time, Salmon's sentimental appraisal of his father differs from, say, Thoreau's, for whom violence was perfectly compatible with and an exemplary sign of John Brown's abiding love for slaves.

It is perhaps unsurprising that Salmon Brown would choose to remember his father as a tender and private man. What I want to stress, though, is the middle ground Salmon's account articulates between nineteenth-century perspectives that viewed Brown's violence as a manifestation of his love and later accounts that will neglect altogether the sentimental context out of which Brown first emerged. Salmon maintains a sentimental reading of his father, but it is a reading from which wrath and violence have been removed. And Brown's daughter, Ruth, does the same when she delivers to Franklin Sanborn a list of her father's favorite scriptural passages in 1882, over thirty years before Salmon's account. The biblical passages that Ruth cites as some of her father's favorites—Proverbs 21:13, Proverbs 22:9, Matthew 5:42—and that ostensibly mandate a loving disposition are themselves often immediately preceded or immediately followed by passages that articulate the violent consequences of failing to nurture a loving heart. As one who follows the Golden Rule, John Brown nevertheless would have understood God's love to be underwritten by threats of violent reprisal; divine justice is configured as mercy for some, punishment of others. It is this important point that Ruth omits. Proverbs 21:13, for example, states, "Whoso stoppeth his ears at the cry of the poor, he also shall cry himself, but shall not be heard." This passage requires that Christians remain open to and willing to aid in the suffering of others but is immediately preceded in Proverbs 21:12 by the following: "The righteous man wisely considereth the house of the wicked: but God overthroweth the wicked for their wickedness," so that the selfish will be objects of God's anger. Likewise, Proverbs 22:9 reads: "He that hath a bountiful eye shall be blessed; for he giveth of his bread to the poor." Christians, according to this passage, must actively work to alleviate those who suffer, giving of themselves and their possessions as an act of compassion and generosity. This passage, however, which encourages an ethic of sympathy, is preceded by Proverbs 22:8: "He that soweth iniquity shall reap vanity: and the rod of his anger shall fall"—and followed by Proverbs 22:10—"Cast out the scorner, and contention shall go out; yea, strife and reproach shall cease." The logic of compassion as it is constructed here is not merely promotional of good deeds; while moral actions are desired, the theological implications of failing to act righteously are described as well. If one refuses to give bread to the poor—if one fails, that is, to extend oneself in the service of one's less fortunate brethren—then one will suffer the penalty of God's anger (Proverbs 22:8) and be cast out from God's favor (Proverbs 22:10). While Ruth Brown cites scriptural passages that underscore her father's compassion for slaves, she segregates these passages from their larger discursive context, in which God's calls for universal love are paired with descriptions of how he punishes those who do not love adequately enough. In emphasizing certain biblical passages over others, Ruth Brown implies that her father had a similarly discerning eye, choosing to focus on God's mercy rather than his retributive wrath. What Ruth Brown does with Scripture, she does with John Brown himself by isolating his compassionate nature from his violent deeds, separating one from the other so that Brown might be remembered not for what he did but for who he was. For Ruth, this meant that John Brown might be immortalized as a kind father and pious Christian.

I do not want to suggest that Salmon and Ruth Brown's descriptions of their father represent the views of all their siblings at every stage of their thinking about John Brown. For example, John Brown Jr. also reflects in 1885 on his father's patriarchal authority within the home. As David Reynolds has observed, John Brown became by the 1830s "the patriarch of patriarchs," a transformation that coincided with his rejection of pacifism and his avowal of violence as a necessary strategy to end slavery.[38] While Brown desired egalitarian relations within the larger social order, he enjoyed absolute dominion over his home and family members, often using the whip when his children disobeyed his directives. Whereas Salmon might work to obscure this feature of his father, John Jr. highlights it, not as a sign of his father's harsh nature but as an indication of his compassion for his children. As John Jr. recounts in a now-famous example, despite his father's occasional severity, he often had tears in his eyes when he whipped his children, suggesting that his sternness was an outgrowth of his compassion.[39] In John Jr.'s view, violence, even against his children, could have a regenerative effect, and in one famous incident, Brown orders John Jr., whom he was beating for a series of infractions, to turn the whip on Brown himself to illustrate, in his son's words, "the Doctrine of Atonement," where "Justice could be satisfied by inflicting penalty upon the back of the innocent instead of the guilty."[40] Though he recognizes his father as a patriarch, John Jr. nevertheless describes John Brown as a compassionate man, and his severity was one way his compassion manifested itself. John Jr., in other words, sees his father's violence to be an expression of love, a view that accords more with Thoreau's account of Brown than does Lydia Maria Child's or even Salmon Brown's. This tension between Salmon's account and John Jr.'s underscores the contested nature of John Brown, even among family members. Where the former seeks to mute his father's violent actions, the latter understands that compassion can be expressed violently, and acts of violence themselves can become signs of a compassionate heart. In punishing his children with the whip, John Jr.'s view suggests, Brown communicates his unbounded love for them.[41]

The examples I have selected, beginning with Lydia Maria Child and ending with Salmon, Ruth, and John Brown Jr., are meant to dramatize the attenuation of apocalyptic sentimentalism as an interpretive strategy supporters used to make sense of this incendiary figure. I am not trying to provide a comprehensive account of the myriad responses to and depictions of John Brown, favorable and unfavorable, that have accumulated over years. Rather, I am aiming to demonstrate how a particular logic in which love and violence/vengeance were inseparably entangled inevitably broke down so that these two impulses became contradictory rather than cooperative. With the erosion of apocalyptic sentimentality, one also sees how a discourse of sentimental love that was vital to mid-nineteenth-century responses is almost entirely missing from scholarly readings of John Brown. And when love and violence do come up, they are often treated as clashing rather than as congruent.

This does not mean, however, that the logic of apocalyptic sentimentalism has disappeared entirely. In the epilogue to this book, I consider a few important cases from the contemporary moment in order to illustrate that this discourse is very much alive in a range of political and cultural rhetorics. And while apocalyptic sentimentality over time became a less prominent feature specifically in discussions of John Brown, there is one notable exception, involving a 1973 conversation between James Baldwin and Frank Shatz. In this exchange, Shatz, a survivor of Nazi-held Hungary, discusses Brown with Baldwin. One of the most important voices to come out of the civil rights movement, Baldwin regards Brown with a great deal of affection and admiration, stating that he was not just helping "the Negroes to freedom" but was instead trying to "liberate a *country*, not simply the black people of that country."[42] Brown's sympathy extends, in Baldwin's view, beyond his dedication to black Americans; his commitment to freedom was all-encompassing so that he sought to free slaves from physical bondage and whites from the psychological bondage of racism. Baldwin, like many defenders of Brown before him, tries to rescue Brown from accounts that treat him as "extreme," stating that "all he was really saying was that men are not things." In language that echoes Thoreau's, Baldwin insists that Brown was "a great American prophet. He was one of the really great Americans, one of the really great people, for *any* country."[43] Neither a madman nor a zealot, Brown was a visionary who understood the true cost of holding slaves and sacrificed himself so that his country might be spared.

And it is this sacrifice that most interests Baldwin as an example of what a white man (in Baldwin's view, perhaps the only courageous white man in the history of "such a cowardly race of people") would be willing to do to save an entire nation from ruin. "There was something special about John Brown," Baldwin explains. "He attacked the bastions of the federal government—not to liberate black slaves, but to liberate a whole country from a disastrous way of life. And as horrible as it may sound, it was an act of love. Love."[44] If, as David Reynolds has argued, Brown really did seed civil rights for black Americans, then it makes sense that one of the foremost spokesmen of the civil rights movement, a full century after Brown, would understand Brown's raid to be a loving act. Baldwin's view is informed by a similar rationale as that of apocalyptic sentimentalism where a violent gesture can confirm the violent actor's loving nature.[45] Baldwin sees the raid as a perfect expression of sympathy and Brown as a paragon—indeed an unparalleled instance—of compassionate whiteness. What made Brown unique to history was that he was willing to "risk everything," and this is the lesson Baldwin believes white Americans must learn. Whether or not the struggle goes "on and on and on" is, Baldwin explains to his white interlocutor, "entirely up to you" (266).

That a selection of antislavery reformers immediately following Harpers Ferry and a major civil rights activist over a century later were both able to regard John Brown's raid as a quintessentially loving act is no coincidence. It may be easier, in other words, to interpret violence as an expression of love when one is operating under dire historical circumstances, as Baldwin and the abolitionists were. The cultural discord generated by debates over race that marked both the antebellum period and the civil rights era is precisely what enabled some to understand the confluence of two seemingly antagonistic impulses—one toward love, the other toward violence—to be a logical development rather than an irrational one. And for antebellum Americans, there is another discord on the horizon, one whose effects end up being far more cataclysmic than anything previously warned about or prophesied.

Endings

The hope among nineteenth-century sentimentalists had always been that sympathy would possess sufficient power to bind together individuals, irrespective of the racial, class, and cultural differences that ostensibly separated them. Perhaps the final irony is that the pervasive expressions of sympathy I have considered in this chapter come from Northerners, not from slaveholding Southerners, and are directed at a radical white reformer rather than black slaves. As opponents of slavery become more desperate, the calculus of apocalyptic sentimentalism continues to shift, so that what was once the ideal target of this discourse (i.e., loveless slaveholders) has changed, and its purpose (i.e., inspiring in these loveless slaveholders feelings of compassion for slaves) is never fulfilled. Instead, America is left with radical abolitionists expressing sympathy for an even more radical insurgent. Rather than cohering the nation, this form of sympathy contributes to its disintegration instead. As the positive reactions to John Brown suggest, sympathy is a powerful unifying agent, but the more emphatically the antislavery contingent sympathetically coalesced around Brown (even as some rejected his violent measures), the deeper the divide that separated North and South. Sentimental love, in other words, ends up being as much a divisive force as it is a unifying one, and in the case of Brown, it has a tremendously destabilizing effect. Rather than binding the nation, love helps destroy it instead.

The concern of this chapter, of course, has not been whether sympathy succeeds or fails but rather how a tradition of apocalyptic sentimentalism provided a framework for understanding John Brown as a deeply sentimental figure and how this framework began to break down when Brown's supporters were no longer able to reconcile actual acts of violence with the deep-seated feelings of love that purportedly motivated them. For many, Brown's rebellion was an exemplary act of sympathy, and it was a religiously inflected sentimental discourse that helped make that reading of Brown possible. Because of the bloodshed for which Brown was finally responsible, however, many of his defenders lost the ability to read love and violence as signs of one another; Harpers Ferry and Kansas shattered the delicate balance that had been established within the apocalyptic sentimental tradition. Indeed, if Brown has become one of the most highly mythologized figures in American history, perhaps the originary myth is the one that posited his violent acts as examples of his love for slaves, a view that many (though not all) ultimately found unsustainable. Responses to Brown like the ones I have recounted in this chapter (as well as others I have not discussed that were deeply critical of him) were typically untidy and frequently contradictory because the constellation of issues Brown's raid spotlighted could not be easily resolved with a single, neat interpretive schema. In light of this, modern scholars who read Brown as a revolutionary hero or religious martyr might expand their conceptual framework so that they see him as the nexus at which nineteenth-century anxieties over race, slavery, liberty, love, violence, terror, and vengeance finally collide and are recast. The discourse of apocalyptic sentimentalism is one framework that makes such a reading possible.

Finally, John Brown signals that the warnings are over; the days when writers used ideas of vengeance to incite change have come to an end. If Brown signifies the separation of love and violence, the American Civil War concludes the tactical uses of apocalyptic sentimentalism. By the early 1860s, threats of woes to come sound absurd when compared to the carnage that has already arrived in the wake of the war. Only violence and bloodshed are left to resolve America's bitter conflicts, but not without first propelling the nation into unimaginable hardship.

CODA

The Civil War and Modern Apocalyptic Sentimentalism

> And perhaps beyond those shrouded swells another man did walk with another child on the dead gray sands. Slept but a sea apart on another beach among the bitter ashes of the world or stood in their rags lost to the same indifferent sun.
> —*Cormac McCarthy*, The Road, 2006

In the fall of 1863, President Lincoln issued a Proclamation of Thanksgiving encouraging citizens at home and abroad to set aside the "last Thursday of November next, as a day of Thanksgiving and Praise to our beneficent Father who dwelleth in the Heavens."[1] The proclamation begins with a reflection on the "blessings of fruitful fields and healthful skies" that had characterized the past year. Such an expression of gratitude must have seemed surprising to many Americans, given the astonishing casualties at Gettysburg, Chickamauga, and Chancellorsville—to name three of the bloodiest battles of the entire Civil War, all fought in 1863.[2] Nevertheless, this declaration of thanks is part of a larger effort by Lincoln to "heal the wounds of the nation and to restore it as soon as may be consistent with the Divine purposes to the full enjoyment of peace, harmony, tranquility and Union."[3] While the principal achievement of this document may have been its creation of a national holiday, the Proclamation of Thanksgiving also identifies the Civil War as a sign of God's disapprobation. Recalling all the blessings God has provided during the year despite the war, the document announces that "they are the gracious gifts of the Most High God, who, while dealing with us in anger for our sins, hath nevertheless remembered mercy."[4] As it is represented here, the war has sacred as well as secular significance. The conflict is not only the result of ideological differences between sectional cultures but also a costly tribulation for the "perverseness and disobedience" Americans have displayed toward God.[5]

By sacralizing the conflict, the Thanksgiving declaration exemplifies how

Northerners and Southerners alike understood the Civil War to be a major event in providential history. For many Americans, the war was a trial through which God would ultimately vindicate the side that he favored. These events, though bloody, were not to be lamented but instead celebrated, for it was through scourging on the battlefield that God's earthly kingdom would finally be made manifest. Speaking about the Confederacy, one Southern pastor declared: "I confidently believe that in leading us through this fiery trial God is preparing a chosen people for a great mission."[6] Union ministers made similar pronouncements about Northern culture, suggesting that a "baptism of fire and blood" would lead to their "day of future glory."[7] This optimistic view of the war is perhaps most powerfully expressed in Julia Ward Howe's "The Battle Hymn of the Republic," which recounts how God "hath loosed the fateful lightnings of His terrible swift sword" against the wicked (i.e., the slaveholding Confederacy); the war, for Howe, is the sign of the "glory of the coming of the Lord."[8] Others were less sanguine, however, seeing the war as an indication of God's disfavor with all of America and as punishment for failing to fulfill its millennial role. And there was ample visible evidence to support this view. As the war progressed, the country began to look more and more like an apocalyptic landscape (as evinced in the photography of Matthew Brady, Alexander Gardner, and others): a once pristine pastoral environment was decimated, the bodies piled up, and late in the war, General Sherman moved like an avenging angel from Chattanooga to Savannah and north again to Charleston, South Carolina, setting the South aflame as he went.[9] Prophesies of fire and brimstone were finally being visited on the nation.[10]

While Americans regularly linked the Civil War to apocalyptic history, what is striking is that these accounts are no longer located within a sentimental structure. If John Brown's raid initiated the separation of love and violence/vengeance, the Civil War marks the moment when the discourse of apocalyptic sentimentalism loses its force. Threatening God's vengeance was part of an antebellum strategy that antislavery writers deployed to catalyze a dramatic transformation in the nation's relationship to race-based slavery. As the event that would accomplish this transformation, the Civil War mitigated the urgency (and desperation) felt by these writers. God's retribution had already arrived. In response to the catastrophic consequences of a war that left so many dead on the battlefield and deeply wounded the nation, new discourses began to emerge that emphasized healing and reunion, replacing those that promoted wrath and vengeance.

This rhetorical shift away from vengeance and toward reconciliation is most dramatically illustrated in Abraham Lincoln's Second Inaugural Address, in which he both marshals and recasts the elements of apocalyptic sentimentalism to dissipate the threat it so often conveyed. In this address, Lincoln holds the Confederacy responsible for the war but resists isolating the South as the sole object of God's fury. "Woe unto the world because of offences!" Lincoln proclaims in a familiar idiom that, like the address on Thanksgiving, positions the war as a providential event and a sign of God's anger. "For it must needs be that offences come; but woe to that man by whom the offence cometh!"[11] While Lincoln acknowledges that "American Slavery is one of those offences," so that the South must absorb a large portion of blame for the nation's current woes, he also concedes that God "gives to both North and South, this terrible war." The Civil War, in Lincoln's view, is a shared burden, not one the South must shoulder alone, and one presumably brought on by Northern offenses as well. Mending the wounds begins, for Lincoln, by demonstrating that the entire nation has been the target of God's disapproving wrath. In a subtle but remarkable gesture, Lincoln democratizes God's vengeance as a way to heal the sectional divide rather than lay blame on one portion of the nation while sparing the other. Here, Lincoln radically adjusts the apocalyptic logic I have outlined throughout this book so that God's wrath, in the form of the war, is an affliction the whole nation must willingly take on and endure together; it is vengeance that has a unifying and palliative effect which begins to bind the nation. Vengeance is targeted at everyone rather than at only those who have failed to love, and because all Americans have experienced God's wrath collectively, they therefore share, as one nation, the same wish that "this mighty scourge of war may speedily pass away." America is unified in its desire for peace. However, if peace does not come, if "God wills that [the war] continue ... until every drop of blood drawn with the lash, shall be paid by another drawn with the sword," then this penalty is one all Americans will bear, for "'the judgments of the Lord, are true and righteous altogether.'"[12]

Having reformulated God's wrath from a threat one side directs toward the other into something the nation experiences collectively, Lincoln fosters national unity without relying on the menacing language of God's vengeance. He revises the rhetoric of vengeance, in other words, so that he can leave it behind. "With malice towards none;" Lincoln famously concludes, "with charity for all; ... let us strive on to finish the work we are in; to bind up the nation's wounds; to care for him who shall have borne the battle, and for his widow, and his orphan—to do all which may achieve and cherish a just, and a lasting peace, among ourselves, and with all nations."[13] Because all Americans have been wounded by the war, they can care for one another with a generous spirit and without grudges, regardless of ideological disagreements. The affliction the nation has suffered is strong enough to overcome the political and cultural differences that might divide its members. The "work we are in" that Lincoln refers to is the work of compassion and love, and of nurturing a spirit of friendship and affection so the nation might be made whole again.

With these words, Lincoln announces that the antislavery tradition of apocalyptic sentimentalism has come to an end. For many, lasting peace could not be achieved with repeated threats to love more deeply; rather, it required cooperation and a shared commitment to perfecting the nation's new birth of freedom. Along with Lincoln's rhetoric, the dissolution of slavery itself helps lay to rest apocalyptic sentimentalism as a structural relationship between love and fear. No longer did abolitionists need to threaten slaveowners to feel right so that slavery would end. In some sense, the prediction of apocalyptic sentimentalists actually came true—the threat is delivered, slavery is abolished, and peace can now be established. By describing the completion of this tradition, I am not suggesting that hostility in the postwar period subsides or that the entangled discourses of love and vengeance disappear for good. I am saying, however, that there is no highly visible, coherent tradition like the one involving the figures I have examined in this study. As history moves on and away from the Civil War, so does apocalyptic sentimentalism.

There have nevertheless been occasional flare-ups of apocalyptic sentimentalism since the Civil War, instances when the discursive construct I have described reemerges in powerful if somewhat altered forms. Such eruptions are to be expected, given that the apocalypse has, over the past 150 years, remained foundational to the way Americans have understood and articulated the significance of major historical moments; the Progressive Era, the Cold War, our so-called Age of Terror, and moments in between have all generated recognizable versions of apocalyptic sentimentality, where ideas of love and warnings of apocalyptic vengeance and destruction are woven into an era's political and cultural imagination. In light of my focus on antebellum uses of terror, I want to conclude *Apocalyptic Sentimentalism* by looking briefly at three examples of apocalyptic sentimentalism since September 11, 2001. Modern America's relationship to terror is marked by a surprising paradox. Since the 9/11 attacks, the nation has been engaged in a sustained fight against any ideology or act meant to inspire terror; indeed, for the past decade, the State has emphatically disavowed terror as being, by definition, anti-American. Despite this disavowal, terror has, since 9/11, been thoroughly incorporated into our own political, aesthetic, and entertainment discourses. The harder we try as a nation to locate the perpetrators of terror on foreign soil, the more we seem to internalize it as a constitutive part of our cultural DNA.

Snapshot 1: Glenn Beck

In a story from 2009 on the fragile state of Mexico, Glenn Beck warns of the possible consequences for the United States if that country fails politically and economically. Following a break during his newscast, Beck announces, "We are a country that is in real trouble," and "the final straw that could break our camel's back could be the collapse of Mexico."[14] Beck's warning is not of a coming religious apocalypse, but his tone is dire and his prophecy resembles those from the antebellum period that addressed the United States' impending ruin. Beck explains that Mexico is the twelfth-largest economy in the world and one of our closest trading partners (including our third-largest oil supplier), and any disruption in Mexico's economic system would unavoidably cause severe distress within U.S. markets. And the major cause of unrest within Mexico's economy is, according to Beck, drug crime, including murders, kidnappings, and beheadings of police officers. Beck warns that if Mexico becomes any more unstable, it could devolve into a "three-sided civil war" so destructive that the violence would inevitably cross the Mexico-U.S. border and become America's problem as well.[15] In less than two minutes, Beck paints a terrifying portrait of collapsing nations, violence, and imminent bloodshed all bearing down on U.S. culture.

And it is the border that emerges as Beck's chief concern. "If Mexico collapses," Beck asks, "isn't anybody think[ing] that there would be a rush of people trying to get out of a new narco-state, that would rush our border, where there is no fence?" Beck's language is telling, as it reveals his anxieties about America's inability to protect itself from foreign invaders. In emphasizing this "rush" against a borderless and thus helpless population, Beck's descriptions of Mexican infiltration evoke scenes from novels like *Zone One: A Novel* and films like *World War Z*, where even seemingly impenetrable barriers are overcome by the undead and the infected who contaminate and ultimately kill the innocent and the pure.[16] There is an obvious racial subtext to Beck's anxieties, despite his attempt to deflect charges of racism (i.e., "you're called a racist for just wanting a fence"). Unlike the tradition of nineteenth-century apocalyptic sentimentalism that so often cautioned against such racialist views, Beck's warnings of fast-approaching cataclysm only reinforce longstanding Eurocentric assumptions about racial and ethnic hierarchies. The threat as Beck describes it stems from cultural infection rather than an angry God, but the terror is, for some Americans, just as acute. Such concern on Beck's part prompts him to wonder, "If things would shake apart ... are we the people that can be peaceful, are we the Americans that can stand arm and arm that can welcome people onto our boat but not panic or allow panic to spread to sink our lifeboat?" While Beck frames this crisis as an opportunity for Americans to display their benevolence, one wonders, given the racial anxieties he has already displayed, if Beck's questions are not, in fact, genuine ones. Do Americans possess enough compassion to welcome the "rush" of Mexicans into Texas, New Mexico, Arizona, and California without "panic"? Beck does not say. What he is sure of is the danger that imperils America because of Mexico's instability. Reiterating this point, Beck concludes this segment with one final warning: "This could be the final lightning bolt in the perfect storm."

Viewers are reassured of Beck's sincerity as he begins his next, related segment about the 2004 disappearance of Yvette Martinez. Beck opens this story by reminding his audience that Martinez "disappeared just a few blocks away from our U.S. border." Immediately following this statement, Beck pauses as the grief he feels over the loss of Martinez interrupts his broadcast. His lips tighten, his eyes drop away from the camera as he tries to compose himself. As if snapped out of his mournful recollections, Beck emphatically reclaims the camera with his gaze and continues his report. But the sadness has found Beck's voice, and he reads with a lachrymose quiver for which he has become known. He tells his viewers of a promise he once made to Martinez's stepfather that he would "not let this story die." With every passing word, Beck becomes increasingly dejected. "I am not a journalist," he announces, "I am just a guy who cares . . ." With these words, Beck is overcome, and all the visible signs of his grief and caring are on display: the tearful eyes, the choked voice, the frustration at being unable to stifle his sorrow. Several seconds pass before he is able to finish his thought: "I'm just a guy who cares an awful lot about my country." Beck completes the segment by interviewing Bill Slemaker, Yvette's stepfather, an interview that, among other things, provides additional "evidence" of the crisis in Mexico.

Beck's tears place him in a sentimental tradition in which crying was an unequivocal sign that one felt right about a particular issue. If one has lingering doubts about Beck's claims regarding Mexico, one need only witness his public display of caring to know that he is a trusted source whose sentiments are heartfelt. Beck begins the segment with a chilling warning about Mexico's instability and ends it by exhibiting his heartfelt compassion for the victims of brutal violence, therefore combining two of the essential elements of apocalyptic sentimentalism: one meant to incite fear, the other to confirm the importance of love. Beck's rhetoric makes two important changes to the standard structure, however. First, in contrast to the nineteenth-century sentimental strategy, in which warnings of a coming disaster are mobilized to inspire love, Beck's love is deployed, in this example, to verify the threat. Beck's dire assessment of Mexico can be trusted, in short, because he has a loving heart. Second, Beck mobilizes a structure of apocalyptic sentimentalism in the service of a decidedly conservative agenda. The discourse I have been examining is not, after all, an ideology as such but a rhetorical construct that might be marshaled for various political purposes. While I have focused on a segment of antislavery culture whose activities are radical rather than conservative, this does not mean that apocalyptic sentimentality itself is inherently a radical or progressive system. Indeed, as one of the most identifiable apocalyptic sentimentalists in modern America (with his frequent warnings and frequent tears), Beck exemplifies the conservative uses of this tradition.

Snapshot 2: The Storms of James Hansen

Few modern discourses have more avidly deployed an apocalyptic tone than the environmental movement, and few figures are more important within this movement than James Hansen.[17] A highly regarded climatologist and director of the NASA Goddard Institute for Space Studies until his retirement in 2013, Hansen was perhaps the single individual most responsible for introducing global warming to the world with his congressional testimony on climate change in 1988. Throughout his career, Hansen has been a prolific writer and activist, working to devise strategies that might stave off further environmental degradation and preserve an environment that has been decimated by sharp rises in temperatures over a relatively short span of time.

In his highly regarded 2009 book, *Storms of My Grandchildren: The Truth About the Coming Climate Catastrophe and Our Last Chance to Save Humanity*, Hansen covers the recent history of climate science and his place in it, surveying the latest scientific data to provide a comprehensive, up-to-date portrait of the current global crisis. The title alone gives some indication of Hansen's perspective. Climate change will have catastrophic consequences if the necessary steps are not taken to reduce atmospheric carbon dioxide, and while there is still an opportunity to do this, time is running short. As Hansen reasserts in the first few pages of the book, "This is our last chance."[18] Hansen establishes another important connection in the title that will frame the argument he makes throughout the book: namely, the relationship between climate change and the types of storms his grandchildren will experience in the future if nothing is done to resolve our current climate woes. Hansen understands the climate crisis, in part, through the lens of his grandchildren and the future they will inhabit. Global warming is, among other things, a destructive process that intersects with and endangers the domestic space—and the people Hansen loves who will occupy America's future homes. Hansen's rhetorical strategy recalls nineteenth-century authors who located apocalyptic vengeance as threatening the home front. For Hansen, today's version of apocalyptic devastation comes in the form of a man-made, carbon-driven, fossil-fueled catastrophe.

In the preface to his book, Hansen states that he became involved in policy-making rather than being solely "focused on the pure science" following the birth of his granddaughter, which inspired Hansen to reconsider his role in stopping global warming. "I did not want my grandchildren," Hansen reveals, "someday in the future, to look back and say, 'Opa understood what was happening, but he did not make it clear'" (*S* xii). As a symbol of this inspiration,

Hansen began showing a photo of his granddaughter during lectures on global warming, prompting newspapers to refer to him playfully as the "grandfather of global warming" (xii). Hansen's metamorphosis from mere scientist into the prophetic voice of global warming occurs, in short, because he loves his grandchild and fears for her future well-being. As evidence for his love, Hansen includes in the book the same photo of his granddaughter that he displayed during his lectures. She is centered and takes up most of the frame; beyond her stand rows of patio chairs, presumably near a pool, and what looks to be a modest beach house, invoking both domesticity and play. The camera's flash lights her alabaster skin and accents her blonde hair but leaves the periphery of the image, including the trees and sky, dark and underexposed, evoking the approach of turbulent weather. The beauty and innocence of this child are the subject of the photo, but it is a beauty and innocence backgrounded by something ominous and foreboding. The storms are coming.

Hansen uses domestic rhetoric in order to narrate his critical engagement with the politics of environmental science, and he returns to this frame at the end of the book in order to reemphasize the gravity of the environmental crisis. Reflecting on the arrival of a new grandchild—this time, a boy named Jake—Hansen remarks that "Jake has no idea what he is in for—that's just as well. He had better first grow up strong and smart" (S 238). Hansen none-too-subtly suggests that the present generation will not fix the problem, and that his grandchildren will inherit and have to repair it themselves. How can one motivate individuals to tackle this growing problem, Hansen wonders—and here he quotes Larry King—when "nobody cares about fifty years from now"? The answer, Hansen says, is with family; "people do care about their children and grandchildren" (238). If the environment is going to be preserved, it is because adults love their families, and especially their children and children's children, and therefore will come to feel a "responsibility to future generations" (238) once they learn to appreciate that today's carelessness will be tomorrow's calamity. As Hansen structures it here, domestic love is the only motivation sufficiently powerful to prevent an environmental apocalypse. However, if this love is not yet activated, then Hansen needs to remind his readers of what is to come, which he does in the paragraphs that follow. He recalls "connecting the dots between global warming and species extinction, based on both the history of Earth and the current unusual rate at which climate zones are shifting" (239). Hansen goes on to describe the coal trains he once saw in Iowa, calling them "death trains." "The railroad cars," he observes, "may as well be loaded with the species themselves, carrying them to their extermination" (239). Hansen's description eerily recalls the Nazi holocaust trains that carried Jews and other "undesirable" populations believed to be hampering the species to the death camps. This logic posits environmental degradation as the newest form of human extermination, an ecological holocaust that does not draw distinctions among race, ethnicity, class, or nation but offers equal-opportunity destruction. While one's love of family should in theory safeguard future generations from environmental calamities, Hansen uses warnings of "global chaos" (275) to incentivize that love and ensure that adults act now to make possible a future "in which we learn to live with other species in a sustainable way" (239). Rather than employing the common antebellum pattern in which threats of destruction follow calls for greater love, Hansen continually oscillates from love to terror and back to love. These impulses are paired and in constant interaction for, as Hansen sees it, only when love of family is strong enough, and fear of environmental catastrophe profound enough, will the current generation work to create an ecologically rich and sustainable future for all their children and grandchildren to inherit.

Snapshot 3: Cormac McCarthy's *The Road*

The first two snapshots discussed here are examples of political discourse that seek to influence governmental policy. They loosely resemble in structure the nineteenth-century tradition of apocalyptic sentimentalism: threats of a coming apocalypse (with God's wrath replaced by the collapse of Mexico and environmental devastation) and appeals for greater love (with love for slaves replaced by love of country, love of family) are paired together in a way that recuperates and modestly revises the antecedent tradition. In this final snapshot, I consider the development of apocalyptic sentimentalism within contemporary fictional narratives. As a fictional mode, apocalyptic sentimentalism undergoes a more dramatic change. Threats of vengeance and pleas for love are not paired together as they are in political rhetoric; rather, in these fictional examples, sentimental interactions involving family occur against the backdrop of apocalyptic devastation. The surrounding apocalyptic landscape works to intensify and fully illuminate the exchanges between members of a family trying to survive in a decimated setting, and the narrative focus on family, in turn, intensifies the destructive repercussions of the apocalyptic event. Some of the more notable film and television examples of this dynamic include *Jericho* (2006), *WALL-E* (2008), *The Walking Dead* (2010), and *Melancholia* (2011).[19] In each case, some form of domestic arrangement (involving members of an intact family, or two sisters and a son/nephew, or even the budding romance between a trash-collecting robot and an initially hostile but ultimately loving robot companion) is negotiated within an apocalyptic context where the family is in constant danger of being annihilated.[20]

The paradigmatic example of modern fictional apocalyptic sentimentalism, however, is Cormac McCarthy's *The Road*. The novel portrays a father and son as they journey toward the coast following an unspecified apocalyptic event that has eradicated all identifiable markers of civilization. In this setting, most of humanity is absent with the exception of the occasional (often shell-shocked) survivor and, more disturbingly, roaming bands of marauders from whom the boy and his father must remain hidden. McCarthy's style is fragmented, gray, and ashen like the world he describes, and the novel derives its poignancy from these two characters' efforts to hold onto a pre-apocalyptic model of family in a world that has lost all meaning and purpose. Domestic activities that would have once been considered mundane become acutely meaningful within the milieu of pervasive devastation, where all that is left are the ordinary rituals of existence. Conversely, events that in the past might have served as highlights in the life of a family—vacations, college graduations, weddings—are rendered absurd in light of the circumstances and are left unmentioned.[21] As the father, for example, cuts the boy's hair (he "tried to do a good job and it took some time") or watches the boy run ("The boy set off down the road. He'd not seen him run in a long time. Elbows out, flapping along in his outsized tennis shoes. He stopped and stood watching, biting his lip"), we see that his metric of meaning has been recalibrated, so that actions and gestures and words that in a prior time would have been unremarkable now constitute the very foundation of their existence as a family.[22] There is no future in this narrative outside of domestic economy.

Even as McCarthy emphasizes the domestic arrangement between father and son, he offers a rewriting of domesticity and the tradition of domestic fiction, beginning with the boy's mother, who kills herself rather than accompany her husband and son. In nineteenth-century iterations, the mother existed as the moral center of the domestic arrangement and the guarantor of virtue among family members. In McCarthy's updated account, the mother commits suicide precisely as a moral act. "We're the walking dead in a horror film," she tells her husband (*R* 55). She even acknowledges that she would "take [the boy] with me if it werent [*sic*] for you. You know I would. It's the right thing to do" (56). The mother makes a moral claim ("It's the right thing to do"), and in doing so fulfills her conventional role as mother, but the devastation they inhabit forces her to dramatically rethink what is right for her family. As she reminds her husband: "Sooner or later [the marauders] will catch us and they will kill us. They will rape me. They'll rape him" (56). McCarthy thus forces the reader to consider whether it is even possible to have moral influence within the family in a postapocalyptic world. This radical revision of the mother figure signals the various ways McCarthy upends many of the conventions of the genre even as he continues to depend on them.

Just as notable as McCarthy's reinscription of the symbolic power of motherhood is his description of actual homes the travelers come upon and the terrible fear they inspire in the boy. Throughout the novel, the boy expresses horror at the thought of having to enter a domestic space, so he and his father remain on the move. In a pre-apocalyptic time (as well as in an earlier literary tradition of domestic fiction), homes were endpoints within which familial love and moral virtue were cultivated and kept safe. But for these nomads in incessant transit, a tenuous morality develops on the road: in their encounters with other nomads; in their arguments about whether to help those in need; in the boy's questioning of whether he and his father are still, and always will be, "the good guys" in the otherwise "cold relentless circling of the intestate earth" (77, 130). The moral truths that in nineteenth-century domestic fiction were often taken for granted are, in McCarthy's novel, propositions that have to be proven and defended. There is no self-evident and agreed-upon morality in *The Road*—not even between a father and his son—and readers are left to wonder if, indeed, there can be such things as love and family and goodness within the "crushing black vacuum of the universe" that surrounds them (130).

If there is one abiding truth in *The Road*, it is that the boy is the sentimental center of this novel. He is the reason his father has not committed suicide, and he embodies a sense of innocence and goodness that the apocalypse does not crush but instead amplifies. The father conveys this fact soon before he dies. "You have my whole heart. You always did," he explains to the boy in what are the first actual words of love the father speaks to his son. "You're the best guy. You always were" (279). This focus is one feature McCarthy's novel shares with the nineteenth-century tradition of domestic fiction: namely, the salvific power of children, a view animated by the child's placement within a nihilistic landscape. The boy's goodness is not motivated by the apocalyptic context but exists independent of it and in confrontation with it. One of the qualities this father loves about his son is that the boy's virtue has not been marred by the historical moment he occupies. And the boy is good not because he is threatened with destruction; he is good in spite of it. Here, then, is one last revision of the apocalyptic sentimentalism that occurs within so many modern fictional narratives. The apocalypse is not the source and motivation for greater love. Love is protection from and a challenge to a world marked by an apocalyptic threat. This is true in *The Road* as well as in the examples of contemporary apocalyptic fiction I listed above and for other works of fiction that are part of this tradition. I began this study by insisting that pleas for love and warnings of apocalyptic destruction were not contradictory but compatible in the antebellum context. It seems fitting that I conclude by surveying the contemporary tradition of apocalyptic sentimental fiction only to make the opposite claim: love and apocalyptic devastation are, in this context, deeply antagonistic.

The preceding snapshots should be seen not as comprehensive readings but as gestures at how certain preoccupations from the nineteenth century have endured into or reemerged within the modern moment. In particular, I wanted to highlight that sentimental and apocalyptic discourses often appear together as part of various political or aesthetic objectives. Given our current geopolitical climate, it is understandable that the family unit, as both a building block of and metaphor for the nation, is imagined as always being in danger, and that this danger is often rendered in apocalyptic terms, whether that apocalypse takes the form of zombie infestation, environmental calamity, or other large-scale catastrophe. The contemporary examples discussed here are not replicas of nineteenth-century apocalyptic sentimentalism; important modifications are made in the course of deploying this rhetorical structure. But they are part of a genealogy that extends back at least to the antebellum period.

Americans presently exist in a complicated relationship to terror. Since 9/11, the nation has been on perpetual high alert for the next act of terrorism, and terror itself has come to be seen as the greatest danger to the so-called American way of life. At the same time, this nation's political rhetoric and mass entertainment are themselves often predicated on, and avidly seek to inspire, a sense of terror in their audiences, and it appears that audiences enthusiastically consume these discourses.[23] While I am not suggesting that an act of terrorism and, say, a call to save the environment that bases motivation on fear are the same thing, I am saying that many Americans show a surprising fascination for, and perhaps even derive a great deal of pleasure from, an affect that they ostensibly find revolting and vehemently disavow. We must be careful to distinguish between the different registers of terror without reducing them simply to an external threat (even though this is one of its registers), especially so we can identify those instances when terror—in the form of rhetoric, entertainment, or as a political act—is generated from within our national borders and directed at other nations or even at other Americans. The apocalypse is one important discursive category by which terror continues to insinuate itself into contemporary American life. Terror in politics, novels, film, and television is nothing new, but the intersection of apocalyptic and sentimental discourses in post-9/11 America is a phenomenon that is increasing, suggesting that Americans are responding to terror at the start of the twenty-first century with a reinvigorated and revised sentimentality. The present moment is, once again, marked by apocalyptic sentimentalism.

Notes

Introduction

1. The *New-York Gospel Herald* was a Universalist publication edited by Theophilus Fisk, and Universalists promoted a set of doctrines that challenged Calvinist orthodoxy. Adopting a populist ethos, Universalists like Elhaman Winchester and Hosea Ballou often preached on universal salvation, an idea that contested the long-standing belief among Calvinists that only the elect received everlasting life. While many Universalists believed in Christ's second coming and final judgment, they also maintained that sinners would not need to suffer endless punishment the way Calvinists had insisted. For an excellent study on Universalist theology and its relationship to Calvinist thought, see Bressler, *The Universalist Movement in America*. For a concise statement on the widespread challenges to Calvinist theology in the antebellum period, see Hatch, *The Democratization of American Christianity*, chapter 6.

2. PAULUS, "Remarks on the Term Vengeance," 59; all original emphases.

3. As the religious foundations of American society were shifting within a rapidly expanding evangelical culture, so too were ideas about a wrathful God. Many would have challenged PAULUS's conclusions, including other practicing Universalists. In an 1841 entry in the *Trumpet and Universalist Magazine*, for instance, one author argues that "Strictly speaking, there can be no such thing as wrath, anger, or vengeance, in the Supreme Being." Challenging accounts like those offered by PAULUS—also a Universalist—this writer contends that wrath and vengeance are fundamentally antithetical and thus external to the Christian God's nature. "Is he not declared to be *love*?" this writer asks, "and are we not told, that he who dwelleth in *love* dwelleth in *God*, and God in him? . . . Those then who represent God as being angry, in the sense in which man is angry, destroy his perfection;—they sweep away with a careless hand his blessedness, and make him the most miserable being in the universe." Notions of vengeance and anger create for this author an untenable paradox that violates the very virtues marking God's perfection. Whereas PAULUS treats love and vengeance as harmonious elements of God's

nature, so that expressions of God's wrath actually serve to promote happiness among his believers, this author expels wrath from the ontology of God, suggesting instead that divine vengeance and anger are symbolic formulations, not literal ones. Disputes like this one over God's nature, especially his inclinations toward wrath and vengeance, highlight an important aspect of America's religious evolution, something I discuss in greater detail later in the introduction but nevertheless want to highlight here. It is against this fluctuating backdrop that apocalyptic sentimentalism emerges and develops ("Wrath or Vengeance of God," 118; all original emphases).

4. Sentimental moral philosophy is not, obviously, reducible to love. However, love is often the affective register through which nineteenth-century U.S. sentimental tradition is read. This book is neither about sentimental moral philosophy as such or the Scottish Common Sense tradition in which this philosophy is rooted, nor is it about returning U.S. sentimentalism to some imagined "proper" origin, but about how scholars who privilege sympathetic affection overlook the functions of vengeance and fear within works of sentimental narration.

5. Fisher, *Hard Facts*, 105.

6. Whether they disparage sentimentalism for its insincere and saccharine parading of emotion or laud it for the way it contests more patriarchal forms of social interaction by privileging the authority of maternal affection, scholars nevertheless continue to treat love as the defining trait of the sentimental tradition. This debate about whether sentimentalism inhibited or enabled improved forms of authority begins with Jane Tompkins's response to Ann Douglas. Douglas mourns the loss of Calvinism's patriarchal authority with the advent of sentimentalism, while Tompkins finds in sentimentalism the emergence of female authority. For a useful summary of this debate, see Wexler, "Tender Violence," in *The Culture of Sentiment*, 9–17.

7. As Joanna Bourke argues, "Fear acquires meaning through cultural language and rites.... Emotions enter the historical archive only to the extent to which they transcend the insularity of individual psychological experience and present the self in the public realm" (*Fear: A Cultural History* 7). The frequency with which figurations of apocalypse appear, especially within the political context of abolition, suggests that the apocalyptic is a cultural language within antebellum America in which terror is expressed and recognized as such.

8. According to June Howard, "When we call an artifact or gesture sentimental, we are pointing to its use of some established convention to evoke emotion; we mark a moment when the discursive processes that construct emotion become visible." With this useful clarification in mind, we might think of the apocalyptic as a visible convention that helps create loving emotions (Howard, "What Is Sentimentality?" 76).

9. Douglass, *Narrative*, 7.

10. According to John Stauffer, only a minority of abolitionists were actually interested in forming interracial bonds. As he argues, Frederick Douglass's friendships with Gerrit Smith and John Brown were radical even within abolitionist circles. See Stauffer, *The Black Hearts of Men*. While these types of interracial bonds may not be common among abolitionists, they were emphasized with greater frequency within the antislavery rhetoric of the 1840s and 1850s.

11. Weinstein, *Family, Kinship, and Sympathy*, 3.

12. Ibid., 4.

13. While Sedgwick revises the Puritan past as a way to eliminate terror from the sentimental landscape, I would suggest that she nevertheless reintroduces an economy of terror back into the novel in the form of racial conflict between Anglo-Saxons on the frontier and indigenous Americans. This transposition of terror from theology to race serves as an interesting prelude to the chapters that follow, where threatening God's impending wrath and warning of slave insurrection come to mean the same thing. In other words, threats of slave violence were often configured as examples of God's fiery judgment, and vice versa. These formulations become a central part of the sentimental structure of the texts that I examine.

14. Warner, *The Wide Wide World*, 241–42.

15. For an interesting study of the changing depictions of Jesus within American culture, see Prothero, *American Jesus*.

16. Writing about the period in question, Elizabeth Clark argues that "the liberalizing trend toward the benevolent, unpunishing God . . . touched all but the most crabbed of orthodox Calvinists, establishing a common ground from which reformers could condemn cruelty and [prepare] a Christian audience receptive to their criticism" ("'The Sacred Rights of the Weak'" 14). For Clark, as for most scholars, Calvinism is pitted against religious faiths that privilege God's love and mercy. It is this notion that also characterizes scholarship on the sentimental tradition as well, which, given its ties to the Scottish Enlightenment, is seen to exist in direct opposition to the so-called spirit of Calvinist thought. For additional scholarship that locates sentimentalism within the Scottish Enlightenment, see Dillon, "Sentimental Aesthetics"; Boudreau, *Sympathy in American Literature*; Merish, *Sentimental Materialism*; Howard, "What Is Sentimentality?"; Ellison, *Cato's Tears*; Camfield, *Sentimental Twain*; Crane, *Race, Citizenship, and Law*; and Martin, *The Instructed Vision*. For a useful collection on liberal religious trends and their influence on American art and culture in the nineteenth and twentieth centuries, see Schmidt and Promey, eds., *American Religious Liberalism*.

17. Prominent Scottish Enlightenment thinkers like Francis Hutcheson and David Hume developed theories of sympathy as part of their epistemological and moral philosophies, but the account of sympathy that had the greatest influence on American sentimentalism came from Adam Smith's *The Theory of Moral Sentiments*.

18. Douglas, *The Feminization of American Culture*, 12.

19. Ibid., 18.

20. Ibid., 13. Douglas is fully aware of Calvinism's shortcomings—"it was repressive, authoritarian, dogmatic, patriarchal to an extreme" (12)—even as she mourns its loss.

21. Bart D. Ehrman has argued that the biblical figure of Jesus should be read within the tradition of apocalyptic prophets. Ehrman suggests that the apocalyptic is foundational to Jesus's teachings, a view many nineteenth-century Americans not only held but saw as being compatible with Jesus's emphasis on love as well. See Ehrman, *Jesus: Apocalyptic Prophet*.

22. United States Supreme Court, *A Report*, 404.

23. Support for slavery was widespread in Southern churches and among Southern

preachers. But many Northern churches remained hostile to abolitionist activity, even when they regarded slavery as a corrupt and immoral institution. In the view of many Northern church leaders, it was best to let Southern churches decide how to address the slavery question. As John R. McKivigan and Mitchell Snay observe, "Despite considerable antislavery progress in many denominations"—particularly among Northern Methodists and Presbyterians—"abolitionism remained a minority viewpoint in the northern church in 1860" (*Religion* 13). McKivigan and Snay's introduction provides a valuable overview of how Northern religious institutions responded to growing tensions over slavery. For an analysis of the crisis in theology over Scripture's inability to provide a coherent response to the slavery question, see Noll, *The Civil War*.

24. Bercovitch, *The American Jeremiad*, 23. For an account of history as a series of crises, so that "to live is to live in crisis," see Kermode, *The Sense of an Ending*, 26. Bercovitch similarly claims that the Puritans saw their place in history to be always in a state of crisis. For an excellent examination of the ways in which crisis and myriad discourses of disaster have shaped America's fundamental understanding of itself with regard to its sphere of power, its economic regimes, its treatment of the environment, and various other related contexts, see Rozario, *The Culture of Calamity*.

25. Edwards, "Sinners," 96.

26. Ibid., 96.

27. Referring to his frequent evocations of fear in his sermons, Edwards says: "Some talk of it as an unreasonable thing to fright persons to heaven; but I think it is a reasonable thing to endeavor to fright persons away from hell. They stand upon its brink, and are just ready to fall into it, and are senseless of their danger. Is it not a reasonable thing to fright a person out of a house on fire? The word *fright* is commonly used for sudden, causeless fear, or groundless surprise; but surely a just fear, for which there is good reason, is not to be spoken against under any such name" (Edwards, *The Works of President Edwards*, 538; original emphasis). For Edwards, inspiring fear was a necessary strategy when it came to saving souls, especially when members of the Puritan communities he addressed failed to appreciate how dire their circumstances were. Antislavery reformers held views similar to Edwards, seeing slavery as the sin for which an entire nation will inevitably have to pay a heavy price.

28. Edwards, "Sinners," 102–3; emphasis mine.

29. The affections, including hope, joy, peace, and especially love, were important components of Edwards's thinking about religious faith and conversion at the height of the Great Awakening. His most consolidated and thorough examination of these affections, and the way in which their veracity could be tested, is articulated in *A Treatise Concerning Religious Affections*, published in 1746. For a very useful account of Edwards's complex study, see Smith, "Religious Affections."

30. Whereas sentimental love is understood to work against hierarchies, Puritan accounts of love appear at times to be dependent on them. For example, in "A Model of Christian Charity," John Winthrop delineates the imperative to build a community of Christian love (always with the threat of God's wrath for failing to do so), but he conceptualizes love as a structure of obligations within a hierarchical social order. Those in positions of power demonstrate love through mercy, benevolence, and charity. Those on

the bottom of the hierarchical relationship exemplify love through submission, gratitude, and fealty. Within the sentimental tradition, by contrast, love is defined in terms of the natural sentiments—the prerational impressions of approval and disapproval that one experiences when observing human actions. Through the push and pull of these natural sentiments, which are antecedent to any relations of hierarchy, one develops moral structures of interpersonal relationality. In the particular account of abolitionist sentimentality that I examine throughout this book, sentimentalism offers a new concept of love that resists hierarchies but nevertheless retains the emphasis on divine retribution so prevalent in Puritan America. See Winthrop, "A Model of Christian Charity."

31. While my focus often attends to the more threatening, dread-ridden quality of the jeremiadic tradition, Bercovitch emphasizes the Puritan sermon's abiding optimism. He argues, "The essence of the sermon form that the first native-born American Puritans inherited from their fathers, and then 'developed, amplified, and standardized,' is its unshakable optimism" (6–7). He concedes: "Not that [the Puritans] minimized the threat of divine retribution; on the contrary, they asserted it with a ferocity unparalleled in the European pulpit. But they qualified it in a way that turned threat into celebration. In their case, they believed, God's punishments were *corrective*, not destructive.... The Puritans did not seek out affliction, but where they found it they recorded it as zealously, and almost as gratefully, as they recorded instances of God's mercies towards them" (8; original emphasis). In the way Bercovitch emphasizes the "corrective" purposes of retribution, I believe our arguments are in strong agreement. For an analysis of how this dynamic tension between optimism and pessimism has organized American apocalyptic literature, see Zamora, "The Myth of Apocalypse."

32. For analyses of the various ways sentimentalism intersected with and enabled (and, at times, frustrated) democratic discourse, see Boudreau, *Sympathy in American Literature*; Ellison, *The Plight of Feeling*; and Barnes, *States of Sympathy*.

33. To the extent that it inspires a commitment to self-preservation, the apocalypse bears on one's bodily existence as well as on one's spiritual well-being. "The emotion of fear," says Joanna Bourke, "is fundamentally about the body—its fleshiness and its precariousness. Fear is *felt*, and although the emotion of fear cannot be *reduced to* the sensation of fear, it is not present *without* sensation" (8; original emphases).

34. The remarkable proliferation of religious denominations and sects was one of the principal features of America's rapidly changing and expanding religious culture in the period I examine.

35. Despite their critiques of Calvinist theology, some Methodists, for example, understood the value of generating fear as a way to guide their congregants to moral action. To this end, Methodist ministers continued to invoke God's vengeance in their sermons. More moderate denominations like the Universalists, who promoted a doctrine of universal salvation, charged Methodists with overemphasizing so-called justice at the expense of God's mercy. Methodists countered these charges by accusing the Universalists with failing to take seriously the doctrine of divine justice. While Universalists did believe salvation was possible for everyone, when Hosea Ballou (a Universalist) concluded that sin was its own punishment and discounted the need for notions of divine punishment to act as a deterrent for sinners, he was criticized by fellow Universalists for

promoting a theological doctrine that abandoned God's reprisal and therefore removed the incentive for Universalist followers to live moral lives. Even a denomination as liberal as Universalism struggled to produce a univocal account of God's judgment (this internal struggle can also been seen with PAULUS and the example from footnote 2). So while each denomination was struggling to clarify and revise certain normative values within Calvinist thought, notions of God's vengeance lingered, though in varying degrees. This was true for Baptists and even some Unitarians. See Holifield, *Theology in America*, 213, 224–26, 229–30, 261–62.

I obviously cannot cover—in an entire book, let alone a paragraph and a footnote—the full complexity of the doctrinal debates that were ongoing in this period. With the above examples, I only gesture toward the types of conversations that were unfolding around the issue of God's wrath and judgment.

36. Carlos Wilcox, "Sermon XIX," 30.

37. The more optimistic of the nineteenth-century religious reformers, postmillennial Christians believed that the slow perfecting of humanity would antecede the installation of God's earthly kingdom. This group is often contrasted with the premillennialists, who believed that Christ's return would trigger a series of tribulations that unregenerate sinners would have to endure before the millennium began. It is the premillennialists who are often associated with the fire-and-brimstone rhetoric I examine in this study, for this was the way they encouraged sinners to reform their ways and flee from the wrath to come.

38. I take "redeemer nation" from Ernest Lee Tuveson, whose important study explores how a millennial logic has organized America's religious, political, and cultural history (*Redeemer Nation*). For the best analysis of the apocalyptic motivations behind the Protestant emigration to America, see Zakai, *Exile and Kingdom*. Zakai argues that "to a large extent, the justifications for and the vindications of the Protestant settlement of Virginia and the Puritan migration to New England were based upon the premises of the apocalyptic tradition or upon the apocalyptic interpretation of history. Indeed, it is hard to conceive of the English colonization of America without the apocalyptic dimension according to which the settlement of America was seen as a divine duty to spread the Gospel in remote corners of the world" (61).

39. *The Apocalypse Explained* and *A Key to the Revelations*.

40. While this broadside predates the period I am investigating, it nevertheless provides a sense of the way Protestant Americans were engaged with and publicly promoting end-times theology (*By the Command*).

41. For just two examples, see Bird, *The Infidel*, and Fairfield, *The Last Night of Pompeii*.

42. See Husch, *Something Coming*, for more on visual depictions of apocalypse in the period I am examining.

43. "Drinking Song" was published by Charles Mangus in the early 1860s and was an adaptation of a poem written by the German poet and philologist Ludwig Uhland.

44. "Whoever takes on the apocalyptic tone," writes Derrida, "comes to signify to, if not tell, you something. What? The truth, of course, and to signify to you that it reveals the truth to you; tone is revelatory of some unveiling in process" ("Of an Apocalyptic Tone" 84). In light of Derrida's claims about the relationship between an apocalyptic

tonality and the revelation of truth, we can see why such a discursive mode would have been adopted by abolitionists. It was one of the principal ways of underscoring and "confirming" the "truth" of slavery's immorality. Of course, those who defended slavery and used a similarly apocalyptic tone to do so would have claimed that *they* were, in fact, revealing some absolute truth about slavery's rightness, necessity, etc. For a thorough analysis of the rhetorical uses of apocalypse, see O'Leary, *Arguing the Apocalypse*. O'Leary argues that apocalyptic rhetoric situates audiences in a temporal setting in which the fulfillment of history is claimed to be fast approaching. Such an approach, O'Leary maintains, allows the rhetor to propose that he has a way to resolve whatever crisis is at hand.

45. Of course, violence was not the only form that slave resistance took, and scholars have examined the myriad ways slaves resisted oppressive plantation life. Violence, nevertheless, remains one of the principal objects of my analysis.

46. Reynolds, *Righteous Violence*, 3.

47. Davis, *Inhuman Bondage*, 205. For important works of scholarship that explore slave resistance within a revolutionary frame, see Genovese, *Roll, Jordan, Roll*; Morgan, *American Slavery, American Freedom*; Davis, *The Problem of Slavery*; Genovese, *From Rebellion to Revolution*; Walzer, *Exodus and Revolution*; Andrews, *To Tell a Free Story*; Aptheker, *Abolitionism: A Revolutionary Movement*; Huggins, *Black Odyssey*; Sundquist, *To Wake the Nations*; Freehling, *The Reintegration of American History*; Horton, *In Hope of Liberty*; Foner, *The Story of American Freedom*; Glaude, *Exodus!*; Furstenberg, "Beyond Freedom and Slavery." While this is only a partial list, it illustrates how many of the landmark works in this field conjoin ideas of slave resistance with notions of revolution.

48. There are obviously problems with the scholarly treatment of Douglass as an index by which nineteenth-century black Americans have been understood. For an excellent critique of reading slave resistance within a heroic frame, see Hartman, *Scenes of Subjection*, 61–70. For scholarship on the revolutionary dimensions of Douglass and *The Heroic Slave*, see Reynolds, *Righteous Violence*, chapter 3; Sale, *The Slumbering Volcano*, 173–97; Sundquist, *To Wake the Nations*, 83–87; and Yarborough, "Race, Violence, and Manhood," 166–88.

49. Scholars have shown a great deal of interest in how evangelicalism in the nineteenth century intersected with and accommodated republican ideology. In addition to exploring some of these moments, I also examine instances when a certain strand of apocalyptic theology existed in tension with and even endangered an expanding sphere of liberty. For more on the confluence of evangelical Protestantism and republicanism, see Noll, *America's God*; Forbes, "Slavery and the Evangelical Enlightenment"; Hatch, *The Democratization of American Christianity*; and Ahlstrom, *A Religious History*, especially chapters 24–30.

50. This is not to suggest that I am advocating submission or subordination as a tactic for resisting racial injustice. Rather, I am trying to explicate the account of resistance-through-submission that some nineteenth-century antislavery texts produced. I also do not want to imply that revolution and religious violence never overlap; in fact, they often do. But there are instances when it is important to maintain some distinctions between these two frameworks of violence and their ideological origins. Ideas regarding slaves' revolutionary agency, which scholars often privilege, tend to submerge the terror that

apocalyptic prophecy is intended to produce as well as obscure the divergent forms of agency that are represented within a religious rather than secular epistemology.

51. See Brodhead, *Cultures of Letters;* and Wexler, *Tender Violence.* Also see Barnes, *Love's Whipping Boy.*

52. Noble, *Masochistic Pleasures,* 23.

53. See Apter, *Dangerous Edge.*

54. Donald Pease has examined how Americans have used the idea of America's place within apocalyptic history to legitimize and justify acts of state violence. See "American Apocalypse."

55. What makes modern-day terrorism so objectionable is its use of seemingly random acts of violence against ostensibly innocent civilian populations. This was typically not a feature of nineteenth-century antislavery politics, although at times terror was engendered precisely by violent acts and not just rhetorical ones. Nat Turner and John Brown, whom I consider at length in this book, are two very famous cases in point. Some might argue today, as many did in the 1830s and late 1850s, that Turner's and Brown's insurgencies unfairly targeted "innocent" civilians. One of the key features, however, that distinguishes apocalyptic sentimentalism from modern-day terrorism is the discourse of love that is such a central part of the sentimental tradition. Turner and Brown may indeed be read as nineteenth-century terrorists, but they are not easy parallels to modern-day terrorists.

56. There is debate about U.S. foreign policy and the extent to which America engages in acts of terror even as it claims to be committed to the eradication of terror-based practices, which it says are illegal. When it comes to terrorism, in other words, the United States may be a perpetrator and not just a victim. See Stanford Law School and NYU School of Law, *Living Under Drones.* For more on U.S. drone use and its relationship to terrorism, see Greenwald, "U.S. drone strikes"; Monbiot, "In the U.S., mass child killings"; and Abé, "The Woes."

57. For a fine study of the rise of terrorism within America's literary and political culture in the late nineteenth and early twentieth centuries, and the way this culture overlaps with and energizes the evolution of industrial capitalism, see Clymer, *America's Culture of Terrorism.*

58. Eastman, *Aunt Phillis's Cabin,* 279–80; original emphasis.

59. Ibid., 280.

Chapter 1. David Walker, Nat Turner, and the Logic of Sentimental Terror

1. According to Cindy Weinstein, "the generic goal" of the sentimental novel "is the substitution of freely given love, rather than blood, as the invincible tie that binds together individuals in a family" (*Family, Kinship, and Sympathy* 8). Love is what unites members of a family and coheres families into larger communities. Shirley Samuels explains that "The reform literature associated with sentimentality works as a set of rules for how to 'feel right,' privileging compassion in calibrating and adjusting the sensations of the reader in finely tuned and predictable responses to what is viewed or read" (*The Culture of Sentiment* 5).

2. As Glenn Hendler argues, "Sympathetic identification works through a logic of equivalence based on affect; any being capable of suffering, regardless of race and age, or any other personal characteristic, can evoke sympathy, especially from a female character (or reader) who has suffered herself" ("The Limits of Sympathy" 688). Notwithstanding the prevalence of these readings of sympathy, I do not want to suggest that scholars have an uncritical view of sympathy and love and the material differences that they obscure between black and white persons. For critiques of sympathy, see Marianne Noble, *Masochistic Pleasures*, chapter 2; Hendler, *Public Sentiments*; and Wexler, *Tender Violence*.

3. Hendler, *Public Sentiments*, 119.

4. Weinstein, *Family, Kinship, and Sympathy*, 66.

5. Camfield, *Sentimental Twain*, 27–35.

6. I do not use "abolitionist sentimentality" and "apocalyptic sentimentalism" interchangeably. Apocalyptic sentimentalism is a particular narrative and rhetorical strategy that certain practitioners within abolitionist and antislavery camps deploy in their arguments. The examples of apocalyptic sentimentalism that I examine in this book all bear on the issue of slavery, but not every antislavery writer who uses sentimental strategies necessarily deploys the discourse of apocalyptic sentimentalism.

7. Despite Michael P. Johnson's claims that the Vesey plot was itself a fabricated conspiracy, Peter Hinks has presented compelling evidence to suggest that Walker was indeed in South Carolina in the early 1820s and may have even participated in the plot's organization. At the very least, Walker probably attended the AME Church in which Vesey and his coconspirators planned their attack. For a full account of Walker's possible relationship to Denmark Vesey, see Hinks, *To Awaken My Afflicted Brethren*, chapter 2. For a useful historical overview of the Denmark Vesey affair, see Pearson's introduction to *Designs Against Charleston*.

8. Walker, *Appeal*, 72 n.; hereafter abbreviated *A* and cited parenthetically by page number within the text.

9. For an excellent discussion of the circulation of Walker's *Appeal* and the ramifications of its presence in the South, see Hinks, *To Awaken My Afflicted Brethren*, chapter 5.

10. Garnet, "Sketch."

11. While many mainstream Southern Methodist churches in the early decades of the nineteenth century were becoming less emphatic in their antislavery stance in order to appeal to the planter class whose membership they sought, the AME Church in cities like Philadelphia and Charleston remained on the front lines of antislavery activism and worked aggressively to counter growing racism within white Methodist ranks as well as within society at large. As far as the AME Church's presence in Charleston, Peter Hinks argues, "Planning for [Vesey's] revolt and preparing the minds of numerous blacks for justifying it certainly occurred in one form or another within the several African congregations and their associated classes." Hinks continues: "While black revolt in the Charleston of 1822 would have been possible without the AME Church, its organizational potential would have been severely curtailed. One can legitimately call the Charleston AME Church the center of the Vesey conspiracy" (*To Awaken My Afflicted Brethren* 37–38). It is within this context that Walker's ideas regarding slave resistance likely formed.

12. For a detailed explanation of the theological origins of Walker's and Vesey's ideas on rebellion, see Hinks, chapter 2. For an extensive analysis of "prophetic ethics" and Walker's relationship to the Hebrew prophetic tradition, see Burrow, *God and Human Responsibility*.

13. Gene Andrew Jarrett maintains that Walker ultimately disavows the practical usage of violence because it contradicts leading black activists who promoted moral solutions to slavery rather than violent ones ("'To Refute Mr. Jefferson's Argument'" 313). Eddie Glaude argues that "Walker was not advocating a destructive expression of anger. Not at all. His intent was to shift the center of gravity in our morality to a place where our justification for action emanates not from custom or habit but from conscience or some principle of thought" (*Exodus!* 40). I have been suggesting, in contrast to claims offered by Jarrett and Glaude, that Walker's calls for violence are not only sincere but practical insofar as they might move readers to change their minds, after changing their hearts, about the morality of slavery. Levine's claims are made in *Dislocating Race and Nation*.

14. *The Confessions of Nat Turner*, ed. Greenberg, 50; hereafter abbreviated *C* and cited parenthetically by page number within the text.

15. The only mention of liberty in the *Confessions* comes from Will, one of Turner's rebels, who expresses to Turner that "his life was worth no more than others, and his liberty as dear to him." Rather than reassuring Will that liberty was the shared objective among all the conspirators, Turner merely asks him "if he thought to obtain it?" Will's reply that "he would, or loose his life" is what "put him in full confidence" with Turner (48). At no point does Turner concede that he believes freedom is a possibility for these insurgents. What makes Will a useful ally, then, is not his commitment to an idea of freedom that Turner himself pursues, but his willingness to fight and die alongside Turner, regardless of Turner's actual motives.

16. Questions of authenticity have surrounded Turner's *Confessions* since the late 1960s, with critics typically doubting the reliability of Thomas Gray's reporting. Against this tradition, Eric Sundquist argues that while Thomas Gray's involvement may "[serve] to contain and suppress Turner's revolt by situating it within a description of fanaticism," it is ultimately Turner, not Gray, who "should be seen to be in control of his text" (*To Wake the Nations* 43, 38). Other scholars, like Sundquist, have offered a more nuanced theory of "authorship" for the *Confessions*, often treating Gray and Turner as collaborators rather than mere antagonists. See Greenberg, "Introduction," *The Confessions of Nat Turner*, 8; Andrews, *To Tell a Free Story*, 72–77; and Parramore, *Southampton County*. In contrast, Wilson Jeremiah Moses reads the *Confessions* not as a collaboration at all but a true statement that Gray faithfully recorded during his interviews with Turner (*Black Messiahs and Uncle Toms* 64). I am not entering into this debate, which is speculative at best. Whether the *Confessions* was Turner's voice or Gray's or some combination of the two is less important than the public portrait of Turner that the text produces and that readers consume as well as the terror that such a portrait generates.

17. In an effort to distinguish Turner's words from Gray's, Anthony E. Kaye argues that there are indeed signposts that expose Gray's editorial presence, most notably those moments when Turner refers to "our blood-stained track" and his "thirst for blood." It is with these "improbable" statements, says Kaye, that we see how "Gray put words in

Turner's mouth" (Kaye, "Neighborhoods and Nat Turner," 9). Seymour L. Gross and Eileen Bender also dispute that Turner would have referred to a "thirst for blood" in his confession to Gray, and doubt that Turner would have had knowledge of the various dramatic and rhetorical conventions that appear in the *Confessions* (see "History, Politics and Literature" 496–98). One could just as easily counter these arguments by pointing out that Turner's confession was principally about inspiring terror, and what better way for an insurgent like Turner to produce terror than by emphasizing his thirst for blood?

18. See especially Tompkins, *Sensational Designs*, chapter 5; and Sanchez-Eppler, "Then When We Clutched Hardest."

19. Readers would have been equally horrified when Turner recounts how his rebels murdered ten children (whose bodies were decapitated and piled together. This particular detail, however, is not included in Turner's statement to Gray). I single out the sleeping infant not because this death was more gruesome than the others but because it serves as a concise example for me to examine the symbolic role of children within the tradition of apocalyptic sentimentalism.

20. *Richmond Whig*, September 26, 1831, qtd. in Foner, ed., *Nat Turner*, 29.

21. *Richmond Enquirer*, September 30, 1831, qtd. in Foner, ed., *Nat Turner*, 30.

22. Brown, *Narrative of Henry Box Brown*, 39.

23. *New York Morning Courier and Enquirer*, September 17, 1831, qtd. in Foner, ed., *Nat Turner*, 23.

24. For more on these debates, see Foner's introduction to *Nat Turner*, 7–10.

25. Thomas C. Parramore emphasizes Turner's rebellion as a colossal tactical failure and Turner as a leader who was "incapable of devising a feasible plan." This view presupposes that Turner's intent was to liberate slaves, which, as I have already suggested, was not the case. See "Covenant in Jerusalem," chapter 4.

26. Sale, *The Slumbering Volcano*, 6.

27. According to Jarrett, one of the ways Walker challenges Jefferson's ostensibly scientific claims regarding African Americans' inherent inability to exist as free citizens is through what he calls a "black revolutionary lexicon" (298–99). Robert Levine maintains that Walker's entire notion of slave resistance is organized in relation to his reading of the Declaration of Independence, a document that ironically not only sanctions but encourages the use of violence against repressive governing regimes (*Dislocating Race and Nation* 107–8).

28. Eric Sundquist typifies scholarly readings of Turner by conjoining the revolutionary to the theological, treating these two categories as not only cooperative but virtually synonymous. "The millenarian tradition that Turner invoked in 1831," Sundquist observes, "intentionally or not, shared with radical abolitionism a theoretical belief in the power of Christianity as an agent of sudden, revolutionary change." And this revolutionary potential of millennial Christianity is best exemplified by the Christian God that Turner and other abolitionists turn to, a figure Sundquist describes as a "revolutionary messiah" (64). Eugene Genovese similarly links the revolutionary and the apocalyptic, which, he argues, produced within the context of early slave resistance "revolutionary terror." Genovese also maintains that Turner spoke "in the accents of the Declaration of Independence and the Rights of Man" (*From Rebellion to Revolution* 9, 49).

29. Sundquist, *To Wake the Nations*, 29. Sundquist does not discount Walker's religiosity but instead enfolds Christianity into a revolutionary framework, creating what he calls a "revolutionary Christianity" (67). For an excellent reading of Walker's use of the Exodus story to claim America as a land fundamentally shaped by the presence of African Americans, see Apap, "'Let no man of us,'" 319–50.

30. Qtd. in Nell, *Colored Patriots*, 8.

31. Scholarly readings seem to take their cue from William Cooper Nell, who in 1855 included Walker and Turner in his book *The Colored Patriots of the American Revolution*. Acceding to Nell's depiction of these figures as black revolutionaries, scholars continue to talk about the *Appeal* and *Confessions* and their account of slave rebellion as expressions of a revolutionary spirit among black rebels, suggesting that black violence is revolutionary violence transposed to a different but nevertheless equivalent set of historical circumstances.

32. Walter Johnson has expressed similar frustration with New Social History's account of agency as an expression of liberal selfhood, where the slave's capacity for making rational, autonomous choices in opposition to the degrading logic of race-based slavery is typically highlighted and emphasized. Says Johnson: "By applying the jargon of self-determination and choice to the historical condition of civil objectification and choicelessness, historians have, not surprisingly, ended up in a mess. They have, in the first instance, ended up with what is more-or-less a rational choice model of human being, and shoved to the side in the process a consideration of human-ness lived outside the conventions of liberal agency, a consideration, that is, of the condition of enslaved humanity." My account of the messianic is, I believe, one such instance where slaves internalized a form of agency that cannot be neatly sorted within a liberal frame ("On Agency" 115).

33. As Maggie Sale explains, citizenship was often understood in masculinist terms during the antebellum period, which might explain Walker's preoccupation with black manhood. Sale offers an important critique of the gender divide that exists in Walker's argument. "While Walker's desire to inspire and even to incite makes sense given his aims and the context in which he was working," argues Sale, "this stance obviously is problematic in relation to those, particularly women, who chose not to flee or overtly to resist slavery because they constituted the primary support system for others. Walker's logic makes no provision for this population, defining refusal to resist as 'a mean, servile spirit,' or even worse, brutishness and semihuman stature" (53).

34. Of course, much of the Christian tradition dating as far back as Augustine is based on self-disavowal. What interests me here is how a discourse of abnegation intersects with and supports a discourse of black empowerment in the antebellum period.

35. Edwards, *Personal Narrative*, 288.

36. Ibid., 291–92.

37. Ibid., 293.

38. Emerson, "Self-Reliance," 143.

39. Qtd. in Mott, "Age of the First Person," 69. It is worth noting that Benjamin Franklin's autobiography was first published in America in 1818, just eleven years before Walker published the *Appeal*. Franklin's autobiography collaborates with Emersonian

notions to inspire a cultural ideology of self-reliance. Franklin—scientist, statesman, Founding Father—is America's quintessential self-reliant man. Franklin's model of self-reliance, however, in which industriousness is a central trait of the self-sufficient individual, differs from Emerson's, even though Emerson is often misread as offering a naïve version of rugged individualism.

40. See especially Douglass, "Self-Made Men," 545–75.

41. For a concise statement on the relationship between Emersonian self-reliance and abnegation, see Buell, *Emerson*, chapter 2.

42. Emerson, "Self-Reliance," 139.

43. Butler, *Psychic Life of Power*, 7.

44. Ibid., 2.

45. Butler addresses the unavoidably circular nature of this argument in the introduction to *The Psychic Life of Power*, in which a discourse exerts a force on a subject, paradoxically treating the subject as if it already exists, when the force itself is the very source of the subject's production.

46. Ibid., 9. For a powerful description of the contradictory nature of subjection, see Spivak, *Outside in the Teaching Machine*, chapter 2.

47. For a lesser-known example in which ideas of black empowerment are constructed in a subordinate relation to God, see Young's "The Ethiopian Manifesto."

48. For more on the theological dimensions of Turner's rebellion, see Harding, "Symptoms of Liberty"; and Sidbury, "Reading, Revelation, and Rebellion."

49. While Turner rejects African religious practices, scholars have nevertheless argued that some of Turner's descriptions (communicating with the spirit, the markings on the head and breast) suggest that non-Christian religious rituals and beliefs influenced the spiritual account of his life leading up to the rebellion (see Sobel, *Trabelin' On*, 161–66). These representations from an African past heighten the drama of Turner's apocalyptic narrative, even if they do not originate in a Christian evangelical tradition. For an excellent examination of the way Turner's rebellion impacted Baptist churches in southeastern Virginia, see Scully, *Religion*.

50. For an analysis of how Turner's prophetic mode in the *Confessions* radically destabilizes traditional literary categories of author, character, and narration, see Scales, "Narrative Revolutions." Scales argues that the narratives produced by Turner and Joseph Smith represent a speaking subject that intermingles with the divine, thus creating a model of subjectivity that does not coincide with the autonomy of the liberal speaking subject. I agree with Scales that one of the crucial features of Turner's narrative is the way his identity and the divine at times become coextensive. My analysis, however, emphasizes how Turner transforms notions of liberal agency through an act of self-abnegation, a transformation that depends in large measure on apocalyptic theology.

51. By the early nineteenth century, no figure had come to symbolize American liberal theory more powerfully than did Thomas Jefferson, and no text was more representative of liberalism's so-called universal egalitarianism than the Declaration of Independence. For David Walker, however, Jefferson reflects the nation's most damaging and invidious assumptions about racial difference, assumptions that Jefferson most notoriously expressed in his *Notes on the State of Virginia* and that, for Walker, undermined the fun-

damental tenets of the Declaration. "Mr. Jefferson," explains Walker, "a much greater philosopher the world never afforded, has in truth injured us more, and has been as great a barrier to our emancipation as any thing that has ever been advanced against us" (*A* 27). It is Jefferson's argument in *Notes*, and not his abstract claims in the Declaration, that have most powerfully shaped America's racial beliefs, and "unless we try to refute Mr. Jefferson's arguments respecting us," Walker concludes, "we will only establish them" (15). While invested in adopting the principles Jefferson expresses in his most famous piece of political writing, Walker nevertheless remains committed to disavowing Jefferson's views as a natural scientist, views, Jefferson says, that confirm "the real distinctions [between the races] which nature has made" (Jefferson, *Notes*, 199).

52. Scholars continue to reject discourses like Walker's and Turner's for being inherently regressive and oppositional to strategies of freedom. Eddie Glaude and Michael Walzer, for instance, have both argued against a messianic logic being part of strategies of liberation. Glaude argues along the lines of Walzer, calling for a vision of freedom that "imagine[s] a nationalist politics without the baggage of political messianism, that is to say, without the desire for the apocalypse, a readiness to force the End, and claims of the unconditionality of the national mission" (144–45). According to Glaude, a politics rooted in the apocalyptic can too easily slide into a form of chauvinism as destructive as the politics one is trying to dispute (80). I agree with Glaude that arguments like Walker's and Turner's that are rooted in political messianism do tend to "force the End" in a manner that modern readers understandably find troubling. What I disagree with is how often scholars have tried to rescue Walker and Turner by locating them within a black revolutionary tradition, a move that makes the forms of violence they express more acceptable because it coincides with America's emergence as a (white) liberal society. I say this, not because I admire or support or sympathize with Turner's and Walker's envisioning of racial violence, but only because I want to describe properly the way examples of power and violence in the *Appeal* and *Confessions* depart from liberal norms.

53. In an especially egregious display of racial acrimony following Turner's insurrection, vigilante groups rounded up and murdered innocent slaves, with victims numbering into the hundreds. For more, see Foner, ed., *Nat Turner*, and Oates, *The Fires of Jubilee*. For an interesting counterpoint to these acts of vigilante justice, see Breen, "Contested Communion." Breen's analysis centers on several Baptist churches located near the Southampton revolt whose white members agreed to allow blacks back into the church rather than excommunicate them, a rare but meaningful instance of magnanimity among white Southerners.

54. Most black authors nevertheless deployed this very discourse, arguing that black Americans met the criteria for inclusion within the body politic. According to Richard Yarborough in "Race, Violence, and Manhood": "Even a superficial survey of nineteenth-century writing and oratory reveals the extent to which Afro-American spokespersons like [Albert A.] Whitman, Douglass, [David] Walker, and [Henry Highland] Garnet saw the crucial test of black fitness to be whether or not black men were, in fact, what was conventionally considered 'manly'" (167–68). The traits that helped to consolidate this stable sense of selfhood for black men included "nobility, intelligence, strength, articulateness, loyalty, virtue, rationality, courage, self-control, courtliness, honesty, and

physical attractiveness as defined in white Western European terms." These values that were championed by the white bourgeois majority to define masculinity were appropriated by black authors to construct their accounts of ideal manhood. African American writers thus colluded, perhaps unavoidably, in reproducing, valorizing, and ultimately adopting as their own those normative structures that were used by white racists to marginalize black subjects as subhuman beings. Black writers, in short, sought to construct a black masculinist identity through many of the same categories that defined normative (and thus white) liberal citizenship.

55. I am careful here not to locate Walker at the start of a so-called African American literary tradition, given that Kenneth Warren and Robert F. Reid-Pharr have argued against retroactively assigning such a tradition when one did not actually exist. Warren argues that the tradition we call "African American literature" organized itself in response to Jim Crow, and its authors were defined by their contestation of the ideological parameters of this social construct. According to Warren's periodization, then, African American literature is a tradition that started much later than the early nineteenth century and has already come to an end. Reid-Pharr compellingly claims that the vast body of writing by black Americans is far too diverse and dynamic to organize within a single black literary tradition. I do, however, want to emphasize that apocalyptic sentimentalism was at least partly influenced by a set of early black texts while stopping short of claiming that these texts compose an original black literary tradition. See Warren, *What Was African American Literature?*, and Reid-Pharr, *Conjugal Union*, especially chapter 1.

Chapter 2. "The Wrath of the Lamb"

1. Stewart, *Religion and the Pure Principles*, 30, emphasis mine; hereafter abbreviated *Religion* and cited parenthetically in the text by page number. Quotations from *Religion and the Pure Principles of Morality* and Stewart's public addresses all come from Marilyn Richardson's edited collection of Stewart's writing.

2. For an analysis that considers the relationship between David Walker's *Appeal*, Maria Stewart's addresses, and the creation of the *Freedom's Journal*, see Garfield, "Literary Societies."

3. It is important to keep in mind that Stewart publishes this essay only several months after Nat Turner's insurrection. Anxieties were indeed high about other possible insurrections, and Stewart, rather than seek to alleviate these anxieties, chooses to intensify them instead. For an analysis of the ways in which Stewart extends the work of Walker and Turner, particularly in terms of the prophetic voice she adopts, the way she engages with the needs of the black community, and her critiques of systemic racism (and not just slavery), see Rycenga, "Maria Stewart, Black Abolitionist."

4. As some scholars have argued, women writers and activists did not always adhere to the divide between public and private spheres. See Baym, *American Women Writers*.

5. Romero, *Home Fronts*, 53.
6. Ibid., 54.
7. Grasso, *Artistry of Anger*, 106.
8. Ibid., 110.

9. Ibid., 110.

10. Ibid., 131.

11. Few critics, however, have considered how protosentimentalist conventions characterize much of Stewart's discourse, and none has explored the dynamic between the affects of love and fear and what this dynamic means for the way we understand sentimentality within early African American literature as well as more broadly. Along with identifying sentimental tropes in Stewart's work, Joycelyn Moody is one of the few scholars to treat the jeremiad and the sentimental as compatible discourses. "Like the jeremiads of the seventeenth-century American Puritans," Moody argues, "African American jeremiads are by definition a sentimental form since they rely on moral suasion, deep feeling, and a shared sense of social justice" (*Sentimental Confessions* 29).

12. Stewart, "Franklin Hall," 45; hereafter abbreviated FH and cited parenthetically in the text by page number.

13. Stewart, "Afric-American Female Intelligence Society," 52; hereafter abbreviated FIS and cited parenthetically in the text by page number.

14. Critics often identify Stewart as the first American woman to appear in public to speak on political matters, but this is not entirely accurate. For an excellent discussion of antebellum female preachers who engaged in political exhortation, see Brekus, *Strangers and Pilgrims*, chapter 5.

15. Brekus, *Strangers and Pilgrims*, 200.

16. Ibid., 201–2.

17. "Combining maternal affection with angry condemnations of sin, and tearful appeals to sinners with acerbic humor," says Brekus about the style female preachers often employed, "female preachers alternately fascinated and shocked their congregations" (*Strangers and Pilgrims* 206).

18. Ibid., 216.

19. Many female preachers held the belief that men were the designated heads of the household and superior to women, a view derived from a particular reading of Scripture. So while these preachers would often critique an array of social injustices, they viewed the patriarchal order as scripturally sanctioned. Stewart, on the other hand, challenges gendered *and* racial disparities simultaneously, and while she occasionally expresses conservative ideas regarding proper womanhood and ideal masculinity, she also proposes more radical notions that threatened prevailing attitudes about gender relations. For more on the conservative views of female preachers, see Brekus, *Strangers and Pilgrims*, 222–23.

20. Stewart, "Meditation I," 37. While Stewart's meditations were not delivered publicly, they provide a useful lens through which to examine and interpret her lectures.

21. Stewart, "Afric-American Female Intelligence Society," 52.

22. Stewart, "Sufferings During the War," 103.

23. The cause of Walker's death is still unclear. While many abolitionists (and some modern critics) believed that Walker was murdered, many scholars concede that he probably died of tuberculosis, which was widespread in Boston at the time.

24. Catherine Brekus argues that female preachers provide a useful test case for charting the changing notions of womanhood in the early nineteenth century. "Female

preachers epitomized the confusion over the proper boundaries of women's sphere" (*Strangers and Pilgrims* 205). Even though her career as a public speaker was brief, Stewart, too, put pressure on traditional ideas regarding appropriate topics for women's discourse. Frances Smith Foster makes the provocative claim that because black women were less constrained by social convention, they enjoyed greater freedom within the antislavery movement to challenge prevailing attitudes regarding gender and race: "In a rather peculiar way, the antislavery movement may have been the one place where black women writers may have found it easier to be published than white women abolitionists did. Social mythology in the United States presented white women with a nearly insolvable conundrum that black women did not have. White women were already stretching their boundaries by writing in public. They had to be quite careful not to appear indecorous or unfeminine, to speak or to even know about aspects of slavery not fit for ladies. That left little or nothing for them to write about beyond platitudes and generalities. Black women, on the other hand, were not expected to be refined, chaste, or ladylike so they could speak more freely" (*Written by Herself* 81).

25. Stewart was affiliated with the First African Baptist Church in Boston, and African American Baptist preachers and lay ministers like Stewart sought religious models through which to imagine the liberation of black Americans. God's retributive wrath as it is expressed in Revelation, an idea to which Stewart repeatedly returns, constitutes one such model. For an account of Stewart's use of Revelation and Scripture more generally to shape her public performance, see Cooper, *Maria Stewart*. Cooper does an exhaustive job of demonstrating that virtually every line of Stewart's lectures is informed by a biblical passage.

26. Stewart, "Meditation I," 37.

27. Stewart, "Farewell Address," 69; hereafter abbreviated FA and cited parenthetically in the text by page number.

28. Carla Peterson also identifies this trend among early black women who desired to enter the public arena. Peterson claims that they "did so by 'achieving' an additional 'oppression,' by consciously adopting a self-marginalization that became superimposed upon the already ascribed oppressions of race and gender and that paradoxically allowed empowerment." While Peterson is not talking about messianic power, her language helps articulate how an avowed subordination was used to generate greater resiliency and strength. See Peterson, *"Doers of the Word,"* 17.

29. Stewart, "The Proper Training of Children," 159–60; hereafter abbreviated TT and cited parenthetically in the text by page number.

30. Stewart, "Masonic Hall," 63; hereafter abbreviated MH and cited parenthetically in the text by page number.

31. Stewart, "Cause for Encouragement," 44; hereafter abbreviated CFE and cited parenthetically in the text by page number.

32. This statement of vengeance, from Romans 12:19, is just one of a number of examples where the New Testament provides the kind of apocalyptic framework that many see as being characteristic of the Old Testament.

33. As Lora Romero points out, "In an era of hypersensitivity to the threat of black on white violence at home and abroad, references in Stewart to the 'many powerful sons and

daughters of Africa' prepared to demand 'their rights' and, if refused, willing to 'spread horror and devastation' (71) make her speeches only slightly less incendiary than *David Walker's Appeal*" (*Home Fronts* 60).

34. Laurel Bollinger similarly argues that Stewart relies on conventional maternity as a way to enter the public discourse. Bollinger also asserts that Stewart offers a more radical account of maternity in her meditations, a point with which I agree. I want to suggest, however, that maternity, crucial though it is, is only one-third of a tripartite representation of womanhood (the other two-thirds being the prophetic and messianic dimensions). See Bollinger, "'A mother in the deity,'" 360.

35. I disagree, for instance, with Joycelyn Moody's argument, in which she states that "Stewart's gender complicates labeling her a jeremiah, for the black jeremiah, like the earlier American Puritan jeremiah, confidently assumes the power of the patriarch. Though she is austere, Stewart does not write or speak with absolute patriarchal authority.... The cultural prescriptions/proscriptions of true women as demure, compassionate, and soft-spoken fully spanned the nineteenth century (and still persist even today) and were patently incompatible with the fire-and-brimstone stridence of the jeremiad" (*Sentimental Confessions* 30). While these injunctions against women using tropes that modern readers have come to identify with the masculine domain did exist, Stewart was part of a class of women who nevertheless employed the apocalyptic as a fundamental part of their discourse. That such a class existed suggests that the divide between the masculine and feminine spheres was more unstable than many scholars would have it. And while Stewart does not simply replicate the authority of the Puritan minister by way of rhetorical mimicry, she nevertheless imbues herself with power precisely by combining the more fiery aspects of the jeremiad with the more compassionate language of mercy, forgiveness, and love. In highlighting Stewart's authority, Opal Moore replicates a similar assumption. "Stewart," says Moore, "speaks in the voice of a man. It is a voice that takes the tone of forceful authority. It is also the voice of creation." While I do not want to rob Stewart of her authoritative voice—that is, I share Moore's view about the potency of Stewart's rhetoric—I do want to point out that Moore treats Stewart's authority as masculine rather than troubling the binary that places the masculine on one side of an ideological divide, the feminine on another. See Moore, "The Productions of Maria W. Stewart," 445.

36. Beecher, *A Treatise on Domestic Economy*, 35–36; hereafter abbreviated *T* and cited parenthetically in the text by page number.

37. Revelation 22:16: "I Jesus have sent My angel to testify to you these things in the churches. I am the Root and the Offspring of David, the Bright and Morning Star" (KJV).

38. Child, "The Black Saxons," 19–20; hereafter abbreviated BS and cited parenthetically in the text by page number.

39. Child's reference to a Robin Hood who specifically fought Norman lords was an idea that first appeared in the nineteenth century.

40. Child, "Slavery's Pleasant Homes," 147; hereafter abbreviated S and cited parenthetically in the text by page number.

41. Jacobs addresses this unique injustice when she reports the birth of her daughter

in her autobiography. "When they told me my new-born babe was a girl," recounts Jacobs, "my heart was heavier than it had ever been before. Slavery is terrible for men; but it is far more terrible for women. Superadded to the burden common to all, *they* have wrongs, and sufferings, and mortifications peculiarly their own" (*Incidents* 77; original emphasis).

42. For an argument that understands violence as the "discourse" that initiates the social life of the slave, see Hartman, *Scenes of Subjection*. Hartman explains that "the material effects of power on bodies [is] an injunction to remember that the performance of blackness is inseparable from the brute force that brands, rapes, and tears open the flesh in the racial inscription of the body. In other words, the seeming obstinacy or the 'givenness' of 'blackness' registers the 'fixing' of the body by terror and dominance and the way in which that fixing has been constitutive" (58).

Chapter 3. Uncle Tom's Cabin *and the Fictionalization of Apocalyptic Sentimentalism*

1. Stowe, *Uncle Tom's Cabin*, 637, original emphasis; hereafter abbreviated *U* and cited parenthetically in the text by page number.
2. The critical consensus is that Stowe's education in the Scottish Common Sense tradition is what enabled her to use "sympathy" so strategically in *Uncle Tom's Cabin*, a view with which I agree, though with one qualification. Stowe's religious background, especially her familiarity with the liberal Calvinist theology exemplified by her father, has just as much of an influence on her ideas of the sentimental as does her reading of the Scottish Enlightenment. In particular, Stowe uses the apocalyptic to fire the imagination so that it extends itself, in a sympathetic act, to the suffering of another. She chooses a religious category in order to ensure that her readers make the sympathetic leap from self to other.
3. Tompkins, *Sensational Designs*, 140. The jeremiad and the apocalypse are not, of course, synonymous. For the Puritans (and for Stowe as well), the jeremiad was the primary mechanism through which the apocalypse was given public expression.
4. Ibid., 125. Tompkins concludes that Stowe saw her book as "an instrument for bringing about the day when the world would be ruled not by force, but by Christian love" (141), a love that was specifically located within the purview of a matrifocal family unit.
5. Coleman, "Unsentimental Woman Preacher," 278, 279; original emphasis. Coleman maintains the perennial opposition between love and fear that has characterized the novel's scholarship. She argues that, in the afterword of the novel's final installment in the *National Era*, Stowe disavows the "bold, decidedly masculine prophetic stance" of the concluding warning and instead reemphasizes her role as a paragon of maternal affection, writing in recognizable fashion that "'the dear little children' who have followed her story 'have her warmest love'" (qtd. in Coleman 278–79). These children, Stowe continues, should "remember the sweet example of Little Eva, and try to feel the same regard for all that she did" (qtd. in Coleman 278). While it is true that Stowe's afterword recuperates the rhetoric of sympathetic love that has become synonymous with sentimental fiction, it is certainly not true that the "closing paragraphs [in the *National Era*] . . . subvert the jeremiad that precedes them by transforming it from direct address

into a mimesis of direct address, a mere playing with the voice of prophecy" (278). Coleman's argument is an amplified version of Tompkins's original intervention. In order for her to continue to claim Stowe as the paradigmatic nineteenth-century literary matron, Coleman must first disavow the residual patriarchy that the jeremiad represents by turning Stowe's fire-and-brimstone language into mere mimicry of her Calvinist forebears. Rather than undermining the novel's concluding jeremiad, however, Stowe's return to the role of matronly womanhood in the afterword conforms to the pattern she already established in the narrative in which love is paired with and supported by fear.

6. Bellin, "Up to Heaven's Gate," 290.

7. It is not surprising that scholars read love in *Uncle Tom's Cabin* as they do, especially given the way Stowe herself described one of the inspirations for the novel. Referring to her eighteen-month-old son Charley's death from cholera, Stowe writes: "It was at *his* dying bed, and at *his* grave that I learnt what a poor slave mother may feel when her child is torn away from her.... I felt that I could never be consoled for it, unless this crushing of my own heart might enable me to work out some great good to others.... [M]uch that is in that book ('Uncle Tom') had its roots in the awful scenes and bitter sorrows of that summer" (Stowe to Eliza Cabot Follen, qtd. in Sanchez-Eppler, "Then When We Clutched Hardest," 66; original emphasis). Stowe's description captures the spontaneous generation of sympathy that occurs over the shared experience of a dying child, and it is this sentimental logic that scholars have used to frame their readings of the novel. Not all Americans were predisposed to sympathize over such scenes, a reality of which Stowe was acutely aware. For Stowe, then, sentimentality was more an instrument of coercion rather than a mode that facilitates sympathetic feelings between already caring individuals.

8. Scholars who see the primary innovation of sentimentalism to be its ability to facilitate cross-racial identifications and who thus assume that Stowe sees such identification as inevitable for all readers do not recognize that in certain moments, Stowe appears less than sanguine about the willingness or likelihood of her readers to sympathize or identify with slaves. See Hendler, "The Limits of Sympathy"; and Fisher, *Hard Facts*, chapter 2. Fisher expresses this very logic of sentimentality when he argues that the "sentimental novel creates the extension of feeling on which the restitution of humanity is based by means of equations between deep common feelings of the reader and the exotic but analogous situations of the characters" (118). It is Fisher's notion of "creating" an extension of feeling that interests me in this chapter, and how Stowe devises strategies that seek to generate sympathy when there are no "deep common feelings" to speak of.

9. In a chapter that considers Stowe within the emergence of liberal Protestantism, Carrie Tirado Bramen argues that Stowe is principally a theorist of "niceness" whose work emphasizes "the love and affection of Jesus" (47), a claim she persuasively develops through nuanced and provocative analyses of "Home Religion" (1870) and especially *Footsteps of the Master* (1877). What Bramen's argument does not acknowledge, however, is that this likeable Jesus only really becomes possible for Stowe once slaves have been emancipated and slavery has been removed from the national landscape. The nice "Victorian Jesus" (41) who constitutes the "embodiment of maternal love" (53) is a postwar, postslavery configuration ("The Christology of Niceness"). For more on the relationship

between evangelical revivalism and abolition, see Abzug, *Cosmos Crumbling;* McKivigan, *The War against Proslavery Religion;* and Daly, *When Slavery Was Called Freedom.*

10. "Some of his sermons," Stowe writes to her son Charles in 1874, referring to Jonathan Edwards, "are more terrible than Dante's hell" (Stowe to Charles, qtd. in Kimball, *Religious Ideas,* 32).

11. According to Gregg Camfield, Stowe saw Common Sense philosophy as an acceptable and most welcome alternative to Calvinist theology. "Typically for a nineteenth-century American," argues Camfield, "Harriet Beecher Stowe arrived in the Common Sense camp by way of her opposition to Calvinist doctrines that she could not reconcile to her own ideas of Christian love and justice" (35). Camfield argues that in light of her misgivings about the more punitive aspects of Calvinist theology, "Harriet turned to a metaphysical tradition founded on John Locke's formidable epistemological challenge to Calvinism so that she could support her own faith" (27). For Camfield, the disavowal of Calvinism constitutes sentimentalism's originary moment. I argue instead that within Stowe's early work, it is the fire-and-brimstone rhetoric of Calvinism that enhanced and supported sentimentalism's commitment to love (Camfield, *Sentimental Twain,* 35).

12. Stowe to Charlie, qtd. in Kimball, 53; original emphasis.

13. Stowe, *Key to* Uncle Tom's Cabin, 233. Other vocal opponents of slavery like William Lloyd Garrison and Henry David Thoreau argued that with the passage of the Fugitive Slave Law, slavery became a national rather than merely regional sin (prompting Garrison to exclaim: "There is no North. A sordid, truckling, cowardly, compromising spirit, is everywhere seen."). Stowe similarly decried the North's decision to embrace this legislation. "So much for the course of a decided antislavery body in union with a few slave-holding churches," Stowe wrote in response to the adoption of the Fugitive Slave Law. "So much for a most discreet, judicious, charitable, and brotherly attempt to test by experience the question, What communion hath light with darkness, and what concord hath Christ with Belial? The slave-system is darkness,—the slave-system is Belial!" (*Key to* Uncle Tom's Cabin 216). See Garrison, "No Compromise with Slavery"; also see Thoreau, "Slavery in Massachusetts."

Also in 1854, Stowe decried legislation proposing to extend slavery into the Kansas and Nebraska territories. In her "Appeal to the Women of the Free States of America," Stowe makes a sentimental appeal that recalls her approach in *Uncle Tom's Cabin.* Arguing that "there is but one feeling and one opinion" that mothers can have at the idea of extending slavery, Stowe insists that they will be the ones to protest and prevent the passage of this legislation. Says Stowe: "There is not a woman in the United States, when the question is fairly put before her, who thinks these things are right." Even as she asserts this claim with confidence, Stowe equivocates, betraying a momentary concern that even the right feelings of American mothers are not enough to ensure they will reject the legislation. "The warm beatings of many hearts have been hushed," says Stowe, "our yearning and sympathies have been repressed, because we have not known what to do; and many have come to turn a deaf ear to the whole tale of sorrow, because unwilling to harrow up the soul with feeling, were action supposed to be impossible." To counteract well-meaning but complacent mothers, Stowe has recourse to the same ideological structure she turns to throughout *Uncle Tom's Cabin,* reminding all her readers that a "conflict is now commencing between the forces of liberty and despotism throughout the world. We, who are Christians, and believe in the sure word of prophecy, now that fearful convulsions and over-turnings are predicted before the coming of Him who is to rule the earth in righteousness. How important in this crisis that all who believe in prayer should retreat beneath the shadows of the Almighty" (Stowe, "Appeal").

14. Stowe, *Writings of Harriet Beecher Stowe*, 158.

15. Tompkins, *Sensational Designs*, 127.

16. Tompkins is the first to foreground in any significant way the salvific nature of Eva's passing. In contradistinction to Ann Douglas, who argues that Eva's death "is not particularly effective in any practical sense," Tompkins maintains that "Little Eva's death enacts the drama of which all the major episodes of the novel are transformations, the idea, central to Christian soteriology, that the highest human calling is to give one's life for another" (128). See Douglas, *The Feminization of American Culture*, 2.

17. Baldwin, "Everybody's Protest Novel," 13, 14.

18. Ibid., 14.

19. This equivalence is troubling: the adult male, Tom, and the child, Eva, are treated as "equal," despite the disparity in their ages, the dissimilarity of their experiences, and the differences in their racial makeup. In establishing a sympathetic bond between Tom and Eva, Stowe obscures the important traits that differentiate their identities. Indeed, this type of obfuscation has been an understandable source of frustration for critics of sympathy. Dana Nelson has argued about the shortcomings of sympathy in establishing equivalences between persons: "Sympathy assumes *sameness* in a way that can prevent an understanding of the very real, material *differences* that structure human experience in a society based upon unequal distribution of power" (*The Word in Black and White* 142; original emphases).

20. I explore in chapter 5 what is probably the most dramatic instance of irony in the apocalyptic sentimental tradition, where acts of violence are understood to be the purest expressions of love.

21. Cathy Davidson regards sentimentalism as a literary antecedent against which the gothic tradition develops. While sentimental and gothic fiction share common preoccupations, the gothic, observes Davidson, exposes the horrors of the domestic space while examining "the different, the exotic, and the bizarre" more earnestly than the sentimental tradition typically does. Marianne Noble argues that the sentimental and gothic traditions "[stimulate] pleasure by exploiting the terror of tortured victims." And while Noble argues that the "core of horror in sentimentality is a gothic image," I suggest that in certain cases (like in *Uncle Tom's Cabin*) the apocalyptic is privileged over the gothic even when they are both deployed simultaneously. See Davidson, *Revolution and the Word*, 224; and Noble, "An Ecstasy of Apprehension," 164. Also see DeWaard, "'The Shadow of Law,'" for a reading of how the sentimental and gothic elements in *Uncle Tom's Cabin* work to expose the legal constraints surrounding black female bodies and augment the psychological terror engendered by the laws that manage and control these bodies.

22. Karen Halttunen has shown the important role played by the gothic—in particular, the image of the haunted house—in the religious imaginations of Lyman Beecher, Henry Ward Beecher, and Harriet Beecher Stowe. Halttunen also argues that the prin-

cipal function of the gothic is to create an "atmosphere of evil and brooding terror, whose purpose is to involve the reader by evoking an imaginative emotional response of fear" that, in turn, compels a reader or auditor into making moral decisions. Given Halttunen's claims about the role of terror within the gothic, and in light of the fact that the gothic and apocalyptic both appear in these scenes with Legree, it would seem, as I argue above, that Stowe is marshaling two of the most powerful nineteenth-century discourses of fear to confront the worst kind of slaveholder. I observe, however, that in *Uncle Tom's Cabin*, Stowe subordinates the gothic to the apocalyptic: the gothic appears in only a few scenes, whereas the apocalyptic appears repeatedly throughout the narrative. Halttunen, surprisingly, makes no mention of the interaction between the gothic and the apocalyptic, nor does she explain precisely how the gothic fits into Stowe's theory of the sentimental. See Halttunen, "Gothic Imagination and Social Reform," 112.

Whether this convergence suggests a more widespread collaboration between the gothic and the apocalyptic in antebellum culture is an interesting question to consider but a line of inquiry that I cannot pursue here. It should be noted, however, that channeling the apocalyptic and the gothic allows Stowe to focus attention on the different dimensions of terror characteristic of these two modes. Generically speaking, the gothic tends to involve supernatural forces that inspire psychological terror, whereas the apocalyptic, with its emphasis on a wrathful God (who is, for a believer, quite "natural" or "real" rather than supernatural), highlights the embodiment of terror, or how God's wrath might ultimately impact one's physical well-being in life and soul after death. While there may be overlap between the gothic and the apocalyptic and the forms of terror they achieve, they should not be seen as collapsible or synonymous, either in Stowe's novel or in other imaginative works that deploy these genres concurrently.

23. Stowe, *Writings of Harriet Beecher Stowe*, 157.

24. Beecher, "Reformation of Morals," 21, 31.

25. Ibid., 25.

26. In an excellent study of biblical prophecy and its influence within American cultural history, Paul Boyer similarly cautions against making firm distinctions between what he calls a "passive *pre*millennialism" and an "optimistic, activist *post*millennialism," especially in antebellum America. See Boyer, *When Time Shall Be No More*, 82–83; original emphases.

27. Powell, *Ruthless Democracy*, 106–7.

28. Samuels, "Miscegenated America," 493; original emphasis.

29. Yarborough, "Strategies of Black Characterization," 65.

30. Kaplan, *The Anarchy of Empire*, 48. The frustration with Stowe's colonizationist solution in many ways begins with Martin Delany, who expressed his outrage soon after the novel's publication (see "Mrs. Stowe's Position"). For important contemporary analyses of Stowe's ending in *Uncle Tom's Cabin*, see Spillers, "Changing the Letter"; Brown, *Domestic Individualism;* Levine, *Martin Delany;* Ryan, *The Grammar of Good Intentions*.

31. According to George Fredrickson, Stowe's views on Africa's privileged place within apocalyptic history were probably first influenced by Alexander Kinmont's lectures on race, in which he describes a millennialist future for Africa in ways that closely resemble

Stowe's vision in *Uncle Tom's Cabin* (see *Black Image*, 110–16). Timothy Powell suggests that Stowe was also influenced by the rhetoric of the American Colonization Society, which "elegantly adorned" its colonizationist aspirations "in the language of divine providence and sentimental benevolence" (111). Stowe's father, Lyman Beecher, himself a supporter of colonization, was, according to Joan Hedrick, also directly responsible for shaping Stowe's initial defense of colonizing missions in Africa (*Harriet Beecher Stowe: A Life* 235). While Stowe does not say much elsewhere in her writing about colonization and in fact begins to revise her opinions once she is attacked by critics for the way she concludes the novel, her statement in *Uncle Tom's Cabin* concerning colonization should be seen as part of a more expansive cultural milieu in which colonization was said to have a providential import.

32. Fredrickson, *Black Image*, 102.

33. Baldwin, *Notes of a Native Son*, 14. For examples of scholars who, like Baldwin, deride sentimentalism for its ostensibly insincere melodrama and for fundamentally misrepresenting reality, see Brown, *The Sentimental Novel in America;* Douglas, *The Feminization of American Culture;* Midgley, "Brutality and Sentimentality"; Jefferson, "What's Wrong with Sentimentality?"; and Berlant, *The Female Complaint*.

Chapter 4. "Can Fear of Fire Make Me Love?"

1. Stowe, *Uncle Tom's Cabin*, 557–58, 559–60.

2. Another well-known example from the novel in which the slave's body is subordinated to the soul comes in Eva's final sermon not long before she dies. In it, she chides her father's slaves for living "idle, careless, thoughtless lives" and implores them to begin caring for their souls in order to gain access to that "beautiful world, where Jesus is." "Each one of you can become angels, and be angels forever," Eva tells her devoted onlookers. It is presumably as angels that they will escape the burden of corporeality and become spiritual beings in heaven (*Uncle Tom's Cabin* 410).

3. Challenging the common scholarly assumption that slavery's demise was inevitable because it violated the "personhood" of the slave and thus conflicted with the key liberal tenets enshrined in the Declaration of Independence and the Constitution, Arthur Riss argues that "Although it may seem reassuring to see 'personhood' as an essential attribute of the oppressed, a pregiven identity that simply needs to be unveiled—liberated from prejudice, ethnocentrism, and irrationality—I am suggesting that 'personhood' only becomes intrinsic and indisputably possessed retroactively. It is precisely because the work of 'personifying' slaves has been completed that this work can be forgotten and so thoroughly erased." Riss's argument about the fundamentally disputed nature of antebellum black personhood is an important one to consider as we explore how Stowe enlists but also critiques humanistic traits to produce sympathetic slave characters. Stowe appreciates that merely assigning such traits to slaves does not necessarily "personify" them, especially because so many Americans sympathetic to slavery believed that blacks occupied a different category of being (*Race, Slavery, and Liberalism* 9).

4. Fisher, *Hard Facts*, 99. For Fisher, one of the main contributions of sentimental fic-

tion to the slavery debates was its attempt to revise accounts of an innately inferior and subhuman black self.

5. Fredrickson, *Black Image*, 75. Together, these scientists promoted the theory of polygenesis, or multiple creations, to "prove" that Negroes and Caucasians did not belong to the same species of man. According to Werner Sollors, the scientific racism of Louis Agassiz was particularly influential in shaping racialist views on mixing blood. Agassiz warned that if Caucasians were to mix with Negroes and other inferior species, Americans might be reduced to an "effeminate progeny of mixed races, half indian, half negro, sprinkled with white blood" (qtd. in Sollors, *Neither Black Nor White*, 131). Stephen Jay Gould maintains that Agassiz's conversion to polygenesis is attributable to his colleagues who supported polygenesis and who strongly encouraged him to adopt these views, and to his first encounter with blacks, whom he had not seen in Europe and who generated "a pronounced visceral revulsion" in him (*The Mismeasure of Man* 44).

6. For an analysis that considers representations of interracial coupling and racial amalgamation in the years between the Revolutionary War and the Civil War, see Lemire, *"Miscegenation."* Lemire explains how kinship ties were often figured through a rhetoric of blood, so that during this interregnum between wars, blood was a powerful metaphor by which to mark the borders of the family. Stowe's novel demonstrates the illusory nature of these blood-based boundaries between races, showing instead how thoroughly miscegenated Southern families often were.

7. These views about the degenerative nature of racial amalgamation, while widespread, were not universal. Those who challenged racial hierarchies often extolled the potential benefits of racial mixing—what was called "hybrid vigor." Both *Uncle Tom's Cabin* and *Dred* appear, at times, to promote this very notion. See Sollors (133–35) for more on this idea.

8. Sollors, *Neither Black Nor White*, 132.

9. Stowe, *Dred*, 38; hereafter abbreviated *D* and cited parenthetically in the text by page number.

10. Characterizing Harry as an aesthete also recalls and counters Thomas Jefferson's claim that American Negroes were incapable of generating or appreciating works of art because their imaginations were naturally "dull, tasteless, and anomalous." Jefferson contends that in his observations as a natural scientist, "never yet could I find that a black had uttered a thought above the level of plain narration; never see even an elementary trait of painting or sculpture." While Jefferson concedes that Africans are more proficient in music than whites, he doubts if they could equal whites in composition or harmony. And blacks, according to Jefferson, had not yet produced any meaningful poetry (despite his already having met Phillis Wheatley and read her poems). For Stowe, then, Harry's aesthetic sensibility signals the complexity of his mind and is an indication of a common humanity shared by whites and blacks. Indeed, Harry's sophistication stems from his racial genealogy; Harry's amalgamated blood, rather than impeding his growth, enables it instead. See Jefferson, *Notes*, 146–47.

11. Harry is not the only example of a slave who displays loyalty toward his enslavers. Tiff, for example, "never seemed to cherish the slightest doubt that the whole force of

the Peyton blood coursed through his veins, and that the Peyton honor was intrusted to his keeping" (*D* 90). While Tiff's sense of self is constructed through a perceived shared heritage rather than a bond created by blood, what is important for Tiff is that the Peyton family has an illustrious history. In a conversation with Old Hundred, Tiff implies he is superior to other slaves because the Peyton family has roots as one of the oldest in Virginia, whereas Old Hundred's family hails from North Carolina and therefore does not possess the same distinguished pedigree (225).

12. Emerson, "American Civilization," 237.

13. Rodgers, *Work Ethic*, 1. Rodgers demonstrates in exhaustive detail the moral ascendancy of labor in the 1840s and 1850s, itself rooted in the earlier Protestant notion of "calling." The popular literature of the time, as Rodgers shows, enthusiastically promoted the virtues of work, and many of these stories were directed at young readers. And Stowe's family was a central part of this conversation about work, particularly Henry Ward Beecher and Catherine Beecher, who commented at length about the value of labor within a Christian culture, stressing the necessity of hard work in the creation of a just and moral society. See especially chapters 1, 4, and 7.

14. Foner, *Free Soil*, 11.

15. Qtd. in Foner, *Free Soil*, 12.

16. Rachel Naomi Klein reads against several generations of scholars who understand Stowe's apparent anticapitalist domestic economy to be operating in direct opposition to the market economy, arguing that "a free and democratic labor system informed [Stowe's] critique of slavery and shaped her analysis of the 'woman's sphere.'" Klein goes on to show that Stowe's views of wage and free labor very much coincided with the views held by most Republicans at the time ("Harriet Beecher Stowe" 135).

17. Mabie, qtd. in Rodgers, *Work Ethic*, 13.

18. For more on antebellum discourses of black labor and the relationship between work and masculine ideals, see Ball, "To Train Them for the Work." Ball's study examines conduct manuals directed at black men for the way they promoted work as a practice to challenge the discourses that supported slavery.

19. In an excellent reading of legal and fictional challenges by slaves for economic rights, Jeffory Clymer observes that Harry's dedication to Nina is particularly pernicious because "Nina frequently gives money to her dissolute brother, Tom, to help him out of tight spots," and Tom frequently threatens to purchase Harry's wife, Lisette. "In a vicious cycle," Clymer shrewdly concludes, "Harry's money not only hardens the manacles of his own bondage, but indirectly deposited in Tom's hands, that same money might send his wife into the same sort of sexualized slavery experienced by his own unnamed mother at the hands of his and Tom's father, Colonel Gordon" ("Family Money" 229).

20. No slavery apologist was more promotional of the paternalistic logic of slavery than George Fitzhugh, whose views were deeply influential throughout the 1850s. Fitzhugh maintained that plantation slavery was a far more amenable arrangement than what factory laborers were subject to throughout Northeastern cities. Northern laborers (whom Fitzhugh argued toiled under a form of "wage slavery") worked in an inequitable system where they were allowed "the least possible portion of the fruits of their own labor" (*Cannibals All!* 25). For this reason, concluded Fitzhugh, a free laborer was "more of

a slave than the negro, because he works longer and harder for less allowance than the slave, and has no holiday, because the cares of life with him begin when its labors end. He has no liberty and not a single right" (18–19).

Fitzhugh was widely read and especially prolific in the middle part of the 1850s, so that his argument endorsing the paternalism of slavery overlapped with Stowe's challenge to it. Stowe and Fitzhugh both portray slavery as a domestic arrangement even as they draw opposite conclusions, underscoring how battles over the morality of slavery were often figured as contests over the moral arrangement of families in the North and in the South.

21. For a reading of how Stowe uses both classical imagery and phrenological sciences to "build the body of Dred," see Sanchez-Eppler, *Touching Liberty*, 28–30. Sanchez-Eppler underscores the challenge of depicting a black character like Dred who is both heroic but could still be sympathetic to readers. Stowe does this, Sanchez-Eppler points out, by muting those physical features that do not conform to white beauty ideals. As I argue later in this chapter, Dred is not meant to be a sympathetic figure.

22. Greenberg, ed., *The Confessions of Nat Turner*, 44.

23. As I have suggested in previous chapters, insurrectionary panic becomes integrated in the rhetoric of abolitionist sentimentality, especially Stowe's. By the mid-1850s, many Southerners dreaded the possibility of slave revolt, a point many scholars of *Dred* have recognized. Even unsuccessful or incomplete revolts caused tremendous panic. Eric Sundquist observes that the revolts of Gabriel Prosser and Denmark Vesey "achieved in the arena of terror and propaganda many of the effects of successful revolts," and this terror haunted many Southerners who felt they were approaching a nightmarish scenario because of slavery (*To Wake the Nations* 43). In fact, several months into the Civil War, Thomas Wentworth Higginson commented that "the most formidable weapon in the hands of slave-insurgents is always this blind panic they create, and the wild exaggerations which follow" ("Nat Turner's Insurrection"). While scholars have appreciated how Stowe plays off of and augments the fears surrounding possible slave revolts, none has discussed how this narrative strategy forms a key aspect of *Dred*'s sentimentality.

24. While I emphasize the apocalyptic contours of Dred, it is unsurprising that scholars have proposed a wide range of frameworks within which to read him, given how extreme a character he is. Cynthia Hamilton argues that "Stowe's Dred is less a man than the embodiment of terrible forces" ("*Dred:* Intemperate Slavery" 273). Similarly, Maria Karafilis recognizes this abstract dimension to Dred, claiming that he "functions as a symbol, a mystical, etherealized prophet figure touched with special knowledge, who is to serve as a 'sign unto this evil nation.'" For Karafilis, however, Dred is not simply an abstraction. Stowe's "complex portrait of Dred depicts him not just as a dehumanized, disembodied spiritual agent of social and political transformation" but as "an actual, embodied agent" and "instigator of social and political change" ("Spaces of Democracy" 44). Karafilis acknowledges the corporeality of Dred's existence, especially in the physical threat he poses to Southern slaveholders, which makes Dred partly human, partly imaginative, and thus a metaphorical construct. Lawrence Buell describes Dred as a "mythic figure at the level of narrative representation" whom Stowe represents as deliberately "improbable," marking her "shift (farther) away from realism" ("Harriet Beecher

Stowe" 199). Rather than see Dred as representing Stowe's shift away from realism or her use of his character as principally a symbolic construct, I suggest that her account of Dred is a response to the failure of humanistic categories to transform enslaved beings into free men.

25. Jeffory Clymer rightly points out that Stowe fails to produce a genuine solution to the problem of Harry's dedication to Nina by having Nina die prematurely. Had Nina lived, it remains doubtful that Harry would have struck Tom and fled to the woods ("Family Money" 229–30).

26. Critics who highlight Dred's revolutionary agency in the novel include Karafilis, "Spaces of Democracy," 44; Levine, *Martin Delany*, chapter 4 and his introduction to *Dred*, xx–xxi; Crane, *Race, Citizenship, and Law*, 74, 76; Rowe, "Stowe's Rainbow Sign," 51; and Nabers, "The Problem of Revolution."

27. It is not until the last few decades of the nineteenth century that paranoid ideas about the sexually rapacious black man take firm hold within the white imagination. Stowe nevertheless preemptively placates these growing anxieties about black men violating the sanctity of female virtue by having Dred disclaim any desire to defile Southern white women. Dred may pose a threat to slaveholders, but he is not, Stowe suggests, morally dissolute. For more on these anxieties in postbellum America, see Williamson, *The Crucible of Race*, chapter 4.

28. Qtd. in Dillingham, *Melville's Later Novels*, 65.

29. Melville, *Moby-Dick*, 135; hereafter abbreviated *M* and cited parenthetically in the text and by page number.

30. At times, Stowe also implies that Dred, rather than being in direct communication with God, may instead be mad like Ahab. Describing Dred's visage, Stowe writes that in his eyes "there burned . . . like tongues of flames in a black pool of naphtha, a subtle and restless fire, that betokened habitual excitement *to the verge of insanity*" (*D* 198; emphasis mine). Even as she highlights Dred's religious devotion, Stowe speculates about his mental stability, as surely antebellum readers would have done. "Dred was," Stowe later writes, "under the inspiring *belief* that he was the subject of visions and supernatural communications" (274; emphasis mine). Claiming that Dred *believes* he is the subject of supernatural communications is not the same as emphatically asserting that he in fact *is* the subject of such visions. Of course, Stowe is not disclaiming Dred's privileged standing as a recipient of God's word either. Nor does she say that he is insane, only that he "verges" on insanity. Given how inflammatory a character Dred is, it is reasonable to assume that Stowe had misgivings about him, especially as someone chosen by God to do his work on earth; hence the subtle suggestion that he might be insane. And yet Stowe also signals his central importance in the narrative, first, by making him the book's titular character, and second, by underscoring Dred as a key component of the novel's sentimental politics.

31. Dimock, *Empire for Liberty*, 116–17. Dimock describes "negative individualism" as a kind of self-punishing subject, where the self is both the "seat of agency" and the "circuit of discipline" (131). "What we might expect to find in Ahab," Dimock argues, "is an individualism that afflicts its bearer, one that apprehends and incriminates, one that dis-

ciplines the self in its very freedom. And that, in fact, is what we do find.... He is both doomed and free: free, that is, to choose his doom" (115).

32. Elizabeth Schultz argues that *Moby-Dick* is informed by midcentury sentimental conventions and emphasizes Melville's sympathy for women's suffering within the domestic sphere. Her reading challenges a tradition of scholars who have read *Moby-Dick* as an antisentimental novel and who have inferred from Melville's work a strand of hostility toward women ("The Sentimental Subtext of *Moby-Dick*").

33. This is not, of course, Melville's last word on vengeance. In his 1855 novella "Benito Cereno," Melville once against takes up the issue as he explores a slave revolt onboard the *San Dominick*. As the chief architect of the mutiny, the slave Babo might interestingly be thought of as a terrorist responding to the terrorism of slavery, so that one form of terror meets and counteracts another. Babo operates according to the threat of further violence; he inspires in the Spaniards aboard the ship the same kind of fear that slave owners inspire on the plantation. In light of this, Babo could be read as Melville's response to the character Dred, though with none of the fire and brimstone. He is both a successor of Nat Turner and a predictor of John Brown. While Babo, however, constitutes a much more direct reference to a racial violence that was only indirectly referenced in *Moby-Dick*, Babo's vengeance onboard the *San Dominick* is more sadistic than apocalyptic. Indeed, Melville might be inventing a new category of vengeance altogether, what we might call "sadistic vengeance" where vengeance becomes an expression of the slave's sadism, replacing Turner's abiding faith in a just and retributive God.

34. For more on the repercussions of Turner's insurrection on the Virginia legislature, see chapter 1.

35. Hedrick, *Harriet Beecher Stowe*, 259; Foster, *The Rungless Ladder*, 85; and Rowe, "Stowe's Rainbow Sign," 50. Other scholars who support this reading of Milly as the moral authority in the novel include Crane, Stratman, Davis, Duquette, Whitney, and Buell. Crane argues that "Dred's revolution is successfully challenged by Milly in a scene that reveals the debilitating effect of the tension in Stowe's divided natural rights sentiment between sympathy and revolutionary wrath." Because Milly foregrounds Christian love, Mary Kemp Davis refers to her as the "most empowered slave speaker in Stowe's novel." It is in Milly, Elizabeth Duquette similarly argues, that Stowe "locates her final moral model, one that tempers emotion with reason and identifies the good of the community as the proper focus of an individual's ethical instincts." See Crane, "Dangerous Sentiments," 203; Stratman, "Harriet Beecher Stowe," 391–92; Davis, *Nat Turner*, 133; Duquette, "The Republican Mammy?" 13; Whitney, "In the Shadow," 566; and Buell, "Harriet Beecher Stowe," 197.

36. Robert Levine has argued persuasively that the development of Stowe's thinking on race and slavery after the publication of *Uncle Tom's Cabin* was due to her continued intellectual engagement with some of the major black figures of her day, including Frederick Douglass, Sojourner Truth, and others. See his *Martin Delany*, chapter 4.

37. See Karafilis, "Spaces of Democracy," 44, and Hamilton, "*Dred*," 277.

38. Of course, Dred does kill an overseer, but he does so outside the reader's view, so that Stowe's audience does not have to witness this act of violence. Nevertheless, when

Stowe describes the events that led to the overseer's death, readers are never given the impression that he is commanded by God to strike and kill the overseer (*D* 209), and this elision potentially complicates the account of Dred's agency I have described so far. It is possible, in other words, that Dred murdered the overseer as a deliberate act, and it is this possibility of a slave acting without the sanction of God that Stowe has to quickly conceal from the reader by describing Dred as an instrument of God and not a self-reliant insurgent.

Chapter 5. Sentimental John Brown

1. Brown was tried for treason (against the Commonwealth of Virginia), murder, and inciting a slave insurrection.

2. Wise, Letter to Lydia Maria Child, 326, n.2, qtd. in Meltzer and Holland, *Lydia Maria Child: Selected Letters;* hereafter abbreviated *L* and cited parenthetically by page number within the text.

3. Larry Reynolds persuasively argues that in addition to America's own revolutionary past, Europe's "revolutionary scene" of the 1840s had a powerful influence in shaping American perspectives on violent resistance (54–55). For accounts that locate Brown squarely within a revolutionary framework, see Reynolds, *Righteous Violence;* Carton, *Patriotic Treason;* Cain, "Violence"; Filler, *The Crusade Against Slavery,* 242; Ruchames, ed., *John Brown;* DuBois, *John Brown.*

4. For a representative study that examines Brown the martyr, see Finkelman, "Manufacturing Martyrdom."

5. Bertram Wyatt-Brown takes up the issue of Brown's sanity in "'A Volcano Beneath a Mountain of Snow.'" While scholars like Wyatt-Brown, David Reynolds, and John Stauffer defend Brown from charges of insanity, there are some critics who still conclude (quite wrongly, I believe) that he must have been insane to raid a federal armory without a sufficient number of men or adequate tactical skill. For such a reading, see Gilbert, "Behavioral Analysis."

6. Nudelman, *John Brown's Body,* 16.

7. Ibid., 17.

8. Barnes, *Love's Whipping Boy,* 114.

9. Ibid., 114.

10. Ibid., 120.

11. Redpath, *Public Life,* 48.

12. For background on Brown's many forms of employment, most of which ended in failure, see David Reynolds, *John Brown, Abolitionist,* chapter 5.

13. Brown, Letter to Mary Brown, 53, qtd. in Trodd and Stauffer, *Meteor of War;* hereafter abbreviated *M* and cited parenthetically by page number within the text. There are numerous typos and misspellings throughout Brown's letters; I quote the text exactly as it appears.

14. Only half of Brown's twenty children survived into adulthood. He lost some children to illness and, in the case of Amelia Brown, to accident. Others perished fighting alongside Brown during his antislavery campaigns in Kansas and Virginia. These losses

always profoundly affected Brown, even if they did not redirect his immediate course of action. When Salmon Brown, John Brown's son, reflects on the three children the family lost while living in Richfield, all within the span of three weeks, he comments, with no small degree of pathos, that this was a "calamity from which father never fully recovered" (*M* 68).

15. According to John Brown Jr., Brown's eldest son, his father had once considered making his family a multiracial one. John Jr. explains that one evening, John Brown pointedly asked his son if he would "like to have some poor little black children that were slaves (explaining to me the meaning of slaves) come and live with us; and asked me if I would be willing to divide my food and clothes with them." For John Brown, incorporating an adopted black child into his family would have constituted a powerful antislavery gesture and symbolized a kind of microcosm of the nation in which races loved and supported one another. "He made such an impression on my sympathies," continues John Jr., "that the first colored person I ever saw (it was a man I met on the street in Meadville, Penn.,) I felt such pity for him that I wanted to ask him if he did not want to come and live at our house." Like many writers before him, Brown understands the home to be a site for transforming racial sympathies and impresses on his son the deep need for familial affection across the color line ("Reminiscences of John Brown, Jr.," qtd. in Ruchames, *John Brown Reader*, 178).

16. I do not want to give the impression that Brown's messianism, because it is love based, is more evolved than the models we have seen in other contexts, such as Turner's *Confessions* and Stowe's depiction of Dred. Nonetheless, Brown's messianic discourse diverges from previous accounts in a way that insinuates potentially problematic racial distinctions. In constructing empowered accounts of black agency, previous authors, white and black, relied on ideas of vengeance to imbue strength in the black subject. While this is an understandable discursive maneuver, given the constraints surrounding nineteenth-century black agency, this strategy associates black power with vengeance and thus with a kind of brutality that potentially marks the black being as savage. Vengeance, then, is a necessary though troubling option. As a white man, Brown is not subject to the same constraints and therefore does not need to rely on such extreme categories to authorize his power. Indeed, it is in some sense Brown's whiteness that makes love such a radical possibility, for it unsettles the racial order as it had been imagined by most white Americans at this time. Brown's love is dangerous precisely because it is directed at black Americans. In contrast, in these other texts, love that emanates from blacks often comes with an accompanying threat of vengeance to energize its power.

17. For an analysis that reads Brown's letters in the manner I am discouraging, see Trodd, "A Less Costly Ink."

18. In Jeremiah 38–39, Ebed-Melech rescues Jeremiah from prison and is spared by God once Jerusalem falls to the Babylonians (KJV).

19. It is in this same letter that Brown announces to his family that he has been "sentenced to be hanged on 2 Decem next." In characteristic fashion, Brown makes this announcement, not in the body of the note, but in the postscript. This rhetorical gesture dramatizes Brown's selflessness. In the letter proper, he encourages his family to nurture sympathy and love for slaves. And he subordinates himself into the postscript to convey

that his own trials are secondary to the slaves' suffering. To underscore this point, Brown concludes: "Do not grieve on my account. I am still quite cheerful" (*M* 138).

20. So readily did Brown's letters circulate among Northern readers that Henry C. Wright wrote in a letter to Henry Wise: "John Brown, the friend of the slave, [has] edited every paper, presided over every domestic and social circle, over every prayer, conference and church meeting, over every pulpit and platform, and over every Legislature, Judicial and Executive department of government; and he will edit every paper, and govern Virginia and all the States, and preside over Congress, guide its deliberations, and control all political caucuses and elections, for one year to come" (Wright, Letter to Henry A. Wise, qtd. in David Reynolds, *John Brown, Abolitionist*, 384).

21. Thoreau, "A Plea for Captain John Brown," 413.

22. Ibid., 396. David Reynolds convincingly argues that the Transcendentalists were the main reason Brown was not lost to history, for they were the only collection of prominent intellectuals who came to Brown's defense immediately following the raid. And none was more important than Henry David Thoreau, who not only spoke in unflinching support of Brown but also inspired other, more influential figures like Emerson to speak out on Brown's behalf. See *John Brown, Abolitionist*, 343–47, 363–67. For a very useful analysis of the shift in Thoreau's thinking from passive nonresistance to violence, see Larry Reynolds, *Righteous Violence*, chapter 4.

23. Langston, Letter from the *Cleveland Plain Dealer*, qtd. in Quarles, *Blacks on John Brown*, 14.

24. Ibid., 12.

25. Parker, Letter from Rome, qtd. in Redpath, *Echoes of Harper's Ferry*, 88.

26. Emerson, "Brown Relief Meeting House," qtd. in Redpath, *Echoes of Harper's Ferry*, 121. For analyses on the radicalization of Emerson and his response to Brown, see Larry Reynolds, chapter 2; Ziser, "Emersonian Terrorism"; and Von Frank, *The Trials of Anthony Burns*.

27. Of course, another reason why more support may have been offered to Brown than to Walker or Turner is because Brown is white. Among the white elite, Brown's actions may have been perceived as "right" not because of some trait inherent to the act itself that distinguished it from what Walker promoted and Turner enacted. Rather, Brown's skin may have helped signify the rightness of his actions while allowing Northern whites to imagine more easily a sense of solidarity with Brown than they could have with Walker and Turner. What Turner achieved in Southampton County could not be perceived as a moral act, not because of the number of dead white bodies, but because of Turner's black skin. While I do not want to imply that this was the main reason Northern whites were able to respond to Brown as they did, I do not want to deny either that Brown's whiteness may have made it easier for other whites to express their support for him.

28. Carolyn L. Karcher provides an excellent overview and analysis of Child's response to Brown, especially Child's struggles to reconcile her pacifist convictions with her praise of Brown as a defender of freedom and loyal servant to slaves. See Karcher, *First Woman*, 416–26.

29. Carolyn L. Karcher maintains that Child "would judge Brown not by external standards, whether religious or political, but by his moral effect on her" (426). I agree

with Karcher's reading, though I think underlying this "effect" is a much more impassioned attachment than Karcher (and Child) lets on.

30. Child, "Letter from a Colored Man," 202; original emphasis.

31. Ibid., 203.

32. Whittier, "Brown of Osawatomie," qtd. in Redpath, *Echoes of Harper's Ferry*, 304.

33. William Lloyd Garrison, himself a pacifist, famously chided Whittier for his short-sighted perspective on Brown, writing in *The Liberator:* "If there is a danger, on the one hand, lest there may be a repudiation of the doctrine of non-resistance, through the sympathy and admiration felt for John Brown, there is more danger, on the other hand, that the brutal outcry raised against him as an outlaw, traitor, and murderer by those who are either too cowardly to avow their real convictions, or too pro-slavery to feel one throb of pity for those in bondage, will lead to unmerited censure of his course. Difficult as it may be to hold an equal balance in such a case, it is still the duty of every one to do so" (qtd. in Redpath, *Echoes of Harper's Ferry*, 309). Even Garrison is struggling here with his own pacifist principles. He chooses to minimize criticisms of Brown rather than have someone like Whittier challenge Brown's methods and thus risk losing this important antislavery symbol.

34. Ransom, *John Brown*; Noble, *John Brown's Blessing*; and Hovenden, *Last Moments*. For concise but compelling analyses of the paintings by Ransom and Noble, see Trodd and Stauffer, *Meteor of War*, 242–44.

35. Governor Wise wrote of Brown: "And they are themselves mistaken who take him to be a madman. He is a bundle of the best nerves I ever saw, cut and thrust, and bleeding and in bonds. He is a man of clear head, of courage, fortitude, and simple ingenuousness. He is cool, collected and indomitable, and it is but just to him to say, that he was humane to his prisoners, as attested to me by Col. Washington and Mr. Mills; and he inspired me with great trust in his integrity as a man of truth" (Wise, "Speech in Virginia," qtd. in *M*, 258). Other notable Southern figures, including John Wilkes Booth and Stonewall Jackson, offered words of high praise for Brown's integrity, if not his deluded decision to invade the South.

36. Melville, "The Portent," 11.

37. In over twenty images that Jacob Lawrence produced of Brown in 1941, for instance, he captures Brown's work as a land surveyor, his violence in Kansas and Harpers Ferry, and his subsequent hanging and martyrdom. But there is not a single image that emphasizes Brown's love of slaves or how this love might have been the motivating force behind his various violent engagements.

38. David Reynolds, *John Brown, Abolitionist*, 65.

39. Stauffer, *Black Hearts of Men*, 91.

40. Brown, Jr., "Reminiscences of John Brown, Jr.," qtd. in Ruchames, *John Brown Reader*, 175.

41. John Stauffer points out the unfortunate ironies of Brown's use of the whip: "He did not recognize," writes Stauffer, "that the brute force he employed against his children (and, later, against proslavery advocates) was of the same sort that masters used to control their slaves" (*Black Hearts* 91). Also see 233–34 for more on Brown as patriarch. While Brown's use of the whip no doubt seems unnecessarily harsh, especially given

present-day shifts away from corporal discipline, Brown whipping his children, in John Jr.'s view, is markedly different than slave masters whipping their slaves. According to his son, Brown uses the whip as a source of instruction for his children, whom he loves, whereas the slave master employed the whip for punitive measures only.

42. Baldwin, qtd. in Banks, "John Brown's Body," 254–55.
43. Ibid., 255; original emphasis.
44. Ibid., 265.
45. David Reynolds, *John Brown, Abolitionist*, x.

Coda

1. Lincoln, "Proclamation of Thanksgiving," 520–21. This proclamation was actually composed by William Seward, Lincoln's secretary of state.
2. There were over 51,000 casualties at Gettysburg, over 34,000 at Chickamauga, and over 29,000 at Chancellorsville.
3. Lincoln, "Proclamation of Thanksgiving," 521.
4. Ibid., 520–21.
5. Ibid., 521.
6. Tichenor, "First-Day Sermon," 103–4.
7. Gaylord, "A Discourse Delivered," qtd. in Moorhead, *American Apocalypse*, ix.
8. Howe, "Battle Hymn," qtd. in Clifford, *Mine Eyes*, 287.
9. Describing the military campaign leading from Atlanta to Savannah, Edmund Wilson argues that Sherman "launched upon an independent exploit which [was] to open a new age in tactics and to set a new record for ruthlessness in the conduct of the Civil War" (*Patriot Gore* 179).
10. As Sherman himself said about the South's slaveholding practices, "God himself has obliterated whole races from the face of the earth for sins less heinous" (qtd. in Wilson, *Patriot Gore*, 185).
11. Lincoln, "Second Inaugural Address," 687.
12. Ibid., 687.
13. Ibid., 687.
14. Beck, Fox News, February 3, 2009. All quotes are taken from this broadcast.
15. Beck does not identify the participating sides in this civil war.
16. Whitehead, *Zone One: A Novel*; Matthew Michael Carnahan, screenplay for *World War Z*, based on a novel by Max Brooks. *World War Z* and *Zone One: A Novel* are zombie narratives that feature scenes in which the undead rush and overcome barriers meant to protect the living. The modern zombie tradition has been read as dramatizing America's anxieties with racial others, and Beck's descriptions are analogous with scenes from these two recent fictional works.
17. The representative example of environmental apocalypticism is Al Gore's documentary *An Inconvenient Truth*, a film that powerfully visualizes the scale of environmental decay through the use of images and graphics charting the rapidity with which the planet's health has declined. In the film, Gore observes that studying the current global climate is like taking "a nature hike through the Book of Revelation."

18. Hansen, *Storms of My Grandchildren*, xii; hereafter abbreviated *S* and cited parenthetically by page number within the text.

19. *Melancholia* is not an American film. I include it here to suggest that perhaps apocalyptic sentimentalism has, and may have always had, a transatlantic scope (Lars von Trier, *Melancholia*, 2011).

20. In a review for the *Los Angeles Times*, Kenneth Turan describes *WALL-E* as "daring and traditional, groundbreaking and familiar, *apocalyptic and sentimental*" (Turan, review of *WALL-E*; my emphasis).

21. The examples I mention (as well as many others that I do not) all share heteronormative assumptions about the configuration of families. Even as these fictional accounts interrogate the internal dynamics of family life within an apocalyptic wasteland, they all presuppose a traditional family unit.

22. McCarthy, *The Road*, 151–52, 201; hereafter abbreviated *R* and cited parenthetically by page number within the text.

23. In *Terrorism TV*, Stacy Takacs brilliantly examines how narratives of terrorism quickly became incorporated into prime-time television series following 9/11, so that these series provided indirect support for the Bush administration's war on terror.

Bibliography

Abé, Nicola. "The Woes of an American Drone Operator." *Spiegel Online International*, December 14, 2012.
Abzug, Robert H. *Cosmos Crumbling: American Reform and the Religious Imagination*. New York: Oxford University Press, 1994.
Ahlstrom, Sydney. *A Religious History of the American People*. New Haven: Yale University Press, 1972.
Ampadu, Lena. "Maria W. Stewart and the Rhetoric of Black Preaching: Perspectives on Womanism and Black Nationalism." In *Black Women's Intellectual Traditions: Speaking their Minds*, edited by Kristin Waters and Carol B. Conaway, 38–54. Burlington: University of Vermont Press, 2007.
Andrews, William. *To Tell a Free Story: The First Century of Afro-American Autobiography, 1760–1865*. Urbana: University of Illinois Press, 1986.
Apap, Chris. "'Let no man of us budge one step': David Walker and the Rhetoric of African American Emplacement." *Early American Literature* 46, no. 2 (2011): 319–50.
The Apocalypse Explained: A Compendium of Ten Discourses, on the Book of Revelation. Broadside. Worcester, Mass.: American Antiquarian Society, 1862.
Apter, Michael J. *The Dangerous Edge: The Psychology of Excitement*. New York: Free Press, 1992.
Aptheker, Herbert. *Abolitionism: A Revolutionary Movement*. Boston: Twayne, 1989.
Baldwin, Elihu. "Sermon XXVII: The Final Judgment. Hebrews, IX 29.—After This is Judgment." In *The National Preacher; or, Original Monthly Sermons From Living Ministers (1826–1828)* 2, no. 7 (Dec. 1827), 108. Accessed through the American Periodical Series Online.
Baldwin, James. *Notes of a Native Son*. Boston: Beacon Press, 1955.
Ball, Erica L. "To Train Them for the Work: Manhood, Masculinity, and Free Black Conduct Discourse in Antebellum New York." In *Fathers, Preachers, Rebels, Men: Black Masculinity in U.S. History and Literature, 1820–1945*, edited by Peter Caster and Timothy Buckner, 60–79. Columbus: Ohio State University Press, 2011.

Banks, Russell. "John Brown's Body." *Transition* 9, nos. 1–2 (2000): 250–66.
Barnes, Elizabeth. *Love's Whipping Boy: Violence and Sentimentality in the American Imagination*. Chapel Hill: University of North Carolina Press, 2011.
———. *States of Sympathy: Seduction and Democracy in the American Novel*. New York: Columbia University Press, 1997.
Bartlow, R. Dianne. "No Throw Away Woman: Maria Miller Stewart as Forerunner of Black Feminist Thought." In *Black Women's Intellectual Traditions: Speaking their Minds*, edited by Kristin Waters and Carol B. Conaway, 72–88. Burlington: University of Vermont Press, 2007.
Baym, Nina. *American Women Writers and the Work of History, 1790–1860*. New Brunswick, N.J.: Rutgers University Press, 1995.
Beck, Glenn. *Glenn Beck*, Fox News, February 3, 2009.
Beecher, Catherine E. *A Treatise on Domestic Economy*. Boston: Thomas H. Webb, 1843.
Beecher, Catherine E., and Harriet Beecher Stowe. *The American Woman's Home*. 1869. Edited by Nicole Tonkovich. New Brunswick: Rutgers University Press, 2002.
Beecher, Lyman. "A Reformation of Morals Practicable and Indispensible. A Sermon Delivered at New-Haven on the Evening of October 27, 1812. Andover, 1814." In *Lyman Beecher and the Reform of Society: Four Sermons*, edited by Edwin S. Gaustad. New York: Arno Press, 1972.
Bellin, Joshua. "Up to Heaven's Gate, Down to Earth's Dust: The Politics of Judgment in *Uncle Tom's Cabin*." *American Literature* 65, no. 2 (June 1993): 275–95.
Bercovitch, Sacvan. *The American Jeremiad*. Madison, Wis.: University of Wisconsin Press, 1978.
Berlant, Lauren. *The Female Complaint: The Unfinished Business of Sentimentality in American Culture*. Durham, N.C.: Duke University Press, 2008.
Bird, Robert Montgomery. *The Infidel; or, The Fall of Mexico: A Romance by the author of "Calavar."* Philadelphia: Carey, Lea & Blanchard, 1835.
Bollinger, Laurel. "'A mother in the deity': Maternity and Authority in the Nineteenth-Century African-American Spiritual Narrative." *Women's Studies* 29, no. 3 (June 2000): 357–82.
Boudreau, Kristin. *Sympathy in American Literature: American Sentiments from Jefferson to the Jameses*. Gainesville: University Press of Florida, 2002.
Bourke, Joanna. *Fear: A Cultural History*. Emeryville, Calif.: Shoemaker & Hoard, 2006.
Boyer, Paul. *When Time Shall Be No More: Prophecy Belief in Modern American Culture*. Cambridge, Mass.: Harvard University Press, 1992.
Bramen, Carrie Tirado. "The Christology of Niceness: Harriet Beecher Stowe, the Jesus Novel, and Sacred Trivialities." In *American Religious Liberalism*, edited by Leigh E. Schmidt and Sally M. Promey, 39–65. Bloomington: Indiana University Press, 2012.
Breen, Patrick. "Contested Communion: The Limits of White Solidarity in Nat Turner's Virginia." *Journal of the Early Republic* 27, no. 4 (Winter 2007): 685–703.
Brekus, Catherine A. *Strangers and Pilgrims: Female Preaching in America*. Chapel Hill: University of North Carolina Press, 1998.
Bressler, Ann Lee. *The Universalist Movement in America, 1770–1880*. New York: Oxford University Press, 2001.

Brodhead, Richard H. *Cultures of Letters: Scenes of Reading and Writing in Nineteenth-Century America.* Chicago: University of Chicago Press, 1993.

Brown, Gillian. *Domestic Individualism: Imagining Self in Nineteenth-Century America.* Berkeley: University of California Press, 1990.

Brown, Henry "Box." *Narrative of Henry Box Brown, Who Escaped from Slavery, Enclosed in a Box 3 Feet Long and 2 Wide. Written from a Statement of Facts Made by Himself. With Remarks Upon the Remedy for Slavery By Charles Stearns.* Boston: Brown and Stearns, 1849. 39. Documenting the American South, University of North Carolina, http://docsouth.unc.edu/neh/boxbrown/boxbrown.html.

Brown, Herbert Ross. *The Sentimental Novel in America, 1789–1860.* Durham, N.C.: Duke University Press, 1940.

Buell, Lawrence. *Emerson.* Cambridge, Mass.: Harvard University Press, 2003.

———. "Harriet Beecher Stowe and the Dream of the Great American Novel." In *The Cambridge Companion to Harriet Beecher Stowe*, edited by Cindy Weinstein, 190–202. New York: Cambridge University Press, 2004.

Burrow, Rufus. *God and Human Responsibility: David Walker and Ethical Prophecy.* Macon, Ga.: Mercer University Press, 2003.

Butler, Judith. *The Psychic Life of Power: Theories in Subjection.* Stanford, Calif.: Stanford University Press, 1997.

By the Command of the King of Kings, and at the Desire of All Who Love His Appearing, at the Theatre of the Universe, on the Eve of Time, Will be Performed, the Great Assize, or Day of Judgment. Broadside. Worcester, Mass.: American Antiquarian Society, ca. 1789.

Cain, William E. "Violence, Revolution, and the Cost of Freedom." *Boundary 2* 17, no. 1 (Spring 1990): 305–30.

Camfield, Gregg. *Sentimental Twain: Samuel Clemens in the Maze of Moral Philosophy.* Philadelphia: University of Pennsylvania Press, 1994.

Carlos Wilcox, A. M. "Sermon XIX: The Unreasonableness and Danger of Indecision." *The National Preacher; or, Original Monthly Sermons From Living Ministers* (July 1827): 17–32. Accessed through the American Periodical Series Online.

Carnahan, Matthew Michael (screenplay). *World War Z.* DVD. Directed by Marc Forster. Los Angeles: Paramount Pictures, 2013. Based on a novel by Max Brooks.

Carton, Evan. *Patriotic Treason: John Brown and the Soul of America.* Lincoln: University of Nebraska Press, 2006.

Child, Lydia Maria. "The Black Saxons." *The Liberty Bell. By Friends of Freedom* (Jan. 1, 1841): 19–44. Accessed through the American Periodical Series Online.

———. "Letter from a Colored Man in Ohio to L. Maria Child." *The Liberator* (December 23, 1859): 202. Accessed through the American Periodical Series Online.

———. "Slavery's Pleasant Homes: A Faithful Sketch." *The Liberty Bell. By Friends of Freedom* (Jan. 1, 1843): 147–60. Accessed through the American Periodical Series Online.

Clark, Elizabeth. "'The Sacred Rights of the Weak': Pain, Sympathy, and the Culture of Individual Rights in Antebellum America." *Journal of American History* 82, no. 2 (September 1995): 463–93.

Clymer, Jeffory A. *America's Culture of Terrorism: Violence, Capitalism, and the Written Word*. Chapel Hill: University of North Carolina Press, 2003.

———. "Family Money: Race and Economic Rights in Antebellum U.S. Law and Fiction." *American Literary History* 21, no. 2 (Summer 2009): 211–38.

Coleman, Dawn. "The Unsentimental Woman Preacher of *Uncle Tom's Cabin*." *American Literature* 80, no. 2 (June 2008): 265–92.

Collins, Patricia Hill. *Black Feminist Thought: Knowledge, Consciousness, and the Politics of Empowerment*. New York: Routledge, 2000.

Cooper, Valerie C. *Maria Stewart, the Bible, and the Rights of African Americans*. Charlottesville: University of Virginia Press, 2011.

Crane, Gregg. "Dangerous Sentiments: Sympathy, Rights, and Revolution in Stowe's Antislavery Novels," *Nineteenth-Century Literature* 51, no. 2 (Sept. 1996): 176–204.

———. *Race, Citizenship, and Law in American Literature*. New York: Cambridge University Press, 2002.

Daly, John Patrick. *When Slavery Was Called Freedom: Evangelicalism, Proslavery, and the Causes of the Civil War*. Lexington: University Press of Kentucky, 2002.

Davidson, Cathy N. *Revolution and the Word: The Rise of the American Novel*. New York: Oxford University Press, 1986.

Davis, David Brion. *Inhuman Bondage: The Rise and Fall of Slavery in the New World*. New York: Oxford University Press, 2006.

———. *The Problem of Slavery in the Age of Revolution*. Ithaca, N.Y.: Cornell University Press, 1975.

Davis, Mary Kemp. *Nat Turner Before the Bar of Judgment: Fictional Treatments of the Southampton Slave Insurrection*. Baton Rouge: Louisiana State University Press, 1999.

Delany, Martin. "Mrs. Stowe's Position." *Frederick Douglass Paper*, May 6, 1853. Accessed through Accessible Archives, www.accessible-archives.com.

Derrida, Jacques. "Of an Apocalyptic Tone Recently Adopted in Philosophy." In *Derrida and Negative Theology*, edited by Harold Coward and Toby Foshay, 25–71. Albany: SUNY Press, 1992.

DeWaard, Jeanne Elders. "'The Shadow of Law': Sentimental Interiority, Gothic Terror, and the Legal Subject." *Arizona Quarterly* 62, no. 4 (Winter 2006): 1–30.

Dillingham, William B. *Melville's Later Novels*. Athens: University of Georgia Press, 1986.

Dillon, Elizabeth. "Sentimental Aesthetics." *American Literature* 76, no. 3 (2004): 495–523.

Dimock, Wai Chee. *Empire for Liberty: Melville and the Poetics of Individualism*. Princeton, N.J.: Princeton University Press, 1989.

Douglas, Ann. *The Feminization of American Culture*. New York: Alfred A. Knopf, 1977.

Douglass, Frederick. *Narrative of the Life of Frederick Douglass, an American Slave*. 1845. New York: Modern Library, 1994.

———. "Self-Made Men." In *The Frederick Douglass Papers*, series 1, vol. 4, edited by John Blassingame and John McKivigan, 545–75. New Haven: Yale University Press, 1992.

"Drinking Song." Published by Charles Magnus, no. 12 Frankfort St., N.Y. Broadside. Worcester, Mass.: American Antiquarian Society, ca. 1860–1867.

DuBois, W. E. B. *John Brown: A Biography*. 1909. Reprint, New York: Oxford University Press, 2007.
Duquette, Elizabeth. "The Republican Mammy? Imagining Civic Engagement in *Dred*." *American Literature* 80, no. 1 (March 2008): 1–28.
Eastman, Mary H. *Aunt Phillis's Cabin; or, Southern Life as It Is*. 1852. Ann Arbor, Mich.: Scholarly Publishing Office, University of Michigan University Library, 2005.
Edwards, Jonathan. *Personal Narrative*. In *A Jonathan Edwards Reader*, edited by John E. Smith, Harry S. Stout, and Kenneth M. Minkema, 281–96. New Haven: Yale University Press, 1995.
———. "Sinners in the Hands of an Angry God." In *A Jonathan Edwards Reader*, edited by John E. Smith, Harry S. Stout, and Kenneth P. Minkema, 89–104. New Haven: Yale University Press, 1995.
———. *A Treatise Concerning Religious Affections*. In *The Works of Jonathan Edwards*, edited by John E. Smith. Vol. 2. New Haven: Yale University Press, 1959.
———. *The Works of President Edwards, in Four Volumes, with Valuable Additions and a Copious General Index*. Vol. 1. New York: Robert Carter and Brothers, 1868.
Ehrman, Bart D. *Jesus: Apocalyptic Prophet of the New Millennium*. New York: Oxford University Press, 1999.
Ellison, Julie. *Cato's Tears and the Making of Anglo-American Emotion*. Chicago: University of Chicago Press, 1999.
———. *The Plight of Feeling: Sympathy and Dissent in the Early American Novel*. Chicago: University of Chicago Press, 1997.
Emerson, Ralph Waldo. "American Civilization." In *The Works of Ralph Waldo Emerson*. New York: Hearst's International Library, 1914. 3: 225–46.
———. "Self-Reliance." In *Selected Writings of Emerson*, edited by Donald McQuade, 129–53. New York: Modern Library, 1981.
Fairfield, Sumner Lincoln. *The Last Night of Pompeii: A Poem: And Lays and Legends*. New York: Elliott and Palmer, 1832.
Filler, Louis. *The Crusade Against Slavery, 1830–1860*. New York: Harper & Row, 1963.
Finkelman, Paul. "Manufacturing Martyrdom: The Antislavery Response to John Brown's Raid." In *His Soul Goes Marching On: Responses to John Brown and the Harpers Ferry Raid*, edited by Paul Finkelman, 41–66. Charlottesville: University Press of Virginia, 1995.
Fisher, Philip. *Hard Facts: Setting and Form in the American Novel*. New York: Oxford University Press, 1985.
Fitzhugh, George. *Cannibals All! or Slaves Without Masters*. 1857. Edited by C. Vann Woodward. Cambridge, Mass.: Harvard University Press, 1988.
Foner, Eric. *Free Soil, Free Labor, Free Men: The Ideology of the Republican Party Before the Civil War*. New York: Oxford University Press, 1995.
———, ed. *Nat Turner*. Englewood Cliffs: Prentice-Hall, 1971.
———. *The Story of American Freedom*. New York: Norton, 1998.
Forbes, Robert P. "Slavery and the Evangelical Enlightenment." In *Religion and the Antebellum Debate Over Slavery*, edited by John R. McKivigan and Mitchell Snay, 68–106. Athens: University of Georgia Press, 1998.

Foster, Charles. *The Rungless Ladder*. Durham, N.C.: Duke University Press, 1954.

Foster, Frances Smith. *Written by Herself: Literary Production by African American Women, 1746–1892*. Bloomington: Indiana University Press, 1993.

Fredrickson, George. *The Black Image in the White Mind: The Debate on Afro-American Character and Destiny, 1817–1914*. Middletown, Conn.: Wesleyan University Press, 1987.

Freehling, William W. *The Reintegration of American History: Slavery and the Civil War*. New York: Oxford University Press, 1994.

Furstenberg, François. "Beyond Freedom and Slavery: Autonomy, Virtue, and Resistance in Early American Political Discourse." *Journal of American History* 89, no. 4 (March 2003): 1295–1330.

Garfield, Michelle N. "Literary Societies: The Work of Self-Improvement and Racial Uplift." In *Black Women's Intellectual Traditions: Speaking Their Minds*, edited by Kristin Waters and Carol B. Conaway, 113–28. Burlington: University of Vermont Press, 2007.

Garnet, Henry Highland. "Sketch of the Life and Character of David Walker." *The North Star*, July 14, 1848. Accessed through Accessible Archives, www.accessible-archives.com.

Garrison, William Lloyd. "The Insurrection." *The Liberator*, September 3, 1831, 143. Accessed through the American Periodical Series Online.

———. "No Compromise with Slavery: An Address Delivered in the Broadway Tabernacle, New York, February 14, 1854." New York: American Anti-slavery Society, 1854.

Genovese, Eugene. *From Rebellion to Revolution: Afro-American Slave Revolts in the Making of the Modern World*. Baton Rouge: Louisiana State University Press, 1979.

———. *Roll, Jordan, Roll: The World the Slaves Made*. New York: Pantheon, 1974.

Gilbert, James N. "A Behavioral Analysis of John Brown: *Martyr or Terrorist?*" In *Terrible Swift Sword: The Legacy of John Brown*, edited by Peggy A. Russo and Paul Finkelman, 107–17. Athens, Ohio: Ohio University Press, 2005.

Glaude, Eddie. *Exodus! Race, Religion, and Nation in Early Nineteenth-Century Black America*. Chicago: University of Chicago Press, 2000.

Gordon, Dexter B. *Black Identity: Rhetoric, Ideology, and Nineteenth-Century Black Nationalism*. Carbondale: Southern Illinois University Press, 2003.

Gore, Al. *An Inconvenient Truth*. DVD. Directed by Davis Guggenheim. Los Angeles: Paramount Classics, 2006.

Gould, Stephen Jay. *The Mismeasure of Man*. New York: Norton, 1981.

Grasso, Linda. *The Artistry of Anger: Black and White Women's Literature in America, 1820–1869*. Chapel Hill, N.C.: University of North Carolina Press, 2002.

Greenberg, Kenneth, ed. *The Confessions of Nat Turner and Related Documents*. Boston: Bedford / St. Martin's, 1996.

Greenwald, Glenn. "U.S. drone strikes target rescuers in Pakistan—and the west stays silent." *The Guardian*, Aug. 20, 2012.

Gross, Seymour L., and Eileen Bender. "History, Politics and Literature: The Myth of Nat Turner." *American Quarterly* 23 (October 1971): 487–518.

Halttunen, Karen. "Gothic Imagination and Social Reform: The Haunted Houses of Lyman Beecher, Henry Ward Beecher, and Harriet Beecher Stowe." In *New Essays* on *Uncle Tom's Cabin*, edited by Eric J. Sundquist, 107–34. New York: Cambridge University Press, 1986.

Hamilton, Cynthia. "*Dred:* Intemperate Slavery." *Journal of American Studies* 34, no. 2 (2000): 257–77.

Hansen, James. *Storms of My Grandchildren: The Truth About the Coming Climate Catastrophe and Our Last Chance to Save Humanity*. New York: Bloomsbury, 2009.

Harding, Vincent. "Symptoms of Liberty and Blackhead Signposts: David Walker and Nat Turner." In *Nat Turner: A Slave Rebellion in History and Memory*, edited by Kenneth S. Greenberg, 79–102. New York: Oxford University Press, 2003.

Hartman, Saidiya. *Scenes of Subjection: Terror, Slavery, and Self-Making in Nineteenth-Century America*. New York: Oxford University Press, 1997.

Hatch, Nathan O. *The Democratization of American Christianity*. New Haven, Conn.: Yale University Press, 1989.

Hedrick, Joan D. *Harriet Beecher Stowe: A Life*. New York: Oxford University Press, 1994.

Hendler, Glenn. "The Limits of Sympathy: Louisa May Alcott and the Sentimental Novel." *American Literary History* 3, no. 4 (Winter 1991): 685–706.

———. *Public Sentiments: Structures of Feeling in Nineteenth-Century American Literature*. Chapel Hill, N.C.: University of North Carolina Press, 2001.

Higginson, Thomas Wentworth. "Nat Turner's Insurrection." *The Atlantic*, August 1861. www.theatlantic.com/past/docs/issues/1861aug/higginson.htm.

Hinks, Peter. *To Awaken My Afflicted Brethren: David Walker and the Problem of Antebellum Slave Resistance*. University Park: Pennsylvania State University Press, 1997.

Holified, E. Brooks. *Theology in America: Christian Thought from the Age of the Puritans to the Civil War*. New Haven, Conn.: Yale University Press, 2003.

Horton, James Oliver. *In Hope of Liberty: Culture, Community, and Protest Among Northern Free Blacks*. New York: Oxford University Press, 1997.

Hovenden, Thomas. *The Last Moments of John Brown*. 1884.

Howard, June. "What Is Sentimentality?" *American Literary History* 11, no. 1 (Spring 1999): 63–81.

Howe, Julia Ward. "Battle Hymn of the Republic." In Deborah Pickman Clifford, *Mine Eyes Have Seen the Glory: A Biography of Julia Ward Howe*, 287–88. Boston: Little, Brown, 1978.

Hubbard, Dolan. *The Sermon and the African American Literary Imagination*. Columbia: University of Missouri Press, 1994.

Huggins, Nathan. *Black Odyssey: The African-American Ordeal in Slavery*. New York: Pantheon, 1990.

Husch, Gail E. *Something Coming: Apocalyptic Expectation and Mid-Nineteenth-Century American Painting*. Hanover, N.H.: University Press of New England, 2000.

International Human Rights and Conflict Resolution Clinic at Stanford Law School and Global Justice Clinic at NYU School of Law. *Living Under Drones: Death, Injury, and Trauma to Civilians from U.S. Drone Practices in Pakistan*. September 2012. http://livingunderdrones.org.

Jacobs, Harriet Ann. *Incidents in the Life of a Slave Girl: Written by Herself*. 1861. Cambridge, Mass.: Harvard University Press, 2000.

Jarrett, Gene Andrew. "'To Refute Mr. Jefferson's Argument Respecting Us': Thomas Jefferson, David Walker, and the Politics of Early African-American Literature." *Early American Literature* 46, no. 2 (2011): 291–318.

Jefferson, Mark. "What's Wrong with Sentimentality?" *Mind* 92 (1983): 519–27.

Jefferson, Thomas. *Notes on the State of Virginia*. 1781. Edited by Frank Shuffelton. New York: Penguin, 1998.

Johnson, Walter. "On Agency." *Journal of Social History* 35, no. 1 (Fall 2003): 113–24.

Kaplan, Amy. *The Anarchy of Empire in the Making of U.S. Culture*. Cambridge, Mass.: Harvard University Press, 2002.

Karafilis, Maria. "Spaces of Democracy in Harriet Beecher Stowe's *Dred*." *Arizona Quarterly* 55, no. 3 (Autumn 1999): 23–49.

Karcher, Carolyn L. *The First Woman in the Republic: A Cultural Biography of Lydia Maria Child*. Durham, N.C.: Duke University Press, 1994.

———. *Shadow Over the Promised Land: Slavery, Race, and Violence in Melville's America*. Baton Rouge: Louisiana State University Press, 1979.

Kaye, Anthony E. "Neighborhoods and Nat Turner: The Making of a Slave Rebel and the Unmaking of Slave Rebellion." *Journal of the Early Republic* 27, no. 4 (Winter 2007): 705–20.

Kermode, Frank. *The Sense of an Ending: Studies in the Theory of Fiction*. New York: Oxford University Press, 2000.

A Key to the Revelations, or an Exposition of the Prophecies, According to Lowman and Faber. Broadside. Worcester, Mass.: American Antiquarian Society, ca. 1808–1816.

Kimball, Gayle. *The Religious Ideas of Harriet Beecher Stowe: Her Gospel of Womanhood*. New York: Edwin Mellen, 1982.

Klein, Rachel Naomi. "Harriet Beecher Stowe and the Domestication of Free Labor Ideology." *Legacy* 18, no. 2 (2001): 135–52.

Lemire, Elise. *"Miscegenation": Making Race in America*. Philadelphia: University of Pennsylvania Press, 2002.

Levine, Robert. *Dislocating Race and Nation: Episodes in Nineteenth-Century American Literary Nationalism*. Chapel Hill: University of North Carolina Press, 2008.

———. *Martin Delany, Frederick Douglass, and the Politics of Representative Identity*. Chapel Hill: University of North Carolina Press, 1997.

Lincoln, Abraham. "Proclamation of Thanksgiving." In *Lincoln: Selected Speeches and Writings, 1859–1865*, edited by Don E. Fehrenbacher, 520–21. New York: Library of America, 1989.

———. "Second Inaugural Address." In *Lincoln: Selected Speeches and Writings*, edited by Don E. Fehrenbacher, 686–87. New York: Library of America, 1989.

Martin, Terence. *The Instructed Vision: Scottish Common Sense Philosophy and the Origins of American Fiction*. New York: Kraus Reprint, 1969.

McCarthy, Cormac. *The Road*. New York: Vintage International, 2006.

McKivigan, John R. *The War against Proslavery Religion: Abolitionism and the Northern Churches, 1830–1865*. Ithaca, N.Y.: Cornell University Press, 1984.

McKivigan, John R., and Mitchell Snay. "Introduction: Religion and the Problem of Slavery in Antebellum America." In *Religion and the Antebellum Debate Over Slavery*, edited by John R. McKivigan and Mitchell Snay, 1–32. Athens: University of Georgia Press, 1998.

Meltzer, Milton, and Patricia G. Holland, eds. *Lydia Maria Child: Selected Letters, 1817–1880*. Amherst: University of Massachusetts Press, 1982.

Melville, Herman. "Benito Cereno." In *The Piazza Tales*. New York: Dix & Edwards, 1856.

———. *Moby-Dick; or, The Whale*. 1851. New York: Penguin, 1992.

———. "The Portent." In *Battle-Pieces and Aspects of the War*. New York: Harper & Brothers, 1866. 12.

Merish, Lori. *Sentimental Materialism: Gender, Commodity Culture, and Nineteenth-Century American Literature*. Durham, N.C.: Duke University Press, 2000.

Midgley, Mary. "Brutality and Sentimentality." *Philosophy* 54 (1979): 385–89.

Monbiot, George. "In the U.S., mass child killings are tragedies. In Pakistan, mere bug splats." *The Guardian*, December 17, 2012.

Moody, Joycelyn. *Sentimental Confessions: Spiritual Narratives of Nineteenth-Century African-American Women*. Athens: University of Georgia Press, 2001.

Moore, Opal. "The Productions of Maria W. Stewart: Rebellious Domesticity and Black Women's Liberation." In *Early America Re-Explored: New Readings in Colonial, Early National, and Antebellum Culture*, edited by Klaus H. Schmidt and Fritz Fleischmann, 441–65. New York: Peter Lang, 2000.

Moorhead, James H. *American Apocalypse: Yankee Protestants and the Civil War, 1860–1869*. New Haven, Conn.: Yale University Press, 1978.

Morgan, Edmund. *American Slavery, American Freedom: The Ordeal of Colonial Virginia*. New York: Norton, 1975.

Moses, Wilson Jeremiah. *Black Messiahs and Uncle Toms: Social and Literary Manipulations of a Religious Myth*. University Park: Pennsylvania State University Press, 1982.

Mott, Wesley T. "The Age of the First Person Singular: Emerson and Individualism." In *A Historical Guide to Ralph Waldo Emerson*, ed. Joel Myerson, 61–100. New York: Oxford University Press, 2000.

Nabers, Deak. "The Problem of Revolution in the Age of Slavery: *Clotel*, Fiction, and the Government of Man." *Representations* 91, no. 1 (Summer 2005): 84–108.

Nell, William Cooper. *The Colored Patriots of the American Revolution*. Boston: Robert W. Wallcut, 1855.

Nelson, Dana. *The Word in Black and White: Reading "Race" in American Literature, 1638–1867*. New York: Oxford University Press, 1993.

Noble, Marianne. "An Ecstasy of Apprehension: The Gothic Pleasures of Sentimental Fiction." In *American Gothic: New Interventions in a National Narrative*, edited by Robert K. Martin and Eric Savoy, 163–82. Iowa City: University of Iowa Press, 1998.

———. *The Masochistic Pleasures of Sentimental Literature*. Princeton, N.J.: Princeton University Press, 2000.

Noble, Thomas S. *John Brown's Blessing*. 1867.

Noll, Mark. *America's God: From Jonathan Edwards to Abraham Lincoln*. New York: Oxford University Press, 2002.

———. *The Civil War as a Theological Crisis*. Chapel Hill, N.C.: University of North Carolina Press, 2006.

Nudelman, Franny. *John Brown's Body: Slavery, Violence, and the Culture of War*. Chapel Hill, N.C.: University of North Carolina Press, 2004.

Oates, Stephen. *The Fires of Jubilee: Nat Turner's Fierce Rebellion*. New York: Harper & Row, 1975.

O'Leary, Stephen D. *Arguing the Apocalypse: A Theory of Millennial Rhetoric*. New York: Oxford University Press, 1994.

Parramore, Thomas C. "Covenant in Jerusalem." In *Nat Turner: A Slave Rebellion in History and Memory*, edited by Kenneth S. Greenberg, 58–76. New York: Oxford University Press, 2003.

———. *Southampton County*. Charlottesville: University Press of Virginia, 1978.

PAULUS. "Remarks on the Term Vengeance." *New-York Gospel Herald*, Feb. 14, 1829, p. 59. Accessed through the American Periodical Series Online.

Pearson, Edward A. "Introduction: Culture and Conspiracy in Denmark Vesey's Charleston." In *Designs Against Charleston: The Trial Record of the Denmark Vesey Slave Conspiracy of 1822*, edited by Edward A. Pearson, 1–164. Chapel Hill: University of North Carolina Press, 1999.

Pease, Donald. "American Apocalypse: The End of Exceptionalism and the Return of Alexis de Tocqueville." In *Apocalypse*, edited by Fritz Gysin, 23–40. Tübingen, Germany: G. Narr, 2000.

Peterson, Carla. *"Doers of the Word": African-American Women Speakers and Writers in the North, 1830–1880*. New York: Oxford University Press, 1995.

Powell, Timothy. *Ruthless Democracy: A Multicultural Interpretation of the American Renaissance*. Princeton, N.J.: Princeton University Press, 2000.

Prothero, Stephen. *American Jesus: How the Son of God Became a National Icon*. New York: Farrar, Straus & Giroux, 2003.

Quarles, Benjamin, ed. *Blacks on John Brown*. Urbana: University of Illinois Press, 1972.

Ransom, Louis. *John Brown Meeting the Slave Mother and Her Child on the Steps of the Charleston Jail on His Way to Execution*. 1860.

Redpath, James. *Echoes of Harper's Ferry*. 1860. Westport, Conn.: Negro University Press, 1970.

———. *The Public Life of Capt. John Brown*. Boston: Thayer and Eldridge, 1860.

Reid-Pharr, Robert F. *Conjugal Union: The Body, the House, and the Black American*. New York: Oxford University Press, 1999.

Reynolds, David. *John Brown, Abolitionist: The Man Who Killed Slavery, Sparked the Civil War, and Seeded Civil Rights*. New York: Vintage, 2005.

Reynolds, Larry J. *Righteous Violence: Revolution, Slavery, and the American Renaissance*. Athens: University of Georgia Press, 2011.

Riss, Arthur. *Race, Slavery, and Liberalism in Nineteenth-Century American Literature*. New York: Cambridge University Press, 2006.

Roberson, Susan. "Maria Stewart and the Rhetoric of Mobility." *Journal of International Women's Studies* 4, no. 3 (May 2003): 56–61.

Rodgers, Daniel T. *The Work Ethic in Industrial America, 1850–1920*. Chicago: University of Chicago Press, 1979.

Romero, Lora. *Home Fronts: Domesticity and Its Critics in the Antebellum United States.* Durham, N.C.: Duke University Press, 1997.

Rowe, John Carlos. "Stowe's Rainbow Sign: Violence and Community in *Dred: A Tale of the Great Dismal Swamp* (1856)." *Arizona Quarterly* 58, no. 1 (Spring 2002): 37–55.

Rozario, Kevin. *The Culture of Calamity: Disaster and the Making of Modern America.* Chicago: University of Chicago Press, 2007.

Ruchames, Louis, ed. *A John Brown Reader: The Story of John Brown in His Own Words, in the Words of Those Who Knew Him, and in the Poetry and Prose of the Literary Heritage.* New York: Abelard-Schuman, 1959.

———. *John Brown: The Making of a Revolutionary.* New York: Grosset & Dunlap, 1969.

Ryan, Judylyn. *Spirituality as Ideology in Black Women's Film and Literature.* Charlottesville: University of Virginia Press, 2005.

Ryan, Susan. *The Grammar of Good Intentions: Race and the Antebellum Culture of Benevolence.* Ithaca, N.Y.: Cornell University Press, 2003.

Rycenga, Jennifer. "Maria Stewart, Black Abolitionist, and the Idea of Freedom." In *Frontline Feminism: Women, War, and Resistance*, edited by Marguerite R. Waller and Jennifer Rycenga, 297–342. New York: Garland, 2000.

Sale, Maggie Montesinos. *The Slumbering Volcano: American Slave Ship Revolts and the Production of Rebellious Masculinity.* Durham, N.C.: Duke University Press, 1997.

Samuels, Shirley, ed. *The Culture of Sentiment: Race, Gender, and Sentimentality in Nineteenth-Century America.* New York: Oxford University Press, 1992.

———. "Miscegenated America: The Civil War." *American Literary History* 9, no. 3 (1997): 482–501.

Sanchez-Eppler, Karen. "Then When We Clutched Hardest: On the Death of a Child and the Replication of an Image." In *Sentimental Men: Masculinity and the Politics of Affect in American Culture*, edited by Mary Chapman and Glen Hendler, 64–85. Berkeley: University of California Press, 1999.

———. *Touching Liberty: Abolition, Feminism, and the Politics of the Body.* Berkeley: University of California Press, 1993.

Scales, Laura Thiemann. "Narrative Revolutions in Nat Turner and Joseph Smith." *American Literary History* 24, no. 2 (Summer 2012): 205–33.

Schmidt, Leigh E., and Sally M. Promey, eds. *American Religious Liberalism.* Bloomington: Indiana University Press, 2012.

Schultz, Elizabeth. "The Sentimental Subtext of *Moby-Dick*: Melville's Response to the 'World of Woe.'" *ESQ: A Journal of the American Renaissance* 42, no. 1 (1996): 29–49.

Scully, Randolph Ferguson. *Religion and the Making of Nat Turner's Virginia: Baptist Community and Conflict, 1740–1840.* Charlottesville: University of Virginia Press, 2008.

Sedgwick, Catharine Maria. *Hope Leslie; or, Early Times in the Massachusetts*, edited by Mary Kelley. New Brunswick, N.J.: Rutgers University Press, 1987.

Sidbury, James. "Reading, Revelation, and Rebellion: The Textual Communities of Gabriel, Denmark Vesey, and Nat Turner." In *Nat Turner: A Slave Rebellion in History and Memory*, edited by Kenneth S. Greenberg, 119–33. New York: Oxford University Press, 2003.

Smith, Adam. *The Theory of Moral Sentiments*. New York: Cambridge University Press, 2002.

Smith, John E. "Religious Affections and the 'Sense of the Heart.'" In *The Princeton Companion to Jonathan Edwards*, edited by Sang Hyun Lee, 103–14. Princeton, N.J.: Princeton University Press, 2005.

Sobel, Mechal. *Trabelin' On: The Slave Journey to an Afro-Baptist Faith*. 1979. Reprint, Princeton, N.J.: Princeton University Press, 1988.

Sollors, Werner. *Neither Black Nor White Yet Both: Thematic Explorations of Interracial Literature*. New York: Oxford University Press, 1997.

Spillers, Hortense. "Changing the Letter: The Yokes, the Jokes of Discourse; or, Mrs. Stowe, Mr. Reed." In *Slavery and the Literary Imagination*, edited by Deborah E. McDowell and Arnold Rampersad, 25–61. Baltimore: Johns Hopkins University Press, 1989.

Spivak, Gayatri Chakravorty. *Outside in the Teaching Machine*. New York: Routledge, 1993.

Stauffer, John. *The Black Hearts of Men: Radical Abolitionists and the Transformation of Race*. Cambridge, Mass.: Harvard University Press, 2001.

Stewart, Maria. "An Address Delivered at the African Masonic Hall." In *Maria W. Stewart, America's First Black Woman Political Writer: Essays and Speeches*, edited by Marilyn Richardson, 56–64. Bloomington: Indiana University Press, 1987.

———. "An Address Delivered Before the Afric-American Female Intelligence Society of America." In *Maria W. Stewart, America's First Black Woman Political Writer: Essays and Speeches*, edited by Marilyn Richardson, 50–55. Bloomington: Indiana University Press, 1987.

———. "Cause for Encouragement." In *Maria W. Stewart, America's First Black Woman Political Writer: Essays and Speeches*, edited by Marilyn Richardson, 43–44. Bloomington: Indiana University Press, 1987.

———. "Lecture Delivered at the Franklin Hall." In *Maria W. Stewart, America's First Black Woman Political Writer: Essays and Speeches*, edited by Marilyn Richardson, 45–49. Bloomington: Indiana University Press, 1987.

———. "Meditation I." In *Meditations from the Pen of Mrs. Maria Stewart*. Washington: W. Lloyd Garrison & Knap, 1879. 37.

———. "Meditation XI." In *Meditations from the Pen of Mrs. Maria Stewart*. Washington: W. Lloyd Garrison & Knap, 1879. 49.

———. "Mrs. Stewart's Farewell Address to Her Friends in the City of Boston." In *Maria W. Stewart, America's First Black Woman Political Writer: Essays and Speeches*, edited by Marilyn Richardson, 65–74. Bloomington: Indiana University Press, 1987.

———. "The Proper Training of Children." In *Two Texts on Children and Christian Education*, edited by Eric Gardner. *PMLA* 123, no. 1 (2008): 159–60.

———. *Religion and the Pure Principles of Morality*. In *Maria W. Stewart, America's First Black Woman Political Writer: Essays and Speeches*, edited by Marilyn Richardson, 28–42. Bloomington: Indiana University Press, 1987.

———. "Sufferings During the War." In *Maria W. Stewart, America's First Black Woman*

Political Writer: Essays and Speeches, edited by Marilyn Richardson, 98–109. Bloomington: Indiana University Press, 1987.

Stowe, Harriet Beecher. "An Appeal to the Women of the Free States of America on the Present Crisis in our Country. By Mrs. Harriet Beecher Stowe." *Provincial Freeman*, March 25, 1854. Accessed through Accessible Archives, www.accessible-archives.com.

———. *Dred: A Tale of the Great Dismal Swamp*. 1856. Edited by Robert S. Levine. New York: Penguin Books, 2000.

———. *A Key to Uncle Tom's Cabin; Presenting the Original Facts and Documents Upon Which the Story Is Founded. Together with Corroborative Statements Verifying the Truth of the Work*. 1853. Bedford, Mass.: Applewood Books, 1998.

———. *Uncle Tom's Cabin; or, Life Among the Lowly*. 1852. New York: The Modern Library, 2001.

———. *The Writings of Harriet Beecher Stowe: With Biographical Introductions, Portraits, and Other Illustrations*. Vol. 15. Boston: Houghton, Mifflin, 1896.

Stratman, Jacob. "Harriet Beecher Stowe's Preachers of the Swamp: *Dred* and the Jeremiad." *Christianity and Literature* 57, no. 3 (Spring 2008): 379–400.

Sundquist, Eric. *To Wake the Nations: Race in the Making of American Literature*. Cambridge, Mass.: Harvard University Press, 1993.

Takacs, Stacy. *Terrorism TV: Popular Entertainment in Post-9/11 America*. Lawrence: University Press of Kansas, 2012.

Thoreau, Henry David. "A Plea for Captain John Brown." In *Thoreau: Collected Essays and Poems*, edited by Elizabeth Hall Witherell, 396–417. New York: The Library of America, 2001.

———. "Slavery in Massachusetts." In *Thoreau: Collected Essays and Poems*, edited by Elizabeth Hall Witherell, 333–47. New York: The Library of America, 2001.

Tichenor, Isaac Taylor. "First-Day Sermon." 1863. In *The Home Mission Statesman*, edited by J. S. Dill, D.D., 88–108. Nashville, Tenn.: Sunday School Board Southern Baptist Convention, 1908.

Tompkins, Jane. *Sensational Designs: The Cultural Work of American Fiction, 1790–1860*. New York: Oxford University Press, 1985.

Trier, Lars von, dir. *Melancholia*. DVD. Copenhagen, Denmark: Nordisk Film, 2011.

Trodd, Zoe. "A Less Costly Ink: John Brown's Prison Letters and the Traditions of American Protest Literature." In *Letters and Cultural Transformations in the United States, 1760–1860*, edited by Theresa Strouth Gaul and Sharon M. Harris, 197–219. Farnham, Surrey: Ashgate, 2009.

Trodd, Zoe, and John Stauffer, eds. *Meteor of War: The John Brown Story*. Maplecrest, N.Y.: Brandywine Press, 2004.

Turan, Kenneth. "*WALL-E:* Groundbreaking yet familiar, part romance, part sci-fi, Pixar's latest work is wonderful and full of wonder." *Los Angeles Times*, June 27, 2008. www.latimes.com/news/nationworld/world/middleeast/la-et-walle27-2008jun27,0,362267.story.

Tuveson, Ernest Lee. *Redeemer Nation: The Idea of America's Millennial Role*. Chicago: University of Chicago Press, 1968.

United States Supreme Court. *A Report of the Decision of the Supreme Court of the United States, and the Opinions of the Judges Thereof, in the Case of Dred Scott Versus John F. A. Sandford.* New York: D. Appleton, 1857.

Utley, Ebony. "A Woman Made of Words: The Rhetorical Invention of Maria W. Stewart." In *Black Women's Intellectual Traditions: Speaking Their Minds*, edited by Kristin Waters and Carol B. Conaway, 55–71. Burlington: University of Vermont Press, 2007.

Von Frank, Albert. *The Trials of Anthony Burns: Freedom and Slavery in Emerson's Boston.* Cambridge, Mass.: Harvard University Press, 1998.

Walker, David. *Appeal, in Four Articles; Together with a Preamble, to the Coloured Citizens of the World, but in particular, and very expressly, to those of the United States of America.* 1831. Edited by Sean Wilentz. New York: Hill and Wang, 1995.

Walzer, Michael. *Exodus and Revolution.* New York: Basic Books, 1985.

Warner, Susan. *The Wide Wide World.* 1850. New York: The Feminist Press at CUNY, 1987.

Warren, Kenneth W. *What Was African American Literature?* Cambridge, Mass.: Harvard University Press, 2011.

Weinstein, Cindy. *Family, Kinship, and Sympathy in Nineteenth-Century American Literature.* New York: Cambridge University Press, 2004.

Wexler, Laura. *Tender Violence: Domestic Visions in an Age of U.S. Imperialism.* Chapel Hill: University of North Carolina Press, 2000.

———. "Tender Violence: Literary Eavesdropping, Domestic Fiction, and Educational Reform." In *The Culture of Sentiment: Race, Gender, and Sentimentality in Nineteenth-Century America*, edited by Shirley Samuels, 9–38. New York: Oxford University Press, 1992.

Whitehead, Colson. *Zone One: A Novel.* New York: Doubleday, 2011.

Whitney, Lisa. "In the Shadow of *Uncle Tom's Cabin:* Stowe's Vision of Slavery from the Great Dismal Swamp." *New England Quarterly* 66, no. 4 (Dec. 1993): 552–69.

Williamson, Joel. *The Crucible of Race: Black-White Relations in the American South Since Emancipation.* New York: Oxford University Press, 1984.

Wilson, Edmund. *Patriot Gore: Studies in the Literature of the American Civil War.* New York: W.W. Norton, 1994.

Winthrop, John. "A Model of Christian Charity." In *The Norton Anthology of American Literature*, 6th ed., vol. A, edited by Nina Baym, 206–17. New York: Norton, 2003.

"Wrath or vengeance of God." *Trumpet and Universalist Magazine*, Jan. 16, 1841, p. 118. Accessed through the American Periodical Series Online.

Wyatt-Brown, Bertram. "'A Volcano Beneath a Mountain of Snow': John Brown and the Problem of Interpretation." In *His Soul Goes Marching On: Responses to John Brown and the Harpers Ferry Raid*, edited by Paul Finkelman, 10–38. Charlottesville: University Press of Virginia, 1995.

Yarborough, Richard. "Race, Violence, and Manhood: The Masculine Ideal in Frederick Douglass's 'The Heroic Slave.'" In *Frederick Douglass: New Literary and Historical Essays*, edited by Eric J. Sundquist, 166–88. New York: Cambridge University Press, 1991.

———. "Strategies of Black Characterization in *Uncle Tom's Cabin* and the Early Afro-American Novel." In *New Essays on Uncle Tom's Cabin*, edited by Eric J. Sundquist, 45–84. New York: Cambridge University Press, 1986.

Young, Robert Alexander. "The Ethiopian Manifesto, Issued in Defence of the Blackman's Rights, in the Scale of Universal Freedom." 1829. In *A Documentary History of the Negro People in the United States*, edited by Herbert Aptheker, 1: 90–93. Secaucus, N.J.: Citadel Press, 1973.

Zakai, Avihu. *Exile and Kingdom: History and Apocalypse in the Puritan Migration to America*. New York: Cambridge University Press, 2002.

Zamora, Lois Parkinson. "The Myth of Apocalypse and the American Literary Imagination." In *The Apocalyptic Vision in America: Interdisciplinary Essays on Myth and Culture*, edited by Lois Parkinson Zamora, 97–138. Bowling Green, Ohio: Bowling Green University Press, 1982.

Ziser, Michael. "Emersonian Terrorism: John Brown, Islam, and Postsecular Violence." *American Literature* 82, no. 2 (June 2010): 333–60.

Index

Italicized page numbers refer to figures.

abolitionists: hostility of Northern churches toward, 195–96nn23–24; rhetoric of wrath found in writing of, 4–5; slavery framed as violation against God by, 4. *See also* antislavery discourse; Brown, John; *and specific authors*

abolitionist sentimentality: apocalyptic sentimentalism compared with, 201n6; Brown as fantasy of nineteenth-century, 155–56; and insurrectionary panic integration, 219n23; tropes of, 72. *See also* sentimentalism

"Address Delivered Before the Afric-American Female Intelligence Society of America, An" (Stewart sermon), 59

Afric-American Female Intelligence Society of America, 66

African American literature, 207n55

African colonization (*Uncle Tom's Cabin*), 113–18

African Masonic Hall, 66

African Methodist Episcopal (AME) Church of Charleston, 37, 42, 201n11

Agassiz, Louis, 124

Al Qaeda, 23

amalgamated blood (*Dred*'s Harry Gordon character), 124–30, 217n10

American Colonization Society, 116

American Renaissance scholarship, 35

antebellum period: apocalypse as recurring theme during, 13, 17; apocalyptic vengeance used to politicize terror in, 3–4; Calvinism orthodoxy challenged during, 11–12; challenging gendered speech acts during, 25, 60–61; citizenship understood in terms of masculinity during, 204n33; enslaved Negroes not recognized as persons during, 56–57; religious violence as challenging racial structures of, 22; "work ethic" significance during, 127, 218n18. *See also* Civil War; United States

antislavery discourse: abolitionist sentimentality as shaper of, 3, 8–9, 72, 155–56; apocalyptic theology as fundamental to, 17, 19–22; fear and love paired within, 3, 6, 26, 27, 98–113, 141–44, 145–49, 165–66; during Harpers Ferry debate, 29, 149, 153–80; messianic violence linked to, 20–31, 38, 44–57, 60–61, 80–81, 131–36, 146–48; rhetoric of wrath in, 1–12, 19, 24–26, 29. *See also* sympathy; *and specific authors*

apocalypse: in "The Apocalypse Explained," 13, *14*; in "By the Command of the King of Kings," *16*; Christianization of Africa as sign of impending, 113–18; in "Drinking Song," 17, *18*; as engine of American literary and cultural history, 31; in "A Key to the Revela-

245

apocalypse (*continued*)
  tions," *15*; in McCarthy's *The Road*, 189–91; as signifying threat and terror, 12–13; Stewart's "domestication" of, 25, 58, 64, 77–78, 93
"Apocalypse Explained, The" (broadside), 13, *14*
apocalyptic sentimentalism: abolitionist sentimentality compared with, 201n6; Beck's use of, 184–87; Brown at Harpers Ferry as culmination of, 5, 24, 28–30, 166, 178–80; and Child's response to Harpers Ferry, 167–71; Civil War as end of, 30–31, 180, 182–84; as developing alongside nineteenth-century religious and cultural transformations, 11–12; Hansen's use of, 187–89; Lincoln's Second Inaugural as recasting, 30, 182–84; McCarthy's *The Road* as, 189–92, 227n22; and Stewart's sermons, 5, 28, 58, 71–75; of Stowe's *Dred*, 6, 24, 100, 140–49; in Stowe's *Uncle Tom's Cabin*, 24, 97–99, 100–119; as tactic to generate love and fear, 146; Walker's *Appeal*'s influence on, 24, 62. *See also* sentimentalism
apocalyptic terror: abolitionist narrative's use of, 22–31; post-9/11 America incorporation of, 31, 184–92; Puritan ministers' use of, 9–11; Turner's *Confessions*' portrayal of, 28, 44–47; vengeance used to politicize, 3–4; Walker's *Appeal*'s use of, 24–25, 37, 39–44. *See also* fear; terror
apocalyptic theology: as fundamental to antislavery agenda, 17, 19–22; and messianic violence, 20–22, 25–28, 38, 44–57, 60–61, 80–81, 131–36, 146–48; Methodist sermons on, 197–98nn35–36; of postmillennial Christians, 198n37; of premillennialist Christians, 198n37. *See also* Calvinist theology; Puritanism
apocalyptic vengeance: Brown's violence as, 5, 24, 28–30, 92, 149, 157–80; as creating sentimental sympathy, 155; description of, 4; multiracial democracy in tension with, 135–36, 140–48; sentimentalism's use of, 3–4, 131; Stowe's revised sentimentalism in *Dred* to include, 140–49; as threat to democracy in *Moby-Dick*, 140, 144. *See also* fear; God's wrath/vengeance; messianic violence
Appeal to the Coloured Citizens of the World (Walker): apocalyptic sentimentalism as organizing principle in, 28; attack of, on slavery, 39–40, 74–75; image of God in, 53; influence of, on apocalyptic sentimentality, 24, 62; messianic violence in, 49–57, 135, 148; power through self-abnegation in, 25, 38, 49; public reaction to, 39, 43; racially integrated nation as goal in, 40, 41–42, 46; sympathy and vengeance in, 24–25, 37, 39–44, 82–83; Turner's *Confessions* compared with, 25, 37–38, 44, 56; violence as revolutionary agency misread in, 38, 48. *See also* sentimental fiction; Walker, David
"Appeal to the Women of the Free States of America" (H. B. Stowe), 213–14n13
Apter, Michael, 22
Aunt Phillis's Cabin (Eastman), 30

Baldwin, Elihu, 1
Baldwin, James, 104, 118, 178–79
Barnes, Elizabeth, 154, 155
"Battle Hymn of the Republic, The" (Howe), 182
Beck, Glenn, 184–87
Beecher, Catherine, 63, 83; *A Treatise on Domestic Economy*, 84–85, 86
Beecher, Lyman: Calvinism of, 26, 101, 115, 119; influence of, on *Uncle Tom's Cabin*, 113, 115, 119; "A Reformation of Morals Practicable and Indispensable," 112
Bellin, Joshua, 99
"Benito Cereno" (Melville), 221n33
Bercovitch, Sacvan, 9
Bible: binary imposed on, 8; and Christ of *Uncle Tom's Cabin*, 112; *Dred* character reads, 133–34; in Stewart's sermons, 209n25; sympathy in, 176. *See also* Revelation, book of
black power: *Dred* and masculine, 123–31; fantasies of, 48. *See also* messianic violence
"Black Saxons, The" (Child): characters and plot of, 86–90; home as place of slave violence in, 64, 92, 140, 168; logic of apocalyptic sentimentalism in, 90
"Blow Ye the Trumpet Blow" (hymn), 174
body: Eva's sermon in *Uncle Tom's Cabin* on subordination of slave's, 216n3; fear and self-preservation of, 197n33
Brady, Matthew, 182
Brekus, Catherine, 65

Brodhead, Richard, 21
Brown, Amelia, 158
Brown, Henry "Box," 46
Brown, John: apocalyptic sentimentality culminating at Harpers Ferry with, 5, 24, 28–30, 166, 178–80; Baldwin's defense of, 178–79; Barnes on violent outcome of sympathetic identification of, 155; "Blow Ye the Trumpet Blow" as favorite hymn of, 174; Child's response to, 92, 156, 166–69, 170–71, 177, 224nn29–30; compassion of, for slave families, 157–64; Curry's *Tragic Prelude* mural on, 172, *173*, 175; daughter's recollections of, 176–77; domesticity of and antislavery violence by, 157–64; Emerson's support of, 164–65, 170, 224n22; execution of, 153; family devotion of, 157–59, 162–64; family tenderness and Puritan severity of, 175–76; as fantasy of abolitionist sentimentality, 155–56; Garrison's support of, 225n33; Golden Rule as justification for, 160, 164, 176; Harpers Ferry actions of, defended as love, 29, 149, 153–80; as instrument of apocalyptic vengeance, 5, 24, 28–30, 92, 149, 157–80; letter of, to wife, 157–59, 162–64; letters of, in prison, 29, 156, 157, 161, 164, 223–24n19; Melville's description of, 153, 157; modern scholarship on Harpers Ferry role of, 154–55; *New York Tribune*'s portrait of, 169, 170, 171, 172, 175; nineteenth-century sentimental sympathy exemplified by, 149, 154, 157–64; and practice of separating love from violence, 156–57; race as factor in support of, 224n27; racial distinctions in messianic discourse of, 223n16; son John's reflections on, 177, 223n15; son Salmon's recollections of, 29, 172, 174–77; sympathetic identification of, and turn to violence, 157–80; Thoreau's support of, 155, 164, 166, 167, 170, 176, 177, 224n22; *Uncle Tom's Cabin* and *Confessions* revised by kissing of black child by, 171; violence of, against "innocent" civilians, 200n55; whipping of children by, 177, 225–26n41; Whittier's poem on, 169–70; Wise on emotional state of, 225n35. *See also* Harpers Ferry
Brown, John, Jr., 177, 223n15
Brown, Ruth, 176–77
Brown, Salmon, 29, 172, 174–77

Brown, William Wells, 47
"Brown of Osawatomie" (Whittier), 169–70
Butler, Judith, 49, 52
"By the Command of the King of Kings" (broadside), *16*

Calvinist theology: apocalyptic sentimentalism as developing during decline of, 11–12; Beecher's, 26, 101, 115, 119; divinity model in, 52; Douglas on opposition of sentimentalism to masculinity of, 7–8; *New-York Gospel Herald* challenges to, 193n1; patriarchal power equated with, 35; "Remarks on the Term Vengeance" regarding manipulation of, 1–2, 4, 29; Scottish Common Sense tradition compared with, 7, 36–37, 213n11; Scottish Enlightenment as opposition to, 36; Stowe's critical stance against, 26, 113; Stowe's liberal Protestantism as replacing, 101–2, 113. *See also* apocalyptic theology
Camfield, Gregg, 7, 36–37
Carton, Evan, 172
Child, Lydia Maria: letter of, to Garrison on Brown, 168–69; response of, to Harpers Ferry, 92, 156, 166–69, 170–71, 177, 224–25n29; sentimental traditions used by, to examine domesticity and slavery, 63–64, 83, 86–93, 140; Turner's *Confessions* as bridge linking Walker to, 38
—works of: "The Black Saxons," 64, 86–90, 92, 140, 168; "John Brown and the Colored Child," 170–71; "Slavery's Pleasant Homes," 64, 86, 90–93, 140, 168
children: in Child's "John Brown and the Colored Child," 170–71; *New York Tribune*'s portrait of Brown kissing black, 169, 170, 171, 172, 175; and relationship between characters of Uncle Tom and Eva, 108–11, 214n19; salvific power of, in nineteenth-century tradition, 191; Turner's *Confessions* on killing of infant, 45–46, 203n19
Christ: apocalyptic tradition of, 195n21; debate over return of, 198n37; Milly (*Dred* character) on love of, 142–43; Stowe's vision of separation of righteous from unrighteous by, 118; *Uncle Tom's Cabin* on freeing slaves through salvation of, 114–18; *Uncle Tom's Cabin* on salvation through, 6, 26, 98–113

Index 247

citizenship: black authors' argument for black, 206–7n54; Sale's critique of gender divide in Walker's argument on, 204n33; Walker's critique of Jefferson's doubts about black, 47, 203n27, 205–6n51, 217n10

Civil War: apocalyptic history linked to, 182; Harpers Ferry as signaling, 153; and Lincoln's Proclamation of Thanksgiving, 181–82; and Lincoln's Second Inaugural Address, 183; as marking apocalyptic sentimentalism's end, 30–31, 180, 182–84; Melville's description of Brown as "meteor" bringing about, 153, 157; Sherman's campaign during, 182, 226n9. *See also* antebellum period; United States

Clark, Elizabeth, 195n16

Cole, Thomas, 17

Coleman, Dawn, 99

compassion: of Brown toward slave families, 159–60; as primary emotional goal of sentimental narration, 3; Stewart's use of sympathetic identification as appeal for, 73–75; *Uncle Tom's Cabin* use of fear of God's vengeance to invoke, 6, 26, 98–100, 102–13; Walker's *Appeal* linking God's wrath to, 24–25, 37, 39–44, 82–83; Walker's use of sympathetic identification to motivate, 37, 40, 41–42, 74–75

Confederacy: casualties suffered by, 181; Lincoln's Second Inaugural Address on shared burden of, and North, 182–84

Confessions (Turner): black subject empowered through self-abnegation in, 25, 38, 49; Brown's kissing of black child as revising infant murder scene in, 171; as connecting African American apocalyptic tradition to Stowe, 38, 44; Gray's editorial presence in, 202–3n17; influence of, on apocalyptic sentimentality, 24; on killing of Travis's infant child, 45–46, 203n19; liberty in, 202n15; messianic violence and terror in, 28, 44–47, 49–57, 135, 146–48; prophetic mode of, 205n50; questions of authenticity regarding, 202n16; as rejecting Walker's vision of racially integrated nation, 46; Uncle Tom contrasted with black males of, 108; violence misread as revolutionary agency in, 38, 48; Walker's *Appeal* compared with, 25, 37–38, 44, 56. *See also* sentimental fiction

Curry, John Steuart, 172, *173*, 175

Dawes, Rufus, 17

Declaration of Independence, 19–20, 42, 43–44, 47, 116, 135, 216n3

Delany, Martin, 47, 57, 71

democracy. *See* multiracial democratic communities

Denman, Lord, 97

Dimock, Wai Chee, 138

domesticity: Beecher's use of sentimental traditions to examine, 63, 83–86; of Brown as recalled by son Salmon, 29, 172, 174–77; Child's narratives shattering tranquility of, 64, 86–92, 140, 168; Child's sentimental fiction examining, 63–64, 86–93; film and television examples of, and apocalypse, 189–91, 226nn16–17, 227nn19–21; Hansen's use of rhetoric of, 187–88; *Moby-Dick* on Ahab's rejection of, 138–39; modern scholarship segregating apocalyptic sentimentalism from, 64; Stewart's yoking of, with apocalypse, 25, 58, 64, 77–78, 93. *See also* families

Douglas, Ann, 7–8, 82, 194n6; *The Feminization of American Culture*, 7

Douglass, Frederick, 20, 47–48, 155; *The Heroic Slave*, 20; *Narrative*, 4

Dred (H. B. Stowe): as agent of God's wrath, 131–36; apocalyptic contours of Dred character in, 219–20n24; apocalyptic sentimentalism in, 6, 24, 100, 140–49; Dred's death in, 144, 145–46, 149; Dred's killing of overseer in, 221–22n38; Dred's reading of Bible in, 133–34; fear as sentimental register in, 6; freed slave community in, 144–45; functions of Dred character in, 144–45; Harry Gordon contrasted with Dred in, 122–23, 130–31, 134–35, 148–49; Harry Gordon's comparison of Declaration of Independence to slave resistance in, 134; Harry Gordon's identity and discourse of blood in, 124–30, 217n7, 217n10; Harry Gordon's "work ethic" and loyalty to half-sibling Nina in, 127–29, 220n25; as highlighting incommensurability of slavery with nineteenth-century norms, 129–31;

implication of Dred's madness in, 220n30; love as missing from Dred's discourse in, 141–43; Melville's *Moby-Dick* compared with, 28, 123, 135–40; messianic violence in, 27–28, 111, 121–23, 131–36; Milly and Dred as sentimental core of, 27, 141–44, 145–49; multiracial democracy in, 28, 135–36, 140–48; slave humanity in, 123–31; slave insurrection as sentimental strategy in, 38; slave insurrection with apocalyptic retribution conjoined in, 93; Stowe's revised sentimentality and apocalyptic vengeance in, 140–49; Tiff's loyalty in, 144, 217–18n11; Turner's influence on, 28, 132, 141, 146–48; *Uncle Tom's Cabin* compared with, 27–28, 125, 130, 132–33, 134, 144–45, 148–49. *See also* sentimental fiction

Dred Scott v. Sandford (1857), 8–9

"Drinking Song" (broadside), 17, *18*

Durand, Asher, 17

Eastman, Mary H., 30

Echoes of Harper's Ferry (Realf), 153

Edwards, Jonathan, 51, 196n27, 196n29; "Sinners in the Hands of an Angry God," 10–11

Edwardsian theology, 100

Emerson, Ralph Waldo: and Protestant view of self, 49, 51; support of Brown by, 164–65, 170, 224n22

Engles, Jeremy, 47

families: Brown on interracial sympathy through devotion to, 157–64; Brown's children on their, 29, 172, 174–77, 223n15; *Dred*'s discourse on interracial, 124–30, 217n6, 217n10; film and television examples of, and apocalypse, 189–91, 226nn16–17, 227n19, 227n21; "generic goal" of sentimental fiction to show ties of, 200n1; Hansen's use of, 187–89;. *See also* domesticity

fear: as acquiring meaning through cultural language and rites, 194n7; as being about body and self-preservation, 197n33; Child's "Slavery's Pleasant Homes" on domestic space as source of, 64, 86, 90–93; *Dred's* Milly and Dred characters' role in pairing love with, 27, 141–44, 145–49; Edwards on his sermon evoking, 196n27; Edwards's "Sinners in the Hands of an Angry God" invocation of, 10–11; as incentive to love, 3; as Puritan community component, 10; sentimentalism's use of, 3–4, 131; as sentimental register by Stowe, 6, 102; Stewart's Christianity as constituted by, 72–73; Stowe's *Uncle Tom's Cabin* on transformation through, 6, 26, 98–113, 212n8. *See also* apocalyptic terror; apocalyptic vengeance

female preachers: changing notions of womanhood reflected by, 208–9n24; hybrid discourse used by, 65–67; imaging themselves as "warriors" and "nurturers," 65; respect for patriarchal order by, 208n19. *See also* Stewart, Maria

feminine speech: African American woman resistance through, 61–62; antebellum-period gender divide between masculine and, 60; female preachers using masculine and, 65–67; Stewart's messianic violence discourse challenging "proper," 25, 60–61, 80–81

Feminization of American Culture, The (Douglas), 7

Fern, Fanny, 62

"Final Judgment, The" (E. Baldwin), 1

Finkelman, Paul, 172

First African Baptist Church in Boston, 209n25

Fisher, Philip, 3, 123

Fitzhugh, George, 218–19n20

Foster, Charles, 142

Franklin, Benjamin, 204–5n39

Fredrickson, George, 118, 124

free blacks: black authors argument for citizenship of, 206–7n54; Sale's critique of gender divide of Walker's argument on citizenship of, 204n33; and Stewart on men's duty to defend slaves, 79–83; and Stewart on moral authority and virtues of women, 75–79; and Walker's charge to men to protect and provide for women, 81; Walker's critique of Jefferson's doubts about citizenship for, 47, 203n27. *See also* slaves

Fugitive Slave Act (1850), 8, 102, 213n13

Fuller, Margaret, 62

Gardner, Alexander, 182

Garrison, William Lloyd: Child's letter to, on Brown, 168–69; "The Insurrectionist," 35; sentimental appeal against slavery in preface

Index 249

Garrison, William Lloyd (*continued*)
of, 4–5; sentimental model of, 57; support of, for Brown, 225n33
gendered speech acts: African American women's resistance through, 61–62; and hybrid discourse of female preachers, 65–67; Stewart's critiques on oppression through, 62–63, 76–77, 82, 210n35; Stewart's messianic discourse challenging, 25, 60–61, 80–81
Gliddon, George, 124
global warming, 187–89
God's love: binary of, and wrath in New and Old Testament, 8; Milly (*Dred* character) on, 142–43; nineteenth-century sentimental discourse on, 1–3, 35–36; Puritan accounts of, 10; "Remarks on the Term Vengeance" on, 1–2, 4, 29; Stewart's apocalyptic sentimentalism and racial uplift as using, 71–75; Stowe's *Uncle Tom's Cabin* pairing of, with fear, 6, 26, 98–113. *See also* love
God's wrath/vengeance: antislavery rhetoric using, 4–5; binary of, and love in Old and New Testament, 8; Edwards's "Sinners in the Hands of an Angry God" invocation of, 10–11; murderous slave as manifestation of, 93–94; nineteenth-century sentimental discourse on, 1–3, 36–37; religious debates over, 193–94n3, 197–98n35; "Remarks on the Term Vengeance" on, 1–2, 4, 29; Second Great Awakening's emphasis on redemptive power instead of, 11–12; Stewart's apocalyptic sentimentalism and racial uplift using, 71–75; Stowe's Dred character as agent of, 131–36; Stowe's *Uncle Tom's Cabin* on transformation through love and fear of, 6, 26, 98–113; sympathy created through terror of, 9; Turner's insurrection perceived as, 46–47; Walker's *Appeal* linking sympathy with, 24–25, 37, 39–44. *See also* apocalyptic vengeance; messianic violence
Golden Rule, 160, 164, 176
Gore, Al, 226n17
Gospels. *See* Bible
gothic novel tradition, 214nn21–22
Grasso, Linda, 61–62
Gray, Thomas, 38, 44, 202–3n17
Grimes, Sarah, 62
Grimke, Angelina, 62

Hale, Sarah J., 17
Hansen, James, 187–89; *Storms of My Grandchildren*, 187–88
Harpers Ferry: apocalyptic sentimentality culminating at, 5, 24, 28–30, 166, 178–80; as apocalyptic vengeance, 5, 24, 28–30, 92, 149, 157–80; Barnes on violent outcome of sympathetic identification at, 155; Brown's sympathy expressed as violence at, 157–80; Child's response to, 92, 156, 166–69, 170–71, 177, 224–25n29; defended as example of Brown's deep love, 29, 149, 153–66; events at, 153; modern scholarship's analysis of, 154–55; practice of separating Brown's love from violence at, 156–57; violence against "innocent" civilians at, 200n55. *See also* Brown, John
Hawthorne, Nathaniel, 17, 35, 136
Hayden, W. B., 13
Hedrick, Joan, 142
Hendler, Glenn, 35–36
Heroic Slave, The (Douglass), 20
Hope Leslie (Sedgwick), 6, 195n13
Hovenden, Thomas, 170
Howe, Julia Ward, 182

Inconvenient Truth, An (documentary), 226
"Insurrectionist, The" (Garrison), 35

Jackson, Rebecca Cox, 58
Jacobs, Harriet, 47
Jarrett, Gene Andrew, 47
Jefferson, Thomas: Declaration of Independence, 42, 43–44, 47, 116, 216n3; *Notes on the State of Virginia* by, 47; Walker's critique of racialist views of, 47, 203n27, 205–6n51, 217n10
jeremiad tradition, 9; Puritan sermon with dread-ridden quality of, 197n31, 208n11; in Stowe's novels, 99, 115, 123, 211–12n5; used by female preachers, 65
Jericho (TV show), 189
Jesus Christ. *See* Christ
"John Brown and the Colored Child" (Child), 170–71

Kansas-Nebraska Act (1854), 8
Kaplan, Amy, 116

"Key to the Revelations, A" (broadside), 15
King, Larry, 188

Langston, Charles Henry, 164, 167
Lawrence, Jacob, 172
Lee, Jarena, 58, 71
Lee, Robert E., 153
Lesley, Peter, 167
Lesley, Susan, 167
Levine, Robert, 43, 47
Lincoln, Abraham: Proclamation of Thanksgiving, 181–82; Second Inaugural Address, 30, 182–84
Lincoln, Salome, 65
love: and Child's response to Harpers Ferry, 92, 156, 166–69, 170–71; as defining trait of sentimental tradition, 194n6; *Dred*'s Milly and Dred characters' role in pairing, with fear, 27, 141–44, 145–49; fear used as incentive to, 3; Harpers Ferry defended as expression of Brown's, 29, 149, 153–66; identified as outcome of sentimental narration, 35–36; McCarthy's *The Road* on, 191; as missing from discourse of Stowe's *Dred*, 141–43; Puritan accounts of, 10, 196–97n30; Stowe's *Uncle Tom's Cabin* pairing of, with fear, 6, 26, 98–113, 212n7; Warner's depictions of judgment as incentive for greater, 6. *See also* God's love

Martinez, Yvette, 186
masculinity: antebellum-period citizenship understood in terms of, 204n33; contrast between *Dred*'s Harry Gordon and Dred's, 122–23, 130–31, 148–49; in *Dred*, 123–31
McCarthy, Cormac, 181, 189–92, 227n22
Meditation XI (Stewart), 59
Melancholia (film), 189, 227n19
Melville, Herman: apocalypse in work of, 17; "Benito Cereno," 221n33; on Brown as "meteor" bringing about war, 153, 157; Puritanical authoritativeness of, 7. *See also Moby-Dick*
messianic violence: antebellum society's racial structures challenged by, 22; *Appeal* on response to slavery through, 49–57, 135, 148; as black-empowerment strategy, 48–49; and *Confessions*, 28, 44–47, 49–57, 135, 146–48; distinctions between revolutionary and, 57;

as exemplifying violence constructed by Walker and Turner, 48–57; as power rooted in Christianity, 21; slave resistance as, 20–21, 38; Stewart's challenge to slavery using, 25, 60–61, 80–81; Stowe's *Dred* on development of, 27–28, 111, 121–23, 131–36; as theory of power and apocalyptic sentimentalism, 21; Turner as symbol of, 38. *See also* apocalyptic vengeance; God's wrath/vengeance; slave violence
Methodist churches: African Methodist Episcopal (AME) Church of Charleston, 37, 42, 201n11; sermons invoking God's vengeance, 197–98nn35–36
mixed-blood status: of *Dred*'s Harry Gordon character, 124–30, 217n10; rhetoric of blood on, 217n5; *Uncle Tom's Cabin* as challenging assumptions about, 123, 125
Moby-Dick (Melville): Ahab's vengeance in, 136–40; debate over attitude toward women in, 221n32; "negative individualism" of Ahab in, 220–21n31; Stowe's *Dred* compared with, 28, 123, 135–40; and vengeance as threat to democracy, 140, 144
Morton, Samuel, 124
multiracial democratic communities: exploration of, in Stowe's *Dred*, 28, 135–36, 140–48; Melville's *Moby-Dick* on vengeance as threat to, 140, 144; Turner's *Confessions* rejecting vision of, 46; *Uncle Tom's Cabin* ending revised by *Dred*'s, 144–45, 148–49; Walker's *Appeal* on goal of, 40, 41–42, 46, 55–56; white sympathy for black brethren for, 41–42

Narrative (Douglass), 4
NASA Goddard Institute for Space Studies, 187
Nazi holocaust trains, 188
Newhall, Henry, 155
New-York Gospel Herald, 193n1; "Remarks on the Term Vengeance," 1–2, 4, 29
New York Morning Courier and Enquirer, 46–47
New York Tribune, 169, 170, 171, 172, 175
9/11 attacks, 31, 184, 192
Nobel, Marianne, 21–22
Noble, Thomas, 170
Northern Baptist theology, 66–67
North Star, 39
Notes on the State of Virginia (Jefferson), 47

Nott, Josiah, 124
Nudelman, Franny, 154–55

patriarchal order: and Brown's authority, 177; Calvinist theology equated with, 35; Douglas on, 82; respect of female preachers for, 208n19
PAULUS, 4, 29; "Remarks on the Term Vengeance," 1–2
Percival, James Gates, 17
Phillips, Wendell, 48, 155
Poe, Edgar Allan, 17
polygenesis theory, 217n5
postmillennial Christians, 198n37
post-9/11 America: apocalyptic sentimentalism used in, 31, 184, 192; and Beck, 184–87; and Hansen's apocalyptic discourse, 187–89; and McCarthy's *The Road*, 181, 189–91; primetime television in, 227n23
power: Calvinist theology equated with patriarchal, 35; fantasies of black, 48; messianic violence as rooted in Christian, 21; Second Great Awakening's emphasis on redemptive, 11–12; Stewart on black women's, 67–68; Stowe on Dred's, 131–36; Stowe's equating of loving mothers with social, 26; Turner's representation of, 38, 54–55; Walker's articulation and concept of, 38, 52–53
premillennialist Christians, 198n37
Proclamation of Thanksgiving (A. Lincoln), 181–82
Prosser, Gabriel, 39, 219n23
Protestantism: apocalyptic motivations behind emigration of, to America, 198n38; early "calling" notion of "work ethic" of, 218n13; masochistic impulses in, 22; merciful Jesus of liberalized, 26; subjection of self in, 51–52; in *Uncle Tom's Cabin*, 101–2
Puritanism: apocalyptic terror element of, 9–11; Brown's, 175–76; fear as component of, 10; love concept in, 10, 196–97n30; in Melville's authoritativeness, 7; in Sedgwick's *Hope Leslie*, 6, 195n13. *See also* apocalyptic theology
Puritan sermon: Edwards's "Sinners in the Hands of an Angry God," 10–11; fear of God's wrath in, 9–10; optimism of, 197n31; purpose of, 9–10

race: as factor in support offered to Brown, 224n27; Stewart's focus on, 62–63, 76–77, 82; in Stowe's *Dred*, 124–30, 217n7, 217n10; theory of multiple creations of, 217n5
racially integrated nations. *See* multiracial democratic communities
Ransom, Louis, 170
Realf, Richard, 160; *Echoes of Harper's Ferry*, 153
"Reformation of Morals Practicable and Indispensable, A" (L. Beecher), 112
Religion and the Pure Principles of Morality, the Sure Foundation on Which We Must Build (Stewart), 59–60, 72, 73, 74, 75–77, 78
religious violence. *See* messianic violence
"Remarks on the Term Vengeance" (PAULUS), 1–2, 4, 29
Revelation, book of: and Catherine Beecher, 85; and Christ in *Uncle Tom's Cabin*, 112; Hayden's course on, 13, *14*; 16:16, 72–73; Stewart's sermons using, 209n25; Turner's rewriting of, 55. *See also* Bible
revolutionary violence: African American writers as linking slave resistance to, 47–48; Declaration of Independence's authorization for, 19–20, 42, 43–44, 47, 116, 135, 216n3; distinctions between theological and, 57; slave resistance as religious violence instead of, 20–21, 38; violence misread in Walker's *Appeal* and Turner's *Confessions* as, 38, 48; Walker's engagement with Jefferson's ideas on, 47
Reynolds, David, 177, 178
Reynolds, Larry, 19
Richmond Whig (newspaper), 46
Road, The (McCarthy), 181, 189–92, 227n22
Roberts, Abigail, 65
Romero, Lora, 61
Rowe, John Carlos, 142

Sale, Maggie, 47, 204n33
salvation: and Second Great Awakening, 11–12; *Uncle Tom's Cabin* on freeing slaves through, 114–15; *Uncle Tom's Cabin*'s use of fear and love for, 6, 26, 98–113; Universalists' doctrine of universal, 197–98n35
Samuels, Shirley, 116

Sanborn, Franklin, 176
Sandford, Dred Scott v. (1857), 8–9
Scottish Common Sense tradition, 7, 36–37, 211n2, 213n11
Scottish Enlightenment: as opposition to Calvinism, 36; sentimentalism's roots in, 7; Stowe's training in, 100, 101, 102; theories of sympathy developed in, 195n17; ties of, with sentimental tradition scholarship, 195n16
Second Great Awakening, 11–12
Second Inaugural Address (A. Lincoln), 30, 182–84
Sedgwick, Catharine Maria, 6, 195n13
self: Emerson's "aboriginal," 49, 51; Protestant subjectivization of, 51–52; Stewart's construction of public, 64–71; Walker on transfers in power and theory of, 52–53
self-abnegation: danger of promoting, as challenge to racial oppression, 69; Stewart's politicized female presence through act of, 67–69; Walker and Turner's empowered rebellious black subject through act of, 25, 38, 49. *See also* submission/subordination
self-reliance model, 49, 51, 204–5n39
sentimental fiction: Child's "The Black Saxons" as, 64, 86–90, 92, 140, 168; Child's "John Brown and the Colored Child" as, 170–71; Child's "Slavery's Pleasant Homes" as, 64, 86, 90–93, 140; "generic goal" of, 200n1; as literary antecedent to gothic tradition, 214nn21–22; McCarthy's *The Road* as apocalyptic, 181, 189–92, 227n22; in modern television and films, 189–92, 226nn16–17, 227n19, 227n21; salvific power of children in nineteenth-century, 191; Sedgwick's *Hope Leslie* as, 6, 195n13; sympathetic identification produced by, 36; Whittier's "Brown of Osawatomie" as, 169–70. See also *Appeal to the Coloured Citizens of the World*; *Confessions*; *Dred*; *Uncle Tom's Cabin*
sentimentalism (nineteenth century): binary between, and hardline Christian orthodoxy, 8; compassion as emotional goal of, 3; Douglas on opposition of masculine Calvinism to, 7–8; evangelical context of, 38; investment of, in fear to drive transformation, 3–4; love and God's wrath in, 1–3, 36–37; love and sympathy as outcomes of, 35–36; love as defining trait of, 194n6; masochistic pleasures generated by, 22; religious violence as undergirding structure of, 20–21, 38; roots of, in white and black forms of representation, 58; scholarship identifying violence in, 21–22; Scottish Enlightenment roots of, 7; Walker's foundational presence in, 58; on women as paragons of Christian morality, 75. *See also* abolitionist sentimentality; apocalyptic sentimentalism
September 11, 2001, attacks, 31, 184, 192
sexual violence: Child's "Slavery's Pleasant Homes" on, 64, 86, 90–93; interracial Southern families constituted by, 91; paranoid ideas about black man engaged in, 220n27
Shatz, Frank, 178
Sherman, General, 182, 226n9
"Sinners in the Hands of an Angry God" (Edwards sermon), 10–11
slave resistance: African American writers linking revolutionary heritage to, 47–48; America's revolutionary genealogy used to justify, 19–20, 42, 43–44, 47, 116, 135; apocalyptic sentimentalism on retributive violence of, 19–22; Douglass's *The Heroic Slave* on, 20; as examples of religious violence not political revolution, 20–21, 38; fictional and historical examples of, 19–20; Stewart on black women's inclusion in, 70–71; through submission, 199–200n50; Walker on God's role in enabling agency of, 49–50, 74–75
slavery: abolitionists on immortality of, 4, 198–99n44; Child's use of sentimental traditions to examine, 63–64, 83, 86–93, 140; Declaration of Independence's conflict with, 216n3; defended as being God's will, 9; *Dred*'s Harry Gordon character and collusion in, 128–29; Fitzhugh's defense of, 218–19n20; messianic violence as response to, 47–56; Stewart's messianic violence discourse challenging, 25, 60–61, 80–81; Stowe's *Dred* highlighting incommensurability of nineteenth-century norms with, 129–31; *Uncle Tom's Cabin*'s conversion solution to, 103–4, 113–18; Walker's *Appeal* as attack against, 39, 39–44, 49–57

"Slavery's Pleasant Homes" (Child): characters and plot of, 90–92; home as place of slave violence in, 64, 90–93, 140, 168

slaves: apocalyptic sentimentalism on retributive nature of, 19–22; Brown's sympathy toward families of, 159–60; Child's "Slavery's Pleasant Homes" on sexual violence against female, 64, 86, 90–93; economic rights of, 218n19; Eva's sermon in *Uncle Tom's Cabin* on subordination of body of, 216n3; humanity and black masculine authority of, in Stowe's *Dred*, 123–31; Stowe's *Uncle Tom's Cabin* on African colonization by freed, 113–18; Stowe's *Uncle Tom's Cabin* on Christian faith empowering, 120–21; Walker on God's role in enabling resistance by, 49–50; Walker's *Appeal* on national integration of, 40, 41–42, 46, 55–56. See also free blacks

slave violence: America's revolutionary genealogy used to justify, 19–20, 42, 43–44, 47, 116, 135; and *Appeal*'s messianic vengeance, 49–57, 135, 148; Child's identification of home as place of, 64, 86–92, 140, 168; as heroic against white masters, 92; as manifestation of God's wrath, 93–94; and messianic violence, 47–56; panic over possibility of, 219n23; as rational expression of Enlightenment, 20; Turner's *Confessions* portrayal of, 28, 44–47, 49–57, 135, 146–48; Walker's disavowal of, 202n13; Walker's warnings of, 82–83. See also messianic violence

Slemaker, Bill, 186
Sollors, Werner, 125
Stewart, Maria: affiliated with First African Baptist Church in Boston, 209n25; apocalyptic sentimentalism as organizing principle in lectures of, 5, 28, 58, 71–75; on Christianity as constituted by fear, 72–73; Christian orthodoxy of, 66–69, 71–75, 81–82; as Christian soldier, 65–67; construction of public self of, 64–71; as contributing to "domestication" of apocalypse, 25, 58, 64, 77–78, 93; on duty of free black men to defend slaves, 79–83; as first public political activist among black women, 65; frustration of, over white American obstinacy, 74; ideological alignment of, with Walker, 60–61; and inclusion of women in resistance against slavery, 70–71; on liars and lying, 78; on messianic violence to challenge oppression, 25, 60–62, 80–81, 82; on moral authority of free black women, 75–79; and notions of womanhood and masculinity, 208n19, 208–9n24; race and gender focus of, 62–63, 76–77, 82, 210n35; as redefining black womanhood, 67–69, 75–79; self-abnegation of, to represent politicized woman, 67–69; sentimental structure of political rhetoric of, 98; Stowe's antislavery discourse compared with, 119; Turner's *Confessions* as bridge linking Walker to, 38; Walker's approach compared with, 58, 60–61, 62–63, 207n3; on Walker's death, 66

—works of: "An Address Delivered Before the Afric-American Female Intelligence Society of America," 59; *Meditation XI*, 59; *Religion and the Pure Principles of Morality, the Sure Foundation on Which We Must Build*, 59–60, 72, 73, 74, 75–77, 78

Storms of My Grandchildren (Hansen), 187–88
Stowe, Charles, 102
Stowe, Harriet Beecher: "Appeal to the Women of the Free States of America," 213–14n13; within canon of sentimental fiction, 24; critical stance of, against Calvinism, 26, 113; Edwardsian theology and Scottish Enlightenment training of, 100, 101, 102, 211n2; fiction of, as providing Brown with public support, 165; influence of Lyman Beecher in writings of, 113, 115, 119; injunction of, to "feel right," 3, 39–40, 98, 99, 111–12, 144; jeremiad tradition in novels of, 99, 115, 123, 211–12n5; Kinmont's influence on, 215–16n31; letter of, to Lord Denman, 97; liberal Protestantism of, 101–2; Puritanism in fiction of, 102; as theorist of "niceness," 212–13n9; Turner's *Confessions* as bridge linking Walker to, 38, 44; Walker's approach compared with, 58. See also *Dred*; *Uncle Tom's Cabin*

submission/subordination: Dred character's reliance on God contrasted with Uncle Tom's, 133; of Eva's sermon in *Uncle Tom's Cabin*, 216n2; slave resistance through, 199–200n50; Stowe's Uncle Tom character as showing, 26–27, 108; used by black women to enter public arena, 209n28. See also self-abnegation

Sundquist, Eric J., 47

sympathetic identification: Barnes on Brown's, 155; expressed as violence by Brown, 157–80; produced through sentimental fiction, 36; *Uncle Tom's Cabin*'s use of fear of God's vengeance to invoke, 6, 26, 98–100, 102–13; Walker's *Appeal* for racially integrated nation through, 37, 40, 41–42, 74–75, 82–83

sympathy: antebellum-period debate over, 5; antislavery discourse production of, 5–6; biblical ethic of, 176; and Brown as exemplar of nineteenth-century sentimentality, 149, 154, 157–64; of Brown toward slave families, 157–64; as outcome of sentimental narration, 35–36; Scottish Common Sense tradition's stress on, 36–37; Scottish Enlightenment theories of, 195n17; Stowe's Dred character as catalyst for, 146; Stowe's *Dred* slave characters as creating, 123–31; Stowe's equation of social power with, 26; Stowe's *Uncle Tom's Cabin* use of, 6, 26, 98–100, 102–13; terror as prerequisite for, 9; variation in antebellum writers' approach to, 57–58; Walker's *Appeal* as linking God's wrath to, 24–25, 37, 39–44, 82–83. *See also* antislavery discourse

Takacs, Stacy, 227n23
Taney, Roger B., 8–9
terror: historical precedents to antebellum period's apocalyptic, 9–12; modern association of terrorism with, 22–23, 184–91; post-9/11 American incorporation of, 31, 184–92. *See also* apocalyptic terror

terrorism: debate over U.S. foreign policy's engagement in, 200n56; as "greatest danger" to American way of life, 192; incorporation of, into prime-time television following 9/11, 227n23; post-9/11 America's response to fear of, 31, 181–92; September 11, 2001, attacks, 184, 192; violence against civilian populations as feature of, 200n55

Terrorism TV (Takacs), 227n23
Thompson, Rachel, 65
Thoreau, Henry David, 155, 164, 166, 167, 170, 176, 177, 224n23
Tompkins, Jane, 7, 26, 99, 194n6
Towle, Nancy, 65
Tragic Prelude (Curry), 172, *173*, 175
Travis, Mrs., 45

Treatise on Domestic Economy, A (C. Beecher), 84–85, 86
Trodd, Zoe, 172
Turner, Nat: apocalyptic sentimentality in writing of, 5; articulation of power by, 38; influence of, on Stowe's *Dred*, 28, 132, 141, 146–48; messianic violence in writing of, 48–57; millenarian tradition invoked by, 203n28; non-Christian religious rituals and beliefs as influencing, 205n49; as rewriting book of Revelation, 55; and scholarship normalizing promotion of violence as revolutionary, 38, 48; as symbol of religious violence, 38; Walker's approach to slave violence compared with, 25, 37–38, 44, 56. *See also Confessions*

Turner's insurrection: constructed as apocalyptic event, 44–45; innocent slaves killed by vigilante groups after, 206n53; violence against "innocent" civilians during, 200n55; widespread panic and terror as chief aim of, 28, 44–47

Uncle Tom's Cabin (H. B. Stowe): on Africa as God's chosen nation for colonization, 113–18; apocalyptic sentimentalism fictionalized in, 24, 97–99, 100–119; Brown's kissing of black child as revising scenes in, 171; Christianization of George Harris character in, 115–16; conversion of Negro heathens as sign of apocalypse in, 101; critical objections to ending of, 26–27, 115–17; Eastman's *Aunt Phillis's Cabin* parody of, 30; ending of, revised by *Dred*'s multiracial community, 144–45, 148–49; equation of social power with loving mothers in, 26; gothic tradition in, 214nn21–22; Hallidays' Quaker household as moral standard in, 111–12; humanity of Haley character in, 105–7, 108, 111; injunction to "feel right" in, 3, 39–40, 98, 99, 111–12; as joining sentimentality to antislavery politics, 26–27; Negro characters returning to Africa in, 26–27, 101, 116–17; pairing of fear and love in, 6, 26, 98–113, 212n7; on relationship between Uncle Tom and Eva characters, 108–11, 214n19; sentimental challenge to Simon Legree character in, 109–10; significance of Eva's death in, 214n16; St. Clare character of, as dramatizing transfor-

Uncle Tom's Cabin (H. B. Stowe) *(continued)* mation and salvation, 102–7; Stowe's critical stance against Calvinism in, 26, 113; Stowe's revised sentimentality of *Dred* compared with, 27–28, 125, 130, 132–33, 134, 145, 148–49; submissive character of Uncle Tom in, 26–27, 108; symbolism of Eva's hair in, 109–11; theological dimension of sentimentality of, 7; Uncle Tom's death in, 120–21. *See also* antislavery discourse; sentimental fiction

United States: debate over foreign policy engagement of, in terrorism, 200n56; post–Civil War shift from vengeance toward reconciliation in, 30–31, 180, 182–84; post-9/11 apocalyptic sentimentalism in, 31, 181, 184–91, 192, 226n16, 227nn19–20, 227n22–23; September 11, 2001, attacks against, 184, 192; so-called feminization of American culture of, 7–8. *See also* antebellum period; Civil War

Universalists, 193n1, 197–98n35

vengeance. *See* apocalyptic vengeance; God's wrath/vengeance

Vesey, Denmark, 37, 39, 42, 132, 201n7, 219n23

Walker, David: African Methodist Episcopal (AME) Church of Charleston's influence on, 37, 42; antislavery discourse of Stowe compared with, 119; apocalyptic sentimentality in writing of, 5; articulation of power by, 38; charges men to protect and provide for women, 81; critique of Thomas Jefferson's racialist views by, 47, 203n27, 205–6n50; as foundational presence in sentimentalism, 58; as linking slave resistance to revolutionary heritage, 47–48; messianic violence constructed by writings of, 48–57; on public reaction to *Appeal*, 39; racially integrated nation as goal of, 40, 41–42, 46, 55–56; and scholarship normalizing promotion of violence as revolutionary, 38, 48; sentimental structure of political rhetoric of, 11, 98; Stewart's ideological alignment with, 58, 60–61, 62–63, 207n3; as surrogate working for God's wrath, 74; sympathetic identification used by, to motivate compassion, 37, 40, 41–42, 74–75; on transfers in power and selfhood, 52–53; Turner's approach to slave violence compared with, 25, 37–38, 44, 56. *See also Appeal to the Coloured Citizens of the World*

Walking Dead, The (TV show), 189

WALL-E (film), 189, 227n20

Walters, Ronald, 149

Warner, Susan, 6

Weinstein, Cindy, 5

Wesley, Charles, 174

Wexler, Laura, 21

Whitehead, Colson, 226n16

Whittier, John Greenleaf, 170l; "Brown of Osawatomie," 169–70

Wide Wide World, The (Warner), 6

Wise, Henry, 154

"work ethic": antebellum-period significance of, 127, 218n18; of *Dred*'s Harry Gordon character, 127–29; Protestantism's "calling" notion of, 218n13

World War Z (film), 185, 226n16

Yarborough, Richard, 116

Zone One (Whitehead), 185, 226n16

www.ingramcontent.com/pod-product-compliance
Lightning Source LLC
Chambersburg PA
CBHW011744220426
43666CB00018B/2894